LISTENING TO BRITAIN

Paul Addison and Jeremy A. Crang teach in the School of History, Classics and Archaeology at the University of Edinburgh. They are the editors of *The Burning Blue: A New History of the Battle of Britain* and *Firestorm: The Bombing of Dresden, 1945.*

Listening to Britain

Home Intelligence Reports on Britain's
Finest Hour
May to September 1940

EDITED AND WITH INTRODUCTIONS AND
A GLOSSARY BY
Paul Addison and Jeremy A. Crang

VINTAGE BOOKS
London

Published by Vintage 2011

2 4 6 8 10 9 7 5 3 1

First published by Great Britain in 2010 by The Bodley Head

Vintage
Random House, 20 Vauxhall Bridge Road,
London SW1V 2SA

www.vintage-books.co.uk

Addresses for companies within The Random House Group Limited
can be found at: www.randomhouse.co.uk/offices.htm

The Random House Group Limited Reg. No. 954009

A CIP catalogue record for this book
is available from the British Library

ISBN 9780099548744

The Random House Group Limited supports The Forest Stewardship
Council (FSC), the leading international forest certification organisation.
All our titles that are printed on Greenpeace approved FSC certified
paper carry the FSC logo. Our paper procurement policy can be found at
www.randomhouse.co.uk/environment

Typeset by Palimpsest Book Production Limited, Falkirk, Stirlingshire
Printed and bound in Great Britain by
CPI Bookmarque, Croydon CR0 4TD

In memory of Angus Calder
(1942–2008)

Contents

Acknowledgements

In editing this volume we have accumulated a number of debts. First and foremost, we are grateful to the National Archives for permission to reproduce the Home Intelligence daily reports. We are also indebted to the Trustees of the Mass-Observation Archive for allowing us to incorporate additional material from these reports located among the papers of Mary Adams at the University of Sussex Library. Thanks are due also to the School of History, Classics and Archaeology at the University of Edinburgh for assistance with editorial costs and to Pauline Maclean for invaluable assistance in preparing the text. For indispensable support and guidance in the construction of the book we wish to thank Bruce Hunter at David Higham Associates and Jörg Hensgen at the Bodley Head.

ORKNEY ISLANDS

SHETLAND ISLANDS

Inverness

Aberdeen

SCOTLAND

Dundee

Perth

Glasgow

Edinburgh

Ministry *of* Information
Regions

■ *Regional offices*

Berwick upon Tweed

NORTHERN

Dumfries

■ **Newcastle** *upon Tyne*

Carlisle

■ *Middlesbrough*

NORTHERN IRELAND

■ Belfast

NORTH

North Sea

Barrow-in-Furness

WESTERN

York

Hull

Leeds ■ NORTH EASTERN

Preston

Manchester ■

Liverpool

Sheffield ■

EIRE

Dublin

Chester

Denbigh
Ruthin

Lincoln

Derby ■

NORTH MIDLAND

■ **Nottingham**

Shrewsbury

Birmingham

Norwich
Lowestoft

Coventry

Leicester

MIDLAND

EASTERN

■ **Cambridge**

WALES

Bedford

Ipswich

N

Gloucester

Oxford

Chelmsford

Colchester

Swansea

Cardiff ■

Avonmouth
■ **Bristol**

Bath

Reading

London
(LONDON) ■

Southend

SOUTHERN

Croydon

Canterbury

Margate

Dover

Weston-super-Mare

Tunbridge Wells

Folkestone

SOUTH WESTERN

Southampton

Brighton

Hastings

Portsmouth

Calais

Boulogne

Exeter

Bournemouth

SOUTH EASTERN

Plymouth

Portland

Penzance

FRANCE

| 0 | | 50 | | 100 miles |

| 0 | 50 | 100 | 150 km |

Introduction

The months from May to September 1940 were among the most crucial in British history. During this period, which incorporated the epic events of the evacuation from Dunkirk, the Battle of Britain and the opening stages of the Blitz, the fate of the nation depended, among other things, upon the readiness of the general public to support the war effort and their confidence that Nazi Germany could be defeated. At this critical point, the Home Intelligence department of the Ministry of Information was tasked with compiling daily reports on the state of popular morale. Covering all regions of the United Kingdom the reports ran from 18 May until 27 September, after which they were replaced by weekly summaries. Published here in their entirety, they provide a unique window into the attitudes and behaviour of the British people during what Churchill described as their 'finest hour'.

In order to appreciate the particular character and qualities of the reports we need first of all to remind ourselves of the circumstances in which they were written and the sources from which they were compiled. At the outbreak of war in September 1939 the government of Neville Chamberlain set up a Ministry of Information (MOI) housed in the Senate building of the University of London. The outcome of half-hearted preparations in the late 1930s, the new Ministry lacked authority in Whitehall and suffered from a difficult relationship with the press, which accused it of censoring and withholding news, and more generally of bureaucratic muddle. Nor, when it was first established, had the MOI any means of investigating or monitoring public opinion. It was talking to Britain without listening to Britain: a one-sided conversation.

After much argument within the MOI it was decided to establish

a Home Intelligence department and in December 1939 Mary Adams
was appointed as director with a brief to establish the necessary
machinery.¹ Adams was one of the many temporary civil servants
whose recruitment to Whitehall during the war introduced an
unorthodox element into the pre-war Establishment. After a
degree in botany from the University of Wales she had gone on
to postgraduate research at Newnham College, Cambridge, and
given a series of radio talks on heredity which fired her with
enthusiasm for the cause of educational broadcasting. Joining
the BBC as an education officer, she became a producer with
the corporation's fledgling TV service in 1936: 'a tiny, vivacious,
brainy blonde with bright blue eyes who always dressed very
elegantly'.² Married to the Conservative MP Vyvyan Adams, a firm
opponent of Chamberlain's policy of appeasement, she herself
was 'a socialist, a romantic communist . . . a fervent atheist and
advocate of humanism'.³

When the television service closed down at the outbreak of war,
Adams found herself without a role. But the BBC's loss was MOI's
gain and the Home Intelligence department was largely her creation.
'In those early days of MOI,' she recalled in 1980, 'you could do
almost anything if you had determination.'⁴ In February 1940 she
defined the purposes of Home Intelligence as follows:

1. To provide a basis for publicity. A continuous flow of
reliable information is required on what the public is thinking
and doing in order that publicity measures may be properly
planned and their effectiveness tested.

2. To provide an assessment of home morale. For this
purpose it is necessary to study immediate reactions to specific
events as well as to create a barometer for the purpose of
testing public opinion on questions likely to be continuously
important, e.g. pacifism.⁵

Adams looked to outside bodies to supply much of the necessary
intelligence. She was an admirer of Mass-Observation (M-O) and
commissioned it to undertake studies of morale for her department.
Founded in 1937 by the social anthropologist Tom Harrisson, the
poet Charles Madge and the documentary film-maker Humphrey

Jennings, M-O employed a range of experimental and unorthodox techniques for assessing popular attitudes. Whereas conventional surveys reported the opinions expressed by members of the public to investigators, 'Mass-Observers' eavesdropped on conversations and reported on behaviour as well as opinion. Many of its early reports had focused on working-class life in the Lancashire town of Bolton ('Worktown' in M-O publications), but with the outbreak of war Harrisson, who was now in sole charge of the organisation, turned the spotlight on the problems of the home front. The message of *War Begins at Home*, M-O's account of the phoney-war period published in March 1940, was unequivocal. A gulf of mutual incomprehension separated the politicians and the civil servants in Whitehall from the broad mass of the British public. Neither the press nor the House of Commons could bridge the gulf: Mass-Observation could.

Though historians now place much reliance on its reports, M-O was often criticised at the time on the grounds that its methods were unscientific. To balance and check the intuitive nature of its reports, Adams somewhat reluctantly agreed to the establishment of a more academic and quantitative type of investigation: the Wartime Social Survey.[6] Organised by Arnold Plant, Professor of Commerce at the London School of Economics, and operating under the auspices of the National Institute of Social and Economic Research, some of its surveys, like its investigation into attitudes towards rationing for the Ministry of Food, were carried out for other Whitehall departments. But it also conducted inquiries into morale for Home Intelligence. Its investigators employed the standard market-research technique of a questionnaire which members of the public were invited to answer in face-to-face interviews. The findings were then reported in statistical form. Contrary, however, to Adams's desire to publicise the Survey, its existence was kept secret.

The initial plan was for Home Intelligence to compile a monthly report on the state of morale, but following the collapse of Norway, Belgium and Holland, and the German invasion of France, there was an immediate demand within the MOI for day-to-day information about the state of public opinion. Adams's department was thus instructed 'to report daily on people's reactions throughout the country, with special reference to morale, rumours, and the reception of ministerial broadcasts and pronouncements'.[7] Meanwhile Churchill had succeeded Chamberlain as Prime Minister and appointed his friend and political ally Duff Cooper as Minister of Information.

In compiling the daily reports Home Intelligence was able to draw on the services of M-O and the Social Survey, but a range of other sources were also employed. The MOI's Regional Information Officers (RIOs) across the country were instructed to report each day by telephone between 12 noon and 2.30 p.m. on morale in their regions. 'Their data,' a brief internal history of the department noted, 'were obtained partly by discussions with their own staff, partly by casual conversations initiated or overheard on the way to work, and partly by a hurried series of visits to public houses, and other places where the public foregathered.'[8] BBC listener research surveys were also utilised as were questionnaires completed by such organisations as W. H. Smith and Sons, the London Passenger Transport Board, Citizens' Advice Bureaux, the Association of Women House Property Managers and the Brewers' Society. Additional information was supplied by the main political parties. Secret sources were drawn upon too. Postal censors provided analyses of letters, Special Branch reports were made available, and RIOs were in touch with Chief Constables.[9]

At the same time, special arrangements were put in place to cover the London region. According to the internal history:

> It was decided to make contact with a number of people in London, in all strata of society, who would be prepared, in response to a telephone call or a personal visit, to report the feelings of those with whom they came into contact . . .
> The types of people approached were doctors, dentists, parsons, publicans, small shopkeepers, newsagents, trade union officials, factory welfare officers, shop stewards, Citizens' Advice Bureau secretaries, hospital almoners, businessmen, and local authority officials.[10]

This network was established by the staff of Home Intelligence, who recruited people known personally to them, who in turn suggested other likely individuals, and about twenty phone calls were made each day to these contacts in order to help construct the London region report.[11] This helps to explain why the daily reports for the capital were more substantial than the reports from other regional offices.

The Home Intelligence reports were compiled each day of the week except Sunday. The general overview at the start of each document was written by Adams herself. The rest, presumably, was prepared with the help of her small staff of assistants.[12] The report was produced at 4.45 p.m. and copies distributed within the MOI and to other Whitehall ministries such as the Ministry of Home Security, the Ministry of Labour, the Ministry of Supply, the War Office and the Air Ministry. The total circulation list in September 1940 came to about 100 copies, of which 25 circulated outside the MOI.[13] A small advisory group was established to provide guidance on interpreting the material. Its membership included Lord Horder, Julian Huxley and Richard Crossman.

In the summer of 1940 the future of Home Intelligence was put in jeopardy when its activities became the subject of a hostile press campaign. A number of people had been prosecuted for spreading 'alarm and despondency' by making 'defeatist' remarks or expressing sympathy with the enemy. The MOI, though not responsible for the prosecutions, had been running a 'Silent Column' campaign urging the public not to pass on rumours. Its attempts to monitor morale could therefore easily be mistaken, or indeed deliberately misrepresented, as part of a government witch-hunt against innocent civilians.

On 25 July the science correspondent of the *Daily Herald*, Ritchie Calder, revealed the existence of the Social Survey and its house-to-house enquiries for the MOI and alleged that the public had often reacted violently against the questioning of their morale. The following day the editor of the *Herald*, Percy Cudlipp, renewed the attack in an article in which he referred to the Social Survey as 'Cooper's Snoopers' and urged that the 'morale and social survey' section of the MOI should be closed down. Several other national newspapers took up the hue and cry. The *Daily Sketch* warned: 'This house-to-house questioning will throw the shadow of the Gestapo over honest and loyal creatures . . . The Ministry must abandon these ill-judged, amateurish inspirations.' The *Observer* commented: 'The idea of sounding opinion by doorstep inquiries can hardly have been produced by a British mind. Nothing could be more unpopular or more futile.'[14] Similar views were expressed by MPs critical of the government in a debate in the House of Commons on 1 August.

These reactions reveal how jealous journalists and MPs were of their claims to represent public opinion, and how little credence they were prepared to give to what were then comparatively novel techniques of social research. Duff Cooper, however, mounted a strong defence of the Social Survey in the House of Commons and the press campaign soon died down. From the point of view of Adams and Home Intelligence the attack on the Social Survey had one redeeming feature. It served as a lightning conductor diverting the attack away from the eavesdropping activities of her department (and those of M-O) that could well have got it into serious trouble if they had been exposed. 'Though no deliberate efforts at conceal-ment were made,' remarked the internal history, 'Home Intelligence worked, as it were, in the shadow of the Survey, its doings unques-tioned and its results confidential.'[15] The 'Cooper's Snoopers' affair, therefore, proved to be a storm in a teacup, and the Social Survey eventually emerged with a clean bill of health from an investigation by the Select Committee on National Expenditure.

For students of history the daily morale reports are a fascinating but problematical source. The quality of the evidence is uneven and has to be sifted carefully in order to separate the wheat from the chaff. Some of the statements about the attitudes and opinions of particular localities, for example, are supported by little hard evidence (31 May: 'Horsham continues "smug"' is a memorable case in point). On the other hand the reports contain many references to specific events, perceptions and behaviour, as well as quantitative infor-mation, of great interest. And although they are, by their very nature, invariably impressionistic, the reports represent a genuine attempt to synthesise the best available sources. They illustrate many of the more mundane details and problems of daily life on the home front, as well as the public's hopes and fears about the progress of war, while also demonstrating a sensitivity to issues of class, gender and national identity. Furthermore, although a single day's report when read in isolation can only offer a glimpse of the unfolding drama, the cumulative effect of the reports when read as a whole is to provide a continuously evolving narrative and a coherent version of events.

Interpretations of the material are of course bound to differ and in the final analysis readers must form their own judgements. In our own view the reports offer a number of valuable insights. We need firstly to recognise that the British people, like the compilers of the daily reports, did not know what was going to happen next and were reacting to events without any of the historical perspective that we now have. They thus give the reader some idea of what it must have been like to live through a period of cataclysmic developments. The reports convey a sense of the diversity of British society and the existence of dissenting minorities. But they also testify to certain dominant themes, such as the stubborn belief, in spite of all evidence to the contrary, in ultimate victory; the more or less constant popular pressure for a more effective prosecution of the war effort at home and abroad; a powerful consciousness of national identity which sometimes showed itself in intolerance of conscientious objectors and suspicion of refugees from the continent; and the growing importance for the civilian population of the war in the air. The home front was indeed becoming a battle front and the reports show that the public increasingly thought of themselves as part of the front line. As Angus Calder wrote in a classic work published in 1969, the Second World War was turning into a 'people's war'.[16] And as Churchill prophesied in a speech to the House of Commons in May 1901: 'The wars of peoples will be more terrible than those of kings.'[17]

A word or two of explanation is needed on the subject of the editing of the documents. Our aim has been to publish an unabridged set of the daily reports, of which there appear to be two virtually complete sets in existence. One is in the National Archives at Kew in INF 1/264, the other among the papers of Mary Adams at the University of Sussex.[18] The text published here is based primarily on the set in the National Archives, but this contains minor omissions which have been filled by documents from the Mary Adams papers. The original text, which seems to have been dictated, contains typos and errors in spelling or punctuation which we have corrected, and inconsistencies of presentation which we have replaced with a more uniform house style. We also decided to highlight the distinction between the introductory summary at the start of each report, and the more detailed summaries from the regions, by putting the introduction in italics. We have sometimes omitted headings where they were repetitive or superfluous. In all other respects the text of the original documents has been reproduced in complete and original form.

For the convenience of readers we have grouped the reports into weekly sections and written for each week an introduction outlining the historical context and background to the main topics discussed in the reports. In addition, where appropriate, individuals and terms referred to in the text are identified in the glossary at the back of the book, and a list of abbreviations is attached.

Paul Addison
Jeremy A. Crang

Centre for the Study of the Two World Wars
School of History, Classics and Archaeology
University of Edinburgh

Notes

[1] Ian McLaine, *Ministry of Morale: Home Front Morale and the Ministry of Information in World War Two* (1979), pp. 49–51.

[2] Angus Calder, *Gods, Mongrels and Demons* (2003), p. 11.

[3] Sally Adams, 'Mary Grace Agnes Adams' in *Oxford Dictionary of National Biography* (1990), online.

[4] University of Sussex, Special Collections, Mary Adams papers, box 7, Mary Adams, interview with Angus Calder, 15 February 1980.

[5] The National Archives, Kew, papers of the Ministry of Information, INF 1/47, 'Note on the Functions of Home Intelligence', by Mary Adams, 9 February 1940.

[6] McLaine, *Ministry of Morale*, p. 53.

[7] TNA, INF 1/290, 'The Work of the Home Intelligence Division 1939–1944', p. 3.

[8] Ibid.

[9] TNA, INF 1/47, 'Home Intelligence Machinery', 16 July 1940.

[10] TNA, INF 1/290, 'The Work of the Home Intelligence Division 1939–1944', p. 3.

[11] Ibid., p. 4.

[12] TNA, INF 1/47, 'Home Intelligence: Organisation and Staffing', by Mary Adams, 17 July 1940.

[13] TNA, INF 1/101, 'Home Intelligence', by Mary Adams, 13 August 1940; University of Sussex, Mary Adams papers, box 1, 'Circulation of "Daily Observations by Home Intelligence"', 28 September 1940.

[14] Mass-Observation online, M-O file report no. 325, 'Report on the "Cooper's Snoopers" Press Campaign, 5 August 1940', pp. 1–2, 5.

[15] TNA, INF 1/290, 'The Work of Home Intelligence Division 1939–44', p. 2.

[16] Angus Calder, The People's War: Britain 1939–1945 (1969).

[17] Quoted in Paul Addison, Churchill on the Home Front 1900–1955 (1992), p. 19.

[18] It should be noted that the National Archives' copy of the Home Intelligence reports was made available on microfilm in 1979 by Harvester Press.

SATURDAY 18 MAY TO SATURDAY 25 MAY 1940

The first of the daily Home Intelligence reports reflected the shock and confusion caused by a fast-moving sequence of military disasters. On 9 April Hitler's forces had invaded and occupied Denmark and Norway. The political crisis precipitated by the defeat of the British expeditionary force to Norway had compelled Neville Chamberlain to step down as Prime Minister on 10 May. His successor, at the head of a new all-party Coalition government, was Winston Churchill. At dawn on 10 May Hitler's armies launched an invasion of Belgium and Holland, accompanied by a drive through the Ardennes into northern France. Within a few days the Allied armies were in retreat. On 15 May the Dutch High Command capitulated. By 18 May the German armies were advancing rapidly towards the Channel coast and threatening to encircle the British Expeditionary Force (BEF), along with the French First Army and the Belgian Army.

On 19 May the French Prime Minister, Paul Reynaud, made a last-ditch attempt to revive his country's military fortunes by replacing General Gamelin with General Weygand as commander-in-chief. That evening Churchill, in his first broadcast as Prime Minister, sought to bring home to the British public the gravity of the situation while still holding out hope of a successful Allied counteroffensive. On 15 May, and again on 22 May, he flew to Paris to give encouragement and support to the French, but no counterattack materialised, and by 25 May the commander of the BEF, Lord Gort, had concluded that he could only save his army by conducting a fighting retreat to the coast, and creating around the port of Dunkirk a bridgehead from which the troops could be evacuated across the Channel.

These are the facts as we know them now, but everyone at the time was enveloped to some extent in the fog of war. Reports were sketchy, but it was obvious that the news was bad, and in the absence of hard information rumour and speculation flourished. It was rumoured, for example, that Italy had entered the war, though this did not happen until 10 June, and that the two Princesses, Elizabeth and Margaret, had been sent to Canada. As Home Intelligence commented, the rumours were mainly home-grown but often attributed, by those who passed them on, to 'Lord Haw-Haw', the nickname for the Nazi propagandist William Joyce who broadcast regularly from Hamburg. Press reports alleged that in Belgium and Holland German parachutists had disguised themselves as peasants or clergymen and been assisted by a 'Fifth Column' of enemy sympathisers among the local population. Home Intelligence noted many rumours of parachutists landing in Britain disguised (for reasons best known to the enemy) as nuns. Rumour also pointed the finger of suspicion at enemy aliens, most of whom were of course refugees from Nazi persecution, and there were signs of growing intolerance towards conscientious objectors. MOI officials clearly felt that the public were in need of more leadership and guidance than they were getting, and looked above all to the BBC and the radio as the most effective means of information and propaganda on the home front.

Home Intelligence reports were often impressionistic and never more so than at this early stage, but the straws in the wind they detected suggested a general toughening of popular opinion, a frustrated activism among those who wanted to see the war prosecuted with greater vigour, and a warm welcome for positive measures. On 14 May Anthony Eden, the newly appointed Secretary of State for War, broadcast an appeal for men between the ages of seventeen and sixty-five to join a new part-time militia, the Local Defence Volunteers, intended to serve as a second line of defence in support of the army. (They were to be renamed 'The Home Guard' in July). 250,000 men put down their names within the first twenty-four hours. At the new Ministry of Aircraft Production Lord Beaverbrook injected a spirit of urgency into the drive to accelerate the output of warplanes. There was an enthusiastic response from garage hands when he appealed to them to apply for work in the aircraft factories, but his call for 24-hour working over the next two weekends proved more controversial.

On 22 May Parliament passed the Emergency Powers Act, which gave the government sweeping powers over labour (of which in the event only limited use was made) as well as property. That same day the War Cabinet decided to arrest Sir Oswald Mosley and other leading fascists under a new emergency regulation, 18B (1A), which gave the government the right to detain without trial anyone suspected of endangering public safety, public order, the prosecution of the war or the defence of the realm.

Although it was reported by Home Intelligence that there was as yet 'no fundamental realisation that the fight is for life', from the outset there was a strong belief in eventual victory: 'Still the phrase is heard on all sides "We shall win the last battle."'

SATURDAY 18 MAY 1940

Civilian Morale

This report has been put together hurriedly from a series of reports sent in by our observers over the last few months. In particular, the material collected since 10 May is analysed and an attempt is made to show the implication for morale of present events.

For the sake of speed conclusions are given first:

Conclusions

On 18 May people are by no means prepared for the shock which awaits them. Many will undoubtedly manage to make themselves feel that bad news is not *really* bad, but many fewer people will be able to do this than in previous months, and the propaganda of events is inescapable.

It is suggested that the *shock* of the news can be offset by doing several things. There will be immediate necessity to ease the burden on each *individual* mind, to relieve *personal* fear, and to steady the bewilderment which by its nature leads to feelings of inferiority and futility.

(1) It is imperative that people should not be rallied by the stock trick of recent years, 'the reassuring picture.'

(2) At the same time it is bad to give people flat facts and to allow the exploitation of personal fears and negative imaginative terrors.

(3) Fear needs to be expressive not repressive.

(4) Thus, while private individual fears are bad, socialised fears can be made positive and turned to account.

(5) Where personal fears exist an attempt should be made to liberate them. The fear of parachutists was strongly felt and privately held, particularly among women. Eden's broadcast offering an active solution (even though a partial one) was something aggressive and all our reports show that the broadcast did much to allay personal fears by transference to corporate action.

(6) People should be made to share their fears: to fraternise: be neighbourly. Street unities should be thought out. Social workers should make personal visits. ARP wardens should call personally. Those who play civic roles should be urged to show themselves. The Queen might tour the streets. It is important to stimulate a feeling of being a united nation (at the level of the street as well as at the level of the Cabinet).

(7) Civilian leaders should be chosen and quickly built up. Some would be national figures, e.g. the Duchess of Kent, Gracie Fields, (for women specially).

(8) Interpreters should be chosen and be constantly at work. It is necessary for the news and for events to be interpreted and explained. Retreat and disillusionment engender bewilderment without the help of interpreted facts. Facts, even bad ones, are some protection against bewilderment and suspicion. Interpreters like Vernon Bartlett should be *constantly* broadcasting, explaining each fresh phase and answering the many questions which remain unanswered hour by hour.

(9) Even at the eleventh hour people are seeking and needing a *positive purpose*, something aggressive, dynamic, beyond themselves, worth dying for, not just survival or 'blood, sweat and tears.'

A Summary of Public Opinion
on the Present Crisis

During the course of this afternoon a brief survey of public opinion was made in London and in the Regions (with the exception of Newcastle where the telephone was out of order).

The opinions expressed from the Regions were, of course, those of single individuals, and may therefore be biased in certain respects. But the consensus of opinions gathered both outside and inside London shows marked unanimity upon the major points.

The facts which most clearly emerge are that people are rather more depressed than frightened by the trend of events and that there seems to be confidence in the ultimate victory of the Allies. Nevertheless the gravity of the situation is generally realised.

There is a strong and widely expressed desire for definite instructions to be issued by the Government about what people could or should do to help the country and themselves at the present time. The feeling is that they would like to be disciplined, and would be glad to be given some precise duty or occupation to carry out.

The following is a brief summary of regional opinion:

LEEDS Morale is on the whole fairly good, chiefly because everyone is working full-time. The new phase of the war and the realisation of facts hitherto unfaced has stiffened resistance.

No rumours are reported.

The campaign of open-air meetings put into effect by the Ministry is having a good response, and there have been no interruptions.

CAMBRIDGE This morning there was optimism over the news, but there was some tension in Clacton and Ipswich over the re-evacuation order. There was also apprehension in Cambridge about troop movements, which were said to be for the purpose of combating a parachute raid. In the Chelmsford area there were rumours of parachute troops having landed, and from the same place it was said that there had been bombing at Harwich. Similar rumours and apprehensions were reported from the King's Lynn area.

People would like more explanation on the radio about the military situation. 'Onlooker' is considered too 'fatherly'.

NOTTINGHAM People are more depressed than frightened, though fear seems to be growing. The opinion is generally expressed that it would be a good thing on this account if the Prime Minister were to broadcast in a day or two.

No rumours are reported from this Region.

WALES Although there seems to be a good deal of depression, people seem to be less frightened than angry. The way in which the news is announced by the BBC is considered to account for some unnecessary alarm, and it is suggested that a reassuring personality such as Mr Duff Cooper or Mr Eden should give a short talk every evening *during*, but not after the news.

A rumour which is given general currency is that there is a large Fifth Column nucleus of German tourists in Eire.

BIRMINGHAM People are more bewildered and worried than they were yesterday, and would welcome instructions about what to do or how to act, providing these were of a *definite* nature. The point is made that Government speakers on the wireless would have a greater response if their appeals were directed to backing up the Services rather than the Government, which is much less of a reality to most people than the Navy, the Army or the Air Force.

MANCHESTER The public is not so much frightened as depressed. Today for the first time the news seems to be bringing home to a good many people the real gravity of the situation. The majority in this area ignored the Government's appeal to treat Whitsun Bank Holiday as an ordinary day.

The public would definitely welcome some sort of instructions about what they are expected to do in the present state of crisis. They would, in fact, like to be *disciplined*.

Rumours in this area are confined to exaggerated apprehensions about refugees arriving in great numbers.

BRISTOL Public morale has been shaken by recent events, particularly in Bristol. In Gloucestershire the news has awakened people; everywhere there is determination to win and a realisation that our backs are against the wall.

There are many evidences of rumours in this Region. At Gloucester aviation works it is rumoured that all men up to thirty-six are to be mobilised at once. At Exeter there has been a large water main burst and rumour has it that sabotage is responsible. Many rumours of air raids occur from time to time; one has it that all areas on the South East coast will be raided to drive people over to the South West where they can be bombed collectively. At Gloucester people are saying we are not making enough aeroplanes as there is not enough material at the two aeroplane factories there to provide full-time work.

People would prefer to know all the news, even if it is bad, and criticise the BBC news bulletins as having too little detail in them. They want German claims denied immediately. Exeter says: 'Bad news should be dressed up'. Plymouth, Exeter, Bristol and other towns are asking when the casualty lists are coming out. They suspect the numbers are so large that the Government dare not divulge them. Questions are also asked about how soon the Local Defence Volunteer Corps can act and why more enemy aliens are not interned.

TUNBRIDGE WELLS People do not seem to be frightened but are certainly more depressed than yesterday. General Gamelin's message has helped to account for this. Nevertheless confidence is expressed everywhere in an Allied victory. Most people seem to be prepared for the news to be temporarily worse during the coming weeks.

There was a persistent rumour on Thursday last that Italy had entered the war on the side of Germany.

SCOTLAND The public are undoubtedly more depressed than yesterday, but at the same time express confidence. The main sentiment seems to be that though we always lose the first battle, we always win the last one. (This point was stressed also by Mass Observation's survey made in London during the early afternoon).

Most people seem to be prepared for worse news to come but expect that this will be only temporary.

Observations made today in London largely confirm the trends of opinion expressed in the Regions. The views of working-class people seemed to be on the whole rather more optimistic than those of other classes. Though there is definite apprehension everywhere, and though the seriousness of the situation seems to be fully appreciated, there is also a feeling of confidence.

SUNDAY 19 MAY AND MONDAY 20 MAY 1940

There has been an increase of optimism since Friday and Saturday. The public is still somewhat depressed but there are no signs that determination is shaken. Information goes to show that opinion is labile, any straws of good news are seized and the press of Sunday and today has on the whole been less gloomy than on Saturday. The impression is gained that there is as yet no fundamental realisation that the fight is for life, although many people have envisaged the possibilities of invasion. We shall be able to take it as a common expression. Still the phrase is heard on all sides 'We shall win the last battle'.

Reports show that many women are frightened and that there is a general desire for more concrete proposals and indeed orders about what the public should do. There is a good deal of criticism in this connection on two points:

1. The machinery for registering mechanics at aircraft factories and Labour Exchanges was not ready when the applications began to be made.

2. That the Local Defence Volunteer Corps has not become organised beyond the receiving of applications.

There is also criticism from two or three Regions that Government factories are not working at full pressure because material is not available.

Village and country morale continues to be higher than urban morale chiefly because there is less realisation of the dangers.

Broadcasts

1. Mr Duff Cooper. Very well received. Detailed criticisms were made but overwhelmingly people thought the two broadcasts were 'a very good idea', 'first rate', 'shows we're being taken notice of', 'just what we want'. These comments are in general line with interviews on another subject which show that opinion is anxious for an *interpretation* of news.

2. The Prime Minister. All comments are favourable. 'A good fighting speech', 'makes you feel we're taken into his confidence', 'he's not hiding things'. There does not seem to be, however, any general realisation that the Prime Minister's speech had any extremely grave import.

Rumours

The number of rumours has increased considerably since Friday although they are still not as widespread as in September. Several need contradiction, e.g. that Princesses Elizabeth and Margaret Rose have gone to Canada, that parachutists have landed in specified areas, that Italy bombed Paris last night.

There are several scares about Fifth Column agents, particularly in relation to vulnerable points for sabotage. Churchill went to France to cheer Reynaud who is in tears. Italy is already marching through Switzerland. The incendiary bombs dropped near Canterbury were aimed at a secret factory in the woods. Haw-Haw is sending secret messages to the Fifth Column by code words in wireless talks.

Weygand's Appointment

The appointment is taken on trust and generally welcomed. Nowhere does it seem to be felt that the appointment indicated bad leadership. The only criticism is on account of Weygand's age.

Points from Regions

SCOTLAND 'Profound disappointment'. 'We're always too late'. Violent realisation that the Maginot Line did not, in fact, extend to the Channel. Churchill's speech received more seriously than elsewhere. Appeal to 'faith in God' considered to be ominous.

TUNBRIDGE WELLS Medway towns fully recognise their peril. Resigned. On the whole opinion 'encouraged and more determined'.

LONDON Growing resentment against Italians. 'If Italy became an enemy resentment would turn to action'. Churchill's frankness about the possibility of being raided appreciated. 'All are glad Bevin is in the Government'. 'A mood of belligerency and resolve'. Special reports indicate that 'subversive elements' and pacifist statements are on the decline and this is coupled with a new sense of responsibility among the middle classes and the intelligentsia. Surveys of working-class opinion in the East End seem to indicate that there is a good deal less realisation of the danger among working-class people. A Lambeth pub-keeper with an extensive clientele reports that 'tails are up'. 'They'll never get here but if they do we'll show them'.

Another pub-keeper with a more educated clientele sends in a special report in which he describes general criticism: 'They've been too dull and slow' (referring to the late Government). He reports a fighting spirit but emphasizes that there is no talk of defeat; what they want is retaliation.

BIRMINGHAM General satisfaction with the new Government. The special edition of a local newspaper announcing on Saturday 'Maginot Line broken' had a very bad effect. Very bitter feeling about COs and strong antipathy to female aliens. 'Shut up the lot'.

Indications for Action

1. Mr Duff Cooper's broadcasts should be continued. It is considered the duty of a Minister of Information to interpret the news or deliberately to delegate that responsibility to someone else.

2. The Princesses should appear in public with careful publicity attached.

3. The public should be told that the situation in Eire is not being ignored. (There is a general feeling that Fifth Column in Eire is a great danger).

4. COs may increasingly become the object of antagonism which may develop in an ugly way. The public should be told that COs do

not make good soldiers and are therefore not wanted in the Army. Their small and decreasing number should be emphasized.

5. There is a general feeling of alarm that Fifth Column members may become armed through the LDVC.

6. The balloon barrage was apparently ineffective over Hamburg and Bremen. What is the moral for our own defences?

7. There is perpetual criticism in general and in detail about BBC news broadcasts. In particular it is felt that minor news stories about small groups of Messerschmitts etc follow inappropriately after important statements on the greatest battle in the history of the world, etc. Many reports criticise the way in which the programmes were interrupted for Roosevelt's speech. The announcement created considerable alarm. (There is some danger of 'Wolf', 'Wolf' here).

8. The opinion has been expressed in various quarters that some fundamental statement on a post-war social policy coming from 'the new Government' would have an effect in rallying the extreme Left-Wing section of youth organisations (16–20). Youth is 'waiting for a sign' and there are indications that young people will continue to withhold cooperation until they get some assurance that the future is being thought about in a constructive way. Reports show that young people are not content with 'We are fighting for our lives; nothing else matters'. Eden is still an acceptable figure among many youth organisations and observations on his broadcast showed that it was very well received. Failing the Prime Minister he would be a welcome substitute for such a statement.

TUESDAY 21 MAY 1940

Morale is noticeably 'brighter' today. There is a consensus of opinion from the Regions and from our own observer corps that there is rather more optimism, but not over-optimism, of the 'Narvik' kind. Opinion is little changed since Sunday and Monday and this is in line with the general newspaper tone, which has tended to stress any optimistic indications, e.g. 'BEF strike at bulge' (Daily Mail), 'Nazi drive to Cambrai slows down' (Daily Telegraph), 'Fierce battle goes on round St Quentin . . . Nazi tanks were destroyed' (News Chronicle), 'Mystery moves by Weygand; is it the counter-stroke?' (Daily Express).

The following notes are indicative of the general feeling:

1. Most people are slightly less worried and slightly more cheerful today, partly because they are beginning to face up to a more serious situation than they have previously visualised. It is thought that we are holding the Germans.

2. Relieved tension is also indicated in the number of people who show less interest in the news today or who have not bothered to acquaint themselves with the newspapers by mid-morning.

3. In general, it may be said that a mental readjustment is taking place. This readjustment is 'healthy' to the extent that many people are facing up to possible unpleasantness, although they do not yet visualise the full seriousness of the situation.

4. Some people have now exhausted their nervous anxieties and are now worrying less because they have worried so much during the last few days. A typical comment is: 'I'm not going to worry any more till they're here'.

5. The effect of Churchill's speech is still apparent. Complacency was disturbed by it and although many people were worried by the serious implications of the speech, others were stirred by it and are now definitely 'facing the facts'. Of 150 house-to-house interviews in the London area, approximately half said they were frightened and worried by the speech; the rest were 'heartened', 'made more determined', 'stiffened'.

6. Morale in villages is still definitely stronger than urban morale.

7. House-to-house visits show that women are, as usual, more pessimistic about the situation. Women are more nervous about air raids, more concerned about their children, more concerned about 'nothing being done'.

8. The belief that Britain will triumph eventually is universal.

Points from Regions

SCOTLAND Prevailing optimism and confidence. Acute anxiety disappearing.

CAMBRIDGE People are waiting patiently upon events but are relieved at the news. Very bad effect created at Luton when garage mechanics applied at aeroplane works and were told that, owing to the lack of war materials, the present staff was not on full production. Communists and Pacifists are less active. Growing feeling that COs should not be allowed to keep on at their jobs in trades.

MANCHESTER Beaverbrook's appeal had a great response but keen disappointment is expressed because so many applicants were turned away. The public continue to ask what they are expected to do in the present crisis.

WALES Strong feeling that all available man-power is not being used. Anti-Italian feeling growing.

LEEDS Miners still tend to be disregardful of the war effort.

READING People will follow any lead the Government gives. The public only asks for something specific to do. Demand for further action over aliens.

LONDON

Morale considerably improved. A general feeling that 'we are holding them', particularly finding expression among the working classes. Influx of Dutch and Belgian refugees not regarded with favour. House-to-house visiting showed that mothers are still saying that they will keep their children near them even if London is bombed. Common expressions are: 'They are safer in London'. 'It's the coast towns which are going to suffer'. 'We are well defended'.

Rumours

Rumours have considerably increased and in some cases are creating alarm. One point emerges strongly: Haw-Haw is quoted as the source of many rumours. Investigation, however, shows that there has been *no* reference by German propaganda to the places or industries quoted in the rumours. There is an urgent request from nearly all RIOs, as well as from the Home Office and individual correspondence, that these rumours shall be officially denied.

The most prominent rumours are that parachutists have landed in specific areas. (A telegram from Warwickshire says that a motor-cyclist dashed into a pub with the news and rode off again quickly). The New British Broadcasting Station said that many parachutists had landed in Great Britain and that it was obvious that Hitler was clever enough to land many thousands more. This station may be the origin of the parachute rumours.

There is evidence, however, that most rumours arise from general chatter and from the anxiety states of the last few days. It is commonly *believed* that rumours are the work of Fifth Columnists. (Most RIOs and individual correspondents express this view.) The following rumours appear to be dangerous:

1. General Gamelin shot as member of Fifth Column.

2. 'German News' says that Nuneaton, Coventry, Stoke, Stafford, Birmingham, Shrewsbury, Walsall, Wolverhampton are to be bombed.

3. The French Army has been annihilated. Amiens, Abbeville, Arras are captured. Boulogne is reached.

4. Haw-Haw is sending messages to Fifth Columnists by code words in wireless talks.

There are definite indications that the whole rumour situation should be dealt with by means of an authoritative postscript to the news. The situation should be analysed and attention should be directed to the danger of repeating rumours and the importance of tracking them to their source. It should be shown that Haw-Haw is not, in fact, giving references to specific places and industries.

Disbelief in News

As usual there is detailed criticism of BBC news broadcasts. There are further demands for news interpretation and for more speeches like Duff Cooper's.

The whole subject of disbelief in news sources will be the subject of a special report tomorrow.

WEDNESDAY 22 MAY 1940

There was a considerable depression in all parts of the country following the 6 o'clock news yesterday. Reynaud's remark that 'only a miracle could save France' appears to have been too baldly given and it had a bad effect. Duff Cooper's speech at 9 p.m. had, however, a most stimulating and counteracting effect though there were some criticisms of his classical references. Only in Manchester was it disliked. The possibility of invasion is faced with anxiety but with confidence in the ultimate outcome. There is a continued demand for truthful news however black it may be, particularly if it can be given out before German claims are heard. The bombing of Germany is welcomed and people are prepared for reprisals. There is a wide demand for more work of wartime importance and disappointment when it is not forthcoming.

Morale in the Regions

TUNBRIDGE WELLS Reaction to bombs and anti-aircraft guns in East Sussex is pleasurable excitement rather than alarm. Duff Cooper's broadcast produced 'new heart'.

READING No panic. Realisation of our vulnerability. Reynaud caused much speculation. Demand for franker news, and clearer differentiation – especially BBC – between official and unofficial, and factual and conjectural. Want stronger action against aliens. Liked Duff Cooper.

BRISTOL Morale improved. Disappointment wide at inability of firms to get Government work. Want more authoritative statements on news, especially to counter German statements subsequently proved to be true. Demand for a lead for action for civilian population. Dorset upset at lack of air-raid shelters. Some anti-Dutch and anti-Belgian refugee feeling.

NEWCASTLE No weakening of morale, though much anxiety about war news. Duff Cooper's speech approved. Spurt in intensity of war production.

BIRMINGHAM 'Only a miracle can save France' (6 p.m. news) put fear of God into people. They were heartened by longer statement at 9 p.m. Reports of industrial production held up and workers sacked through lack of supplies. Duff Cooper's speech 'good'.

MANCHESTER Rural areas quiet, urban anxious. They regarded Duff Cooper's speech as 'soothing syrup' and did not like it. 'French have let us down but will stage a come-back'. A Trade Union row is brewing about Beaverbrook appeal.

NOTTINGHAM Duff Cooper's speech welcomed. He balanced Reynaud. People are ready for reprisals. In Newark, heavy losses in Norway have stiffened pro-war feeling.

CAMBRIDGE Depressed by 6 o'clock news. Cheered by Duff Cooper at 9 p.m. Request for Duff Cooper weekly or even more often. Air activity off Harwich had no effect on population who are used to it. Women more anxious everywhere than men.

LEEDS Morale good. 'Rock-like calm'. Duff Cooper's speech welcomed. Grave but necessary. Growing anti-alien feeling. Internment of Dutch refugees advocated.

CARDIFF People stunned by bad news. Morale better since then. Reynaud came as a shock. Duff Cooper counteracted it. Less uneasy afterwards. Bernard Stubbs's eye witness account of an air raid much criticised as 'individualist.' Individuals do not matter now. Much feeling that we have been let down by France and by our own High Command. Beaverbrook's 24-hour shift speech criticised: 'too late now'. Everyone wants full-time war work. Request for armed guards at Post Offices, Town Halls, Police Stations, Railway Stations – to increase confidence. Growing anti-alien feeling, especially anti-Italian. Dutch and Belgian refugees had good effect locally. Religio-pacifist Welsh press now calling Germans 'barbarians'.

EDINBURGH Today's news of Arras is welcomed. Ready for further sacrifices if there is intention to take military initiative. Bombing of Germany welcomed although our own risk is increased.

BELFAST No alarm. Growing anti-Fifth Column feeling. Difficulty over arming anti-parachute troops is fear of arms reaching subversive elements. Depressing effect of Reynaud counteracted by Duff Cooper. Dutch and Belgian refugees welcomed, but need for rigid precautions stressed.

LONDON

General anxiety but confidence in the ultimate issue. Women more depressed than men. The possibility of invasion openly faced. Some suggestions that France's mistakes have been due to treachery. Occasional half-joking defeatist remarks heard. Reynaud's speech as reported in 6 o'clock news produced severe depression, satisfactorily counteracted by Duff Cooper. News of recapture of Arras this afternoon caused rise of spirits but people do not accept good news readily for fear of its subsequent contradiction. Much Fifth Column suspicion. Elderly clergyman booed in Hyde Park as Fifth Columnist. Innocent people may soon be molested. WVS have started a housewives' service to aid ARP work in Hornsey. Women unable to leave their homes are training in first-aid and putting up HS outside their houses to show they will take in the slightly wounded to save wardens' time. Fitting of new gas-mask filters has produced no alarm whatever. Unemployed workers at Dagenham complain that not enough effort is being made. London shows same reactions as the provinces but more quickly and to a greater degree.

Rumours

In general the rumour situation remains unchanged. There are still a very large number, some undoubtedly emanating from the German wireless, and others which are simply fatuous originating in imaginative and excitable minds. There is ground for believing that many of both sorts are widely believed. Among those reported today, and which seem to be of significance, are stories that Mr Churchill went to Paris to prevent the French Government from 'packing up there and then', that there are a million colonial troops in France to suppress disorder in the French Army, that Mussolini is planning to enter the war on 25 May, (this being the 20th anniversary of Italy's entrance into the last war).

There are persistent rumours about General Gamelin – that he has shot himself – about a German invasion of Wales through Eire, and there is the usual crop of parachute and bombing rumours from all parts of the country. A large number of others which have been reported, some purporting to have been put about by the German radio, are for the most part fantastic but harmless.

THURSDAY 23 MAY 1940

In general there is a noticeable increase in cheerfulness and general calm, a distinct decrease in pessimism and nervousness. The intense gloom which affected London particularly yesterday is not conspicuous today.

However, there is little over-optimism.

Today's reports suggest that there is a growing basis for a more durable morale. People are rallied not simply by what appears to be better news, but also, though to a lesser extent, *by facing up to the facts and by feeling that they are now taking a more active part in the war.*

There is an increased tendency to say that there has been disgraceful neglect in the past, that something must have been badly wrong at the top. With this goes a new feeling that a big effort is going to be required and that the new government is tackling the problem realistically. Verbatims reflect this:

> *'Well, everyone's in it now.'*
> *'I'm prepared to do anything.'*
> *'It looks as if we're going to do something really big now.'*

Many of these reactions come from the Emergency Powers Bill, which has had an excellent reception, particularly from men and from working-class people. In certain districts there is criticism e.g. 'We're imitating the Nazis now it comes to the point.'

The importance of the new Bill is that it has made people more conscious of their part in the war and of the seriousness of the situation. It is a nail in the coffin of wishful thinking. In the minds of many the Bill means compulsion, and there is a growing tendency for compulsory powers to be welcomed. The Bill provides an important background for action (the kind of background which has been lacking so far). It is important that the Bill should constantly be interpreted, explained, and followed up by suitable propaganda. As far as one can judge people feel the Bill makes for national unity, and for that reason it has been welcomed.

London morale still lags behind that of provincial towns and of the countryside. In London some social workers express doubt about the effect of air raids upon the working-class population.

54% of the electorate voted in the Middleton by-election. A notable increase over recent by-elections. Fascist candidate lost deposit.

Points from Regions

SCOTLAND The Emergency Powers Bill is received with general satisfaction. 'The Bill was overdue.' 'The Government means business.' The call to complete Identity Cards called forth some alarmed comment. It was thought that more explanation of the need should have been given.

WALES The EPB well received. 'Just what was wanted.' Some confusion about the need for filling in the Identity Cards. 'What for?' 'To whom will they have to be shown?' 'Why are photographs not attached?'

No need for special posters. Large crop of rumours yesterday.

NORTHERN IRELAND EPB well received. Increase of work now expected. Readiness to meet any new demands. Meeting of 500 Belfast dockers at the Coal Quay to consider the question of expediting coal discharge. Demand for further action about parachute corps.

CAMBRIDGE Decreased rumours. General approval for EPB.

READING Considerable growth of rumours, many of which would appear to breed defeatism.

TUNBRIDGE WELLS EPB welcomed. Strong favourable comment on Bevin's position. Some uneasiness in coastal towns, but few signs of evacuation. Rumours prevalent.

BRISTOL Support for EPB but strong demand for immediate cooperation by the public. 'We are all anxious to be up and doing.' 'Tell us exactly what to do, and we will do it.' 'Reveal the working machinery of the new act.'

Disruptive elements quiescent.

BIRMINGHAM EPB everywhere welcomed. Enthusiasm waiting to be canalised into concrete action.

LEEDS EPB welcomed. Continued praise of Duff Cooper's broadcast.

NEWCASTLE Very favourable reception for EPB. 'It should have been introduced earlier.' 'It will help production.' 'It will prevent skilled men moving about from one place to another.'

MANCHESTER EPB excellently received by labour and employers. Anxiety about savings alleviated by Kindersley's broadcast. Some evidence that Communist opposition is declining.

LONDON

Duff Cooper's speech still talked about enthusiastically. EPB well received on the whole. Some criticism received from the suburbs. A social worker reports 'an air of false security'. 'Optimism shoots up directly when the news gives half a chance.' Fewer people carrying gas masks than a week ago.

Rumours

There are generally speaking fewer reports of rumours today, and there are none that would appear to be of major importance. With the exception of one quoted in Nottingham by a local councillor to the effect that the BEF are withdrawing from Belgium, all the rest are concerned with hypothetical nuns, bombs and parachutists. Nevertheless, a good many of these have a very unsettling effect and there seems to be no difficulty in their gaining ground. A large number of those which are brought to our notice are still reported as having their origin from the German wireless. One in particular which seems to be causing some alarm to the inhabitants at Twickenham is to the effect that Kneller Hall, the Military School situated in the district, would be one of the first places to be bombed. It may be worth noting in this connection that there is said to be a considerable amount of Fascist feeling in this area.

FRIDAY 24 MAY 1940

There is little change on yesterday except that optimism is slightly down, anxiety is slightly up. There is general recognition that the situation is extremely serious but there is no diminution in confidence in ultimate victory. The possibility of invasion is being faced up to by a few people but there is no general realisation that this may be a possibility.

The acute tension of a week ago has been relieved and there is a tendency for people to believe that they now know the worst. Opinion, however, is unstable and detailed reports over the last fortnight show in a striking way the day-to-day swing of public feeling: anxiety, optimism, pessimism, bewil-derment chase one another over succeeding days. There has been no steady trend of public feeling over the whole period of the invasion. Public opinion is pinned to day-to-day incidents: headlines about the recapture of Arras bring relief; the next day bad news about Boulogne brings temporary gloom. This swing in itself is evidence of a continual nervous tension and the conclu-sion emerges that some steadying, general, forward-looking, slightly long-term attitude would help many people to face the sparse and conflicting news which threatens their morale.

Women, as usual, show more signs of nervous tension than men.

London continues to have a lower morale than the provinces. Londoners are more mobile, more subject to news changes by placards and evening editions. This London situation requires attention since the first real shock is likely to fall on London. London therefore needs a firmer and more stable background tone instead of a less-integrated and more changeable emotional tone.

A new feature today is the great increase and sometimes intense violence of criticism against the French. 'The French are letting us down'. 'I thought the Maginot Line came right up to the Channel; the French hid all that'. 'It's the French keeping everything dark all these months, censoring every-thing, putting all the Opposition into jail'. The French are now becoming the scapegoat and observer reports today indicate that there is a prevalent feeling that if we are defeated, the French will have been to blame. There was plenty of evidence during the last few months that there was no nation-wide feeling of affection and brotherliness for our ally. Confidence in French social structure as well as in the power of French arms has been badly shaken. The consequences of this may be dangerous.

No one knows what has happened to General Gamelin: it is vitally impor-tant that the dangerous rumours about his fate, which are tied up with the whole position of France as a stable social unit, should be put to rest by some factual statement. Liberal and left-wing criticism of the French treat-ment of minority opinion is coming to the fore again and this time it is finding a place in the opinions of ordinary non-political people.

The arrest of Mosley and other Fascists has overwhelming approval. Our observers report that they have seldom found such a high degree of approval for any Government action. The most frequent comment is that it should have been done long ago.

Peace News *today has an important article. The following statement is made: 'The Pacifist movement must not confuse the right to bear its witness*

*and take its punishment with the right to say what it likes and go un-
punished. If it wants relative freedom . . . then it must reject the notion that
its business is to impede the Government in the prosecution of the war . . .
we need a new sense of responsibility, of devotion and of discipline'.*

Points from Regions

All Regions show the following:

1. Great satisfaction at arrest of Fascists.

2. Demand for more work to implement Emergency Powers Bill.
When this is not forthcoming there is much dissatisfaction.

Most Regions show a demand for BBC news bulletins giving more
space to important but unpleasant military events and less to isolated
aerial exploits.

SCOTLAND Suggestions for action against Communists reported.
Criticism of large number of French troops in Glasgow. General
opinion of public 'bewilderment'.

BELFAST Public steady. Position of Eire generally thought unsatisfactory from UK security standpoint.

WALES General public calm but concerned. Arrest of Fascists will
reduce activities of 'Swansea Loyalists' as self-appointed guardians
of public safety.

NEWCASTLE Slight increase in anxiety particularly among women.

MANCHESTER Public mystified and anxious. 'Tanks seem to go where
they like'. Arming of police welcomed.

LEEDS Grave and anxious but no panic. Many spontaneous offers to
shelter refugees. Success of recruiting of Local Defence Volunteers
has reduced ARP recruiting.

NOTTINGHAM Public puzzled but willing to cooperate.

BIRMINGHAM Uneasy. Demand for further acceleration of calling-up and armament activity is common. Poor people and small shopkeepers worried about Emergency Powers Act fearing they will be sent to make munitions, their shops shut, and their savings taken.

READING Danger appreciated but no panic. More aircraft demand.

BRISTOL Reactions very mixed in South West. Cornwall worried particularly about large numbers of unknown aliens who have piled into the county since war began. Bristol and Plymouth – no change. Wiltshire nervous but not panicky. Dorset – no alarm. Appreciation of Air Marshal's broadcast last night was wide.

TUNBRIDGE WELLS Grave but not despondent. German statement that Dover had been bombed gained no currency whatever.

CAMBRIDGE Calm but growing indecision. Evacuation of women and children from East Coastal towns would be welcomed.

There is growing local feeling against the Cotswold Bruderhof. If parachutists landed locally Bruderhof might be lynched.

Rumours

There is a general prevalence of rumours again today; although in the main these are wild and illogical there are one or two which seem to call for immediate action. The most important of these is that it will shortly be impossible to cash cheques owing to the run which is being made on the banks (this matter has already been reported to the Treasury, by whom, it is understood, action is now being taken). Another report stated to be generally current along the East Coast is that the whole of that district is to be evacuated to the West. This is attributed to last night's German radio.

There are, as usual, a large number of rumours dealing with

subjects connected in some way with military activities, many of these no doubt because of their circumstantial nature are reported to be having alarming effects on the civil population. There are, for instance, reports of new kinds of weapons such as armed gliders, delayed action gas cylinders and amphibious channel crossing tanks. In Deptford there has been a resuscitation of the story which seems to be worrying a good many people of a gas which paralyses the will power. It has also been stated (in Bolton last night) that British casualties in France already amount to 100,000.

There is a rumour also about the inefficiency of the present civilian gas masks and it is stated that the new filters are for protection against an hitherto unknown gas. Whether or not this belief is generally prevalent, it seems desirable that some kind of reassurance should be given on this point, in view of the extreme rapidity with which such reports circulate.

Rumours of a civilian character are many and various and among those of importance are the story of a West Country clergyman who is stated to be instructing school children not to report parachutists. From Bristol, Dorset, Plymouth and Wiltshire there are reports of prominent men having been arrested, and there seems ground for believing that these stories are very widely believed. It is suggested by the Bristol RIO from whom this was received that they are so numerous to suggest a deliberate campaign to undermine confidence in public men throughout the Region. From the same sources there are reports that Haw-Haw announced on the wireless the number of barrage balloons at Bristol, and the fact that there would be no necessity for the completion of an aircraft factory now in erection at Swindon. There is, however, no confirmation that either of these reports were in fact broadcast from Germany.

In addition to these examples there are the usual crop of stories about 'hairy handed nuns', parachutists etc., including one about a house full of blind refugees who were alleged to be in possession of machine guns. The true facts of this incident have been explained by the Secretary of the National Institute for the Blind. The explanation is, of course, perfectly reasonable and bears no likeness whatever to the rumour.

In general it seems that the number of rumours may be on the increase, the fact that there are so many makes it increasingly necessary for all of them to be examined carefully so that in appropriate cases denials can be issued immediately by the proper authorities. As those of a military character seem on the whole to be the most frightening, though no doubt often the most incredible, there would seem to be an urgent necessity for some means of denouncing this type of canard regularly, either by means of the wireless or the press.

Clearly the presence of rumours is symptomatic of an underlying condition of ignorance, bewilderment or distrust. Rumours may be spread deliberately (Fifth Column activity) or may be the product of idle and irresponsible gossiping.

There was a strong prevalence of rumours last September; they have again emerged as an important factor in public morale.

Two facts should be appreciated:

1. Rumours are not recognised as such but are *believed*.

2. The great majority of rumours have a *local* context.

The great majority of rumours at the present time are about parachutists and Fifth Column activities. The origin of many of these statements (e.g. three parachutists landed last night near Ashford) is fully believed to be 'the German wireless'. In fact a close scrutiny of the monitored broadcasts shows that specific rumours have *not* originated from Hamburg. There is no mention by Lord Haw-Haw of specific places like Stoke-on-Trent, the local cinema at Woodbridge, the ARP posts in Weston-super-Mare, etc. On the other hand, the New British Broadcasting Station (the short-wave German station situated near Cologne) has on various occasions described the descent of parachutists in England and has provided other material which might be considered to be a source of specific rumour. It should be remembered that the NBBS pretends to be situated in this country and to represent the interests of the British people. It is not easy to hear but the local press is inclined to report what the NBBS says about a specific locality (e.g. 'Worthing was mentioned last night on the German wireless and we are going to be told next week what Worthing citizens think about the war.')

Rumours during the last few days have tended to emphasize some aspect of our own feebleness or futility, e.g. unchecked landing of parachutists, inability of the police to cope with parachutists, inefficiency of anti-aircraft batteries, dislocation of services, etc. This kind of rumour is clearly unhealthy for it is an unconscious reflection of privately held opinion. The following rumours sent in by our observers illustrate this point:

> The police have definitely been told that catching parachutists is none of their business; they can only report it to military authorities.
>
> A balloon barrage broke away in Sussex and they say it took the anti-aircraft guns seven hours to shoot it down.
>
> The boys are all coming back from Belgium without boots.
>
> Five parachutists came down in Suffolk and it was hours before they were caught.

Other rumours are of a general kind and are found more or less unchanged in various parts of the country, e.g. General Gamelin has been shot as a Fifth Columnist.

That Haw-Haw is sending messages to Fifth Columnists by code words in wireless talks.

It is important to remember that certain statements gain currency from German broadcast bulletins which have been in the habit of getting their news in first. The British public heard from the German wireless that Gamelin had gone. They also heard that the Germans had taken Amiens and Arras twelve hours before they got the news from the British press and wireless.

The German invasion of Norway and Denmark, Holland and Belgium was preceded by a great mass of rumours circulating in those countries. A deliberate whispering campaign in Holland led Dutch civilians and soldiers to believe that they were about to be invaded by Great Britain. After the invasion wishful thinking promoted the spread of rumours that British troops had landed by plane in Rotterdam, etc. Evidence from Denmark shows that the spreading of rumours is a technique of Fifth Columnists. The wrong date is attached to a forthcoming occasion – the occasion being a probable one. The date becomes fixed as probable also and the public becomes confused and bewildered or even falsely confident.

The rumour situation is becoming so serious that it becomes imperative for the whole matter to be discussed in detail. It is useless to warn people against *repeating rumours*; most people only repeat what they believe to be true and they repeat it because they have nothing more positive to talk about and their time is not being actively filled. Enemy agents may be at work and there is malicious gossiping but evidence before us at the moment suggests that most rumours are passed on by idle, frightened, suspicious people.

SATURDAY 25 MAY 1940

There is definite evidence of increasing confusion. Today the strongest optimists (working-class men) are often qualifying their remarks with slight suspicion or doubt about the way things are developing. There is public uneasiness: a fortnight's waiting filled with troughs and peaks of depression and optimism is now beginning to produce bewilderment and disquiet. The first shock is over, and people are beginning to feel that large questions ought to be capable of some answer.

1. The opinion has been strongly held that Weygand had 'something up his sleeve' and the necessity for secrecy was appreciated, but many people are now asking what is the reason for the inexplicable inability of the French Army to check the enemy on French territory.

2. Depression is quite definitely up, but on the whole the main trend is towards fatalism, as if people's minds were prepared for almost anything in the way of bad news. Complacency has practically disappeared.

3. Reports from East Norfolk, South-east Essex and the North Riding show that there was public excitement over the raids but no panic. Events were taken calmly. There has been no movement of the population.

4. There are further reports which show that the morale of women is considerably lower than that of men.

5. The King's speech had a steadying but not a deep effect. It was generally liked but most frequent comments were on the improvement in His Majesty's delivery and on the slightly impersonal note of the broadcast.

6. Many people expressed the opinion that the mobilisation of man-power and woman-power is still not being tackled realistically. Many people expected immediate Government action following the Emergency Powers Act. Common verbatims are: 'I am still waiting to be told what to do.' 'I'm ready to do anything, if they'd only tell us what.' 'I can't believe that I'm not wanted.'

A small statistical survey of opinion on the EPA showed 60% strongly in favour, 15% no opinion, 24% favourable under the circumstances, and a statistically negligible percentage antagonistic.

Class and Sex Differences in Morale

An analysis of reports over the whole period of the invasion shows:

1. That men are more optimistic, less anxious and less doubtful than women. This is true not only in a quantitative sense but in a *qualitative* sense also.

2. Upper classes show more disquiet and slightly less optimism than working class. There is more *doubt* among the working class.

3. It can be shown that tension is greatest among middle and upper-class women, and least among working-class men.

4. It should not be forgotten that working-class women are less well informed, and better able to put aside future fears than women in the better-off classes of the community, but these generalisations do not enable one to express any opinion on possible breakdowns in morale among working-class women. A number of social workers consulted are of the opinion that working-class women are more likely to show panic than other classes of the community.

Points from Regions

Although there seems to be general confidence about the ultimate outcome of the war, there is considerable confusion in most of the Regions about the present military situation in France. Coincident with this is a feeling of tension and expectation of a coming counter-attack; unless this materialises fairly soon the effect on morale would seem to be to increase general uneasiness. At the moment, however, the public on the whole seems to be fairly calm and determined.

BRISTOL Uneasiness about France's military effectiveness, and at the same time a sense of relief that we have at last 'woken up'. A general understanding of the necessity for all to take their part in the war effort.

The effect of Haw-Haw is considered in this Region to be extremely insidious, and this danger is underestimated by the BBC and the Government, who do not fully appreciate to what extent this propaganda is believed.

BIRMINGHAM The public are worried by the absence of successful Allied counterattack, and by the apparent inability of the Allies to stop Nazi penetration towards the coast. Though their anxiety on this score is to some extent, however illogically, lessened for the moment by the King's speech, which is said to have pulled them together; this was said to be a 'grand effort'.

In some sections of the community there is a rather defeatist feeling among people who are not very well off and who have not much idea of what we shall lose if we do not win the war.

The alarmist headlines of the national daily papers in the last few days have been a subject of comment in this area. Criticism is made of the fact that there is too little comment or refutation of German claims.

MANCHESTER There is evidence of increasing support for the Government among the working-class section of the public. The King's speech was 'deeply moving'. Rumours are said to be increasing in both number and danger, and suggestions are made that ridicule by the BBC and press would be the most effective way of dealing with this situation.

READING Although tension is increased there is no suggestion of panic, but the continued absence of the eagerly awaited Allied offensive is causing a good deal of apprehension. There is a growing anxiety about bombing and parachute troops – fears continue to be fed by rumour.

The action taken against potential Fifth Columnists is strongly approved, and it is considered that these precautions should be carried to even greater lengths.

Opinion on the King's speech is that it was 'just what was wanted'.

CAMBRIDGE In spite of the fact that bombs fell in two places in this area this morning, morale seems to remain firm and people have taken this event with calmness.

The inexplicable inability of the French Army to check the enemy has caused considerable uneasiness. This is to some extent allayed by a hope that Weygand 'has something up his sleeve'; unless this hope is soon fulfilled the consequent reaction is likely to be most unfavourable.

The King's broadcast was a great success and was considered to have been well timed.

NOTTINGHAM The King's speech was extremely well received.

From this Region alone anxiety is expressed about the lack of reassuring information from Narvik. Our apparent inability to capture the town seems to be causing dubious speculation about the effectiveness of our Norwegian forces.

LEEDS Morale is unchanged by events of the last twenty-four hours. There is confidence and no panic, though rumours seem to be rather more prevalent. Some of these are attributed on what would seem fairly circumstantial evidence to the activities of Fifth Columnists, and intensification of action against such people is being widely suggested.

EDINBURGH The absence of any explicit news about the military situation in France is having a confusing effect, and the urgent need for some regeneration of confidence in the Allied armies is necessary. Absence of news about the situation is causing some depression, though in the main opinion is firm and hopeful.

The King's speech was well received, so too was the arrest of Sir Oswald Mosley.

TUNBRIDGE WELLS The capture of Boulogne had a very depressing effect on public opinion, though this was to some extent offset by the King's speech which was very well received. The rapidity of the German advance, however, gives rise to an uneasy feeling that all is not as it should be with the Allied Command. There has been some apprehension about parachutists. The activities of the Defence Volunteer Corps are encouraging feelings of confidence.

NEWCASTLE In spite of the air raids last night in this Region, there have been no signs of panic or alarm.

The BBC's explanation for the withholding of details about the French military situation is welcomed, though criticised on the grounds that the wording of it was too 'indirect and guarded' to be reassuring.

The King's speech was well received.

CARDIFF Feeling is definitely disturbed by our apparent inability to check the German advance, and by the possibility that this may mean that our own troops will be cut off, but nevertheless there is confidence in our ultimate success.

The rapid formation of the Defence Volunteer Corps has had a stimulating effect on public opinion.

BELFAST The event which seems to have had most effectiveness in this Region is that of the Dublin Military Court case in which were revealed the elements of the Nazi intrigue. This has led to the belief that the secret operations are all the more dangerous and widespread in character than had hitherto been realised. The rounding up of certain members of the IRA and a similar swoop in Britain is generally approved.

The King's speech was very well received.

LONDON

In the London area feeling is generally much the same as that noticed in the Regions. There is a certain amount of apprehension and still further confusion about the military situation. This seems in terms to breed pessimism, though there is no doubt that the general feeling is still determined. The effect of the King's speech has been (a) to stiffen the resistance of people who already realised the gravity of the situation, and (b) to depress and destroy the complacency of those who had not yet realised it. On the whole, the speech was extremely well received.

Feeling in the main seems to combine fatalism, determination and depression, all of which will seem to be attributable to the extreme state of uncertainty about the present situation, although it is realised that this must continue at any rate for the next few weeks. It is understandably difficult to adjust one's mentality to meet the circumstances without some trend of heart.

Rumours

Although no rumours have come to hand today which can be said to be of outstanding importance, there is evidence that a great many are still being circulated, some of which seem to be put about deliberately. Of this type the following is typical: cinema managers in the Exeter district have been told by some of their regular patrons that the showing of the film 'Hitler, Beast of Berlin' should be abandoned next week as Haw-Haw has threatened that Exeter will be bombed if it is shown. This story is apparently widely believed.

A story which is liable to have extremely undesirable repercussions and which is said to be generally current, is that 'the whole stores of the BEF at Boulogne' were left behind when our troops evacuated the town.

Other rumours which, if they are widely propagated, may easily lead to disquiet, unless they are either contradicted at once or confirmed and fully explained, are that all police are to be armed, and that the carrying of respirators is to be made compulsory.

Today there has been the usual crop of parachutist and nun stories, as well as numerous repetitions of General Gamelin's suicide or execution.

The fact that nothing of outstanding importance has been reported today does not indicate that the stories already in circulation are having any less effect, and it is highly desirable that as many rumours as possible should be traced and exposed, since the difficulty of suppressing them is obvious. There seems to be a widespread feeling that the powers of the BBC and the press are not being properly used for this purpose, and there is no doubt that if some form of comprehensive or individual denial could be made *during* the 6 and 9 o'clock news bulletins and could subsequently be confirmed in the following morning's newspapers, a good many of the more harmful rumours would be disproved.

MONDAY 27 MAY TO SATURDAY 1 JUNE 1940

Operation Dynamo, the evacuation of the British Expeditionary Force from Dunkirk, began on the evening of 26 May, but an official news black-out was maintained until the evening of 30 May. While RAF Fighter Command sustained heavy losses fighting off the Luftwaffe in the skies above and around Dunkirk, the BEF and the French First Army battled to maintain a perimeter around the approaches to the port, and the ships of the Royal Navy, commanded by Admiral Sir Bertram Ramsay from his headquarters in Dover, began lifting British troops from the beaches and the harbour. They were assisted by the 'little ships': privately-owned small boats requisitioned by the Admiralty, and a variety of other craft, including lifeboats, fishing vessels, barges and pleasure steamers, whose crews responded to an appeal broadcast by the BBC.

The plight of the BEF was intensified on 28 May by the decision of King Leopold of the Belgians to order the surrender of the 300,000-strong Belgian Army, which had been defending a part of the perimeter. After protests from Reynaud, Churchill agreed on 31 May that French as well as British troops would be evacuated. By 1 June more than a quarter of a million Allied troops had been transported across the Channel. Home Intelligence reported that morale in general was still holding firm though pockets of defeatist talk were detected in Godalming and Fulham. 'The whiter the collar,' the Regional Information Officer for Reading observed, 'the less the assurance' – a judgement reaffirmed two months later in the report for 20 July. Bizarre rumours continued to circulate, with the Chief Constable of Hartlepool and the Professor of French at Newcastle among those suspected of spying for the Germans.

Already there were scattered air raids and the threat of invasion loomed. Most of the children evacuated at the outbreak of war had since returned home. Now a second wave began and the government scheme for the voluntary evacuation of children was extended to east coast towns like Yarmouth and Lowestoft. Fifty thousand children were moved by train on 2 June. Adults were on the move as well: from Tunbridge Wells it was reported that all the removal firms were booked up. The Minister of Information, Duff Cooper, and the Minister of Labour, Ernest Bevin, gave morale-raising broadcasts and the MOI's regional office in Cardiff distributed copies of the 'Keep Calm and Carry On' poster, which had been stockpiled at the outbreak of war and held in reserve for use in emergencies. But it was news of the rescue of the BEF that did most to relieve anxiety. 'Women wept at corners in Leeds when returning BEF marched through town,' Home Intelligence recorded on 1 June. On 2 June Anthony Eden announced in a broadcast that four-fifths of the BEF had been saved.

MONDAY 27 MAY 1940
(INCLUDING SUNDAY 26 MAY)

Reports show a certain steadiness of morale over the weekend. This is partly due to acceptance of what is believed to be a deliberate policy of restricting news. One gets the impression that opinions are being withheld and emotions held in suspense deliberately. It must be remembered, however, that this suspension of feeling (which gives an appearance of steadiness and calm) is arrived at partly at the expense of identification with the events in France. Official statements about the undesirability of liberating news give people an excuse *for not carrying on with the process of facing up to the facts. The result is a small but significant increase in fatalism. Absence of news as a deliberate policy may increase this. Absence of news must be combined with a continuous interpretation of the background situation if morale is to be kept good and the public* identified with the war effort. *By the withholding of news the public has been given a mandate to delay judgment and not to worry. There is distinct advantage, however, in preventing by these means the violent day-to-day swings of opinion and feeling. A slackening of the news tempo has certain definite advantages at the present time.*

On the other hand, the continued detailed publication of German claims and communiques in the press has an effect of cancelling out this relief and detachment.

Anti-French feeling commented upon last Friday has not during the weekend found such overt expression. This may be the result of the news blanket. There have been a number of comments upon the dismissal of the French generals, the most frequent being that this shows that something must have been very seriously wrong at the top. There is, at the same time, relief that mistakes have been discovered and culprits replaced. The net feeling is vague disquiet.

Morale in the provinces and in the countryside continues to be noticeably higher than in London.

Reports from the Regions indicate some satisfaction over the development of plans for the mobilisation of man-power.

'The whiter the collar the less the assurance' is the report of our Regional Information Officer at Reading.

Points from Regions

NEWCASTLE (Northern) Everyone knows where Friday's air raid was. Enquiries as to whether new legislation prevents men leaving important jobs need answering. Nineteen members of Durham Light Infantry are telling alarming stories of wiping out of a DLI battalion at Boulogne, and of confusion among wounded, etc. at the quayside; the result is some public anxiety and anger. Cinema attendances poor, especially on the coast.

LEEDS (North Eastern) Upset caused locally because sirens in North Riding are said to have gone off after bombs were dropped. Comment: 'We're alright, but people at the top are wrong'. Jubilation in Hull at Fascist round up and demand for further action.

NOTTINGHAM (North Midland) Satisfaction at Ironside's appointment. Upset at demand for 12 bore cartridges for anti-parachute troops, on account of their known ineffectiveness compared with rifles and revolvers.

CAMBRIDGE (Eastern) Very good attendance at churches. Local air raids taken calmly. Complaints about excessive personal 'phone calls, also excessive number of calls from London newspaper offices for first-hand interviews. Eastern Regional Commissioner wishes to discourage these.

READING (Southern) Church attendances up. Bitterness towards Germans increases, thanks to refugee stories. Allied counter offensive anxiously awaited. Oxford optimistic. Demand for sub-machine guns for parashots in Guildford. Defeatist talk in Godalming on Saturday due to rumour that the RAF had been entirely flown back to defend Britain.

BRISTOL (South Western) Good response to Mr Bevin among local trade unionists in aircraft factory. Some anxiety over the hills and moors in the west as parachute landing sites.

CARDIFF (Wales) Satisfaction at dismissal of fifteen French generals: 'House needed putting in order'. Sunday services well attended. Increasing demand for round up of Communists as well as Fascists. Criticism of excess RAF bulletins in contrast to other Services.

BIRMINGHAM (Midland) Some surprise at the lack of air raids and parachutists: 'They think Allies have something up their sleeve'. Harold Nicolson's broadcast about rumour widely welcomed and needed.

MANCHESTER (North Western) Excellent spirit in factories. Rumours still growing. Nicolson's broadcast thought not to have had enough punch. Dill, Ironside change accepted as good evidence of new drive.

EDINBURGH (Scotland) West Coast expecting severe treatment in raids, after MacDonald's statement. Broadcast request for 12 bore cartridges unsettling as further lack of arms comparable with those of enemy. Complaints from Glasgow on lack of action in organising parachute Defence Corps. Stiffer attitude to aliens demanded. Eire regarded as possible seat for enemy action.

TUNBRIDGE WELLS (South Eastern) Evacuation of school children being taken very quietly. Rumours common in Brighton area only. Current gossip that wounded are bringing back stories of a hasty and ignominious retreat. Some confusion in coast town hospitals as to what is to become of the wounded whom they are now taking in.

BELFAST (Northern Ireland) German violation of Eire as a possibility has made people nervous. Division of opinion over conscription; majority against it for fear of disloyalist section.

LONDON

Suspense; people getting on with their own affairs; some fatalism while waiting for news. More cheerfulness shown than on Saturday: 'We have turned a corner'. Undercurrent of anxiety is present, especially among women who realise the sacrifice of life: 'We shall win

– but at what a price'. Sunday services well attended; some emotion-
alism displayed. Evacuation talked of on housing estates. Mothers
wish their children should get out before anything happens.
Bermondsey very 'tough'. People will defend themselves to the last.
Parents there would resist compulsory evacuation. They say of
Fascism: 'Your child is not your own'. Labour conditions normal.
Bevin's speech approved by officials, employers and workpeople.
'The country's moving', is heard everywhere. Nicolson's speech was
approved by educated classes; not listened to by working classes
who listen regularly to Haw-Haw at 9.15. Serious defeatist talk in
Fulham working-class and ARP posts due to rumour of King and
Government about to go to Canada. Cinema audiences thin.
Comedies and musicals preferred to serious and war pictures. New
internment of aliens approved. BBC suggested as possible source of
spying. Mistrust of the French expressed.

Rumours

Fewer rumours have been reported today, but those which have
come in show an increase in Fifth Column stories. There is no doubt
that a great many people believe that many rumours are being circulated by Nazi agents, a theory to which credence is given by the
nature of the stories themselves which often seem to have no other
point than to create confusion and alarm. Typical of these is the
report that the full forces of the RAF are to be withdrawn from
France and used for Home Defence purposes.

Another tale of the same sort is that Mr Churchill's visit to France
was to ensure that they would not conclude a separate peace; the
obvious implication being that this was at least a possibility.

It is still being stated, and apparently widely believed, that many
stories are being put about by Haw-Haw. Whether this is true or
not the effect on those who believe this is to make them regard
Haw-Haw as a kind of omniscient being.

There are the usual fatuous inventions today, such as that the Isle
of Wight has been invaded, that bombs were dropped in Barking on
Friday, and that the population of Herne Bay is to be evacuated. In
addition to these there have been repetitions of nuns, parachutists,

bombings, etc., and also a report that the Duke of Windsor has gone to America.

TUESDAY 28 MAY 1940

At the time of writing (4.15 p.m.) our reports do not show the full impact of the Belgian news, although we have enough information to show that public opinion is stunned, bewildered, anxious and recriminatory.

Before the news seeped through there was a definite increase in gloom and depression over yesterday. This was partly accounted for by last night's broadcast news which hinted at 'increasing gravity', 'German brutality', etc., but provided no background information. The effect of this was to produce mystification and a feeling of sinister portent.

The news this morning remained, for most people, a rumour. Even this afternoon reports from the provinces show that the news is still held by some as a rumour. These morning rumours caused many workpeople to stop work and seek confirmation, and many telephone calls were received at this office.

The early afternoon brought forth a deepening anxiety and the first question on all lips has become: what is the fate of the BEF? For the moment this has obscured invasion fear which was becoming prevalent yesterday. The second reaction is an inquiry about the state of Home Defence and the third dominant feeling is bitter recrimination directed against King Leopold.

At the same time reports show, in spite of extreme anxiety, no panic, and if anything an increased determination. All observers agree that people have had the greatest shock of the war but that the atmosphere is not defeatist and that people are still saying widely that we shall pull through in the end. This stock formula provides a persistent background for morale over the last fortnight. There is some danger of taking it at its face value.

Attention is drawn to the following points:

1. Newspaper placards were prohibited yesterday. Last night and this morning, however, pencilled placards and chalked blackboards have been freely displayed and the headlines on them have been of the same order as before.

2. There is evidence that many rumours come from the Belgian and Dutch refugees arriving in London. Observations in reception areas show that, while inhabitants are perplexed that refugees have been sent to vulnerable areas, the effect of refugee stories has on the whole been good (i.e. has stiffened morale).

3. Many complaints are received about BBC news bulletins. Objection is taken to the way in which individual exploits of RAF pilots occupy most of the news time. It is understood that objection is also felt by RAF personnel.

4. A gas mask count has been taken at two places in London consistently since September, 1939. The figures show the following percentages:

Date	Carrying masks
September 4	70%
October 30	59%
November 9	34%
February 5	6%
March 31	1%
May 10	13%
11	14%
12	20%
16	13%
17	9%
26	20%
27	20%
28	20%

No absolute validity is claimed for these figures. Their value is comparative.

Points from Regions

NEWCASTLE (Northern) Some grumbling in middle class at Hexham that French have let us down. In Newcastle writing on pavement in chalk 'We shall soon be there' in German reported. Increased anxiety about Home Defence. General public increasingly keen on spy hunting. Among suspects are Chief Constable of Hartlepool, a Professor of French at Newcastle, and local RIO.

LEEDS (North Eastern) Good response to overtime demand but a desire for orders rather than requests. A demand for more round-up of Fifth Columnists, some criticism of British Secret Service. Local RIO suspected of being a spy.

NOTTINGHAM (North Midland) Perplexity after last night's news bulletin. Some relief that it was Belgians and not French who surrendered. Considerable criticism of newsreel horrors, refugees etc. People felt this would make public rather choose Hitlerism than war.

CAMBRIDGE (Eastern) Public now demanding full news of happenings in Belgium after their patience and hints of gloom.

READING (Southern) News of Belgium desertion spread quickly by word of mouth. As yet little bitterness against Belgium. Increased questioning about state of our defences (guarding of aerodromes, tunnels, bridges, etc., isolated petrol pumps). German Army communiques attracting more attention as their accuracy and moderation are realised in comparison with German air and naval claims.

BRISTOL (South Western) Reaction to special editions announcing Belgium news anxious, stunned, but no panic and no lack of determination. Some feeling against Belgian refugees reported.

CARDIFF (Wales) Married women feeling strain most, strong feeling against IRA and Communists following finding of parachute in Dublin. 'Keep calm and carry on' posters are being distributed.

BIRMINGHAM (Midland) Ordinary people still believe our islands impregnable. Already a whispering campaign against Belgium: 'They must have let us down'. Resentment that BBC made no statement at 8 when they must have known. Duff Cooper's speech was welcomed. Local feeling in favour of stopping racing. None in favour of stopping variety.

MANCHESTER (North Western) A lead from Prime Minister is anxiously awaited and also news of possibility of saving BEF.

EDINBURGH (Scotland) People expecting catastrophic news though there is no defeatism. Local anxiety among women about erection of numerous gas detectors without explanation. Demand for information about Britain's defences.

TUNBRIDGE WELLS (South Eastern) Isle of Thanet very worried at fall of Belgium. Voluntary evacuation occurring. Bridges to mainland said to be mined. Hundreds sleeping in tunnel shelters in last few nights. Evacuation also occurring at Deal; no panic anywhere.

BELFAST (Northern Ireland) News of Leopold's order spread like wildfire. Official silence widely criticised, complaints that too much man power has been used up on non-essential civilian work. Food rationing reductions accepted without complaint.

Today's Rumours

Though fewer rumours have been reported today, in view of the large number which have come in to us during the last few days, it cannot be assumed that they have decreased. In the early part of the day the Belgian surrender was thought in many places to be a rumour, and was consequently accepted with some reserve.

Today's rumours are in much the same vein as usual. Some are of a military character, and the origin of this type is generally said to be 'someone who has returned from France'. While none in this category are of much importance, some have been passed on to MI7a.

There is still a strong belief that Haw-Haw is a source of rumours, more particularly those in which localities are mentioned by name; as, for instance, a story that the Standard Works at Coventry are to be bombed. Although we have no confirmation of Haw-Haw having said this, he is widely believed as the source of the story.

Stories about nuns and parachutists are little in evidence today, but there are others no less fantastic from various parts of the country. In spite of reactions to Belgium's surrender, the character of rumours has not noticeably changed. Many are of the deliberately alarmist sort, though these do not arise out of the new situation, and are for the most part clearly the fictions of a lively imagination.

WEDNESDAY 29 MAY 1940

The shock of the news is still apparent but people are, if anything, calmer. Bad news has had a sobering effect. Personal anxieties and fears have largely become absorbed in deep concern over the BEF, a concern which is growing slowly as a fuller realisation of the situation sinks in. There is as yet, however, no full realisation of the news. The morning newspapers brought no enlightenment; some said 'the BEF is trapped', others 'the BEF fights its way out'. One newspaper describes (Evening Standard, lunch edition) Allied resistance to 'desperate efforts' on behalf of the enemy.

There is still great indignation against Leopold although this would appear to be declining.

The Minister's broadcast at 9 o'clock was favourably received. Reports indicate that people were impressed by his confident manner and that his speech had a steadying effect. The general opinion was that he spoke the truth grave though it was. The increasing prestige of the Minister and his abilities as a broadcaster are becoming obvious in our reports. The people are beginning to rely on him to tell them how the situation should be looked at. This growing reliance on the Minister to tell the truth is a very important factor in morale. It clearly becomes imperative that under no circumstances should he 'let people down'. It would appear that people are becoming increasingly prepared to receive the 'whole truth'. Morale is still high and under these conditions the whole truth (the worst of the bad news) can be told. The bad news about the BEF is still, in most people's minds, the result of 'betrayal'; this is a legitimate conclusion from press reports. This sense of 'betrayal' is one of the factors which is still preventing a complete acceptance of the full implications of the bad news.

However, morale is still stable in the sense that confidence in ultimate victory is generally expressed, although phrases which indicate that victory is inevitable are not common. There is no defeatism and many of our regional reports indicate that resolution has stiffened and that anger is growing.

For the first time there appears to be a levelling up of opinion in London, provincial towns and the countryside.

Points from Regions

NOTTINGHAM (North Midland) Duff Cooper's speech widely approved. 'Personal link between Government and people'. Defection of Leopold is suggested as sign of Fifth Column activities in upper strata of society.

CARDIFF (Wales) No anti-French feeling traced. General reaction to Leopold is one of making allowances for strain of past 14 days. Local Communist meeting broken up by loyalists who sang 'God Save the King' and took the collection for the Mayor's Concert Fund.

BELFAST (Northern Ireland) Cry of treachery at Leopold's surrender has ceased. Most people now suspend judgement. Stir caused by resignation of Parliamentary Secretary to Ministry of Home Affairs who considers Ulster Government has been slack over recruiting measures. Isolated opinions favour National Defence Council for Ulster similar to that just formed for Eire.

MANCHESTER (North Western) Feeling against Belgium very bitter, especially against Leopold; it is reacting against refugees. DC's speech had excellent effect. Local press cooperating well in dispelling rumours.

BRISTOL (South Western) Local satisfaction at French references to Belgian treachery. Coastal people calm in spite of Germans on other side of Channel. Local miners are to give up their holiday week. Traders have offered to release any trade secrets for Government. Prosecution of 'jitter-bugs' urged. Secretary of Bristol Development Board thanks MOI for taking public into its confidence and calming excited feeling. Complaints in Gloucester of sensational and frightening headlines in *Daily Express* and *The Mail*. Satisfaction about further food restrictions.

LEEDS (North Eastern) DC's speech 'best yet.' Remarks about French and rumours of their defection appreciated. Growing feeling against aliens. Strong feeling against Belgian refugees. Requests for more vigorous bombing of Germany: 'give them a taste of their own medicine'. Criticisms of odds against which our planes are fighting and of excessive number of news bulletins.

READING (Southern) Leopold condemned as a super-Quisling. All people ready for any demands on energy, money or time by Government. Undertone of criticism of late Government for having underestimated Germans.

TUNBRIDGE WELLS (South Eastern) Anti-Belgian feeling outweighed by feeling Leopold has let them down. Stories by wounded in Kent hospitals show no defeatism though men faced terrific onslaught. Idea that every rumour-monger is a Fifth Columnist is growing. Only in extreme South East coast towns (Margate, Ramsgate, Deal) is there grave anxiety. People drifting away in voluntary evacuation but no panic. Newsreels criticised for showing devastation produced by enemy but little of our effort.

CAMBRIDGE (Eastern) Troop movements on the East Coast have aroused mild excitement and relief that military authorities are active. Business in Fenland came to a standstill yesterday with depressing news, but has picked up today. Appreciation of DC's broadcast widespread.

BIRMINGHAM (Midland) Forty people consulted gave strongest possible praise for DC's broadcast. A 24-hourly repetition of similar speeches is urged. Engineering and aircraft firm report 100% attendances generally for seven-day week and increased keenness following news of RAF exploits using their products.

EDINBURGH (Scotland) Individual attitude is one of eagerness to take part in national effort. Bitter comments on Belgium's capitulation. DC's broadcast created 'a certain confidence'. Demand for more refugee round-ups. Position of Eire causes anxiety. Criticism of excess RAF news.

NEWCASTLE (Northern) Public criticism of Leopold reported from seven centres. Criticism of French has disappeared. Three centres report steady and cheering influence of DC's speech.

LONDON

'East End considers West End too gloomy. All have fierce fighting spirit.' Isle of Dogs dockers unemployed through losing Scandinavian trade uncomplaining. They back the Government and say 'We must all pull together'. Working-class mothers will not leave their houses now without their children as 'it's air-raid time'. Women volunteering more for ARP work. Suburban women without much to do might panic in air raids. They should be drawn into local schemes. Evacuation still unpopular. Islington say their children were badly treated before. Housing Manager suggests new scheme to win their co-operation with the Government. One mother should accompany every twenty children and supervise them in their billets. After a month she could come home and another mother would take her place, thus disorganising only one household at a time. ARP scheme on Cowley estate of 2,000 tenants, very poor unskilled labourers. Tenants are asked to volunteer as shelter marshals. If they have a part to play they are not so likely to panic. Feeling against Leopold divided. Some bitterness against Belgium even to the extent of saying the Belgian refugees should be sent back. Working-class people on the alert for Fifth Column activities. Greenwich, people quiet. Resent Fifth Columnists going to Isle of Man to have good time when they save up to have a holiday there.

Today's Rumours

It should not be assumed because fewer rumours have been reported today, that they are decreasing in number. On the contrary, our evidence suggests that this situation is becoming more serious.

In particular the dangerous persistency of stories seeking to undermine confidence in the *entente cordiale* and in the French Army is of increasing gravity and one which calls for immediate action on the widest possible scale.

Rumours of a military character are given additional authenticity by the reported conversation of soldiers lately returned from France, to whom various alarming stories are attributed. It seems urgently desirable therefore that some means should be devised of verifying, and when necessary contradicting, such stories, or putting them in their proper perspective.

In view of the fact that Haw-Haw is still widely believed, however incorrectly, to be the source of many rumours, particularly those referring to localities by name, the cooperation of the BBC would be extremely valuable in giving publicity to denials of such rumours.

There are, as usual, a number of sinister and ludicrous stories circulating today, such as that 'Mentally defective patients are being recruited for a suicide corps', that 'London is being heavily stocked for a siege', and that 'The Germans dug through under Switzerland and came up in Toulouse'.

Although it is clearly unnecessary to take action for the suppression of fantasies such as these, there are so many borderline cases where the effects of a seemingly improbable rumour might become serious, that it is necessary, wherever possible, to make an effective contradiction of such stories.

THURSDAY 30 MAY 1940

The position of the BEF is uppermost in the public mind. Many people think the Army will succeed in fighting its way out with heavy losses. Few appear to believe the situation is hopeless. The net feeling is one of suspense. There is not as much expression of opinion as yesterday and while some people are more depressed, others are less so. Thus there is still no complete adaptation to the situation nor a complete realisation of its implications. Nevertheless more people are facing up to the possibility of invasion and many people speak of it as certain. This is as true of the countryside as of the towns for rural defence preparations are now getting under way and there are plenty of local evidences of defence measures.

Morale, however, remains good. There is no defeatism and a general confidence in ultimate victory. At the same time a defensive attitude is becoming apparent and nearly all our reports show that the people are actively enquiring about the state of Home Defence. There is a very large degree of ignorance about the number of military men available, and discussion takes place about whether key points are being actively protected, about the conduct of civilians when air raids come or troops land, about the availability of food supplies. Confusion reigns here and people are heard to be saying that they propose to stay where they are because of the impossibility of deciding where to go for safety. Many people still regard London as safer — because better protected — than other parts of the country. There is a certain amount of voluntary evacuation from the South East Coastal towns and the Ministry of Health report a good response to evacuation proposals in fourteen East Coast towns. Our own observers report that many more people will want to send their children by the end of the week.

There is evidence that people are extremely anxious to be told precisely what to do; they are prepared for orders and are confused by the voluntary principle.

A small survey undertaken to discover whether people approved of racing at the present time showed two out of five approving, two out of five disapproving, one out of five no opinion. A similar survey made to ascertain reactions to variety programmes on the wireless showed an overwhelming majority in favour of continuing them even under emergency conditions. Many say they will be more necessary than ever.

Soldiers returning from Belgium are talking freely about their experiences, particularly in pubs. The effect of this is not good.

Certain localities report considerable 'spy scare' and the situation in a few places has become slightly hysterical. Examples of local inefficiency figure highly in our reports and morale may weaken if attention is allowed to focus on these deficiencies.

A detailed report of the Middleton and Prestwich by-election, 22 May, showed that the percentage of stop-the-war opinion (stationary at about 10% in by-elections since Christmas) had declined although observers found it difficult to elicit opinion on this point. There was strong anti-Fascist feeling which resulted in a very high poll for the Government candidate. The 'grievance figure' had declined remarkably and there was a clear indication that electors were prepared to forget their personal grievances, or, at any rate, to consider it unpatriotic to state them. A negligible percentage expressed the opinion that the war could be stopped after a short fight; the great majority thought the war would go on for a long time.

Anti-Italian feeling is recorded from certain districts.

Points from Regions

NOTTINGHAM (North Midland) Good reaction to David Grenfell's broadcast: 'A miner talking to miners'. BEF officer's broadcast was thought good but excessive Eton and Sandhurst voice criticised. Bus conductors are stopping alarmist chatter by women about evacuation. Common opinion is that children are not safe anywhere so why bother to evacuate them.

CARDIFF (Wales) Military officer's broadcast greatly appreciated: 'plain and unvarnished'. Criticism of mention of places in Ministry of Health Evacuation broadcast. Wounded returning to Wales are 'bubbling with rage'. No defeatism.

BELFAST (Northern Ireland) Recapture of Narvik produced good reaction. 'We can hit back'. Widespread enthusiasm for Ulster Defence volunteers. Restriction on aliens welcomed. Chancellor's statement on war costs 'in the proper tone'.

MANCHESTER (North Western) People are restive, as their spare time is not being used when they have volunteered for voluntary services. Many towns prepared for refugees and nothing has happened. Consequent anti-climax has produced difficulties in collecting clothes and bedding.

BRISTOL (South Western) Anxiety over BEF is mingled with pride. Recent events have ruffled and stimulated West Country people to greater effort.

LEEDS (North Eastern) Employers in Hull anxious for more war work. Yorkshire miners entirely behind national effort. Some scepticism about 100% excess Profits Tax and equality of sacrifice: 'We get 45/- but the bosses are still doing well'. Leopold's surrender has encouraged feeling Fifth Columnists are at the top and not the bottom.

EDINBURGH (Scotland) Anti-war groups, including Communists, are now silent. Industrial cooperation good. No opposition to surrender of holidays, though Glasgow would like them later in relays. More bitter feeling against Leopold. In Glasgow people would not accept Belgian refugees. BBC news this morning announcing superiority of French over German tanks evoked bitter comment: 'Why are Germans at the coast?'

NEWCASTLE (Northern) Harold Nicolson's broadcast about definite possibility of German landing has produced anxiety. In South Shields women are having large sums of money with them. (? Fear of having to make a hasty move or a moratorium.) Return of wounded has brought home reality of war.

READING (Southern) High morale of returning contingents have encouraged people. Some apprehension where police have warned householders near aerodromes to take precautions against enemy descents.

CAMBRIDGE (Eastern) Evacuation is main comment. No alarm at extension of towns involved or at exclusion of other towns, e.g. Norwich. Ministry of Health reports 61% of children registered in fourteen East Coast towns – 38% in four Medway towns. Lowestoft evacuating 80%; Yarmouth 50%.

BIRMINGHAM (Midland) Some anxiety about supplies for BEF and Home Defence. Criticism of BBC reports of minor sporting events, e.g. cycle racing.

TUNBRIDGE WELLS (South Eastern) Voluntary evacuation from Thanet very rapid. Furniture removers fully booked up. Only business shopkeepers report is returning coupons. Margate Food Office had yesterday 2,000 applications for transfers.

LONDON

People still upset over capitulation of the King of the Belgians. Difficulty in 'smiling it off'. St Pancras reports people worried about money. *Docks*. Dock labourers and seamen confident; sure they are going to win. Women-folk not so confident; tend to be afraid of air raids. Much discussion today of Sir Stafford Cripps going to Russia. Dock labourers consider Russia has behaved badly and do not approve of our sending an envoy. They all want more news. Labour Exchanges of London report situation normal but Sunday work accepted cheerfully. Local Labour Exchange reports worried over 200 Cypriots in London who are British subjects. They work requisite number of weeks to claim benefit and then leave their employers for no reason. Bad feeling is being caused by this. Power machinists in demand for Government orders for battle dress. Girls go to other jobs at higher pay when needed for Government work. The Labour Exchange official hopes new emergency powers may stop this state of affairs. A demand for the internment of Czech refugees, as the latter have Communist tendencies. Observers in close contact with the Communist Party and manual labourers who profess Communism state that these elements are now backing the war effort and reluctantly admit we must destroy Hitlerism.

Today's Rumours

The number of rumours we have received today shows an increase over the last few days. The most persistent and most disquieting is one of varying form, but the gist of it is that there is danger of a rift in Anglo-French relations. This story is amplified today by its association with Croix de Feu rumours, of which the following is typical:

The French Army from the high command down to the ranks is riddled with members of the Croix de Feu. Gamelin is alleged to have been the head of it, and the reason that the French are not fighting with the dash of the last war, is because general discontent in their ranks is fostered by members of this association.

Another rumour which, although it is less well documented, seems to have a no less alarming effect, is that Italy has actually entered the war. Today's version of this story is that Raymond Gram Swing stated on the wireless that according to a Reuter message, England and

France had been informed of Mussolini's intention to enter the war, though when this would happen, he, Mr Swing, did not know. It has since been found that this statement was not issued by Reuters, although it is believed to have been put out by another agency.

Haw-Haw continues to be regarded as a fountain head of rumours, more particularly those which refer to hitherto unannounced evacuations and threatened bombing of special objects or localities. Such is his influence, that it appears that rumours attributed to him are far more readily believed than those which are said to have other sources.

Nuns, parachutists, paralysing gases, bombings, etc. are widely reported today; the more circumstantial of this type of rumour states that ten out of fourteen destroyers failed to return after an engagement in the Channel last night.

FRIDAY 31 MAY 1940

*Morale has, if anything, improved since yesterday. This is mainly due to relatively optimistic press reports about the BEF (*News Chronicle: *'Thousands of BEF Men Successfully Withdrawn from Trap'. *Express: *'Tens of Thousands Safely Home Already'. *Mirror: *'Navy Fight for BEF – Thousands Home'). Only the *Herald *is relatively pessimistic. It is also due to the fact that the public has largely recovered from the original shock of the news.*

There is a general calmness, allied with a new feeling of determination. 'The mistakes of the past can now be remedied and we can start all over again.' Observers report a general resolution to throw all reserves of strength into the war effort at home, although misgivings are expressed about the comprehensiveness of our war effort.

A general realisation of the possibilities of invasion has come to the countryside with the barricading of roads, removing of signposts etc.

Anger at Leopold's betrayal is on the whole declining, and on the whole has found much more active expression in the press than in the conversation of ordinary people. Suspicion and mistrust has shifted from Leopold to 'high quarters', and our observers report some further anti-Chamberlain feeling (already remarked by RIO in Reading yesterday). There is also some evidence that suspicion in becoming more general is beginning to attach itself to

'Royalty'. The Duke of Windsor is frequently mentioned and note should be taken of the persistent rumours about members of the Royal Family being in Canada.

There is a tendency to criticise local arrangements for Home Defence, and in particular to accuse Home Defence personnel of being 'too old'.

Points from Regions

NOTTINGHAM (North Midland) Doubt as to whether seven-day week will really increase production reported. Many think Navy will be able to deal with defence of our coastal towns. Nottingham Education Committee report worry over attitude of teachers to war.

CARDIFF (Wales) Return of soldiers from France is converting impersonal attitude of population to one of anger and hatred. Doubt about wisdom of showing generally to women and children pictures of the 'German way' of dealing with ambulances and hospitals. BBC news thought to have increased recently in dignity and character. Industrial response to continuous work is excellent. Men agreed to shelve grievances. Port Talbot concerned about lack of visible anti-aircraft defence.

BELFAST (Northern Ireland) Energy of Northern Government in dealing with Home Defence welcomed and public uneasiness allayed. No undue alarm at threats of invasion.

MANCHESTER (North Western) Criticism of lack of equipment for BEF strong. Local feeling that Italy will be frightened off by US and USSR.

BRISTOL (South Western) Criticism of BEF equipment strong and general worry about stores, etc. left behind is causing speculation. No anger against Belgian people but reaction against Leopold growing. Some discontent at sudden preparations for invasion as these are taken as a sign of muddling unpreparedness after eight months of war.

LEEDS (North Eastern) More concern about BEF than about general war progress. Much local anger against several Public Health officials for butter rationing offences. Labour Exchanges report many cases of men in good jobs seeking war work at financial loss. Anti-Communist Economic League's meeting at Keighley well received.

EDINBURGH (Scotland) No resentment at lack of French counter-attack. Little anxiety about Italy. Glasgow people ask why Unity Mitford is not interned. Talk on BBC at 7.55 this morning criticised as unduly depressing when news following turned out not to be so bad.

NEWCASTLE (Northern) Evening paper reports of Gram Swing's broadcast about Italy caused great excitement in Newcastle, partially relieved later by London statements. Bank managers appreciate broadcast statement about deposits, as some people had withdrawn these. Excitement at Scarborough following order to fishermen to join their drifters and sail for an unknown destination.

READING (Southern) A round robin from prominent Oxford people suggests BBC news bulletins be reduced to two per day. They feel serious loss of concentration and nervous energy in public from listening to repetition of same news. They also suggest evening papers be limited to one edition for same reason. Portsmouth criticises publication of inaccurate and unauthentic foreign news, e.g. casualties in bombing of Rotterdam. Demand for stronger protection of aerodromes etc. Great criticism of BBC appeal for 12 bore shot guns: 'Why not import many sub-machine guns from America?' From Parkeston Quay comes note: 'a good supply of public shelters lessens fear and improves morale'.

BIRMINGHAM (Midland) Strong requests for cancelling of horse and greyhound racing and football, especially from Worcester local racing centre.

Kidderminster reports concern at German technicians in sugar beet factories and careless talk common about RAF depot at Hartlebury. Request for more news about French war effort.

CAMBRIDGE (Eastern) West Norfolk concerned about alleged Fascist activities. Harwich, Clacton and Felixstowe are very worried about talk of civilian evacuation. If this is going to be done it is hoped that as much notice as possible will be given and announcement made reassuringly. Some people at Clacton are already moving their possessions. Some concern in St Albans that manager of North Metropolitan Electric Supply Co. is a German.

TUNBRIDGE WELLS (South Eastern) Bognor and Chichester continue active as holiday centres. East Kent less complacent. Horsham continues 'smug'. Old ladies in Lewes are arranging for free baths for soldiers as a war service.

READING – additional note: Guildford: surprise at arrest of Borough Surveyor. His German wife is popular reason given. Some suspect him as source of Haw-Haw rumours about Guildford Cathedral and camps.

LONDON

Police report states people accept censorship now as necessary to the successful prosecution of the war. They would welcome an earlier release of news items. Last night's talk on evacuation not properly understood by working women. Should be in simpler language. Fulham suggests definite orders would be a relief, as women doubt the point of German attack and think children may be as safe here as anywhere else. Further evidence that low income class resents the sending of aliens to 'comparative safety and leisure in the Isle of Man while our children, aged and infirm remain in this country.' Much Fifth Column feeling in Croydon and Purley. Most aliens accept new restrictions with good grace. Intelligent criticism of RAF exploits too often repeated in the BBC programmes. Working class appreciate them, however, and say 'they give us something to hold on to'. All Housing Managers report people chiefly troubled by high prices. Camden Town women say BBC cooking courses likely to be too expensive and so do not listen to them. Meat rations not fully purchased in several poor districts. Euston Commissioner for Crown Lands office reports not sufficient shelters for her tenants. Has own scheme for supplementing

ARP service among tenants and does not fear panic. Greenwich, Fulham and Deptford women would be glad to take in refugees, especially unaccompanied children. Taxi men and other manual workers' trades declare they are behind the present Government. 'We may have to fight Churchill after; but he's the man for us now'. Appreciate Bevin and Morrison in Government. All want some proof that EPB really means to take over property and will not shelter the rich. Labour Exchanges report conditions normal; no excitement, no grievances. Voluntary basis of service still in operation.

CARDIFF (Postscript) The appointment of Lord Tredegar, whose Fascist sympathies are well known, as Commander of the paratroops at Newport (Mon.) is causing great anxiety.

Today's Rumours

Although the most prevalent of these is concerned with the imminent intervention of Italy in the war, and in many cases of them actually having joined the side of Germany already, there is very little evidence to suggest that this is anything more than an utterance of a possibility which is in many people's minds. The only suggestion which has so far been put forward for this news being authentic is the rather confused reference said to have been made to this subject on Saturday night in Raymond Gram Swing's broadcast from America. From the general prevalence of this rumour it seems that if, in fact, Italy does go to war against us, this will cause no surprise; it is to be hoped therefore that the currency of this story may perhaps act as a buffer against the inevitable shock which the public will get if this does happen.

The invasion of Eire is also rumoured in a large number of places. This story seems to be gaining ground so rapidly that it seems desirable that some kind of announcement should be made about the preparations of the Government of Eire and of our Home Defences to withstand any such attack.

There has been no repetition today of the tension in Anglo–French relations which has featured consistently among the rumours of the last few days. The absence of this is due no doubt to the high tributes paid by the press yesterday and today to the fighting qualities of the French Army in Flanders.

The usual number of rumours attributed to Haw-Haw have appeared today, together with tales of nuns, parachutists and so on.

Among others which are less usual are stories that people in Margate and Ramsgate are taken to the Police Station if they are found to be without their Identity Cards, and that the Russians have invaded Germany.

These are the most credible of a large variety of wholly implausible stories.

SATURDAY 1 JUNE 1940

The return of the BEF has given great emotional relief and many observers report extreme elation succeeding the grave depression of the last few days. Reports from nearly all Regions show that where men of the BEF have returned home morale is stiffened.

In the present state of elation there is some danger that the general war situation is not being faced entirely realistically. There is however a strong undercurrent in conversation which shows that the evacuation must be regarded as a retreat.

The public mind is considerably occupied by practical evacuation considerations.

There is less rumour; evidence points to the anti-rumour campaign having had a successful beginning. Our special observers in the field report that interviewing has become more difficult; the police intervened on several occasions when their advice was sought on the bonafides of investigators.

There is evidence that listeners have considerably more confidence in broadcast news than they had two months ago (Listener research survey).

Points from Regions

NOTTINGHAM (North Midland) Satisfaction at Home Defence measures but public would like further details. 'Chatter bugs' still too common. Strong steps against them asked for. Public still agitated about number of people with German connections at large who are contacting officials. Hotels and bars unusually empty last night due to defence barricades and questioning of motorists on outskirts of Nottingham.

CARDIFF (Wales) In Swansea and South West industrial areas feelings 'a bit flat', possibly due to excessive loyalist activities of 'League of Swansea Loyalists' who have upset and frightened people. RIO suggests visit of prominent politician to Swansea to rouse new hopes and enthusiasm. Feelings towards Italy mixed; some depressed at thought of another enemy, some pleased at our 'firmer attitude'.

BELFAST (Northern Ireland) General opinion expects early entry of Italy into war. This has not seriously influenced morale. Attempt attributed to IRA to bomb cinema in Londonderry regarded as justification for tightening home defence.

MANCHESTER (North Western) Over-emotional pleasure at escape of BEF. Stabilisation by a realistic broadcast is needed to crystalise the elation into resolution. Malcolm MacDonald's speech has had excellent effect in the schools. Penrith: 'Some fear that lonely parts of Cumberland are good points for attack, local working class would like a much more active offensive'.

BRISTOL (South Western) Returning troops circulate stories of our numerical inferiority in aeroplanes. Plymouth: 'Anxious but tough'. Penzance and West Cornwall: 'Uneasy about our retreat, no panic but many long faces'. Cheltenham and Gloucester: 'Removal of signposts has made people face possibility of invasion, demands for details of our defence preparations'. Criticism common of local defence forces especially of 12 bore cartridges. In West Cornwall volunteers are known as the 'Suicide Squad'. Penzance: 'Permission to buy ammunition here is refused but six miles away it can be bought freely'. Trowbridge: 'Anxiety over supposed Germany Colony at Staverton'.

LEEDS (North Eastern) Women wept at corners in Leeds when returning BEF marched through town. No air raids expected for a fortnight. Many have stopped carrying gas masks. Anti-alien feeling checked by authoritative police statement that all are watched. Suggested arming of police welcomed. Slightly stronger feeling that 'those not on war work do no harm by taking a holiday'.

EDINBURGH (Scotland) Difficulties about overtime work are said to be fostered in Port of Glasgow and Greenock by people of Irish origin. Certain trades unions said to be encouraging men of military age to transfer to super-priority government work. Approval at resignations of group commandants of LDV in Angus. Still some doubts about quality of LDV leadership.

NEWCASTLE (Northern) Attitude of women to evacuation of children more reasonable than last September but directives still needed. Dissatisfaction among volunteers that they are not taken on at once for war work owing to lack of details at Labour Exchanges etc.

READING (Southern) Local units of RAF upset at amount of adulation BBC give them. Some nervousness that masses of heterogeneously clothed troops returning may contain spies and Fifth Columnists.

BIRMINGHAM (Midland) Criticism of gloomy broadcasts and news of evacuation: 'too much harassing, too little glory'. BEF men complain of excessive publicity of RAF: 'few were over firing zone'. They fail to appreciate RAF work in harassing lines of communication. Corrective publicity suggested. Absence of road signs causes little difficulty to motorists thanks to hotel advertisements indicating town ten miles away. Chief Constable of Stoke-on-Trent criticises strongly gloomy headlines in local evening paper.

CAMBRIDGE (Eastern) Norfolk, Suffolk and Essex coasts need enlightening about the evacuation policy. RIO suggests statement by Regional Commissioner saying evacuation 'by no means improbable' and giving directions to public if it takes place. Difficulties around Norwich and Ipswich in getting petrol makes people think fear of invasion is great; authoritative Petroleum Board statement would be welcomed. Local military defence measures have produced reassurance.

TUNBRIDGE WELLS (South Eastern) Criticism of Communist tradesmen for evacuating wives and children. Feeling against Germans very bitter in Maidstone because German incendiary bombs ignited oil on water in which sixty Maidstone men were swimming. Local Authorities at Dover object to *Daily Mail* alarmist report of unofficial evacuation. RIO has issued a message to publicans at request of brewers telling them how to stop defeatist talk.

LONDON

Little change generally today though great satisfaction at return of BEF without any hysteria. Confidence in Lord Gort widely expressed. A Hospital Almoner: 'Patients falling off – their thoughts are occupied elsewhere, those who come realise situation is grim. No defeatism'. Chelsea Works Secretary: 'People more cheerful; proud of our men; crowd watching BEF trains on loop lines enthusiastic'. Pinner CAB: 'People anxious about future but cheerful and calm, main worries are financial. WVS and other voluntary war work going well in this district. Duff Cooper splendid'. Catford and Blackheath: 'People well prepared but not neighbourly enough.' Kensington: 'Upset at bureaucratic confusion in dealing with offers of houses for Hospitals and Convalescent Homes'.

Today's Rumours

Evidence continues to accumulate showing the extent to which Haw-Haw is believed to be a source of rumours. This allegation has been repeatedly investigated but has been found in almost every case to be quite untrue. There is a peculiar similarity about the remarks attributed to him; these, almost without exception, refer to knowledge of 'secret' military or industrial centres which are threatened with bombing. There is, however, little to suggest that these rumours have had any serious effects in the neighbourhoods to which they have been said to refer.

Though not apparently widely circulated, a London rumour alleges that hospitals reserved for the wounded of the BEF are hopelessly ill-equipped and badly organised. The Ministry of Health has been informed of this matter.

There were repetitions today of the rumour of France's probable defection from the Allied cause, and of the imminent evacuation of the entire East Coast. Nun spies, butcher boy parachutists and other hybrid phenomena were also reported, though in rather fewer numbers than of late.

MONDAY 3 JUNE TO SATURDAY 8 JUNE 1940

By 4 June 338,226 Allied soldiers, of whom 222,658 were British, had been rescued from Dunkirk. All their transport and heavy equipment had been left behind and as Churchill told the House of Commons that same day: 'Wars are not won by evacuations.' Describing recent events as 'a colossal military disaster', he warned that Britain might have to continue the war alone. 'We shall fight on the beaches,' he declared, 'we shall fight on the landing grounds, we shall fight in the fields and in the streets, we shall fight in the hills; we shall never surrender.' The speech, reported on the news that evening, was not one of Churchill's wartime broadcasts, though he did record a version of it after the war. 'General view of present broadcasts,' reported Home Intelligence on 7 June, 'is that Duff Cooper stands out above the others.'

On 5 June, the nine o'clock news was followed by the first of a series of broadcasts in the 'Postscript' series by the Yorkshire novelist and playwright J. B. Priestley, who paid tribute to the little pleasure-steamers which had taken part in the 'epic of Dunkirk'. Home Intelligence, however, reported strong feeling against the RAF on the part of returning soldiers of the BEF who claimed that the air force had been conspicuous by its absence during the evacuation.

Meanwhile the Battle of France entered a new phase as the Germans launched a fresh offensive along the 'Weygand Line' of the Somme and the Aisne. The French put up strong resistance but were driven steadily back towards the Seine leaving Paris, which had suffered a major air raid on 3 June, defenceless. One hundred and forty thousand British troops, including the 51st (Highland) Division, remained in France, but attempts to reconstitute the BEF were thwarted by the speed of the German advance.

At home Ernest Bevin announced measures to prevent employers from 'poaching' workers employed in essential war industries such as engineering, coal-mining and agriculture. Some antipathy was reported towards Belgian refugees who were alleged, among other things, to be disagreeable people causing a shortage of butter. Rumour had it that the Chief Constable of York had been arrested as a German, and Haw-Haw was alleged to have stated that the Darlington Town Hall clock was two minutes slow, as indeed it was. In an attempt to suppress the more alarming rumours of disaster and defeat, printed newspaper placards were forbidden and replaced by pencillings and chalkings, though it is not clear why this was likely to make any difference. The Ministry of Information's Anti-Lies Bureau swung into action and Scotland Yard were asked to send an officer to reprimand a Mrs Watson, of 145 Empire Court, Wembley, for spreading the rumour that officers had fought to be evacuated before their men at Dunkirk.

MONDAY 3 JUNE 1940

The emotional relief and elation to which attention was drawn in Saturday's report continue. It is remarked that morale is almost 'too good' in certain Regions, an effect which is the result of (1) the stimulating influence of the returned BEF and (2) the failure to realise the full significance of the Flanders evacuation.

Relief at the successful evacuation continues temporarily to overshadow the fear of air raids and invasion at home.

Preoccupation with civilian evacuation has not lessened: the value of evacuation is questioned by some; others urge that the Government should decide and then issue compulsory instructions; many working-class households in London seem determined to resist the evacuation of their children and protest that London is as safe as anywhere.

A growing feeling against Belgian refugees has been noticed; some of this appears to be due to the preferential billeting rates for foreign refugees. The story that they have taken up accommodation which the BEF required in crossing the Channel is also responsible for some antagonism.

The return of our soldiers from Flanders and their dissemination throughout the country has everywhere stiffened morale, but it has brought to the forefront certain critical discussions. In particular the BEF are found to be stating on all sides that the RAF was not in evidence during the retreat. These first-hand stories are throwing some doubt on the truthfulness of the broadcast news reports of RAF exploits. Another subject assuming considerable importance is criticism of those responsible for the inadequate mechanical equipment which has been the cause of so many unnecessary casualties. When the present mood of emotional relief has died down this subject may assume considerable critical importance.

Anti-Italian feeling has strongly increased.

Points from Regions

NOTTINGHAM (North Midland) Entry of Italy into war expected but no dismay at the prospect. A war veteran suggests a 'Dunkirk Medal' similar to Mons Medal of last war; this he thinks would have great psychological value. Some criticisms of BBC for announcing reverses as though they were victories: 'tone too congratulatory'. Kettering: good effect on local morale from Canadian troops billeted there. Their toughness and efficiency awaken feelings of true Empire cooperation.

CARDIFF (Wales) Criticism of broadcast of effect of economic strain in Germany as enhancing excessively present feeling of elation. Eden's speech warmly praised. Returning troops question 'Where are our aeroplanes?' This has raised bitter criticism of previous Cabinet. Request that 'I was Hitler's prisoner' be re-broadcast at 9.30 p.m. this week, as 11 p.m. was too late for many. Returning troops demand stronger measures against aliens. New evacuees warmly welcomed in South Wales valleys.

BELFAST (Northern Ireland) Eden's speech 'reassuring'. Probability of Italy's entry into war much commented on and satisfaction expressed at our threat of strong measures. Lively interest in energetic steps of Eire authorities to strengthen Home Defence.

MANCHESTER (North Western) Eden's broadcast 'timely and effective'. Entry of Italy into war expected and will produce no consternation here. A few French officers have been insulted in streets by mistake for Belgians. French Consul is issuing special badges.

BRISTOL (South Western) BEF men's stories of sky black with Nazi planes and few British ones creating disquiet and distrust of Air Ministry news bulletins: 'Are they minor exploits only?' Offers of service to Employment Exchanges yield unsatisfactory answers unless people offering are on Unemployment Register. Frustration results and patriotic ardour is damped.

LEEDS (North Eastern) Ministry of Labour officials report 'no absenteeism from yesterday's Sunday work'. People seem to be waiting without panic for Hitler's next step. Feeling in Halifax against Irish labourers. Demand in South Yorkshire for better protection of local pits against Fifth Columnists. Shortage of engineers intense in Leeds. Still dissatisfaction on holiday ban for non-war workers: 'Soldiers get leave; why not civilians?'

EDINBURGH (Scotland) Attitude towards Italy becoming defiant. Uncertainty in West about attitude of Eire Government. A clear statement broadcast by De Valera would relieve many loyal Irish in Scotland. Growing feeling for conscription for Civil Defence and war work, so as to settle conflicting claims. Glasgow employers willing to obey direct orders from Ministry of Labour. ARP exhibition at Stonehaven had remarkable response.

READING (Southern) Maurice Healy considered too propitiatory towards Italy last night. 'Why tolerate Mussolini's abuse? Let us take initiative and make him choose between real neutrality and belligerency'. Returning BEF troops stimulate discussion on our lack of planes. Home Defence precautions, hold-ups on roads and BEF stories are waking people up but complacency is still by no means eradicated. Satisfaction at more soldiers on guard at key points. Criticism of tendency to accept a uniform too readily as a credential; registration cards should bear a photograph.

BIRMINGHAM (Midland) Criticism that newspaper reports make BEF appear a rabble and do not stress the martial side of the picture. BEF soldiers reported to have said that RAF were not in evidence over battle front.

CAMBRIDGE (Eastern) Invasion fears rather less: 'was Harold Nicolson exaggerating?' General approval at evacuation of children from coastal towns. Still need for authoritative guidance to adults on subject of voluntary evacuation.

TUNBRIDGE WELLS (South Eastern) East Grinstead phlegmatic after bombs last night: 'it is a pity no more damage was done, as people were left quite unperturbed and unaware of dangers ahead'. Complaints that AA village signs and names on AA boxes are inadequately obliterated. Returning BEF are making strong criticisms of lack of RAF planes.

NEWCASTLE (Northern) Strong complaints by North Shields trawler men at removal of their Bren guns. Previously they had one gun per ship; now one per four or five ships. Durham firms annoyed at manner rather than fact of commandeering wagons for mounting machine guns. Gateshead firm has had to cut down production from sickness, thanks to extra-long hours.

LONDON

Much gossip everywhere and among all classes surrounding stories of the BEF. Returning men have warm praise for Navy but strong criticism that RAF 'was conspicuous by its absence'. They express appreciation and comradeship for French and Belgian soldiers. Hostility expressed by West End staff towards new BBC announcer. 'Too pompous and heavy; almost as if the Nazis had taken over already.' Richmond Citizens' Advice Bureau reports much discontent locally as women who have suffered financially because of the war, offering themselves for munitions work, are told there is none for them. They resent being helped by Unemployment Assistance when they could do national work. This is also reported as being a source of grumbling by the Business and Professional Women's Clubs. Richmond: 'growing anti-alien feeling leading to refusal to allow Belgian refugee children to join play centre. Shop assistants becoming insolent to people with foreign accents. Refugees expressing fear. Local grumbling amongst poor people that refugees are given more money than old age pensioners and unemployed.' Paddington, Marylebone, Kensington: 'amongst all classes dislike of Belgians is growing. They cause shortage of butter and are disagreeable people. Children being received in London areas from which own children are evacuated. Would rather keep own children. Why should our ships be used to carry Belgian refugees when they are needed for our own people?' Discontent also expressed that more money is paid for billeting Belgian refugee children than English ones. Hammersmith, Dulwich: 'people booing Belgian refugees in streets.' Downham Community Centre: 'people full of rumours, inclined to be panicky. Few have wireless and feel cut off from events.' Evacuation not backed up. 'We want to die together.' Chelsea Borough Housing: 'Very few children registered for evacuation here. Fathers chiefly against it as they say country is as dangerous as London.' Praise heard everywhere for Mr Eden's speech as 'it explained the situation.' Criticism of delivery.

Today's Rumours

There is little to add to what was said on Saturday about rumours, except that fewer were reported today.

It is widely and persistently stated that men of the BEF, returning from Dunkirk, are extremely bitter about the absence of British aeroplanes, and the meagre help given them by the RAF during the embarkation from the beaches.

In some cases this feeling is said to be directed towards the personnel of the RAF who have been publicly jeered at by soldiers who have returned from France. Evidence of the strength and spread of this feeling is very marked and its repercussions, unless checked by some statement, or explanation of the facts, are likely to be most unfortunate in both military and civilian circles.

In general, rumours follow the same trend as usual; the majority are juvenile, imaginative fictions of an alarmist nature; a few have a more practical, or at least, understandable basis. It is said, for instance, that the Germans have been using dum dum bullets. This has been 'confirmed' by interviews in the press with men who are said to have witnessed this fact.

There are more rumours again today of impending evacuations from the East Coast towns, new gases, parachute nuns, and so on; but for the first time Haw-Haw seems to be rather less in evidence than of late.

TUESDAY 4 JUNE 1940

The dominant topic of conversation today is the Paris air raid which has affected people in a special way. Paris, for this purpose, is London and the reality of air raids on London has been brought home. The newspaper reports of the raid were fairly restrained; in fact our reports show that this restraint was often looked at with suspicion. People were puzzled that only 17 out of 300 planes were brought down: they believed with some confidence that a very large proportion would be brought down in a raid on 'the capital'. They have largely forgotten Baldwin's once familiar tag 'the bomber will always get through'. An important reaction, however, has been the desire for retaliation. Verbatim reports show that there is an active desire for revenge and the fear of consequences is not entering into public calculation.

The BEF is falling to a lesser place in public consciousness and it is now possible to say in general terms that the retreat is accepted as a 'victory', as a 'lasting achievement', as a sign that 'we cannot ultimately be beaten', that 'we shall always turn a tight corner to our advantage'. It is thus evident that the press has overplayed the event with consequences which require detailed attention.

Now that public attention is no longer strongly focused on the BEF there are signs of a return to the oscillation of public opinion which has been remarked over the last three weeks. This frequent oscillation cannot, under any conditions, be regarded as a really healthy sign.

A valued reporter just returned from a comprehensive tour in Wales and Northern and Eastern England confirms yesterday's assessment that morale on the whole is 'too high'. There is no defeatism but at the same time there is still an inadequate realisation of the facts of the situation. There is no doubt that people are prepared to face facts but they cannot do so unless facts are given their proper value and are adequately assessed.

Anti-French feeling has strongly declined today: there seems no doubt that this is one of the results of the Paris air raid and the identification of Paris and London as capitals. The French are suffering what we shall soon suffer. The French are, therefore, more nearly ourselves than at any previous time.

Duff Cooper's air-raid behaviour, (as reported in the press), has received comment in many of our reports today. It is said that apparently he was not obeying instructions designed for civilian protection!

Points from Regions

NOTTINGHAM (North Midland) Criticism of use of petrol by public for shopping and pub crawling. Visitors from London contrast lack of preparedness for aerial attack and much greater calmness of population in this Region as compared with London. Paris air raid has created interest and speculation rather than alarm.

CARDIFF (Wales) Some criticism of references to ample supplies of bread and butter by Duff Cooper in Paris. Also criticism of his

account of officials leaving shelters before 'All Clear' signal. Evacuees
have been kindly received by South Wales women and social workers
report that their arrival has had a good effect on their morale.
Industrial work continues maximal.

BELFAST (Northern Ireland) Publication of local names in casualty
lists is increasing determination and stimulating war effort rather
than diffusing depression. Satisfaction at recruiting drive for Ulster
units. No upset at Paris bombing. General opinion favours severe
retaliation.

MANCHESTER (North Western) Broadcasts by Labour leaders are
having excellent effect. Sporadic coal strikes have stopped but subversive Communist elements are still having their say. Another speech
from a trusted miners' leader would help.

BRISTOL (South Western) Forty editors in the Region have informed
RIO of BEF stories of aerial inferiority. There is some consequent
public uneasiness. Many complaints of 'joy-riding'. Still complaints
that there is no work for public anxious to help war effort. Many
South Western people think public is still not taking the war seriously enough.

LEEDS (North Eastern) At Halifax workers compelled an employer
to open factory for Sunday work. No anti-French feeling in Leeds.
Great satisfaction at round-up of Fascists yesterday. Labour Exchanges
report increasing release of men for war work. Dyers' Union has
given one week's strike notice to local large firm (Baldwin's) because
firm will not pay extra 2/6d per week demanded.

EDINBURGH (Scotland) BEF speaking freely of lack of planes and
also giving news of friends killed in action before War Office has
time to inform next of kin. West Fife miners refuse to forgo their
holidays; this has produced threats of a boycott by East Fife householders. Complaints made about unguarded points of importance.
Growing tendency to trust BBC news rather than newspapers. Duff
Cooper's broadcasts greatly appreciated and discussed but hope
expressed he will keep out of films (Mr Attlee's cap is said to have

had a depressing effect on picturegoers.) MOI criticised for lack of publicity for British naval and air leaders.

NEWCASTLE (Northern) Keen interest in local Home Defence measures. Ashington older retired miners eager to return to work. Same at Seaham Harbour. Three centres report difficulty in getting petrol. Complaints common that when people answer broadcast appeals local offices have no information available.

READING (Southern) Growing stories of RAF v. BEF controversy. Southampton welcomed French troops enthusiastically. Disquiet in Isle of Wight over nationality of an aeroplane shot down. No official information as to whether it was Allied or enemy. A resident at Wargrave reports that about 1 a.m. on Friday he heard a violent anti-British propaganda talk in French on wave-length between 1975 and 2000. Name of station he thought was 'Poste Francais Revolutionnaire'. Nervousness about aliens and Fifth Columnists continues. Employers hesitate to take aliens on. High wages in dockyards and factories are taking men from rural areas and from less highly paid but no less important jobs.

BIRMINGHAM (Midland) Worcester and Hereford report BEF men cat-calling at films extolling RAF. Other centres report failure of BEF men to realise importance of RAF work behind the line.

CAMBRIDGE (Eastern) East Coast towns rather anxious at blowing up of piers by Army. Still some private adult evacuation going on. Many people still feel State is not using them for national work as they would like to be used.

TUNBRIDGE WELLS (South Eastern) Police raid on BUF at Canterbury very popular. Canterbury people reported quiet and determined. Dover townsman says: 'We don't leave Dover until Channel is full of German seamen'. Public are returning to Brighton hotels. People in munition centre at Dartford very steady.

Reaction to Paris air raids in most parts is one of rather sober fatalism: 'It brings it nearer, doesn't it?' There is no panic and very poor response to evacuation. 'If we are going to be killed, let's all be killed together.' Excellence of non-alarmist reports of Paris air raids is stressed. Neither poor nor suburban people showed fear. Evacuation issue is confused because of Belgian refugee children arriving to be billeted in evacuation areas. People say: 'Why not keep our own children?' Some Croydon residents have evacuated in response to a request because aerodrome is so near, but not the majority.

Today's Rumours

The rumour situation seems to be easier again today. Rumours are fewer but are generally speaking less irresponsible. There is, as yesterday, a preponderance of stories about the BEF's disparagement of RAF activities in France. These stories are widespread, some of them are well authenticated but a good many amount to no more than hearsay.

Rumours from the Eastern Region continue to foreshadow general evacuation of East Coast districts.

There is a rumour from Newcastle that the issue of petrol coupons will be stopped as from tomorrow. It is said that in some parts of the district there is considerable difficulty in getting petrol.

The Chief Constable of York is said to have been arrested as a German. This is a repetition of a rumour that was circulated several days ago and it is a type of rumour which has lately been extremely prevalent.

From Guildford it is said that troops passing through certain stations on their way back from France have been throwing live 303 bullets to children as souvenirs. This matter has already been taken up by the Military Authorities. It is typical of the sort of rumour which has been circulating since the return of the BEF.

Spies, parachutists and Haw-Haw have all been lying low for the last few days, and feature hardly at all in the rumours we have received today.

WEDNESDAY 5 JUNE 1940

The final evacuation of the BEF has brought with it a certain feeling of depression. There is a deflation of tension without a corresponding increase in resolve.

The grave tone of Churchill's speech made some impression and may have contributed in some measure to the rather pessimistic atmosphere of today. It should be remarked, however, that only the Daily Mirror *and the* Daily Worker *gave Churchill's speech headline value ('We Never Surrender', 'Not Blind to Colossal Military Disaster'). The contents of the speech were on the whole expected but some apprehension has been caused throughout the country on account of the PM's reference to 'fighting alone'. This has led to some slight increase in doubt about the intentions of our ally. Consequently our close study of anti-French feeling shows that it has increased over yesterday (when the Paris air raid had brought close identification with the French). That a swing in feeling has so slight a cause is in itself a matter of anxiety.*

News of bombing reprisals was welcomed and many people are demanding the bombing of Berlin.

The Paris air raid continued to hold attention and the revised casualty numbers and the fresh figures given for attacking planes and bombers brought down brought suspicious comment. Many people remarked that the disaster had been purposely minimised.

The BEF continue to express their feelings about the RAF.

There are signs that Fifth Column hysteria is reaching dangerous proportions in some towns and villages: there are fewer rumours but more accusations.

A small statistical survey shows that there is a tendency to attribute Hitler's success so far to his own superior efficiency and preparedness rather than to blame our own deficiencies. The answer to a question designed to test confidence showed that two-thirds were confident that whatever Hitler's next step might be we should be able to deal with it effectively; one-sixth were doubtful; very few indeed were pessimistic. These results show that recrimination is still very low and that there is a substantial body of fully-confident opinion. These are excellent bases for a sound morale and the conclusion is inevitable that this morale is ripe for canalisation in a positive and aggressive direction.

Points from Regions

CARDIFF (Wales) Churchill's speech 'very impressive'. Success of French Military Mission's description of France's sacrifice, and consequent responsibility of this country for maximum war effort. Discontent among LDV owing to lack of information about their duties.

BELFAST (Northern Ireland) Criticism of reference in Churchill's speech to 'fighting alone'. Growing demand for stricter precautions against Fifth Column activity and control of aliens. Agitation about vital defence matters in Northern Ireland reaching Germany through Eire.

MANCHESTER (North Western) Churchill's speech well received. Tribute to RAF welcomed in view of BEF's recent criticisms. New BBC announcer 'depressing and too emotional'.

BRISTOL (South Western) Keen interest in anti-Fifth Column action. Local preparations for dealing with parachutists.

LEEDS (North Eastern) Industry pre-occupied with holiday question. Emphasis on necessity of rest periods for workers engaged twelve hours daily, seven days a week. Situation intensified by labour shortage. Leeds and Hull report satisfaction at arrest of Fascists. Huddersfield weavers threaten to strike owing to employment of Austrian-Czech worker. Wakefield Council dismisses COs from all its services. 100% increase shown in Doncaster Miners' War Savings last week.

EDINBURGH (Scotland) Apprehension of Scotland being Hitler's next victim, as no indication of this has been given by Germany.

High spirits of BEF soldiers inducing feelings of optimism, more obvious among men than women.

NEWCASTLE (Northern) Continued complaints about lack of equipment for LDV, and in slowness of their organization. Speculation among employers as to Minister of Labour's proposals for enforcing over-time.

READING (Southern) General satisfaction at rounding up of Fascists. Perturbation of rural community facing prospect of having to harbour evacuated sheep. Some nervousness expressed about ability of France to withstand impending German attacks.

BIRMINGHAM (Midland) Churchill's speech has had 'excellent effects'. Signs of determination among workers to make up deficiencies in war material.

CAMBRIDGE (Eastern) Position of Italy continues to cause speculation, but not apprehension. Resolution adopted at Ministry's Advisory Committee advocated stronger measures against Fifth Columnists. Criticism of Government's evacuation announcement on ground that it offers no directive for public action in the event of substantial aerial attack or attempted invasion.

TUNBRIDGE WELLS (South Eastern) Criticism of reference to 'fighting alone' in Churchill's speech. Some tendency still to regard Dunkirk as a victory. Proposed anti-gossip week at Chatham promised every support.

LONDON

Substantial failure reported in all districts of Government's evacuation plans, particularly as these apply to children under five. General admiration for way in which Dunkirk evacuation was carried out, but much resentment about alleged lack of troops' equipment. Strong criticism is also made of inequalities in allowances made to soldiers' wives and maintenance cost of German prisoners, the latter being 3/6d more than the former. Need is expressed in poor districts for creches where young children can be looked after while their mothers are working, as in some places neighbours are refusing responsibility of taking in other people's children for fear of air raids. A certain number of large firms and factories are inaugurating campaigns of their own to encourage their workers to make the maximum war effort. Criticisms made of the new BBC announcer who was described as having a 'plum pudding voice', and was compared unfavourably to Haw-Haw.

Today's Rumours

Rumours seem less in evidence than yesterday; several Regions report that rumours have either died down or greatly decreased, and the majority of those in circulation are of little significance. No single subject of rumour is abroad in remote Regions simultaneously.

Lord Haw-Haw is alleged to have stated that the Darlington Town Hall Clock is two minutes slow, which in fact it is. Eastern Region has supported a long-lived rumour to the effect that Bremen announced that the Hoffman Ball Bearing works at Chelmsford would not be left standing after 2 June.

The suppression of the names of arrested Fascists in the Leeds area has given rumour-mongers plenty of scope in supplying them.

Two parachutists are said to have been caught in Sussex, and round Birmingham it is widely stated that spies are being apprehended, and the informants rewarded with £5.

Little has been forthcoming about the BEF and imaginative stories of new British invisible rays and flame throwers, and unfounded rationing restrictions make up the total.

THURSDAY 6 JUNE 1940

News of the fresh offensive has brought anxiety but people are in a tired state of mind and reaction is distinctly slower. Several observers report that some people are finding it increasingly difficult to listen to the news: they have become somewhat desensitised. Comment on the news is cautious and restrained as well as generally apprehensive. There is some suspicion, too, in the remark that the present French communiques ('unimportant strategic withdrawals') have a dangerous similarity to those made just before the breakthrough at Sedan.

There is some ground for suggesting that, from the point of view of morale, the new German attack has come in time to prevent a wave of depression which yesterday's reports showed was developing.

This morning's air raids on Britain were received calmly and the early communiques were warmly approved. The effect of this prompt news on the spread of rumours was noticeable.

Personal grumbles have fallen to a low place in public conversation: national grumbles (lack of planes, etc.) have obscured them.

Yesterday at Mansfield a civilian was fined ten guineas and five guineas costs for falsely attributing a rumour to Haw-Haw. The case has received wide publicity.

Over the whole country newspaper placards have been replaced by pencillings and blackboard chalkings. The degree of irresponsibility they display is considerable but their effect is certainly less prejudicial to public morale than printed posters. False statements have been noticed, e.g. 'Italy has come in', 'Big German Defeat', 'All the Good News' but nevertheless morale continues steady!

Sir Hugh Elles's broadcast was widely commented upon but stirred no great feeling. Typical comments: 'very interesting', 'quite useful', 'of course you should stay at home and barricade yourself', 'not bad but I've had enough of that kind of thing', 'a good broadcaster'. Informed comment suggests that the broadcast was not sufficiently realistic. One correspondent wrote 'I wasn't very greatly interested: he should have told us what to do now'.

STELLAR BULLETIN An eminent astrologer and his publisher, both capable of spreading alarmist reports, have predicted that Monday and Tuesday, 10 and 11 June, are 'fatal days'. Large-scale invasion is indicated and danger to the Royal Family to whom it would be hazardous 'to cross water'.

Points from Regions

NOTTINGHAM (North Midland) Some local evacuation of monied people on a small scale. Dutch and Belgian refugees not popular as it is felt that they should work for their food, also unpopularity due to Fifth Column fears. Dissatisfaction at America's attitude has diminished in last week with rising hopes that she will help actively.

CARDIFF (Wales) Remotest areas still apprehensive about parachute invasion. Wide popular misapprehension about extent of France occupied by Germany as newspaper maps only show northern France and this appears largely occupied. Uneasiness that food stores in Wales will not allow for great influx of evacuees and refugees from South and East. Many requests for repeat broadcast of 'I was Hitler's prisoner', and several suggestions that broadcast 'Information to the enemy' should be repeated earlier than 10.30 when most industrial workers are in bed.

BELFAST (Northern Ireland) Following Ulster PM's conference with British leaders, hopes high that Ulster–Eire border will be more strictly guarded. Six typical listeners comment thus on Haw-Haw's onslaught on British morale: 'By exaggeration and ranting he defeated his own purpose; his silliest broadcast yet'.

MANCHESTER (North Western) Bevin's new EPs acceptable to both employers and men. Coal trade hope miners retain freedom to move from pit to pit. Fifth Column hysteria growing; needs damping down. Evacuation of wealthier classes fairly common. Belgians and wealthier Dutch Jewish refugees unpopular. Public sceptical about help from America.

BRISTOL (South Western) French military officer received magnificent reception from 8,000 Aero workers whom he addressed at Bristol. West Country holiday resorts still anxious about methods of rapid instruction of public on beaches in times of emergency. Need for mobile loud speakers stressed. Voluntary local evacuation negligible. Pacifist literature read mainly by small groups under influence of Quakers; public opinion hostile to these views.

LEEDS (North Eastern) Churchill's speech well received. Working classes all favour getting help from Russia if possible. Five educated Roman Catholics all strongly opposed Russia, however.

EDINBURGH (Scotland) General annoyance at delay in revealing full number of casualties in Paris air raid. Growing feeling that there are too many news bulletins and too much repetition. Two persons when challenged by sentries suddenly produced Identity Cards from hip-pockets. Danger of this practice is stressed as sentries may think they are reaching for 'something else'.

NEWCASTLE (Northern) Public very interested but calm following incendiary bomb locally. Anti-war activities weaker in last two weeks. Probably following hostility of crowds. Protest by unemployed occurred at open-air meeting when importance of greater production was emphasised.

READING (Southern) French troops warmly welcomed on South Coast and French speakers generally in demand. A comprehensive balance sheet of losses on both sides in the Battle of the Ports would be welcomed, as statements so far have been piece-meal. Satisfaction at increased local defence measures. Criticism of voluntary system of local defence. Aliens dismissed from factories in Weybridge and Newbury on demand of fellow workers. False air-raid alarm at Basingstoke last night caused (1) increased black-out (2) people went into street (3) people phoned local Exchange.

BIRMINGHAM (Midland) Still some criticism of French allowing first German breakthrough. Publicity of causes of breakthrough would be welcomed. CO milkman chased by crowd of angry women at Cannock.

CAMBRIDGE (Eastern) Air-raid warning early this morning caused no undue alarm. Prompt broadcast of Air Ministry's communique widely welcomed. West Norfolk suspicious about Fifth Columnists. Hugh Elles's broadcast 'timely'.

TUNBRIDGE WELLS (South Eastern) People in raided area of North Kent calm and steady. Comment general on slackness of sentries; several people record how they have walked into places supposed to be guarded by sentries. Popular impression is that armed civilians are better sentries than soldiers. Armed sentries in Kent are using unshielded lights to stop traffic. It is pointed out that motorists have every excuse for ignoring such lights.

LONDON

Air raids near Greenwich and Deptford this morning taken with interest and calmness; no panic; people's great relief was that their children were safe. Many observers report a widespread feeling that French are proposing to sue for a separate peace. This may be due to misinterpretation of Churchill's speech or some think to deliberate malicious talk. French war communiques are distrusted as people feel they have proved over-optimistic in the past. Sir Hugh Elles's talk was well received; no apprehension raised by it: 'just what we wanted to know'. 'Good home truths'. One query was 'who are the properly authorised people who will give us information?' Evacuation figures improving in some districts. It is automatically assumed that under-fives will stay at home as they cannot be evacuated with schools. Factories report no complaints at overtime work and growing enthusiasm for Home Defence. Feeling against aliens still very strong. Some complaints of harrowing newsreel pictures, hospitals bombed, etc. One report of defeatist talk in the City: 'why not give in to Hitler now?'

Today's Rumours

Rumours continue to show a slight decrease; the majority, which are still wild and obvious inventions, do not appear to be widely believed. Others of a circumstantial nature are excepted more readily. The following extract from the Log Book of the Anti-Lies Bureau gives examples of this type, and indicates the actions which have been taken in each case.

Source and Area	Rumour	Action
G.M. Robertson, Wimborne	Cranford school caretaker at 4. a.m. on June 1st heard Haw-Haw threaten Wimborne.	Checked. No such broadcast at that hour. Informant asked for wavelength, set etc., and told that such language was foreign to Haw-Haw's technique. MI5 Radio Security Dept also informed.
H.J. Keefe, Wembley	BEF officers fought to be evacuated before their men. Story spread by a Mrs Watson, 145 Empire Court, Wembley.	Informed Scotland Yard, and asked them to send an officer to reprimand and warn Mrs Watson.
Mrs Sprigge, Dorking	Rumours against local chemist, radio shop, school and aliens.	RIO informed that if rumours are sufficiently current material will be supplied to him for issue to the local press or authorities.
Librarian of London Corporation	Reports concern of himself and colleagues at inability to check borrowers of Ordnance Survey and other detailed maps of England.	Home Office advised. Points for their consideration are drafted in cooperation with London School of Economics Librarian. MI5 informed after discussion between these two departments. Ministry proposal was agreed and sent to Joint Executive Committee of Government Departments.

FRIDAY 7 JUNE 1940

People are still anxious but there is an undercurrent of cheerfulness. Several of our reports contain indications that the news from France is received with a certain scepticism, others show indications of detachment. These evidences of detachment seem to be due to an emotional weariness of perpetual crises. In this connection it is interesting to note that the East Suffolk inland villages which are the subject of special observation are beginning to show more strain.

Suspicion of strangers appears to be steadily increasing in all areas and rumour is on the decline.

Points from Regions

NOTTINGHAM (North Midland) Unanimity of approval of Cripps as ambassador to Russia. Sixty-five wounded BEF men interviewed all expressed strong approval of French soldiers: 'Splendid in a tight corner'. French are recorded as saying: 'English not serious enough; still many young men at home doing nothing'. Also strong French feeling against our COs. No criticism of withdrawal of newspaper placards. Chalking-up limited. Local air-raid alarm taken very calmly. Grimsby makes following suggestion: many civilians refused to take cover wishing to see the sights. Too many unofficial cars on roads; they may obstruct ARP vehicles and emergency traffic. Unshielded lighting of matches should be prohibited. Householders should black-out their sleeping quarters as lights turned on suddenly when a warning is given stand out dangerously. Confusion about car lights in warnings. Police instructions vary as to whether these should be on or off.

CARDIFF (Wales) No antagonism towards France; rather guilt that we have left them too much to do. Great welcome for French Military Mission. Strong recommendation that it should visit areas where there is anti-French feeling. Wide wish for complete cooperation with Russia. Feeling towards America rather angry. Continuation of Gram Swing type of commentator recommended. Anti-war organisations steadily losing ground. Growing anti-Italian feeling. No reactions to poster prohibition.

BELFAST (Northern Ireland) Anti-Belgian refugee feeling growing; main ground is food shortage. Circulation of *Daily Worker* ten dozen; *Peace News* six dozen; *Action* not handled. Chalking-up of placards has produced very little reaction.

MANCHESTER (North Western) Speech by Lord Derby on French war effort received great ovation. Restricted luxuries order well taken but demand for further action. Motor pleasure driving much criticised. Cars common outside Road Houses every night.

BRISTOL (South Western) Still some lack of faith in our communiques and preference for statesmen's speeches. Growing resentment against those responsible for lack of equipment for BEF. Effect of prosecution of rumourists most salutary.

LEEDS (North Eastern) Today's main interest, last night's air-raid warning. Taken very calmly. Much criticism of large number of people still doing useless work and slowness of authorities to use up available labour on vital work. Resentment on holiday ban for non-urgent workers grows. Almost all BEF men interviewed express warm admiration for French. A few violent left-wingers still regard France bitterly. Anti-war organisations on the wane.

EDINBURGH (Scotland) Growing discontent against leaders of Chamberlain Government. Widespread wish for complete alliance with Russia. Working-class Edinburgh women say they will fight Germans in streets if men can't stop them. BEF soldiers warm in praise of French. No anti-French feeling but some doubt about French internal politics. Anti-war groups remain fairly strong and some public criticism of lack of police action against them.

NEWCASTLE (Northern) Calm during last night's air alarm. No anti-French feeling noticed in Region. Gram Swing popular. A desire for continuance of this type of talk expressed. Chalking-up causes no reaction. Little comment on Cripps's mission, such as there is is favourable.

READING (Southern) Hugh Elles's broadcast generally welcomed. Some anxiety about how soon BEF can get out to help French. If Germans forced French lines it is suggested Duff Cooper should broadcast explaining that this is only part of a gigantic operation and that even a serious initial breakthrough may be rectified by resistance further back.

BIRMINGHAM (Midland) Broadcast of statement by German prisoners about their own lack of protection from RAF have been criticised as 'propaganda'. Anti-war journals seem very unimportant in this Region. Requests for continuance of Gram Swing type of broadcast. Chalking-up of little importance, though newspapers would like to be able to have placards for special occasions. Very little voluntary evacuation.

CAMBRIDGE (Eastern) Public strikingly calm in air-raid alarm last night. Attitude to Russian mission 'perplexity'. Traces of anti-French feeling apparent last week have now vanished. Attitude to America 'resigned'. Public indifferent to cessation of placards. Chalking-up has produced no special reaction. Some voluntary evacuation of adults on East Coast.

TUNBRIDGE WELLS (South Eastern) Only reaction in towns where last night's air-raid warning occurred is disappointment that they were not mentioned in Air Ministry's account of raid. Anxiety at Horsham about failure to camouflage local landmarks. Growing confidence in French Army. Aliens in business in Tunbridge Wells complain anti-alien feeling is ruining them. Eastbourne much calmer with evidence of local military activities. Tonbridge worried about local ARP inefficiency. No chalking-up reported.

LONDON

Public continue calm. Reactions to broadcast speeches: Sir Hugh Elles: general feeling good but not striking. Priestley's postscript very popular. Ronald Cross very good indeed. General view of present broadcasts is that Duff Cooper stands out above the others. In new housing estate lack of neighbourliness still very marked and a potential cause of lack of confidence, thanks to lack of companionship. A common comment on wireless news is that it is too long and many people switch off after ten minutes thus failing to hear the talks. From Wimbledon comes report of great satisfaction with new Old Age Pension scheme. A false alarm on a housing estate of parachutists occasioned by a flock of pigeons resulted in about half the tenants rushing to the roof and the rest rushing to the shelters in the basement. In the melee several women fainted. These people are normally calm and collected. They seem to need more advice as to what to do and how to do it on such occasions.

SATURDAY 8 JUNE 1940

Cheerfulness with an undercurrent of anxiety (in London) and detachment (in the provinces) is the prevailing feeling. It is clear, however, that opinion, on a state of affairs about which there is considerable ignorance, is mobilised around press reports. Judgement is lacking and waits on events.

Air raids appear to have been taken calmly; many people remained in bed during the warnings.

Points from Regions

NOTTINGHAM (North Midland) Public more cheerful. No evidence of anti-French feeling. Confidence in Weygand: 'Old but tough'. Newspaper placards not missed; general opinion is we are better off without scare headlines. Many people slept through air-raid alarms, no upset at them. Criticism that sirens at Grimsby followed the sound of planes. School children not upset, school attendances good, though pupils very sleepy. Grimsby: 'Equanimity of the people extraordinary'. America regarded rather as a useful source of supplies than as a valuable belligerent.

CARDIFF (Wales) Anxiety great at present battle. General feeling 'All right so far'. Further requests for continuance of American broadcasting commentator. Increasing criticism of Chamberlain and Baldwin. Criticism of numbers of pleasure parties in motor coaches still on the road.

BELFAST (Northern Ireland) Increasing Home Defence measures greatly welcomed. Criticism of lack of leadership in ARP continues. People puzzled by Italy's hesitation. Her entry awaited with a fatalistic shrug.

MANCHESTER (North Western) Many feel Hitler is having his 'Battle of the Somme'; others anxious at falling back in good order by French. Pleasure expressed at activity of French Air Force. Heatwave is making many people anxious about holidays. Much comment on £5,000 pension for Lord Simon.

LEEDS (North Eastern) Air raids have caused annoyance rather than alarm. General disquiet at present siren system, and upset in Goole because dock and railway lights were left burning while German planes passed over. Growing feeling that women should be given more work; still 2,000 unemployed women in Sheffield. Public regard America as opportunist and would welcome help but do not expect it. A stronger wish for Russia's friendship rather than America's. Many requests for American broadcast commentator. Refugees not popular, response to evacuation registration poor. Shortage of Civil Defence volunteers persists.

EDINBURGH (Scotland) Morale of working women seems to have improved. Growing anti-Italian feeling. Italian shopkeepers in Glasgow may fare badly if Italy comes into war. Some anti-Jewish feeling. Little voluntary evacuation. Women and children are taking early holidays. Slum dwellers in Edinburgh may evacuate to a caravan colony at Port Seton which would make a fine bombing target. Excessive air warfare reports in the news are arousing suspicion.

NEWCASTLE (Northern) No panic or undue excitement at air-raid warnings on Tyneside, Durham, etc. On Tyneside dancing continued in many halls. At Bishop Auckland and Chester-le-Street people tended to collect in the streets to watch ARP activities. Spy mania increasing in some parts. Criticism among Local Defence Volunteers that platoon commanders have little or no military knowledge, while men under them have big experience. Further reports show public favourable to Cripps's visit to Russia. Little comment on stopping American commentaries, such comment as there was favoured continuing.

READING (Southern) Public mainly reassured about Weygand line. Minority sceptical. Growing impatience with Italy and resentment at any suggestion of conciliation by Allies. Intervention of Mussolini would be welcomed rather than feared. Industrial responses to heavy work excellent. Little concern about air activity, though some evacuation from Isle of Wight. Public dissatisfied at lack of care for welfare of large numbers of BEF camped at Oxford. Alterations in reserved occupations welcomed. Criticism of delay in call-up common.

BIRMINGHAM (Midland) New BBC announcer widely criticised as depressing. Wide apprehension about Fifth Column, spies seen all over the place. Strong feeling for interning more aliens.

CAMBRIDGE (Eastern) Air-raid warning taken calmly by public. No alarmists' rumours after it. Criticisms at Peterborough (just outside Region) where bombs are reported to have exploded in the street because no siren sounded until after explosion. General feeling against any further evacuees in this Region.

TUNBRIDGE WELLS (South Eastern) General feeling is that news is 'not too bad'. A quite common tendency has been noted for the public to criticise Baldwin and Chamberlain very vigorously. Many think Hitler will invade first Eire and then Cornwall and some of public are bringing back the evacuated families from Cornwall. Folkestone Information Committee projects a training course in leadership morale.

MONDAY 10 JUNE TO
SATURDAY 15 JUNE 1940

On 10 June Italy declared war, imperilling Britain's bases in the Mediterranean and the lines of communication with India and the Far East. In North Africa skirmishes broke out along the frontier between the Italian colony of Libya and Egypt, which was nominally a sovereign state but in practice a military stronghold of the British Empire. The RAF began to bomb Turin and other industrial towns in northern Italy and Home Intelligence reported 'evangelical old ladies in Tunbridge Wells satisfied at bombing of Italian Catholics'.

The consequences for the small Italian community in Britain were harsh. Thousands of Italian males were arrested and interned. Italian cafés, restaurants and ice-cream shops were attacked, their windows broken and their premises looted. According to Home Intelligence such incidents were the work of 'hooligans' and feelings towards Italy were more complex, but in the main the general public's attitude was said to be one of contempt.

France was now on the brink of collapse. On 10 June the government quit Paris. On the following day Churchill, on his fourth visit to France as Prime Minister, found Reynaud and Weygand resigned to defeat. Paris was declared an open city and German troops entered the capital on 14 June. The previous day the War Office announced that about 6,000 men of the 51st (Highland) Division had been captured by the Germans at St Valéry-en-Caux.

At home there was much argument over the role of the Local Defence Volunteers and criticism of the fact that as yet they were acutely short of rifles and uniform. For the time being they were employed mainly as an auxiliary police force on the alert for Fifth Columnists, a threat that continued to be taken seriously. Home Intelligence recorded the inconvenience suffered by motorists who found themselves stopped at road blocks by LDV patrols demanding to see their Identity Cards. In the North East there was 'much talk about shooting of motorists, especially if shooters should be LDV men'. On the night of 2–3 June the LDV had shot and killed four motorists in separate locations.

'A special study shows that women are increasingly more anxious and depressed than men,' Home Intelligence remarked on 12 June. This was a persistent theme of the reports in these early months, as was the claim that morale was higher among the working classes than the middle classes.

MONDAY 10 JUNE 1940

Anxiety has deepened over the weekend and optimism about the outcome of the battle is very much less in evidence. There is general realisation of the critical nature of present operations. There is disquiet on several counts: Weygand's standfast order is taken as an SOS (comparisons with Gamelin's 'Conquer or die' are obvious); reports on the progress of the battle invite comparison with those of the Sedan breakthrough; there is a feeling that 'the full story behind events in France has not yet been told'.

People's comments vary with the source of news and some confusion has been caused by the different tone of the wireless and of the various newspapers. The public is becoming quick to notice and comment upon conflicting statements. The indiscriminate machine-gunning of a South Coast town was reported in the press and denied on the wireless, while later editions of the newspapers still carried the old story. There was some criticism also of this morning's bulletin on the naval engagement in northern waters. On all sides the question was asked 'What does this hide?'

The course of events in France is dispelling the superficial expression of anti-French feeling. That feeling, however, is still latent and may have to be reckoned with in the future. At present Weygand is always mentioned with confidence in our reports and the Gamelin situation has been lost to consciousness.

There are over-optimistic references to the help which America will give. Interviewed, many people said they thought America would send large numbers of planes in the immediate future.

A constant source of dissatisfaction is the failure of professional and middle-class people (especially women) to become fully absorbed in the war effort. A defect in mobilisation is obvious from many of our reports.

Our observers report a growth in the feeling which has been latent for some time of 'the inevitability of German aggression'. It has been a particular objective of German propaganda to foster this feeling and extreme care should be taken to eliminate from press and wireless anything which gives support, whether direct or indirect, to this feeling. The trajectory of events is powerful enough without the addition of ill-considered embroideries.

The low poll at the Newcastle by-election was due largely to the opinion that the election should never have been held.

Points from Regions

NOTTINGHAM (North Midland)Well-to-do people are thinking about possible evacuation but are rather ashamed of it. Feeling towards America rather bitter: 'Only interested in dollars'. Business circles show definite anti-Russian feeling but realization of need for cooperation. Strong growth of pro-French feeling thanks to stout French resistance. Most people very willing to help Belgian refugees, though Dutch are considered wealthy enough to fend for themselves.

CARDIFF (Wales) Great satisfaction at Home Defence measures in practical form. French residents show a little bitterness at disproportionate size of our war effort. Maurice Healy's postscript, it is suggested, should take more thought of women as they are more anxious and nervy than men. Priestley's postscript not popular: 'clever generalities leading nowhere'. Folded newspapers showing headlines are used instead of placards. Very little chalking-up. Great discontent about 1,000 Irishmen employed on building defence works in Anglesey. They openly express anti-British and anti-Royalist feeling. 'A useful Fifth Column nucleus'. The work is at Port Rhosneigr.

BELFAST (Northern Ireland) Priestley's broadcast not making a deep impression, 'Did not put steel into us'. Growing anti-alien feeling. ARP still lacking in efficiency and it is felt greater use of local engineering facilities is called for in munitions production.

MANCHESTER (North Western) Vulnerability of Ireland causing anxiety; public sceptical about De Valera's ability to cope with it.

BRISTOL (South Western) Aircraft workers showing great enthusiasm in response to Bevin's appeal. Most towns demand stronger bombing of Berlin. Luxury rationing cheerfully accepted though it will mean stocks going down to half.

LEEDS (North Eastern) Growing demand for bombing of Berlin. This morning's Admiralty announcement felt to be unsatisfactory in view of German claim of victory. Much talk about shooting of motorists, especially if shooters should be LDV men. A number of people, serious-minded, fear France may give in if Germans break through effectively.

NEWCASTLE (Northern) One centre reports great satisfaction at efficiency of ARP on Friday night. Some interest aroused by New British Broadcasting Station, though its propaganda value is considered small.

EDINBURGH (Scotland) Criticism of slowness of call-up. Chalking-up of newspaper bills only occurs in main city streets. Some feeling about mounting war debt to America. A continuance of broadcast of Gram Swing would be welcome. Bombing of Berlin received with enthusiasm. More details would be appreciated instead of lengthy reports of RAF exploits behind the lines.

READING (Southern) Still too much RAF news: 'Their exploits fill the papers but don't stop the Germans'. Request that BBC should stress official and unofficial news items more carefully, and that voluntary system should be abandoned in favour of compulsion for ARP and LDV. Growing impatience with motorist joy-riders at weekends. Criticism that milestones in New Forest are turfed over and not removed and that there are still too many hotel signs about.

BIRMINGHAM (Midland) Requests for information about equipment situation of BEF to allay anxiety very common. Much criticism of haphazard way that road hold-ups of motorists are done by police and military. From Newport, Shropshire, comes suggestion that private businesses should close from Saturday to Tuesday and that workers therein should relieve factory workers for their essential holiday. From this town, too, comes request for trained observer attached to French Forces to describe their activities to us.

CAMBRIDGE (Eastern) Further reports show air raids have had no serious effect on morale. Each successive night fewer people left their houses for garden shelters. Steady private evacuation of adults continues from coastal towns. Directions wanted by public as to their actions if strangers ask the way.

TUNBRIDGE WELLS (South Eastern) Request for a clear definition of our material gains, if any, in Norway. Voluntary evacuation of South East coastal towns is estimated at 20%. At Folkestone only 50% of inhabitants are said to remain. Bus companies may have to shut down. Private car owners in Kent and Sussex cannot get more than one to two gallons at a time, even for three gallon coupons. People assume this to be due to threat of invasion. Contradiction of statement about machine-gunning of civilians in a South East Coast town with substitution of 'searchlight units' has shaken public's faith in our news. People point to circumstantial stories in press describing how public pick up bullets in the street, etc. Increasing precautions taken by public over telephone calls of official information.

LONDON

The public is quiet but expectant. Gravity of the situation is realized though no evidence of lack of confidence in the final result has been discovered. Pinner and Harrow: some anti-French feeling reported, particularly from old ex-servicemen. Reactions to news of evacuation on Thursday; surprise but willingness to abide by the Government's decision as 'they know best' (Stepney and Bow). Shoreditch and Bethnal Green report some confusion as to whether evacuation is to the east or to the west as they were originally to have gone east. News from Norway has produced dismay and some confusion in view of previous broadcasts. Priestley's broadcast fairly well received. Mixed reception for Hugh Dalton. Morden: many comments that allowances for aliens exceed those to wives of our soldiers.

TUESDAY 11 JUNE 1940

The grave events of the past twenty-four hours have occurred so rapidly that not all of them have influenced public feeling. The evacuation of Narvik and the British naval losses associated with this have passed almost unnoticed in the stronger reactions aroused by Italy's entry into the war and the evacuation of Paris by Government Departments.

Nowhere has the entry of Italy created any surprise. Among the majority of the population the feelings are militant anger, disgust, bitterness and even relief. Contempt for the Italian fighting qualities is very common and many people hope that the Allies will take the offensive against their new enemy rather than wait for Mussolini to attack. The more thoughtful people are more doubtful. They see the intervention of Italy as an added difficulty and describe the view that Italy is a new liability to Germany as 'wishful thinking'. Further, many of them personally like Italy and the Italians. The public do not expect set-backs in military or naval actions against Italy. If these are to be anticipated it is essential that they should be prepared for them.

Two views are apparent among the public about the evacuation of the Government staffs from Paris. Some people remember their precautionary evacuation in the last war; others point out that evacuation of a Government has in the past few weeks often proved to be a preliminary to military collapse. There is no anti-French feeling reported, but rather a wave of sympathy for the people who have received a stab in the back in addition to having to fight 'the Battle of France'.

The evacuation of Narvik is not treated as a serious matter by the public. They feel that it was of little use anyway. On the other hand, several reports point out that Admiralty communiques suggested Admiralty ignorance at the details of the British losses and some people are disturbed that the German news 'got in first'. They are also surprised at the reappearance of the Gneisenau.

The great majority of the public welcomed Duff Cooper's speech and appreciated his 'dressing down' of Italy. A small and intellectual minority were very critical of the big drums. Many people stayed up to listen to Roosevelt hoping that his 'important announcement' would be a declaration of war. Their feelings when this did not come were those of mild disappointment as they appear to have known that their hopes were really wishes.

Points from Regions

NOTTINGHAM (North Midland) Duff Cooper received with great enthusiasm: 'the plainest and bravest speaker we have'. Satisfaction at dressing down of Mussolini. Considerable evacuation of well-to-do children so that mothers may take jobs.

CARDIFF (Wales) DC's speech widely commended. Severe criticism of 6 p.m. news. Very strong anti-Italian feeling. Many windows broken in South Wales valleys. Welcome of evacuees continues very good. Mr Hibberd is much missed by public.

BELFAST (Northern Ireland) DC's speech 'courageous' but did not wholly dispel anxiety. Roosevelt did not make deep impression. Some anti-Italian demonstrations in Belfast. British Legion organising plans for tracing rumours to source and notifying police. General enthusiasm for National Savings Week.

MANCHESTER (North Western) Surprising numbers stayed up for Roosevelt. General comment: 'there was little he could do'.

BRISTOL (South Western) Roosevelt said 'all that was possible'. Italian cafe smashed at Exeter. Weymouth and Dorchester very depressed about British naval losses.

LEEDS (North Eastern) Commonest emotion at the moment is sympathy for France. In Leeds disgust at dilatory way LDV is being armed. Some anti-Chamberlain feeling.

EDINBURGH (Scotland) DC's speech 'magnificent'. Only critics were 'a few frosted academics who do not like beating the big drum'. Looting of Italian shops due rather to hooliganism than to anti-Italian feeling. This will have to be watched for fear of its repetition in air raids. A big wave of sympathy for France, with some comparisons of our lack of preparedness.

NEWCASTLE (Northern) DC especially popular among working classes. He is developing a 'fan' following. Roosevelt listened to by many; they liked his speech but were disappointed at no declaration of war. Two centres report voluntary evacuation of wealthier classes. Ice-cream shops wrecked at Ashington and Middlesbrough.

READING (Southern) Hope widely expressed that Allies will take the initiative against Italy. Some worry at efficacy of RAF due to falling off of number of enemy air losses reported. Furious dissatisfaction of men in one aircraft firm owing to their being kept on short time from lack of raw materials. The men telegraphed Lord Beaverbrook a fortnight ago and their telegram has not been answered. PPU activities considerably less. COs continue unpopular.

BIRMINGHAM (Midland) DC's speech made profound impression, but people demand early positive action against Italy to take their measure and to prevent them getting their tails up.

CAMBRIDGE (Eastern) Mystification and anxiety at lateness of Admiralty news of naval disasters at Narvik, particularly as Admiralty itself appeared to have been in the dark.

TUNBRIDGE WELLS (South Eastern) Roosevelt: 'a fine piece of oratory but what did it all amount to?' Disappointment at nothing more than a promise. DC's speech 'most impressive and forceful statement he has made yet'. Only criticism is it belittled significance of Italy rather too much. On the whole the effect was extremely reassuring. Voluntary evacuation from Ramsgate, Thanet, Dover and Folkestone now practically complete. Only essential workers remain.

LONDON

Main subjects of public interest are Italy (see general report) and evacuation. People disturbed by mysterious Admiralty reports of naval battle and losses and annoyed that German bulletin was out first. DC's speech in the main warmly approved; critics however were equally warm. Mothers were only concerned about evacuation. Large volumes of correspondence containing accounts of defeatist talk – 'we'll be as well off under Hitler' – have been received by the *Daily Mail* from all parts of England. The letter-writers express indignation at the commonness of these remarks. In Soho demonstrations were on a very small scale only, though there were many public sightseers. Police kept the crowds well under control though there were some broken windows. Evacuation: in Gillingham, Chatham, Gravesend and Rochester parents are refusing to allow their children to go to Wales for fear they should be compulsorily evacuated to Canada and the Dominions from there. In Richmond there have been a number of enquiries about the possibility of evacuation of children and adolescents to Canada and the Dominions. There is more evidence that compulsory evacuation would be accepted by many people in good grace. Paddington, Islington, Finsbury, Westminster and North Kensington report that public would welcome a country Nursery School scheme for children under five. Housing Estate Managers support this view and are extremely anxious as large numbers of young children on many estates may be a cause for parental panic in air raids. Motorists in Chatham area report extreme difficulty in finding the way as the public are patriotically obstructive.

WEDNESDAY 12 JUNE 1940

The gravity of the situation is generally realised but there is a background of determination untouched by the course of events.

1. France. *The Battle for Paris drives out other topics. Maurois' broadcast had a great effect. It left most people feeling that the situation was 'desperate', the fall of Paris 'inevitable'. Concern is expressed that 'we are not doing all we can for France now', 'It looks as if we're hanging back'. Reports from working-class districts show that many people wonder why we are not sending more material aid immediately. A minority point out that the fall of Paris would not mean the end of the French.*

Suspicion about the news from France is general. 'They are hiding something from us' is a familiar expression. The accuracy of German communiques is frequently commented upon.

2. Italy. *There is a dangerous tendency to treat Italy with scorn (the cue having been taken from official broadcasts). The bombing of Libya was received with satisfaction and it is hoped that the entry of Italy into the war will provide us with an opportunity of taking the initiative.*

Middle-class opinion is increasingly critical of Duff Cooper's Italian broadcast. It was considered 'theatrical', 'unsuitable', 'dangerous'. There is evidence, however, that the speech was in line with the more aggressive, 'tougher', less sophisticated working-class feeling. At the same time it should be noted that the anti-Italian demonstrations were mainly the work of hooligans.

3. Evacuation. *There has been a very high degree of voluntary evacuation from certain coastal towns (over 60% of households in Ramsgate, Margate and Broadstairs). Our observers report that compulsory evacuation of children would be accepted with good grace. 'If the Government wanted us to send the children out they ought to order us all to do it'.*

4. Morale of Women. *A special study shows that women are increasingly more anxious and depressed than men. Evacuation problems press directly on women and food prices are a continual underlying worry.*

5. Recrimination. *'Chamberlain must go' is increasing although not strongly. The Civil Service is now being mentioned as bearing a special responsibility for past errors. The voluntary system (e.g. of recruiting) is coming in for a good deal of criticism.*

6. Rumours. *Although quantitatively rumours are less, they are still exercising strong emotional effect especially in villages.*
    Two rumours are prominent today: a recrudescence of the statement that the two Princesses are in Canada (in spite of today's photographs) and a club rumour that 'there has been a scandal in the Home Office'.

Points from Regions

NOTTINGHAM (North Midlands) It is suggested that scare war articles in *Daily Mirror* harm morale and should be censored or stopped. Requests have been made that news of air raids in counties should state whether alarms only were sounded or whether bombs were dropped as well, as this uncertainty breeds rumour. Some people suggest systematic jamming of Haw-Haw.

CARDIFF (Wales) André Maurois well received but increased anxiety. Coal miners have agreed to a Sunday night-shift. BEF men at Wrexham hooted RAF item at cinema.

BELFAST (Northern Ireland) Disquiet caused by continued attacks on Ulster Government for alleged weakness in war effort. They have now gone too far, causing unnecessary alarm. Citizens asking for more specific advice on air-raid conduct.

MANCHESTER (North Western) Satisfaction at our initiative against Italians. General view about America is that their help cannot be in time to be of great value.

BRISTOL (South Western) TU leaders say war with Italy will strengthen left-wing determination for victory. Workers were suspicious as long as Government courted Mussolini. Now all danger of an anti-Russian line-up has passed. Motorists on Salisbury Plain refused directions by villagers. *Daily Mirror* anti-Haw-Haw campaign has made several people listen to him for the first time. Returning BEF without equipment has produced anti-Chamberlain feeling in Somerset. Country people feel that COs should be put to work at 2/- a day.

LEEDS (North Eastern) Anti-Chamberlain feeling common. Continued demand for bombing of Germany. Uneasiness continues that too many potential Fifth Columnists are not under lock and key.

EDINBURGH (Scotland) West of Scotland workmen not satisfied at vague threats of compulsory action under EPA with no evidence of real action. They ask '*Are* strikes prohibited? *Are* compulsory transfers to take place?' Criticism of lack of detailed news about naval losses and about yesterday's newspaper report that hundreds of German planes had dropped bombs in this country in the last two days. Passage of homing pigeons between Ireland and West of Scotland causing anxiety as a potential method for Fifth Column Irish communications. Prohibition is suggested.

NEWCASTLE (Northern) Some slight increase of anxiety in an area normally very unexcitable.

READING (Southern) Seaport opinion asks what is behind recent increased submarine sinking. Newbury beginning to suggest stopping racing to save petrol. Irritation continues with anything which hampers industrial war effort, e.g. lack of orders in an aircraft factory. Interest in America lukewarm. Suspicion that BEF is held back by lack of materials creates growing anti-Chamberlain feeling.

BIRMINGHAM (Midland) Wide criticism of the ineffectuality of our war effort. This takes two forms: first, criticism of the voluntary system of recruiting for special duties and, secondly, criticism of the appalling ineffectiveness of the Civil Service. This is particularly common among business managers.

CAMBRIDGE (Eastern) No alarm at extension of date and area for evacuation. Much less anxiety among parents to get children away since evidence has appeared of extensive military preparation on coast line. Increasing evidence that public strike a balance between Allied and German communiques.

TUNBRIDGE WELLS (South Eastern) Increasingly warm feeling for French and demand for reassurance that we are giving them all the help we can. Folkestone depopulated by evacuation. Eastbourne less so.

LONDON

Anxiety somewhat increased and gravity of situation realized. Demand that we should give more help to French is common since Maurois' speech. Main feeling for Italians is one of contempt. Working-class people continue to applaud Duff Cooper's speech though more intelligent people are more critical. Evacuation is main topic of talk among the poor. It is doubtful if even all those who are registered will go, as the rumours of a possible German landing in Ireland followed by invasion of Wales and Cornwall make the mothers doubtful as to whether there is any advantage whatever in moving their children. The mothers themselves show a growing feeling against compulsory evacuation. Insofar as it is articulate they feel it is a manifestation of the very thing we are fighting against – the right of the State to break up family life and to take away one's children.

THURSDAY 13 JUNE 1940

Depression and pessimism are at a high level but reaction is 'flat' and without high emotion. People are waiting for the fall of Paris which is regarded as inevitable although the feeling is widespread that this will not mean the end of the war either for France or for ourselves.

At the same time belief in ultimate victory is still general although this belief is now qualified by such comments as: 'We might as well commit suicide if we didn't go on believing in victory', 'I dare not contemplate anything else but victory', 'I suppose in the end we shall win', 'The cost of winning does not bear thinking about'.

Nevertheless morale is still good: over-confidence has everywhere disappeared and there is a determined facing-up to the course of events. Long-continued anxiety is having a bad effect on the morale of middle-class women: 'Women who have work to do get along alright; those who sit at home and listen to the news all day are decidedly jittery'.

There is a high degree of questioning about the amount of our help to France and great anxiety that all possible aid shall be sent (even at the expense of our own home defences) immediately to France.

Italy occupies second place in public reaction. Contempt at Italian intervention is high and the public is still thinking in terms of energetic aggressive action on our part. All news of such action is welcomed and already there is surprise that our attack has not been more formidable and widespread.

A statistical survey of Margate, Ramsgate and Broadstairs (conducted over the week 4–9 June) enabled an estimate to be made of the state of morale of those visited. A generalised assessment shows:

	Good	Medium	Bad	Don't Know
Total interviewed	68%	27%	3½%	1½%

Breaking down this result according to sex we find:

	Good	Medium	Bad	Don't Know
Men interviewed	81%	18%	1%	0
Women interviewed	60%	33%	5%	1½%

A further analysis shows that morale is lower among women over 40. It should be remembered that there is a high degree of voluntary evacuation from these towns which has probably had the effect of leaving behind those with higher morale.

The Communist candidate at Bow and Bromley (Lansbury's old seat) polled 506 votes (losing her deposit). Total poll slightly higher than of late (32.5%). The Communist failed to record local Pacifist tendencies, although stop-the-war feeling was still fairly high. (This section of the electorate did not go to the poll.) The Communist election cries were anti-Chamberlain and anti-upper class and emphasis was laid on domestic issues.

Points from Regions

NOTTINGHAM (North Midland) Landladies welcome BEF, billeted on them. Some ill-feeling between soldiers and civilians because soldiers criticise young civilians, and old soldiers of last war criticise unsoldierly appearance of Army today. Satisfaction at 300 planes from America. Strong criticism of unnecessary dismalness of five-minute religious feature just before 8 a.m. news. The lugubriousness of the Scottish gentleman too often resembles a preparation for the worst.

CARDIFF (Wales) Anti-gossip propaganda having excellent effect. Severe criticism from many quarters at frivolous BBC broadcast adjacent to the 6 o'clock news announcing the entry of Italy into the war.

BELFAST (Northern Ireland) 'Go to it' broadcast widely welcomed by industrial, agricultural, aircraft and shipyard workers. Public approval of decision of Grand Orange Lodge to cancel 12 July demonstrations so that war work may go on. Satisfaction at penalties for spreading alarmist and depressing statements. In spite of Sabbatarian feeling crops are to be gathered on fine Sundays.

MANCHESTER (North Western) Regional Committee making a drive on ARP with newspapers helping, but Local Authorities lukewarm about voluntary scheme. No evidence of increase of class feeling. Evacuation to Dominions scheme attracting interest; details hoped for. Farmers anxious about autumn shortage of labour.

BRISTOL (South Western) Rumour-mongering less. Demand for detailed casualty list of Calais fighting.

EDINBURGH (Scotland) Strong feeling among ex-servicemen that LDV is amateurish and ill-equipped. In some parts volunteers cannot be got for day duties while suitable men are idle and drawing unemployment assistance.

LEEDS (North Eastern) Strong anti-Chamberlain feeling on account of our apparent inability to help France. Business people in Leeds think we shall soon be fighting without France as our ally. Still criticism about number of men who are not being drafted into war work. Working class criticise BBC for putting on a record about hanging the washing on the Siegfried Line immediately after the 6 p.m. news. Song considered badly out-of-date.

NEWCASTLE (Northern) Desmond McCarthy's talk on Robinson Crusoe depressed less intellectual section of population. Wealthier people are leaving Scarborough where considerable activity at night is producing signs of strain in the civilian population.

READING (Southern) Rumours slumping heavily due to anti-rumour campaign, publicity given to prosecution, cooperation of regional press, sobering gravity of situation, and greater flow of news since Italy came in. Details demanded of loss of *Glorious* and accompanying ships. Air-raid warnings taken calmly on coast. Workers complain that alarms without bombs unnecessarily slow their work.

BIRMINGHAM (Midland) Widespread complaint of BBC news bulletins on grounds of excessive senseless repetition and out-of-date background material. Wolverhampton Corporation dismissed for the duration COs. Leamington Rotary Club withdraws support of 'lifts for servicemen' labels on cars on account of parachute menace.

CAMBRIDGE (Eastern) Military preparations at Clacton and Harwich have aroused apprehension; in other coastal towns the effect has been the reverse. Private evacuation continues.

TUNBRIDGE WELLS (South Eastern) Children in Preparatory Schools at Tunbridge Wells are being evacuated in large numbers to Somerset. Thanet towns very depressed. More than 50% of inhabitants now voluntarily evacuated; remainder have come to the conclusion that the Government does not intend to take any measures to remedy their plight. Evangelical old ladies in Tunbridge Wells satisfied at bombing of Italian Catholics. Public presses for strong punishment of officials who leave maps and documents about. General feeling is that police are not bestirring themselves enough in dealing with Fifth Columnists and Pacifist organisers.

LONDON

Public anxiously awaiting news from France. They watch the number of miles the Germans are reported to be from Paris and translate it into terms of London. The working classes appear to expect the fall of Paris but think the Germans will then over-reach themselves and come to a standstill. Evacuation is still the main topic of interest. Those under five who have arranged to go to Nursery Schools have gone willingly, though most mothers like to keep their youngest with them. The 13½ and 14s are not being registered as the present conditions of evacuation forbid their returning to London so that families will lose their earning capacity for the rest of the war. West Ham women are staying away from their houses for short periods only so as not to be caught in raids. Five hundred Belgian refugees kindly received in Southall. Inhabitants have found them surprisingly nice, though families who have husbands or sons in the Army are critical of the young Belgian refugees of military age. All poor-class areas report strong appreciation of Duff Cooper's speech. Shoreditch and Bethnal Green 100% delighted: 'Why are we paying MPs £600 a year to criticise a fighter like him?' Yesterday's gas mask count 3.30 to 4.30 p.m. Nottinghill Gate: of 408 people 13.3% were carrying masks (11.1% of the men and 15.5% of the women).

FRIDAY 14 JUNE 1940

1. Anxiety and tension are increasing. Reynaud's appeal to America has caused many people to express the fear that the French may collapse at any moment. Many enquiries are made about the state of French morale and there is a growing fear that we shall soon be left to fight alone. Questions are urgently asked about the extent of our immediate aid to France.

2. In certain districts women are showing increasing signs of strain.

3. There is increasing criticism of our apparent lack of effort. This finds expression in criticism of the Government which is only partly retrospective. There is some confusion in the distribution of blame and the present Government as well as 'Chamberlain' are being attacked both because of inefficient and inadequate preparedness and because the 'Germans are successful in aggression'. This confusion is unhealthy especially as it is found in association with a guilty admiration for Hitler's fulfilment of his prophecies. It is widely remembered that Hitler said he would be in Paris by 15 June. There is thus some danger of increasing fear, tension points and pockets of defeatism.

4. There is increasing criticism of the LDV and a strong feeling is growing that the voluntary system should be given up both for the LDV, ARP and industrial recruitment. There is a feeling that the determination of the public to win is not being supported by adequate material preparations. Phrases like 'We will never surrender'; 'We will fight in the streets, on the hills . . .' are being criticised in the light of inadequate mobilisation of men and materials.

5. Rumour. *New rumours are of a kind which show increased alarm and apprehension, e.g. the Government are going to Canada, Rumania has stopped oil supplies to France and Britain.*

Points from Regions

NOTTINGHAM (North Midlands) Miners making tremendous efforts to increase output. Some criticism of ploughing-up policy as many landowners are just scratching worthless ground to get the subsidy.

Order of Area Commander putting Nottingham dance halls out of bounds to officers has created much resentment. People on Lincolnshire coast worried at state of coastal defences.

CARDIFF (Wales) Continued resentment against last Government and growing outcry that we should make more use of our man-power. Three parachutists baled out near a congested area causing consternation among women. Arrival of police allayed tendency to panic.

BELFAST (Northern Ireland) Much dissatisfaction with Anderson's statement about Ulster–Eire border. Strong feeling that rigid safe-guards against passage of dangerous persons over border are needed. Hope expressed that Anderson will consult Ulster Government at once. Criticism of Home Defence and ARP persists.

MANCHESTER (North Western) Public increasingly impatient, demanding acceleration of our war effort. They would accept any orders but are disinclined to volunteer. Response to appeal for Civil Defence volunteers most disappointing. Birkenhead reports confirm lack of faith in voluntary system. Fear expressed that reticence about smoke-screens will cause crop of wild rumours.

BRISTOL (South Western) Public anxious lest French statesmen are becoming a little hysterical. 'Tell the truth' speeches by French offi-cers in the area widely welcomed and more are demanded. Public apprehensive as so many BEF men have been seen without rifles, while French troops have them. Apparently, on arrival in England BEF rifles were collected. If this were explained view that British troops dropped rifles and ran for it would vanish. Opposition to horse and greyhound racing almost unanimous, including even Cirencester. Bristol manufacturers demand conscription of labour. A stranger to the Region travelled 360 miles in the West Country without difficulty, thanks to hotel and other private advertisements on the road, and the clearness of the white lines on the roads leading to towns. Exeter welcomes evacuees: 'cleaner than the last lot'. St Austell makes strong criticism of our poor effort in France. French are staking all while we have half a million unemployed.

LEEDS (North Eastern) Much dissatisfaction with maintenance of LDV being left to voluntary contributions. 'Why no Government funds?' Much bitter comment on Juliana's evacuation to Canada.

EDINBURGH (Scotland) 'We are not doing all we can to help France.' Montrose British Legion organises anti-rumour plan. Edinburgh attempts to form 'Sixth Column' to discover Fifth Columnists. This is not regarded favourably by police.

NEWCASTLE (Northern) Constant complaints about lack of proper equipment for LDV. Many groups show exceptional keenness and buy ammunition out of their own pockets to get shooting practice. Strong criticism of Government parsimony in not providing this or refunding money spent.

READING (Southern) We are to blame as much as the French for the present situation. Feeling strong that declaration of war by America would force doubting neutrals, e.g. Turkey and Spain, to come in with us. Minister of Health's statement on evacuation not well received. His arguments lacked conviction. If coast is to be invaded the sooner we evacuate unnecessary civilians, the better; otherwise we shall have streams of refugees as in Holland, Belgium and France. Everyone is tired of the voluntary principle. If Government wants volunteers among youths conscript them. Same applies to industry. Firms still complain they have volunteered for Government work for months but nothing has happened yet.

BIRMINGHAM (Midland) Criticism of our lack of effort continues, especially the slowness of the call-up and the failure to conscript men to deal with the emergency.

CAMBRIDGE (Eastern) Minister of Home Security's appeal to the public to keep away from East Coast has created a little alarm but more thoughtful people recognise the necessity for this precaution. Coast resorts deeply worried at grave prospects now that all holiday business has stopped.

TUNBRIDGE WELLS (South Eastern) Seaside resorts concerned at curtailment of pleasure trips to coast and many now look forward to complete loss of business.

LONDON

People realise how serious the situation is. Fall of Paris has shaken them considerably; though they are calm they show dismay and a growing anger at our lack of men and equipment. Recrimination against the previous Government, especially Chamberlain, is heard, and there is questioning as to whether the French will capitulate. Disappointment is expressed at America's lack of concrete help and at our failure to use all our man-power. Difficulty reported in getting ARP volunteers in South London. In Albert Docks Italian shops attacked by hooligans with nothing better to do. Older people expressed disgust at this. Poplar women angry at able-bodied men spending their time at greyhound racing. Greenwich and Deptford report possibility of our not being victorious is now being considered by some people. West Ham Mission have opened as a substitute for schools. Evacuation in the City of London: only 6% of those registered turned up. Some improvement in evacuation attitude reported following BEF stories of the true horrors of war and showing of newsreels of these horrors.

SATURDAY 15 JUNE 1940

The fall of Paris has brought some slight relaxation of tension. The heart is heavy and sadness broods over conversation. There is relief that Paris has been spared by withdrawal and opinions about the strategic value of the capital are confused. There is disquiet but no feeling of panic.

Paris has brought to the forefront the whole problem of evacuation. Pertinent questions are being asked about our own preparations and there is clear evidence of a popular demand for further instruction and information. Many people are asking whether the Government have a well-considered evacuation scheme or whether the blow, if it falls, will find us without a plan.

Hitler's expected 'peace offensive' finds a place in many conversations and Harold Nicolson's speech was generally welcomed.

There is some evidence that Dutch and Belgian refugees are somewhat demoralised by the course of events and their attitude is having a bad effect on those in contact with them. Hitler's 'prophecies' are getting a wide currency and the tendency to discuss his phenomenal powers needs immediate discouragement. Such phrases as 'He's a genius', 'What's the date for London?', 'He's uncanny', are frequent in overheard conversations.

Criticism of our war effort is strongly on the increase. Blame falls on various authorities: vaguely, 'those at the top'; specifically, the Civil Servants, Chamberlain, the voluntary system. The LDV is considered amateurish and ill-organised. On all sides there is a demand for recruitment without equipment and the mobilisation of willing civilians. Reports from several working-class organisations show that there is serious discontent at the obvious inability to mobilise man-power.

Nevertheless the determination to win is untarnished 'even though we fight alone'.

Points from Regions

NOTTINGHAM (North Midland) Strong feeling that some form of preliminary military training should be compulsory for young men employed in shops and elsewhere. Eden criticised as being too slow. Suggestion that sports broadcasts should be stopped owing to their likelihood of making unfavourable impressions on the French. Demand that Duff Cooper should broadcast 'at least once a week'.

CARDIFF (Wales) Drilling of new recruits should be begun without delay, and without waiting for uniforms and equipment which should be ready after the first few weeks of their training. 'More sober' tone of BBC news is welcomed.

BELFAST (Northern Ireland) Munition workers keen for increased output. Leading factories work two twelve-hour shifts daily. British Legion and regimental associations are to cooperate in forming special detachment of volunteer defence force, for guarding vital points at night.

MANCHESTER (North Western) Uneven working of the voluntary system is criticised, and more definite orders would be welcomed. Public opinion is ahead of Government action in continuing to permit racing, sporting fixtures, luxury motoring, etc.

BRISTOL (South Western) Criticism of stock speeches by public men. Demand for deeds rather than words, particularly in handling campaign against Italy. Strong resentment expressed in Bath at full-pay holidays for 4,000 evacuated (Admiralty) Civil Servants. Similar criticism of joy-riding holiday-makers from Taunton and district; disgust expressed by local residents. Cornish ARP and LDV arrangements said to be badly organised and quite inadequate; the latter's potential resistance no more 'effective than pea-shooters', partly owing to shortage of rifles. In Penzance no public or private shelters, and very few gas masks to be seen.

LEEDS (North Eastern) Criticism on all sides of dilatory methods of Government in organising industrial man-power: 'What would the French think if they could walk through Leeds now and see all the BEF lying about and civilians still undisturbed by war?' 'Why are so many not yet called up?' 'Why are there so many idle women?' 'What is wrong with the War Office?' These remarks are given as typical.

EDINBURGH (Scotland) Precision of Hitler's timetable increasing tendency towards fatalism. Newspapers criticised for sensational treatment of this week's bad news. Widely expressed preference for BBC's bulletins.

NEWCASTLE (Northern) Evacuation from Scarborough continues, though this is less noticeable among the poorer classes. Heavy gunfire heard there yesterday caused some alarm.

READING (Southern) 'Steady growth of a demand for the substitution of business-like compulsion for amateurish voluntary system. This applies to everything, from evacuation to the LDC.' Evacuation has so far gone satisfactorily, and it is thought that this would be stimulated by reports of emergency evacuation in France.

BIRMINGHAM (Midland) Frequent rumours of the presence of enemy aircraft in the vicinity are attributed to careless talk by the Observer Corps. These stories continue in spite of official Air Ministry denials.

CAMBRIDGE (Eastern) There is some resentment, mostly among men, at the alarm caused to their wives by irresponsible conversation among members of the BEF who have returned from France. The effect of this is to induce a fatalistic attitude. There is some nervousness at the possibility of the civil population being evacuated, though this subject is not at present discussed very widely.

TUNBRIDGE WELLS (South Eastern) Dartford factories are said to be slack for want of material and Sunday workers receive double pay for less work than they do ordinarily. At a Sevenoaks meeting to discuss voluntary savings it was suggested that the Government should indicate the articles on which it would be considered patriotic to spend one's money. Concern was expressed at the adverse effect on trade which was likely to result from misguided restrictions on spending.

LONDON

People returning from Paris say there was talk in France that the French are carrying the whole of the battle and the British are not doing their share. Considerable anxiety everywhere that we are not helping as much as we should. More anger against lack of preparedness and even talk of 'Lynching Chamberlain and the old gang if things get very bad'. Paddington reports map of London superimposed on map of Paris (*News Chronicle*, Thursday) has made great impression on working people. 'More propaganda of this direct type might wake people up.' Most social workers report lack of understanding of true significance of events. People still 'living for the moment' in many poor districts. They suggest talks given to small groups of these people by responsible people known in the neighbourhood. These talks must be in language they understand. Many people of this type find wireless voices too impersonal and language too academic to affect them personally. Stories brought home by BEF wake families to realization of danger and have affected evacuation figures. CAB Secretaries report 'Terrifying effect' of sentence in MacDonald's evacuation speech in House, e.g. 'the Government cannot absolutely guarantee the children's safety'. Women ran about housing estates crying and wanting to get children back. Children's enthusiasm to get away into country for 'Holiday' has decided many parents to register them. Care Committee workers report 'The people simply don't know what is happening. If the authorities want to prevent panic among women and children in crowded working-class districts, compulsory evacuation will be necessary'. Children under five have shown great terror in air-raid tests (Chelsea).

MONDAY 17 JUNE TO SATURDAY 22 JUNE 1940

The week began with yet more bad news from France. On 16 June, in a desperate bid to persuade the French to continue the war, the British government proposed an Act of Union between the two countries. When the Reynaud Cabinet rejected the offer and resigned, a new government was formed under Marshal Pétain. The following day he announced that France would seek peace terms. The reaction, Home Intelligence reported, 'has been one of confusion and shock, but hardly surprise'. Anti-French feeling revealed itself in phrases such as 'we're better off without the French' and 'we should have looked after ourselves all along'. The fighting in France continued for another few days but on 21 June Hitler presented a French delegation with armistice terms which they accepted the following day. For the British one of the few redeeming features of the situation was the successful evacuation of a further 136,000 British troops from such French ports as Brest, Cherbourg, St Malo and St Nazaire.

'What General Weygand called the Battle of France is over,' Churchill told the House of Commons on 18 June. 'I expect that the Battle of Britain is about to begin.' In what was to become one of his most celebrated speeches he expressed his unshakable confidence in the ability of the British armed forces to repel and defeat a German invasion. 'Let us therefore brace ourselves to our duties,' he concluded, 'and so bear ourselves that, if the British Empire and its Commonwealth last for a thousand years, men will still say, "This was their finest hour."' He repeated the speech over the radio that evening but sounded tired and the broadcast lacked the fire of his parliamentary performance. 'Churchill's speech was awaited anxiously,' Home Intelligence noted, 'and when heard was the subject of varied reactions. What he said was considered courageous and hopeful and the speech was welcomed for its frankness . . . On the other hand there was widespread comment on his delivery and his references to France have brought a recrudescence of anti-French feeling.'

In a Sunday evening 'Postscript' on 16 June, J. B. Priestley expressed the wish that all children of Britain could be sent across the seas to the Dominions, leaving the adults to fight back against the Nazis with easier minds. Home Intelligence recorded strong popular support for the idea and the announcement on 20 June of a voluntary, state-assisted scheme prompted a rush for places, with 210,000 requests over the next fortnight. Since air raids were already frequent, and the threat of invasion was looming, fears for the safety of children were inevitable but not necessarily a sign of low morale. From the Midland region there were 'many reports of talk among working and lower middle classes that "they would be just as well off under Hitler"', but such expressions of defeatism were outweighed by the strength and frequency of demands for the more effective prosecution of the war. With 650,000 men and women still unemployed the government was under attack for failing to use its powers to mobilise and arm every able-bodied citizen. As one critic put it: 'The Jerries will arrive to find many still in the streets with their hands in their pockets.' According to the North Midlands office, 'Nottingham women want to be armed with rifles and hand grenades.'

The most unpopular feature of the government was the continuing presence in high office of 'the old gang': Neville Chamberlain and his closest political allies. Chamberlain, who was a member of Churchill's War Cabinet, had become the scapegoat for military defeat after Dunkirk, and his pre-war record as an appeaser of Nazi Germany gave rise to the suspicion that he was still in favour of peace at any price or even perhaps a potential traitor.

MONDAY 17 JUNE 1940

Over the weekend throughout all parts of England there was a feeling of gloomy apprehension. As usual this was most obvious among the middle classes and the women, and least obvious among the working classes. Coupled with this was a large volume of criticism of our voluntary active and passive defence measures. Everyone felt that compulsory conscription for the LDV and ARP was essential, and that we could still do more towards increasing our industrial war effort. In many parts there was outspoken criticism of our former Government.

The collapse of France was everywhere considered as a possibility.

The reaction to the capitulation of the French, as announced on the 1 o'clock news, has been one of confusion and shock, but hardly surprise. From all parts come reports of bewilderment and great anxiety. Two questions are uppermost in people's minds. The first is the fate of the BEF. Will a second Dunkirk be possible? What of those of the BEF who were in the Maginot Line? The second great question is, what is happening to the French Navy and Air Force? Are they going to fight on with us? If not, things are indeed black. Two centres in London report a short-wave broadcast from America between 2 and 3 p.m. stating that the French Air Force and Navy continue to fight. These reports have had a most heartening effect.

Throughout the country there is a demand for immediate leadership and guidance as to our attitude. The public are ready and determined to follow the Prime Minister if he gives the word, but if that word is not given there are signs that morale may change rapidly for the worse. Some reports express fear that our Government may go abroad, others that the Government itself may give in. A few feel all is over. The public expect to hear tonight from either Duff Cooper, Churchill, or even the King, what attitude we are going to adopt and what can be done to save the country. Unless one of these leaders speaks tonight, it is certain that a defeatist attitude will gain ground, and the divorce of feeling between the people and the Government will be gravely accentuated.

Points from Regions

(Over the weekend, before one o'clock news)

NOTTINGHAM (North Midland) Stronger feeling against Chamberlain Government: 'half hearted elements in high places'. Increasing indignation at slowness of call-up: 'turn playing fields into drill grounds; don't wait for rifles'.

CARDIFF (Wales) Collapse of France expected; no condemnation but rather self-criticism. Growing feeling against weekend joy-riders in private cars.

BELFAST (Northern Ireland) Germany expected to violate Eire's neutrality. Early statement by Churchill hoped for.

MANCHESTER (North Western) Voluntary recruiting for Civil Defence unsatisfactory. Evacuation of women and children to Dominions (J.B. Priestley's suggestion) has caught popular fancy.

BRISTOL (South Western) Widespread feeling for expulsion of all Chamberlain's ministers, even amongst staunchest Tories. Evacuees given excellent reception. Ex-servicemen in passive defence services indignant that they are banned from joining LDV.

LEEDS (North Eastern) Growing and impressive volume of criticism of 'the authorities'. BEF openly criticise War Office. Organisation of LDV. Failure of mobilisation of man-power and woman-power widely criticised. Popular joke at Harrogate is 'Germans won't bomb Harrogate because of the Air Ministry'.

EDINBURGH (Scotland) Rising anger at our general unpreparedness for acute trouble, especially persistence of voluntary principle.

READING (Southern) Demand for definite instructions and leadership grows, and attempts at recruiting for ARP provoked questions as to why Government does not conscript everybody. Middle class like idea of sending children to Canada. Criticism of old National Government is fed by angry stories of lack of material by BEF and lack of equipment for LDV. Call-up still thought much too slow. Public would welcome a heartening broadcast by Churchill or Duff Cooper immediately.

BIRMINGHAM (Midland) People have a sense of frustration; they want something to do but have no lead. Working class supports idea of Canada for the children.

CAMBRIDGE (Eastern) General and grave feeling that man-power is still not being utilised to the full.

LONDON

The public generally anticipated the capitulation of France. The West End was filled with people last night going to cinemas, with a general air of expectancy. Much criticism of Saturday night's speeches. Voices too old – depressing and devitalising (Grigg, Kindersley and Amery). Business and professional women extremely annoyed at their non-mobilisation by Government. Evacuation continues normally.

TUESDAY 18 JUNE 1940

Morale is little changed since yesterday although the Prime Minister's short broadcast had a steadying effect. His speech was referred to widely in conversation and it was generally recognised that the Prime Minister was unable to say more. 'An interim lead' sums up the comments. Although there is still confusion there is some tendency to think that the situation is not quite as catastrophic as it seemed at first. In some districts the shock is reported to be over and determination is rallying.

Recovery takes the form of an urgent demand for strong leadership and for more realistic measures for Home Defence. Allied with this demand is continued criticism of 'those in authority', 'those at the top', 'cumbersome old machinery'. Anti-Chamberlainism is very strong in certain quarters especially among industrial workers.

There is extremely little anti-French feeling and the PM's remarks about 'the French people' are fully in line with public opinion.

There is increasing restlessness among those who are still immobilised. Reports show serious dissatisfaction that willing help is untapped ('spurned' is the word frequently used).

Reports from working-class districts show an increasing dissociation of leaders and led: many women say about Hitler 'He won't hurt us: it's the bosses he's after: we'll probably be better off when he comes'.

From certain areas (Cornwall, East Yorkshire, London) defeatism is reported but, in the main, there is determination to carry on with the war and to fight to a finish. Many people express relief (of a quite unrealistic kind) that at last 'There are no more Allies'. At the same time there is a good deal of wishful thinking about Russia, Turkey and America. Many men are prepared to 'turn this island into a fortress' and would be glad to see many women and children and 'if necessary the Government' go to Canada. The number of women making enquiries about taking or sending children to the Dominions is hourly increasing.

An attempt to assess answers to the question 'Do you think the war will go on?' showed that about 75% expected the war to continue, 15% did not expect the war to continue, 10% doubtful (84% men compared with 65% women thought the war would continue). The enquiry was conducted yesterday afternoon and evening. A further question designed to test reaction to fighting alone showed that approximately 50% contemplated with confidence fighting alone (25% doubtful, 25% could not contemplate this situation with anything like confidence). Gas-mask carrying has increased by about one-third over last week.

Points from Regions

NOTTINGHAM (North Midland) Compulsory evacuation of children to Canada much discussed. People receiving persuasive cables of invitation from Canada. Nottingham women want to be armed with rifles and hand grenades. Forcibly expressed desire from many parts for Government to use compulsory powers to the full, in conscripting labour and defence forces. Grimsby district ask for more ARP films as an excellent antidote to panic.

CARDIFF (Wales) Almost universal opinion that every fit man should be put into training and armed as soon as possible. Reduce reserved occupations to a minimum. If necessary send children and non-effectives abroad. In North Wales invasion of Ireland is widely envisaged.

BELFAST (Northern Ireland) Volunteers continue to enrol for Ulster Home Defence forces. Good response to salvage campaign for scrap metal and waste paper.

MANCHESTER (North Western) Public ready to make this country a fortress, but say that unless they are organised 'the Jerries will arrive to find many still in the streets with their hands in their pockets'. Delay in arrangements for evacuating women and children to Canada is causing bitter comment of the 'too late as usual' type.

BRISTOL (South Western) Wide feeling that our supply departments have failed. 12,000 men employed at GWR workshops at Swindon asking why no armaments are being made there for machinery is quite suitable. In Cornwall compulsory billeting of evacuees from Poplar is causing friction. Strong desire for industrial conscription, though manufacturers allege Civil Service could not do it efficiently or rapidly. They suggest trade organisations for the job.

LEEDS (North Eastern) Most of public are criticising our war effort and particularly Chamberlain and 'the old gang'. People demand that whole nation should be armed. 'We have half a million ex-servicemen in the country who should be armed at once'.

EDINBURGH (Scotland) Distrust and suspicion of previous Government is growing and there is even some spread to the present Government. 'Are we doing everything that can be done?' Not only people in executive positions but also ordinary working classes are demanding that Government should take over and make use of every able-bodied man. It is suggested Government should order all private gardens to grow at least 50% foodstuffs. 150 volunteer motor mechanics in Edinburgh ready for aircraft work are still marking time.

NEWCASTLE (Northern) Newcastle and Scarborough report growing anger against members of previous Government still in Cabinet.

Restlessness among people in less important reserved occupations and among middle aged ex-servicemen who feel Government should give them a chance to do more to help. Workers at Cargo Fleet Ironworks near Middlesbrough have offered to work sixteen hours a day if necessary. Public need educating about what a peace with Germany now would really involve. Nicolson's broadcast was a step in this direction.

READING (Southern) Demand for strong leadership from Government in Civil Defence and preparedness is unabated. In Southampton and Portsmouth registration of children continues very slack. Criticism of slowness of call-up gathers force in all quarters.

BIRMINGHAM (Midland) Working classes blame Mr Chamberlain and ex-Government for our present difficulties. Much feeling at delay in conscription for ARP and other services. Too many people still doing nothing for war effort. 'The willing horse is getting fed up.' Considerable criticism of BBC news, particularly the continuous repetition of 'stale stuff'.

CAMBRIDGE (Eastern) Public urging that every sort of man-power should be tapped and used. No desire to wash previous Government's dirty linen in public if only present one will get on with the job. Many centres enquiring about overseas evacuation for women and children. Move appears to be popular even with working classes.

TUNBRIDGE WELLS (South Eastern) General feeling that Government has not grappled effectively with situation. Thousands eagerly waiting to be told what to do to serve. Great criticism of BBC for monotonous and needless repetition of stale news and for use of *Herr* Hitler and *Signor* Mussolini. Public expect ten days comparative peace until after Hitler's Versailles speech.

LONDON

Divisional Controller of Labour reports atmosphere strained in most districts yesterday, calm today. Marylebone District segregated large number of women aliens from British subjects to prevent expression of feeling of being crowded out. Canning Town Works: tension yesterday, normal today. Kodak Works, Harrow: staff depressed but not panicky. Hampstead: influx of Belgian refugees asking to be moved out of London. Very emotional; know what war is; might panic and upset local people. NCSS: many enquiries yesterday and today about possibility of sending children at once to the Dominions. Hampstead, Poplar, Pinner, Harrow, Richmond report same enquiries. Mothers would like to go with children in some cases. Other women volunteering to accompany parties. Isleworth: suggestion 3–4,000 dentists over age eligible for commissions should be used in national emergency. Welfare Supervisors (representing 10,000 workers) report definite statement should be made soon about holidays. This question agitating staffs. Men in many districts rushed to Recruiting Offices yesterday and today. Were turned down and told to wait for registration. Much dissatisfaction the result and criticism of present Government. Much criticism also growing of Chamberlain and old leaders. Even accused of treachery.

WEDNESDAY 19 JUNE 1940

On the whole there is slightly less depression today but people are reluctant to discuss the situation and are awaiting the publication of Hitler's terms to France.

Churchill's speech was awaited anxiously and when heard was the subject of varied reactions. What he said was considered courageous and hopeful and the speech was welcomed for its frankness. 'He gives bad news frankly', 'Cool and businesslike', 'The sort of facts and figures we want'. On the other hand there was widespread comment on his delivery and his references to France have brought a recrudescence of anti-French feeling.

The latency of anti-French feeling must never be forgotten. A few days ago sympathy swamped it but it found indirect expression in a common phrase 'At last we have no Allies, now we fight alone'. There has never been much sympathy with the French point of view but there are some indications that the present wave of anti-French feeling is bringing to the surface antagonism against 'French politicians', 'Corruption in high quarters', 'Traitors'.

This feeling finds some parallel in active criticisms of our own leadership. Accusations of 'inefficiency' are common but as yet there is no universal scapegoat. 'There's been inefficiency somewhere – you mark my words', 'Why haven't we enough armaments? That's what I want to know'. Among a higher level of appreciation there is continued criticism of 'the Civil Service', 'those in charge of the LDV', 'Chamberlain'.

Joubert's broadcast was welcomed for its practical tone.

Press photographs of Princess Juliana and her children in Canada have come in for scathing comment.

The raid in Cambridgeshire was received calmly. (It will be the subject of a special report tomorrow).

There are undoubtedly pockets of defeatism and overheards record a number of phrases like 'if we're going to lose, why go on?', 'I suppose we can only wait for Hitler now', but in the main there is a dogged determination to see the thing through. It should be recorded, however, that in many working-class districts this determination is accompanied by some anxiety about the efficient conduct of the war and about the credentials of 'those at the top'.

Points from Regions

NOTTINGHAM (North Midland) Complaints about vague nature of past reports of bombing on English soil (particularly *Daily Telegraph* of 11 June – 'in last few days hundreds of German planes have dropped bombs in this country in the hope of immobilising our fighters'). This causes alarmist speculation. Criticism that returning BEF had not proper railway warrants for leave. A gunsmith reports he cannot dispose of his stock of guns to police or Government. Public questioning about possibility of removing names from shops of Nottingham Co-operative Society.

CARDIFF (Wales) Growing feeling for evacuation of women and children abroad. Commonest question is still 'What of the French Navy?' Growing anxiety in Western counties about possibility of invasion from Eire. Presence of evacuees makes public ask 'Are Government taking invasion fear seriously?' People enquiring about desirability of storing an iron ration. 'Is this unpatriotic?' An authoritative statement would be welcomed. Growing opinion among workers that Russia will soon be more actively in war on our side. MOI pamphlet on invasion hoped to be available in Welsh, or alternatively that translations will be available as public posters.

BELFAST (Northern Ireland) Increasing irritation at Eire neutrality while Eire depends on British aid for defence. Disappointment that Government has not placed more war orders in Ulster which has 60,000 unemployed.

MANCHESTER (North Western) Anxiety common about fate of French fleet and Air Force, also potentiality of Italian submarines to interfere with Atlantic shipping. Growing demand for conscription for Home Defence, ARP and big labour battalions to deal with bombing damage.

BRISTOL (South Western) Some anxiety on coast about possibility of invasion from Eire. News of German terms to France eagerly awaited; comment is 'I expect we shall hear it first from Haw-Haw'.

LEEDS (North Eastern) Growing campaign that race meetings and the like should be stopped. Still much criticism on the lack of Government vigour. BEF men in Leeds last night said 'If real trouble starts in England, and if civilians are not armed, we will go home to defend our families'. One soldier said 'There'll be real mutiny among the lads if they think their own folk are not being protected'.

EDINBURGH (Scotland) Public still feel strongly need for more active and obvious defence measures. General public in Glasgow, and Dundee, still not sufficiently alive to situation. Glasgow observer suggests Dominion troops should be marched through the streets instead of being moved unobtrusively in trains. West of Scotland suspicious of Eire since ambiguous De Valera speech. Feeling that Irish potato diggers should not be allowed in Scotland this season.

NEWCASTLE (Northern) Evacuation of children to Canada is seriously discussed for the first time, though mainly among middle classes. Many well-to-do people evacuating from Scarborough. Ashington anxious that loss of French coal market may cause unemployment. Two Communist meetings in Durham abandoned owing to hostile attitude of public. MOI invasion pamphlet well received.

READING (Southern) Public restive at slow call-up. Mayor of Southampton asked to start drilling men himself. Portsmouth public houses organise anti-Haw-Haw league to stop listening. Tickler's, Aspro's and firms on Slough trading estate organising their own private defence forces with great enthusiasm. They borrow LDV rifles during day and ex-NCOs train them.

BIRMINGHAM (Midland) Many demands for more complete armament of LDV. Public advocate LDV being placed under regular officers or ex-NCOs rather than the squire or the local amateur. Working men trust experienced NCOs far more than retired colonels or majors. Some part of public expect Hitler to demobilise much of his army and blockade us rather than invade us.

CAMBRIDGE (Eastern) Public took widespread raiding last night very calmly and today have settled down quickly to their normal work. Majority remained in their own homes. Few alarmist rumours as a result of the raid.

TUNBRIDGE WELLS (South Eastern) First air-raid alarm in Tunbridge Wells taken very calmly. No evidence of hotel residents wishing to leave as a result. Great confidence in our AA defence and RAF. Today a rush to ARP depots to get contex filters for gas masks.

LONDON

Ex-servicemen disturbed by 'Large number of young men about streets and getting exemption'. Slight anti-French feeling expressed since Mr Churchill's phrase 'Holding France to her Treaty obligations'. Shopping districts, people subdued: 'just carrying on'. Wandsworth: better-class people discussing evacuation to Dominions. This reported also from St John's Wood. Poorer districts, Hammersmith, Fulham, Lambeth: working class talking a great deal about scheme but not anxious for children to go unless they have relatives in Australia or Canada. Silvertown, Venesta Factory (1,600 workers) calm today after guns audible last night. Most people slept through them. Some dismay expressed at civilian casualties, but reason

given 'They must have gone outside to look instead of taking cover'.
Air Marshal's speech gave just the right directions they were needing.
Evidence that it calmed fears. Venesta Factory dissatisfaction that 120
volunteers for LDV still not armed. Men's enthusiasm being lost;
grumbling spreading through factory. Hammersmith: serious
complaints of local Labour Exchange treatment of volunteers for
National Service. Hampstead: some anti-Semitic feeling rising at Jews
talking about leaving the country. This is not reflected in other districts.
St John's Wood reports 'Local Jews excessively patriotic'. Willesden:
complaints that men registered but not yet called up cannot get
employment, hardship cases reported. Fulham: evacuation well
backed up. People now taking it 'very seriously knowing there is
no possibility of the children coming back this time'. Lambeth:
'Scheme for evacuating under-fives badly needed'. Islington: children
sent to Murcott, Islip, Oxfordshire are complaining about billets
and urging mothers to fetch them home at once. 'Some of the
teachers have told them they were as well off in London'. Housing
Manager afraid mothers will be trying to bring their children back.
Mitcham: complaints that district is arbitrarily divided into 'Neutral'
and 'Danger' Areas. Line of demarcation divides same street. Mothers
in 'Neutral' part anxious to get children away, causing local trouble.

THURSDAY 20 JUNE 1940

*There continues to be a slight improvement in the atmosphere of depression
which followed the French capitulation. There is a decline in interest in
Hitler's expected peace terms, but this is coupled with a definite increase in
anti-French feeling, showing itself in such phrases as 'We're better off without
the French', 'We should have looked after ourselves all along'. If the French
capitulation ultimately includes the French Navy and Air Force some Regions
anticipate a growth of very bitter feeling.*

*The air raids and warnings last night have on the whole been taken very
calmly: 'not as bad as we expected'. At the same time areas where bombs fell
before sirens sounded are very critical and this reinforces a widespread demand
for making ARP a compulsory rather than a voluntary service. The raiding in
Wales has strengthened the popular belief that evacuation is not synonymous*

with safety and the value of 'scatter' as a rational air-raid precaution needs emphasis. One Region is very critical of the newspaper methods of presenting air-raid news. It is too alarmist and emphasises the number of casualties, rather than their minute numerical proportion. Two Regions report demands by the public for full details of the night's air raids in the 7 o'clock news 'as a reward for hours of discomfort in the shelters'.

Several Regions report pockets of defeatism especially among lower-middle-class women and the small 'white collar' men. Their reasoning is 'suppose we do lose the war, what difference will it make to us; we could not be any worse off under Hitler; it's the bosses he's after.' At the same time, from the better artisan classes, from the workers, and from young business men in all the Regions come increasing volumes of criticism of the delay by the Government in utilising their services. Their enthusiasm is repeatedly being damped by unsympathetic treatment in Labour Exchanges, and by lack of keenness and efficiency among local leaders of the LDV. There are indications that their feelings may find an outlet either in the organisation of private 'armies' or in an intensified anti-Government anger at what they consider to be 'a betrayal by bureaucracy'. Such remarks as 'arm the civilian population as a whole', 'make ARP and LDV compulsory', 'why doesn't the Government use its compulsory powers instead of talking about them?', have become increasingly common in the past week. It is possible that these two groups – the unenthusiastic selfish minority and the enthusiastic but thwarted majority – might, unless dealt with both by propaganda and by utilisation of their enthusiasm, coalesce to form a large body of people who were definitely convinced that democracy had let them down.

Points from Regions

NOTTINGHAM (North Midland) Continued feeling that Government should make greater use of Emergency Powers to harness the strength of the country. Air raids in Lincolnshire taken very calmly; neither raid was as bad as people expected. In Peterborough great dissatisfaction that no siren was sounded until bombs had actually dropped; also criticism that Peterborough has not been made a protected area. Duff Cooper's speech liked but considered a little too literary. Suggestions that all officers should now wear battle dress as England is now a battle front.

CARDIFF (Wales) Public conduct during first air raid in South Wales excellent, people very calm. DC's broadcast 'really good'. Much criticism of BBC remarks about bad German economic position; public sceptical and sarcastic.

BELFAST (Northern Ireland) News of raid in South Wales makes public expect raiders in Northern Ireland soon. Uneasiness following resignation of Parliamentary Secretary to Ulster Finance Ministry, and his call for reconstruction of Ulster Government.

MANCHESTER (North Western) Some suggestion that Hitler has lost his touch; he should have given Pétain a quick honourable peace and then betrayed him. ARP functioned smoothly in Region's first raid. Public reaction was pride that we are all in it.

BRISTOL (South Western) Air raid in Taunton area caused excitement but little alarm. It may well have a healthy effect on ARP complacency throughout the Region. Demands on all sides that every male member of public should be armed. DC's speech had 'poor reception' owing to long quotation.

LEEDS (North Eastern) Last night's air raid found people increasingly calm. Men in all walks of life express suspicion of those in high places; very intense criticism of voluntary ARP and LDV. 'Government makes good speeches but still acts too slowly'. Business men and working classes make demands: 'Train the men and arm the people', 'Train us now in mufti without arms if necessary'. High ARP officials in Leeds, York, Hull and Bradford express view that ARP should be compulsory. Harrogate and Bridlington are reported to be the most defeatist towns in the Region.

EDINBURGH (Scotland) Anti-French feeling is once again appearing. Air-raid warning in Dundee last night produced every example of imprudent public behaviour. Cross section of Glasgow firm showed overwhelming majority in favour of overseas evacuation. Under £5 a week people were divided 50/50 as to whether mothers should accompany children; over £5 a week people insisted that mothers should go.

NEWCASTLE (Northern) Improvement reported in public behaviour at Middlesbrough and West Hartlepool where bombs were dropped last night and in Newcastle and Durham where there was a warning; no panic and no evidence of evacuation of these towns. Much confusion about motor-car lights in air raids. Repeated authoritative statements needed. Town and County Councils have sent messages to PM welcoming his speech and pledging their support. Many criticisms about Government delay in utilising services of individuals, and about slow call-up following registration.

READING (Southern) If France gives in to German demands public resentment is likely to be very great. Growing hostile criticism of 'selfish' attitude of America. PM speech has done a lot of good. Care is, however, necessary that no more optimistic speeches are falsified by subsequent events. Instances of this are suggestions on BBC that Germany will be facing a severe famine next winter, that petrol stocks in Germany are nearly exhausted and that American help is soon likely to be substantial.

BIRMINGHAM (Midland) DC's speech very well received, especially by the women. Many reports of talk among working and lower middle classes that 'they would be just as well off under Hitler'. Also further continuing criticisms of administration and some demand for action against members of late Government for 'bungling'.

CAMBRIDGE (Eastern) Raids taken calmly. In West Suffolk public upset that bombs were dropped before warnings were sounded. Public over a radius of fifty miles know which Cambridgeshire town suffered special damage on Wednesday. Strong feeling against indiscriminate use of cars for joy-riding, particularly those used for visiting places of entertainment. DC's broadcast 'Not up to his usual standard', 'Too prosy'. Widespread scepticism and impatience at use of history as a background for present events by statesmen. Public do not doubt their own spirit or courage; their fear is for our own Government's inefficiency and slowness in making the best use of the country's resources.

TUNBRIDGE WELLS (South Eastern) Public taking air-raid warnings calmly and sensibly. They are getting to bed early so as to get as much sleep as possible. They feel strongly that 8 o'clock news should reward them with full details of the night's raid after they have spent four or five hours in shelters. Villages still concerned at LDVs' lack of equipment: 'Where are the five million rifles from the last war?' 'Why is ammunition concentrated in dumps which could be destroyed instead of distributed to the LDV?'

LONDON

Duff Cooper's speech criticised on the whole. Considered 'vague and too poetical' after Churchill's realistic talk. Some feeling reported that 'France has failed us'. Camden Town people did not understand suggestion about union with France. Guy's Hospital: many old people asking advice as to whether they should get out of London now. MOI pamphlet considered 'a good idea' by many people, but on the whole 'disappointing'. Federation of Women's Employment reports 'inundated with enquiries about employment from women of professional class and well educated type – ages 25 to 60. Discontent felt when no employment available.' Industrial Welfare Society reports some signs of over-fatigue shown by juveniles at present rate of work. Wandsworth and Battersea registration for evacuation still going on but many people saying 'London is as safe as anywhere'. 'Dominions evacuation would be more popular among working class if mothers could go too'. Care Committee worker, Cowley estate: 'rush of volunteers for ARP work on the estate, showing change of attitude since last week.' Enquiries still made everywhere about French Navy. Chiswick: strong complaint that 'women whose husbands are prisoners in Germany lose their allowance after 6 weeks.' UAB and PAC allowances 'quite ridiculous in view of increased cost of living'. Typical remarks made by such women are these: 'the Government have taken our husbands – they won't get our children'. This is having bad effect in neighbourhood. Suburbs and residential districts of London report hundreds of enquiries about Dominions scheme for evacuation.

FRIDAY 21 JUNE 1940

The atmosphere of waiting continues; in this lull there is some disinclination to speculate about the immediate course of events although the fact that the French are continuing to fight keeps alive the hope that the French Navy and perhaps the French Air Force will continue to fight with us. There is no pronounced growth in anti-French feeling.

Suspense has brought restlessness and observers report many instances of personal irritation. In some cases this has heightened personal anxieties, in others there is an increase of criticism. It is important to notice that this criticism finds expression in anger at past and present inefficiencies here and not in bitterness or anger against the enemy.

A detailed study of public reaction to the recent air raids reinforces this conclusion. Air raids were taken calmly but there was no strong anger directed against the Germans nor was there strong pity for the victims. There was a certain amount of criticism directed against ARP arrangements and a certain amount of surprise that so few planes were shot down. Over-confidence in the technique of defence is still a factor which must be reckoned with. Some Regions report that the raids acted as 'a mild tonic'; the effect of the tonic, however, was endogenous, not exogenous.

There was no strong reaction to Sir Hugh Elles's broadcast. When questioned this morning many people could not recall what he said: many remarked that 'he must be very tired'. There were no adverse comments.

Many reports show how great is the public hunger for leadership and there is a growing feeling that 'this Government is much like the last'. 'Fine speeches are all very well but what we want to know is what to do.' There are indications that the time is growing limited for the successful mobilisation of the public under strong leadership.

Points from Regions

NOTTINGHAM (North Midland) Great satisfaction at resignation of obstructionist War Minister in America, Mr Woodring. Changed attitude of Hearst Press considered to be due to pro-British public opinion in America. Attention is drawn to notices in church porches as a source of information for parachutists as to their whereabouts.

Complaints from Anderby (Lincs.), where bombs were dropped, that ARP volunteers have never been called together for training. Visit by Press Officer to Lincolnshire reveals wide areas unprepared and unprotected; flimsy wire entanglements on coast near Mablethorpe but many miles of coast untouched; isolated wires across fields but nothing on a general scale; no evidence that LDV are being mobilised in any force; hardly any guns seen except a few machine-guns near aerodromes.

CARDIFF (Wales) No bitterness against French, but universal self-recrimination which takes the form of anti-Chamberlain feeling. Sir Hugh Elles's broadcast much appreciated. BBC news still much criticised for continuous repetitions of air battles. Increasing complaints that contex fittings for gas masks are not available in this Region, though they are said to have arrived in Bristol. Workers expecting good news from Russia soon.

BELFAST (Northern Ireland) Public pleased at proposed appointment of Minister of Public Security, as it is hoped that will improve Civil Defence. Sporadic demands for conscription. Limited listening to New British Broadcasting Station; public do not take it seriously.

MANCHESTER (North Western) Long delay in bulletin with details of air-raid damage gave rumour an unbeatable start. Some foolish behaviour (turning on of lights, etc.) reported. Much disappointment at meagre outcome and long delay over Dominion emigration. Growing feeling that after all this Government is much like the last.

BRISTOL (South Western) Many and vague rumours of places bombed, and some alarm thereat. Public believe that Channel Islands are being compulsorily evacuated following search for billets for Channel Island people. RIO requests information to allay or confirm this rumour. It has led to the view among many people that the Germans have captured the Channel Islands. Swindon draws attention to public notices 'keep your cars on the road and keep men in employment' yet radio appeals to public to keep cars off roads and save petrol.

LEEDS (North Eastern) Mild air raids in this Region have acted as a tonic. Criticism of voluntary system of ARP etc. is general. Much feeling against advertisement headed 'Let us brace ourselves to our duty'. Public say 'we are braced already, why doesn't the Government tell us what to do. Fault lies in high places, not with us working people.'

EDINBURGH (Scotland) Public optimistic about America's ultimate entry into war. West of Scotland reports free discussion about large convoy of ships in Clyde. It is felt their presence constitutes an invitation to the enemy to come and attack them. Vague rumours on position of Duke of Windsor causing distress; concise authoritative statement needed. Little public reaction to invasion pamphlet; 'useful, but it ought to have been signed by important people'.

NEWCASTLE (Northern) Three centres report abbreviated official communiques about air raids gave rise to impression that damage to property and life was much greater than it really was. DC's last speech not received favourably everywhere: 'Too many important speeches too close together'. Invasion pamphlet widely approved: 'clearly written, easily understood, meets a genuine need'. Section about firms organising their own defence has caused much discussion and enquiries to police about possibility of getting arms. More information on this score urgently needed.

READING (Southern) Hugh Elles's broadcast increased public confidence that we shall beat off enemy attack. Some discussion and doubt as to how we will then defeat Germany. Public dislike stress laid on Germany's economic difficulties as they do not believe statements and BBC is giving them a sop. Southampton air raids of nights before last received very calmly; Anderson shelters very efficient.

BIRMINGHAM (Midland) Continued complaints about slowness of call-up: 'men lose their enthusiasm waiting'. Important members of Regional Advisory Committee report great distrust among working people of present leadership, particularly about elements of last Government still in Cabinet.

CAMBRIDGE (Eastern) Public know we had air losses in recent raids but Air Ministry has not announced these. It is suggested if only one RAF casualty had been announced without revealing locality many people would have been satisfied. Raiding of South Wales has checked civil evacuation. Public evidence of dislike of broadcast slogans that we are *bound* to win; also criticism of remarks about Germany's bad economic position. Sir Hugh Elles welcomed. Personnel of ARP and LDV are demanding increasingly proper military discipline, also some lack of confidence in local LDV leadership. Chelmsford ARP personnel cannot get steel helmets while Marconi Works in neighbourhood has surplus of 3,000 helmets for its own employees.

TUNBRIDGE WELLS (South Eastern) Thanet residents will welcome more signs of military activity. People still very critical about shot-guns for LDV, especially since they know of tremendous strength of German equipment. Public desire explanation of present position of Duke of Windsor; common question 'Is he a Fascist?'

LONDON

Waste of capabilities of trained women and consequent defeatism considered dangerous to morale. Women's Employment Federation reports that 9,055 women (majority London and Home Counties) registered as having special qualifications. 3,841 still seeking work, of which 2,337 are totally unemployed; rest unsatisfied. 'These women causing nests of defeatism in London.' Sir Hugh Elles's speech considered dull. 'These things have been said so often before. Not enough punch.' Harrow, Kodak Factory: 'Anti-French feeling growing very strong since capitulation. People remember at end of last war our soldiers said they would rather fight with the Germans than with the French'. With growing anti-Chamberlain feeling a desire expressed that Lloyd George should take his place in the Cabinet. 'Lloyd George is the only man who would get there before Hitler'. Feeling from many districts that LDV is not being armed quickly enough. City: 'Churchill's leadership inspires confidence and hope of ultimate victory'. Many complaints about BBC's new interval signal: 'like the tick of doom'. Hammersmith: bitterness growing against Belgian refugees: 'getting better treatment than the British; reason the butter ration is reduced'. Concern expressed in several localities (Silvertown, Harrow, Pinner) about the Duke of Windsor. 'Is he safe? Is he a traitor?' Silvertown Factory Management rebuked members of staff repeating rumour. New sense of responsibility over gossip noticed in consequence. Welfare Supervisor: 'All working well on seven day week and anxious to help. Pleasure expressed at arrival of Australians and new confidence shown because of it.' Venesta Factory arranging own defences. Street defences planned in East End. Talk of Government possibly moving, reports that 'people would crumple if this happened, but would be glad if Princesses got safely to Canada'. From every district reports state that people chiefly concerned with evacuation, either to Dominions or within this country. Much speculation as to which is more dangerous – town or country. Old people want lead as to whether to move now or not. West Ham: 'People afraid of raids; will not go far from home; not attending clubs and social centres. Should be induced to go about normally'.

SATURDAY 22 JUNE 1940

There has been little change in morale during this period of waiting. People have got over the shock of the French collapse and are quite calm.

There is a revival of interest in Hitler's terms to France, and there are a number of rumours about their nature. There is no evidence, however, that these rumours are having a particularly damaging effect.

There is a clear realisation of the danger of invasion and from some Regions come reports that the public think preparations for it have improved. An insistent demand continues for cooperating more fully in the war effort, and there are many expressions of opinion which show that compulsion would be considered advisable and acceptable.

Air raids were taken philosophically, although, particularly in the South-Western Region, they gave rise to uncontrolled rumours. There is criticism of the midnight news reporting the beginning of the raid: it promoted nervous apprehension. Observers report that one of the main reactions in raided districts is weariness through broken sleep with consequent depression.

Certain areas report a slight return to an attitude of disassociation and mental evasion.

Besides waiting for Hitler's terms people are still waiting for a strong lead.

Points from Regions

NOTTINGHAM (North Midland) People going about calmly at their businesses. Banks increasingly willing to lend to farmers. Growing tendency to regard Pétain as a Fascist, particularly since it is known he was ambassador to Spain and, therefore, presumably a friend of Franco. Increasingly cordial feeling towards America, partly because of hospitality offered to children, partly because of arrival of material and partly because of changes in US Government.

CARDIFF (Wales) Continued demand for conscription for ARP and LDV and also for cutting off of luxury supplies at the source.

BELFAST (Northern Ireland) Public believe Northern Ireland now much better prepared for emergencies; great keenness to play a part in Civil Defence. Explosion on waste ground in Belfast last night believed to have been due to a bomb which owner wished to get rid of.

MANCHESTER (North Western) Stirrup pumps and sand have proved most effective in dealing with incendiary bombs. Much satisfaction at strengthening of police and AFS; position still unsatisfactory about volunteers for ARP and LDV.

BRISTOL (South Western) Region full of rumours about districts bombed. Exeter anxious about AA Defence.

LEEDS (North Eastern) Still much criticism of authorities. Very poor attendance at ARP meeting addressed in Leeds by Lord Harlech. Public demand abolition of voluntary system for ARP. Keighley ARP organiser arrested under Defence Regulations; this has stimulated interest in Fifth Columnists.

EDINBURGH (Scotland) News of last night's raids caused little comment. Main interest centred on terms of French peace.

NEWCASTLE (Northern) Public becoming 'philosophical' to air-raid warnings. Intense irritation over conflicting instructions about lights on cars. ARP personnel anxious to be armed. Doubts about powers of police and military to order people off streets in air raids. At Stanley (Co. Durham) Communists had to have personal protection from crowds.

READING (Southern) Many rumours about extent of air raids. Considerable demand in Reading for passages for children to the Dominions.

BIRMINGHAM (Midland) Satisfaction at accelerated rate of registration, but many would like wider conscription for service. Still inadequate removal of road indications, particularly where road names give clues to their direction; estate agents' boards and tradesmen's vans also may reveal localities.

CAMBRIDGE (Eastern) Sporadic raiding in early hours today made little impression on civilian population.

TUNBRIDGE WELLS (South Eastern) Arrival of Empire troops cheering. Hooper's broadcast last night much appreciated: 'Like Duff Cooper he speaks to us in our own language.' Great success of lectures explaining Civil Defence schemes. No serious bank withdrawals, but rather the reverse. No anti-French or anti-Russian feeling detected. Middle-aged volunteers of both sexes at Labour Exchanges very disappointed when their offers of service are turned down. Invasion pamphlet well received, only two criticisms: it is a little too wordy and Section 7 makes no mention of Ministry of Information messages to Information Committees.

LONDON

Some return of children evacuated to Wales reported. Many questions asked about Duke of Windsor. Lorry drivers are reported to be giving details of air-raid damage which arouses surprise when compared with meagre press statements.

Action Points

For the information of the authorities concerned the following points have been extracted from the various reports received today by Home Intelligence Division:

Naval Intelligence Anxiety is expressed about the ability of spies to land with refugees at coastal villages, as the only local check is made by the village PC and harbour master. It is suggested that some more adequate form of supervision should be set up to deal with this possibility.

MI7 Exeter is anxious about its AA defences as there is said to be no barrage or searchlights. Strong criticism is made of inadequate defence arrangements.

Air Intelligence Short official bulletins about raids are regarded with distrust and give rise to many alarmist stories; though the inability to provide details is appreciated, reports of a rather more circumstantial nature would do much to dissipate dangerous rumours.

Home Security Lack of information on the liabilities of compulsorily evacuated persons with regard to standing charges (rents, rates etc.) is causing serious anxiety on many parts of the East Coast. Much inconvenience is being caused by a conflict of orders about lights on cars during air raids. It is emphatically urged that there should be a national announcement of the police powers in this matter. This applies also to responsibilities of the police for clearing streets of pedestrians.

Criticism is made of the fact that factories other than those engaged in armament work, but which may perhaps be doing vital export trade, do not receive anything like the same encouragement in the form of 'Comforting words to their employees' as those engaged in munition making etc: 'Factory workers like ourselves could do with a little encouragement, by being told that our work *is* important, even though it may seem to be rather trivial at the moment'.

Yesterday's *Daily Mirror* photograph of an undamaged Anderson shelter which withstood a nearby bomb explosion has made an excellent impression, and it is suggested that this photo should be more widely publicised.

As railway carriages appear to be fruitful sources of gossip, it is suggested that all railway companies should be encouraged to display anti-gossip posters in their carriages.

Ministry of Transport There still seems to be much confusion about the removal of direction signs: 'Many roads in this area (Birmingham) are so clearly labelled as to a give a complete guide to the direction which should be followed.' It is thought that the instructions about this matter are not sufficiently definite.

Ministry of Supply Manchester reports that the demand for stirrup pumps and sand far exceeds the supplies of either, and urges that some form of control of manufacture is essential in the case of the former.

Ministry of Agriculture Many town dwellers are eager to spend such holidays as they may have in some form of agricultural work, but it is said that local Exchanges have been uncooperative in this matter, and some guidance on the way in which this work can be obtained would be widely welcomed.

National Savings Portsmouth Information Committee say the National Savings campaign would be helped by suspension of the Hire Purchase system. Many people whose wages have recently been increased are buying more extensively than before instead of lending their savings.

MONDAY 24 JUNE TO SATURDAY 29 JUNE 1940

The capitulation of France was followed by a lull in the fighting on land. On 28 June Russian troops marched into Romania and occupied the northern provinces of Bessarabia and North Bukovina, but this was too remote an event to cause more than a flicker of interest in Britain. At home the Germans were ratcheting up the war of nerves with sporadic air raids over many parts of Britain. The Channel Islands, from which British forces and about a third of the civilian population had already been evacuated, were bombed on 28 June and forty-four civilians killed. The RAF, meanwhile, was engaged in a strategic air offensive intended to pinpoint oil refineries, aerodromes and other key military targets. Neither the British public nor the Air Ministry realised the limitations of precision techniques at this time.

There was much speculation about the fate of the French fleet. Its commander, Admiral Darlan, had promised Churchill that he would not hand it over to the Germans, but in spite of this the Prime Minister and the War Cabinet feared that French warships would end up in German hands, with disastrous consequences for the Royal Navy. Meanwhile General de Gaulle had arrived in England with a handful of supporters and a determination to continue the war. On 28 June the British government recognised him as 'leader of the Free French', though not as the head of a government in exile. A few French warships had already made their way to British ports along with their crews.

'The effect of French "capitulation" has in no way minimised the prevailing determination to "fight to a finish",' Home Intelligence reported on 24 June, 'although there are signs of increasing doubt that we shall now be able to obtain "absolute victory".' Morale reports, however, continued to indicate a popular demand for stronger leadership at the top and greater use of compulsory powers in industry and the armed forces. If Churchill was already the dominant figure in the imagination of the public this was not yet evident in the reports.

The most highly rated broadcaster of the week was Anthony Eden, the Secretary of State for War.

One of the most striking features of the reports was a growing optimism over the failure of bombing to create panic or to undermine morale. There was, however, much criticism of the government for inconsistency in the use of sirens to warn of raids. 'Sometimes there have been sirens and no bombs, sometimes bombs and no sirens, and sometimes both,' the regional office in Cardiff recorded. Lack of sleep was another complaint, but there was growing confidence in air-raid precautions and praise for the Anderson shelter. At the Cowley estate in Stockwell, Home Intelligence observed, tenants were 'busy making shelters comfortable with carpets to sleep on, furniture, beds for children, pictures of King and Queen, artificial flowers, Union Jacks etc.' Air raids, the Birmingham regional office reported, were being taken very calmly: 'At Stoke a man took an incendiary bomb to the Police Station in a bucket, and his only complaint was that the police retained bucket.'

MONDAY 24 JUNE 1940

Sunday was a day of rumours about the armistice terms. Their acceptance by the French Government did not come as a surprise. The effect of French 'capitulation' has in no way minimised the prevailing determination to 'fight to a finish', although there are signs of increasing doubt that we shall now be able to obtain 'absolute victory'. Nevertheless the common feeling throughout the country is one of strong resolution (apart from the pockets of defeatism to which attention has repeatedly been drawn).

At all levels of society the opinion is bitterly and vigorously expressed that the French people have been betrayed by 'the politicians'. Indignation against French leaders grew strongly over the weekend: it increased after the announcement of the terms. There are no signs that this indignation is directed against the French people with whom there is considerable sympathy.

The speed with which the French situation has moved to its climax has caused bewilderment and confusion and the political complexion of Pétain's government required time for its proper appreciation. That appreciation has now penetrated the popular mind and the effect of it is to bring to the front those doubts about our own leadership which have been finding expression in criticisms of Government action. There is no escaping the tenor of our reports: leadership is in jeopardy.

From all Regions demands for more 'instructions' are reported — particularly on evacuation and general preparedness. There is a strong desire to get non-combatants, especially children, out of the country. The word 'blockade' is frequently mentioned but now the phrase means the blockade of this country. Dangers from Eire are often discussed and there is a rapidly growing feeling that the Government should take positive action before it is too late.

Our reports show some increase of anti-Semitic feeling due in certain Regions (Leeds, London) to accounts that wealthy Jews are 'panicking to the USA'.

Points from Regions

NOTTINGHAM (North Midland) Considerable gloom caused by French capitulation. Bordeaux Government harshly criticised. Hope of good results from de Gaulle's broadcast. Some lack of confidence in measures taken to prevent invasion. Civil Service criticised for excessive use of red tape in connection with National Service. Official mind must adjust itself to higher speed necessary for war efficiency. Feeling that money is being spent too freely on luxury articles, and that petrol is being used for too much joy-riding.

CARDIFF (Wales) Although people are calm and agree that war must be fought to a finish there is some doubt, in view of the present circumstances, of the way in which we are to obtain absolute victory. Uneasiness expressed about preparations for aiding Eire should invasion be attempted in that quarter. 'People are in a very receptive mood for instructions', and the BBC should devote more time to these and less to entertainment.

BELFAST (Northern Ireland) Disgust, but no surprise, expressed at French acceptance of armistice. Bitterness against Pétain Cabinet, but sympathy for the French people. Danger of invasion from Eire thought to be increasingly likely. Suspicion that 'another Casement plot is being hatched'.

MANCHESTER (North Western) France's signing of armistice regarded as 'another betrayal'. De Gaulle's broadcast made a good impression, but hope of our gaining control of the French Navy and Air Force is disappearing.

BRISTOL (South Western) Strong criticism of Pétain's capitulation, but sympathy with French nation. Recent raids have increased awareness of need for private ARP arrangements. Inadequacy of news bulletins about air raids causes many rumours. More precise mention of localities might avoid this difficulty.

LEEDS (North Eastern) Resentment and bitterness against Germany increases, and is coupled with similar feelings against Civil Service and to some extent the Government, for tardy allocation of war work. Anti-Semitism is said to be seriously increasing; this is due partly to rumoured attempts of rich Jews to leave the country.

better on wireless than University voices'. Silvertown Factory: 'Other Labour MPs besides Cabinet Ministers should give talks, especially Greenwood, to stop suspicion that Labour Ministers are only figure heads'. Suggestion made by workers that 9.00 p.m. news should be given at 8.00 or 8.30. p.m. to allow more sleep when nights are disturbed by warning. East End woman collecting toys and books for children in shelters. Informal visits by officials to factories suggested as helping morale. 'People feel someone is interested in them.'

FRIDAY 28 JUNE 1940

There is little change in the level of morale. People are calm and on the whole confident; there is, however, a growing feeling of 'bored expectancy' caused by 'Hitler's breathing space'. The public is settling down to air raids and they are most frequently referred to as 'a bore'.

Complaints that sirens are not sounded early enough continue: other ARP arrangements come in for general praise. Attendances at school and factory are being affected by night raids.

There is little public reaction to the Russian move: it has simply added to the general bewilderment about the course of events.

Dissatisfaction at the continued immobilisation of man-power and woman-power is still in evidence. The cutting edge of enthusiasm is in danger of being blunted as much by press stories of incompetence and muddle as by the trajectory of events.

Among intellectual circles fear is expressed that the country will be divided by a peace offensive.

The spirit of the people, however, is still calm, determined and fundamentally healthy: there is a fertile field for strong leadership.

Points from Regions

Only four Regions comment on Russia's attitude to Romania. One of these records that people are muddled and confused on the subject. The other three state that the main public attitude is one of indifference, thanks apparently to the personal unpopularity of

King Carol and to his recent Axis sympathies. The tendency is to regard the matter as part of the Hitler–Stalin carve-up.

Regions continue to report an undercurrent of resentment and distrust at the presence of appeasement politicians in the Cabinet, in spite of the published statements this morning.

NOTTINGHAM (North Midland) More informed sections of public are stressing the need for limiting anti-French feeling, on account of the danger of its persisting after the war. Some irritation reported at what is thought to be one-sided reporting of our aerial successes. In spite of Geoffrey Shakespeare's clear and specific broadcast instructions many people still think that in the evacuation of children to Canada there is to be a differentiation between the rich and the poor. Night air-raid alarms in Leicestershire are causing fatigue among factory workers, and a 'go-to-bed-early' campaign is asked for.

CARDIFF (Wales) It is hoped among the public that Churchill will secure the bulk of the French fleet for us. People are still uneasy about our precautions for dealing with an invasion from Eire. From Cardiff come complaints at its small supply of barrage balloons, compared with Bristol and Birmingham. Some anti-French feeling is noticed.

BELFAST (Northern Ireland) Announcement of fine response to appeal for accelerated output has had a stimulating effect. Nevertheless there are still complaints that Northern Ireland is not being given a full opportunity to put all its industry into the war effort. Sharp controversy over proposals for united defence organisation for Northern Ireland and Eire.

MANCHESTER (North Western) Spirit of munition workers is excellent, though they realise increasing odds against us. Many complaints about neglect and mismanagement of LDV. Correction of error in report of Tuesday, 25 June: sentence should read: 'Communist activities greatly decreased in munition factories during last fortnight.'

BRISTOL (South Western) People much encouraged by Morrison's statement on supply, though there is feeling that previous situation must have been very bad for such improvement to be possible. Rumours about raids & ARP continue common. There is still some discontent at the slowness of the military call-up.

LEEDS (North Eastern) Local registration for evacuation to Canada is very heavy indeed. Still a popular view that authorities have not yet properly got to grips with the problem of conscripting manpower. Much evacuation from Bridlington, where bombs fell on Wednesday night. Indignation is reported there that no sirens were sounded, though eight bombs fell.

EDINBURGH (Scotland) Glasgow reports complaints that balloons were late in going up in recent raids, though great skill of searchlight operators was praised. Little apprehension is expressed about future raids.

NEWCASTLE (Northern) Bitterness felt on French capitulation has diminished as a result of news from French Colonial Empire. Scheme for overseas evacuation is on the whole welcomed. From Teesside it is reported that people are going down to their air-raid shelters about 9 p.m. and settling down for the night, even though no alarm has been given.

READING (Southern) Continued reports stress demands by public for greater drive in Home Defence. Newspaper criticisms of the Civil Service are being reflected in public comments.

BIRMINGHAM (Midland) Dissatisfaction in part of Region where bombs were dropped last night because no air-raid warning was sounded.

CAMBRIDGE (Eastern) Main effect of air raids so far has been loss of sleep; many people are readjusting their habits to limit as far as possible their sleep loss. Many suggest that employers should give their staff a rest period. Some reports express fear at lack of elasticity in LDV organization.

TUNBRIDGE WELLS (South Eastern) View is common among the public that two or three nights' disturbed sleep will quickly lead to a breakdown, and it is suggested that public should be informed that many people, for example sailors, work on a four-hour shift system throughout the night indefinitely without ill effect. Comments are still reported that the authorities are far too polite when making reference to Hitler.

LONDON

Cowley Estate, Stockwell, reports tenants busy making shelters comfortable with carpets to sleep on, furniture, beds for children, pictures of King and Queen, artificial flowers, Union Jacks, etc. Women scrubbing floors and laughing: 'wish Hitler could see us now!' Tenants plan to have 'open night' to show off their shelters to their neighbours. Collecting money to buy sand buckets. 'All pleased to have something to do themselves.' Fulham Housing Estate has democratic system in operation of shelter marshals and their helpers chosen by tenants. System worked well on Monday night and people who did not leave their beds then decided to do so next time as they had 'missed the fun'. Notices of lectures on ARP and self-help posted up in prominent place by Estate Manager, resulting in excellent attendances. Parents with children billeted in Devon 'very satisfied'. Lambeth: 'Confusion in some people's minds between warning signal and All Clear.' Siemens, Woolwich: 'Workers putting their hearts into their work in spite of long hours. Those guilty of careless talking or spreading rumours are dealt with at once.' Chiswick: 'Difficulty of getting volunteers for ARP night duty as people have to work by day and cannot do without their sleep.'

SATURDAY 29 JUNE 1940

Although the optimistic trend of the last few days continues events have brought about increasing confusion in the public mind. The Russian move, the situation in Syria, the whereabouts of French ex-Ministers, American politics and uncertainty about the sounding of sirens have all combined to increase bewilderment and suspicion. The commonest verbatim recorded is

'There's something behind all this' or 'I wonder what's the real truth'. People are asking for enlightenment and instruction.

In coastal Regions considerable confusion about evacuation exists and this has added to the general uncertainty. Many middle-class families of small means are enquiring what their position will be under compulsory evacuation and there is evidence that provisional plans for last-minute evacuation are being made by family groups. There is more anger at the Channel Islands raid than over any previous raid on this country but press accounts have left an impression of planless evacuation and of a defenceless civilian population. Stories of jettisoned food and supplies have brought critical comment.

Air raids were taken calmly and the public is becoming increasingly 'shelter-conscious'.

There is much speculation on the French situation particularly in those places where French soldiers and sailors mix freely with the civilian population. On the whole these men have been very well received by British civilians but the mixture of races and opinions among the French forces has been the subject of much speculation and enquiry.

Against this background of uncertainty the British Government's recognition of General de Gaulle has given encouragement and stability to the public.

There is a strong rumour that Hitler's efforts against this country will begin on Monday and his prediction that 'all will be over by August 15th' is widely repeated. People do not 'believe' the prediction but it is freely passed from mouth to mouth and evidence shows that the 'inevitability of Hitler' is an important factor in public morale.

There is no change, however, in recent generalisation: morale is healthy and the confidence and determination of the people is ready for mobilisation and for translation into vigorous action.

Points from Regions

Concern and indignation are reported from several Regions at the bombing of the Channel Islands immediately following their demilitarisation. Manchester reports much anxiety among the 9,000 Channel Island child evacuees there. There is speculation about whether the Germans will use Jersey as a base for air attacks on England.

Many Regions express concern and some confusion about the sounding of air-raid warnings. Cardiff states that the south part of the Region has been raided nightly for the past few nights and sometimes there have been sirens and no bombs, sometimes bombs and no sirens, and sometimes both. The public wish to know what is the policy about the sounding of sirens. At 9.32 this morning an enemy plane flew over Bristol; the public watched this with great interest, as no sirens had been sounded. Rumours are rife in the Region that sirens are to be discontinued. Leeds reports a rumour that sirens will now be sounded only immediately before a raid and this is disturbing women and children who think that they will not have time to reach shelters. Newcastle reports that alarms have been sounded only after bombing although the presence of enemy planes was well-known before that; many requests have been received for a statement on the present Government policy about the sounding of sirens. Cambridge reports that the absence of sirens has, on the whole, had a good effect, though many people are convinced that enemy planes have been over and are surprised that there have been no warnings. There is in this Region a very wide belief that the Government's policy on sounding sirens has been modified and this has caused some apprehension among women. Night flying for training purposes seems to be contributing towards disturbed sleep.

NOTTINGHAM (North Midland) People seem to be discriminating more between the French Government and the French people and to be criticising less. General disappointment at the news from Syria. No great concern at the fate of Romania which is regarded as 'another poor dithering sheep about to be dismembered by the wolves'. In spite of official denials there are further reports of mistrust of Hoare's activity in Spain. Republican nomination in America is well received.

CARDIFF (Wales) People anticipate a turn of events in our favour in connection with Russia. Many suggestions have been received that LDV barricades should have red and *yellow* lights to distinguish them from road repair works.

MANCHESTER (North Western) Recognition of de Gaulle widely approved, but following Syrian news a common comment is 'too late again'. Very little interest in fate of Romania.

BELFAST (Northern Ireland) Hope is expressed that Beveridge's survey of man-power will include Northern Ireland, so that Ulster's 60,000 unemployed may be rapidly absorbed in war work. Hooper's broadcast welcomed as a warning against both over-confidence and fatalistic defeatism. Many people are reported to think that there is some ground for Haw-Haw's attack on BBC and British newspaper editorials for glossing over unpleasant facts. Majority view is that news should be more candid when things are going badly: 'we can take it'.

BRISTOL (South Western) Anti-gossip campaign in Plymouth is having good effect.

LEEDS (North Eastern) Chief air-raid warden of Hull reports no weakening of morale as a result of recent raids. Industrial fatigue is stated to be not yet noticeable in the Leeds area. The militarisation of the coastal zone is popular.

EDINBURGH (Scotland) The Eastern District Commissioner's scheme of volunteer labour reported yesterday has had a remarkable response (140 recruits on first day, 700 on second, and 711 on the third). German broadcasts on fine social conditions in Germany are stated to be having an effect; even members of Forces contrast the alleged superiority of German working-class conditions with those in this country, and a small section of working-class people are reported to be saying quite openly that only the rich have anything to lose by a Hitler victory.

NEWCASTLE (Northern) Information Committee at Sunderland express unanimous view that morale is being affected badly by publicity for 'no holidays and unlimited overtime' to increase production, while there are still 6,000 unemployed in the town.

READING (Southern) Indications that parts of French Empire are obeying Bordeaux are reviving anxiety about the French fleet. News that Government is ready to apply compulsory evacuation when necessary is generally welcomed as showing decision in leadership. Southampton, however, is anxious for fear that this should happen before it is militarily necessary.

BIRMINGHAM (Midland) Further demand for improved armament of LDV, as public believe its importance has much increased as enemy planes are about so frequently.

CAMBRIDGE (Eastern) West Norfolk intensely concerned about the fate in northern France of the 7th Battalion Royal Norfolk Regiment.

TUNBRIDGE WELLS (South Eastern) Kent and Sussex optimistic that as 'Hitler never comes in by front door', he may not start with them. Still a few complaints about inefficiency of LDV. People living in Kent are reported to be garaging their cars near London to avoid leaving them behind in the event of evacuation.

LONDON

Surbiton: 'people's confidence increased since the putting up of barricades on Kingston by-pass. Movement of population in district due to some people going out to the West and others coming in from the South and South East Coast. Local feeling that Belgian refugees billeted in neighbourhood should do useful work.' Clapham: 'people cheerful on whole, though bus drivers and some AFS workers express some defeatism.' Shepherd's Bush: 'continuing local grievance that Belgian refugees have privileges denied to English people. This causing much grumbling.' People answering appeal to work on land during holidays reported snubbed at local Labour Exchanges. Divisional Controller of Labour states that appeal was made before machinery existed to deal with it. Resulting irritation and annoyance on the part of both officials and public. 'Lack of proper camouflaging of important buildings in various districts' reports Welfare Supervisor of large dairy. Brixton: 'Certain press publicity has inspired confidence in Anderson shelters. Those who owned one used it on Monday night, whereas many other people did not leave their beds.' Barking: 'neighbours getting together and arranging communal use of stirrup-pumps and plans for taking in neighbours if houses are destroyed. Local people worried by foreigners rowing ashore from ships anchored in Thames. On Thursday seven Dutch seamen came ashore and joined in talk in the "Crooked Billet", River Road, Creek's Mouth, Barking – small public house in lonely neighbourhood near large power station. Other people present very apprehensive.' Suburban reports show middle classes still enquiring about Dominion evacuation scheme and large percentage anxious for their children to go.

MONDAY 1 JULY TO SATURDAY 6 JULY 1940

On 3 July 1940 French warships in Plymouth and Portsmouth were seized and later that day action was taken against the main French fleet at anchor in the Algerian port of Mers-el-Kebir near Oran. On the orders of Churchill and the War Cabinet, a naval force under the command of Admiral Somerville was despatched to the anchorage and the French admiral in command presented with four options: to join the Royal Navy, sail to a British port, sail to a French port in the West Indies, or scuttle his ships within six hours. When all four options were rejected Somerville opened fire. One French battleship was blown up, a number of other warships badly damaged, and 1,297 Frenchmen killed. In military terms the attack was only a partial success, and it is still a matter for debate whether such ruthless action was necessary, but Churchill's statement on the affair won the acclaim of the House of Commons on 4 July. As Home Intelligence reported, the attack on the French fleet was also good for morale: 'This sign of aggressive action on our part has been generally welcomed and even the fact that many French sailors lost their lives has been allowed to pass with little comment.'

At a time when most air raids were still of a minor character and casualties light, it was recorded that people were responding calmly to the threat, but there were many rumbles of discontent. The absence of the RAF during air raids was a common complaint, but the reality was that Fighter Command could not afford to risk precious resources in minor engagements. Another fertile source of controversy was the system of air-raid warnings. Under the existing system, run by Fighter Command in conjunction with local police and civil defence services, there were four different types of warning, distinguished by colour. A yellow message ('Preliminary Caution') gave a confidential advance warning of an attack to the police, civil defence services, government offices, and large industrial concerns, in a particular district or districts.

It could be cancelled out by a white message ('Cancel Caution'). A red message ('Action Warning') then activated air-raid sirens and hooters – the siren emitting a low moaning sound that rose to a high-pitched wail – to warn the public of an imminent attack. This was cancelled by a green message ('Raiders Passed'), when sirens and hooters sounded the 'All Clear'.

From the public's point of view 'siren policy' was inconsistent and confusing. Sometimes the sirens gave adequate warning, sometimes too little. Sometimes bombs fell without any sirens sounding at all. If consistency was hard to achieve this was partly because the author-ities were torn between conflicting objectives. They had a duty to protect the public by giving them adequate warnings of air attack. But the government was worried by the interruptions to war production caused by public alerts during the wave of night air attacks that devel-oped towards the end of June. Workers on nightshift were spending three or four hours in air-raid shelters before the 'All Clear' sounded, whilst dayshift workers were deprived of sleep. The authorities, there-fore, sought to reduce the number of red warnings, but they faced a difficulty after dark. Factories and workshops were allowed some external lighting at night but as this could assist the Luftwaffe in locating targets, it was automatically switched off when a red warning was activated. If no red warnings were issued, the lights would remain on for the benefit of the enemy. On 2 July the Home Secretary, Sir John Anderson, announced that workers in factories would be encouraged to work on after the red warning and not take shelter until the sound of bombs could be heard: this marked a shift in policy from safety first to production first. Later in the month, on 25 July, a new night-time 'purple' message was introduced that required premises with exempted external lighting to extinguish their lights without sounding a public alarm. In order to retain a system based on four messages, the green and white messages were amalgamated into one. The warning system was thus complicated and, in the absence of a clear-cut explanation of siren policy, the public remained perplexed.

On 1 July the Ministry of Information announced that the Germans had occupied the Channel Islands. 'Some feel they should have been held at all costs like the Ypres salient in the last war,' Home Intelligence reported. The following day the merchant ship *Arandora Star*, which was transporting enemy aliens expelled from Britain to Canada, was torpedoed and sunk off the north-west coast of Ireland. 467 Italians and 175 Germans were killed, a tragedy that drew attention to the shameful treatment of aliens and also highlighted the perils of a transatlantic crossing. Home Intelligence began to detect second thoughts about the desirability of evacuating children to Canada.

The Duke of Windsor, the former King Edward VIII, was currently in Portugal after escaping from France through Spain. Malicious rumour now cast him in the role of a future Nazi puppet ruler of Britain in place of his brother King George VI. 'The fear of "appeasement",' remarked the daily report on 6 July, 'is strong in certain sections of the community, and the movement against certain Ministers is gaining ground.' It was a prescient comment. During the evacuation from Dunkirk three Beaverbrook press journalists – Michael Foot, Frank Owen and Peter Howard – had written under the pseudonym of 'Cato' a political polemic in which they accused Chamberlain, Baldwin and other pre-war ministers of failing to rearm Britain and, in effect, of betraying their country. Published on 5 July 1940, *Guilty Men* sold, as Foot wrote later, 'like a pornographic classic', and gave a renewed impetus to the campaign to remove the 'men of Munich' from office. Churchill, however, resisted the demand for a purge. Chamberlain, who had broadcast on 30 June warning the enemy that 'we will fight him in the air and on the sea, we will fight him on the beaches . . . we will fight him on every road, in every village and in every house, until he or we are utterly destroyed', remained in the War Cabinet until October 1940, when terminal illness forced him to resign.

MONDAY 1 JULY 1940

The present lull in the tempo of events, popularly called 'Hitler's breathing space', is not having the effect of strengthening morale. During the weekend there was some increase in the feeling of bewilderment and suspense and rumours were again a feature of the morale landscape.

There has been a decrease of interest in news and widespread comments that the news is 'unintelligible'. In many of our reports there are strong requests for authoritative interpretations of the news and for guidance in appreciating it. Many people appear to be hoping for a Balkan war as a method of staving off the invasion of Britain; others regard it as a further complication likely to react unfavourably to us. Many people are enquiring about the Cripps mission to Russia. A study of reactions to the announcement of Chamberlain's broadcast in the Sunday press showed that many people thought the broadcast was to be a resignation. Comments on the broadcast: 'Nothing new', 'Quite good', 'On the defensive', 'He sounded very tired', 'Did he break down at the end?', 'He was right once'. The broadcast did not bring to the fore any strong anti-Chamberlain feeling.

Air raids were taken calmly; the siren controversy continues.

The wide circulation of sales catalogues comes in for surprised and critical comment which takes the form of enquiring 'Why does the Government allow it?', 'I thought the Government didn't want people to buy more things', 'What frightful waste of paper'.

There is still resentment that plans for Dominions evacuation are not further forward.

Points from Regions

Chamberlain's speech produced a diversity of comments from the Regions, in which no constant theme can be traced. There was, however, unanimity about his delivery. He seemed tired, an old man, and emotional.

The question of sirens is still exercising the public. Bristol reports public doubt about the siren sounding policy and adds that on Sunday heavy raids occurred without sirens, while today warnings were given although no bombs fell. Leeds reports that there is uneasiness in Bridlington and Sheffield on account of the general belief that sirens are not going to be sounded until the very last minute. Newcastle records further complaints from a number of centres at the failure to sound sirens until enemy aeroplanes are overhead, and in some cases until they have dropped their bombs and departed. It is pointed out from Newcastle that special constables and LDVs have instructions only to act on the sounding of the sirens. Reading reports a little restiveness at the dropping of bombs when and where no warnings have been sounded. Cambridge states that the siren controversy is acute. On the one hand, the early sounding of sirens allows people to become accustomed to sleeping in their shelters; on the other, the advocates of limited siren sounding point to the loss of output and wages which results in factories if workers spend an excessive amount of time in shelters. It is added that if sirens are not sounded most people presume that aircraft engines heard overhead are mainly German and this is causing rumours. An authoritative statement is asked for at once on siren policy, and numerous enquiries have been received today asking for a broadcast tonight.

NOTTINGHAM (North Midland) Recent raids in Derbyshire are stated to have improved morale considerably. Rumour is rife about the presence of the Duke of Windsor in Spain; some take this as evidence of his Fascist sympathy. Loughborough asks for brighter air communiques, and likes eye-witness accounts. An editorial article in a daily paper calling for volunteers for coastal defence construction is commented on critically; labour should be conscripted for this work if it is urgently needed.

CARDIFF (Wales) In spite of lack of sleep people remain cheerful. There is much disappointment that only two Welsh names appear on the Advisory Committee for overseas evacuation, while Scotland has its own committee; Wales has willingly welcomed many thousands of English evacuee children and feels therefore that it deserves more consideration. Flying columns of troops have greatly increased public confidence in our ability to deal with invasion.

BELFAST (Northern Ireland) Reaction to Lord Craigavon's conditional offer to cooperate with Eire on defence has been mixed; Unionists say cooperation is impossible unless Eire enters the war on Britain's side, while Nationalists demand political union of the two countries first. Hence party tension over partition is intensified. Reports are going about that Malcolm MacDonald has been negotiating in Dublin and people are wondering if partition was discussed, or only defence.

MANCHESTER (North Western) Criticism still common at the lack of preparedness of our Island Fortress. People regard the present road barriers and barbed wire as useless against tanks. Fate of French fleet is still much discussed.

BRISTOL (South Western) Local suggestion that anti-tank trenches should be dug by public has been widely welcomed. A report that bombs struck a shelter in this Region without damaging it has increased confidence. Occasional cases of defeatism are reported among isolated businessmen and some of the poor people, but the great majority are for 'sticking it out', on the ground that we should be no better than slaves, that the trades unions would go the way of those in Germany, and that if we stick it Hitler will collapse in a few months.

LEEDS (North Eastern) Criticism of the higher administration continues to be common. 'Whitehall tells the country to be calm; Yorkshire tells Whitehall to be efficient, bold and enterprising'. A fatalistic belief in Hitler's timetable is still prevalent and people say quite calmly 'he starts his Blitzkrieg on July 2.'

EDINBURGH (Scotland) Much comment on Tayside at failure of our fighters to engage German raiders last night, especially when one was caught by searchlights. Explanation is asked for. There is some sceptical criticism of the official reports of our continually successful raids on Germany and their continually unsuccessful ones on us.

NEWCASTLE (Northern) As a result of the scheduling of the northeast as a coastal Defence Area there has been some confusion as to whether residents therein may visit towns outside for shopping. Members of ARP personnel are stated to be spreading a number of rumours about the details of raids.

READING (Southern) Portsmouth has joined Southampton in expressing doubt about the new evacuation situation. In rural areas many people are stated to be still only half awake to our present dangers.

BIRMINGHAM (Midland) Reports from observers among the working classes indicate that the belief that they would be no worse off under Hitler is still persistent. Miners in South Staffordshire are stated to have been told to slow up their efforts because so many export markets have been closed down.

CAMBRIDGE (Eastern) From the Chelmsford area comes a growing demand for Anderson shelters now that it has become a Defence Area.

TUNBRIDGE WELLS (South Eastern) Some resentment recorded among public at Harold Nicolson's references to 'shiver sisters and chatterbugs'; most people do not doubt their own courage to take on what lies ahead. Some criticism also of our advice to German citizens to take cover in our air raids, as many regard this as a sign of weakness on our part.

LONDON

From all reports two main points emerge: (1) Unanimous approval of Priestley's postscript and agreement with what he said. (2) Widespread belief in rumour that war will be over in month or six weeks. London Passenger Transport Board states mechanical staff, responsible for maintenance of rolling stock, both road and rail, unconvinced of importance of their work in national emergency. Want instead to produce war material. Propaganda urgently requested to encourage men to continue their work as usual and that their contribution is a vital one for the national war effort. Harrow: Labour Exchange Manager reports 'difficult to pacify spate of women wanting to undertake war work.' Hendon: 'People still feel they are not told enough news and that bad news is being withheld.' Bethnal Green: 'School teachers' efforts to get children back to schools meeting with success. Few children now on streets. People calm and quite optimistic, but some worried about Post Office Savings in the event of invasion. Asking if they should draw their money out now.' Guy's Hospital: 'Out-patients coming in regularly. This indicates calm. Most people think we will be victorious.' West Ham: 'Most people opposed to Dominions evacuation. Will not agree to children going without parents. If scheme for family evacuation were contemplated it would probably have good reception.' Paddington: 'People with relatives back from France came to register for evacuation. Lack of imagination prevents most others from doing so. Medical examinations started among school children for Dominions.' Highbury, Pollard's Factory: 'Stopped doing work on Sundays but working full time. LDV formed but without equipment. Staff enthusiastic about this, fire squad and first aid party.' Willesden, Guinness's: 'Strong feeling we all ought to be doing something superhuman. Not enough evidence that we are going all out. Should be piling up sufficient reserves to oppose Hitler who has obviously plenty in reserve.' From many districts reports show that children are trickling back from Reception Areas since air raids began.

TUESDAY 2 JULY 1940

There is little change in morale: people are still waiting, most with 'grim determination', others with increasing nervous tension, some with restless criticism.

There is an increase in rumour, and yesterday (the day before Hitler's threatened invasion date) there were many reports of parachute landings and invading troops. Today there is still much talk of the imminence of invasion, often supported by references to 'official' statements that the invasion is only a matter of hours (Nicolson, Chamberlain).

In spite of this atmosphere of tension people are not depressed. Many people say they think our defence preparations are inadequate but at the same time they say 'We shall beat them off', 'We'll teach them a lesson', 'Let them come'.

There is evidence that political exhortations and 'wireless pep talks' are not being well received. People are asking for more information and above all for positive guidance. Ellen Wilkinson's broadcast, however, although in the nature of a 'morale' talk, was widely commented upon as 'young and vigorous', 'giving a lead'. Many people heard her for the first time: 'They ought to make her a general; she would tell us what to do'.

Reports from some rural districts show that the departure to Canada of the wealthy and influential has been strongly criticised.

The indiscriminate internment of aliens is strongly deprecated in intellectual circles and the distress which internment has brought is being reflected in morale.

Air raids are taken calmly and morale is high in districts where there have been continuous warnings, e.g. Bristol. There is little evidence that air raids are affecting morale adversely although there is need for further definition in siren policy.

Points from Regions

Siren policy continues to be criticised. Grimsby welcomes the reduction in alarms. Boston, however, is apprehensive at the lack of sirens, and a denial of any change in policy by the Nottingham ARP Controller has been received with scepticism and derision. From Cardiff comes the complaint that fighter planes are conspicuous by their absence during raids, and this is looked upon as a potential source of anti-RAF feeling such as followed Dunkirk. Bristol reports that employers of labour are asking for a limitation of sirens to avoid industrial fatigue. Leeds reports perturbation in the district because people no longer trust the sirens. In Sheffield there is a common belief that sirens are not being sounded so that industry may continue. Hull reports general indignation because on five nights last week aeroplanes roared overhead and on some of these nights bombs were dropped and yet no sirens sounded. Many people in Hull are passing the nights in their cellars because they cannot trust the sirens. From Thornaby-on-Tees comes the report that public uncertainty about sirens has led to the appointment of street patrol of two men to watch each night for air raids, as a private venture. Reading reports that bombing unaccompanied by warnings continues to be taken calmly. At Stoke uneasiness is said to be developing about the non-sounding of sirens. The town has twice been bombed with only a yellow warning. In working-class streets, private vigilance committees are being formed to look out for hostile raiders. Cambridge states that people are in some degree reconciled to the modified siren system, though there is no lessening of the belief that many of the aeroplanes heard at night are German.

Requests that news bulletins should be broadcast only at 1 p.m. and 9 p.m. continue to be received, and Information Committees stress the bad effect which continued listening to repetitive news has on women.

Rumours of places bombed and parachutists seen continue common.

J. B. Priestley's broadcast on the subject of martial music has been widely welcomed and many suggestions have come in that parades of troops would have a very heartening effect on the public.

NOTTINGHAM (North Midland) There is a general movement to get children to bed earlier and many families are camping out in air-raid shelters, to the delight of the children.

CARDIFF (Wales) Ellen Wilkinson's broadcast considered highly appropriate. MOI film 'Behind the Guns' now showing and is popular.

BELFAST (Northern Ireland) De Gaulle's action in appointing French commanders has revived questioning about fate of French fleet. Hore-Belisha's speech advocating national defence policy for Ireland received critically by majority, because it ignores neutrality of Eire. Big increase in shelters arranged in Belfast. Loan of £50,000 by Ulster firm to Belfast for war expenditure has had excellent effect on public feeling.

MANCHESTER (North Western) Fatigue among people as a result of night raiding is becoming more marked. Possible invasion of Eire is much discussed and there is no confidence in the powers of the Eire government to resist invasion.

BRISTOL (South Western) Bath has reacted admirably to this morning's raid. From Cornwall come complaints of inadequate defence and of the small strength of the LDV. After a succession of night raids and alarms Bristol remains steady and trade and business are normal.

LEEDS (North Eastern) It is not uncommon to find people in this Region who say that though Germany cannot beat Britain, it is impossible to see how Britain can beat Germany. A large German bomber flew low over Hull yesterday and no one troubled to go into shelters; crowd outside Labour Exchange cheered when AA guns went into action. Leeds newspapers and public are campaigning against 'useless' building, i.e. building for peacetime purposes.

EDINBURGH (Scotland) A report from Aberdeen states that crowds flocked to see a burning school immediately after the 'All Clear' siren on Sunday; had the raids been renewed they would have been in grave danger. Enquiries are being received about arrangements for looking after children whose parents have been killed in air raids.

NEWCASTLE (Northern) The cancellation of the traditional local holiday on Tyneside last week produced no dissatisfaction. In Sunderland reports state that rivalry is growing between the LDV and ARP personnel. LDVs are ordering wardens off the streets during air raids.

READING (Southern) Reading Information Committee consider that Chamberlain's broadcast has strengthened neither him nor the Government; the Conservative and business elements were as strongly in favour of his resignation as the Labour contingent. The opposition to Chamberlain is not retrospective but represents nervousness as to whether even now the Government is as resolute and efficient as it should be. The question as to whether workers would really be worse off under Hitler is still being discussed in a comparatively small section of the community. Impatience at the withholding of news, particularly naval and merchant ship losses, and the names of places bombed, is making itself felt, and suggestions have been received that an explanation of the service needs for this reticence would be welcome.

BIRMINGHAM (Midland) Parachutist rumours were rife yesterday before the official denial.

CAMBRIDGE (Eastern) Coastal evacuation by the elderly and infirm is brisk. The belief is still common that today is the day for invasion.

TUNBRIDGE WELLS (South Eastern) Voluntary evacuation from Folkestone was accelerated by the first police notice; a second message broadcast from loudspeaker vans was often imperfectly heard and this created some alarm and indignation. Free railway vouchers are being issued to voluntary evacuees. The *Folkestone Express* and *Hythe Reporter* have ceased publication. Not all are confident that the Government will find them work and shelter, but some of the poor look forward to a holiday at Government expense.

LONDON

Further evidence from all districts that people are not outwardly nervous of air raids and that last week's warning increased their confidence in themselves and their shelters. More reports of appreciation of Priestley's Sunday night talk. News of bombing in Wales very disturbing to parents with children evacuated there. Clerkenwell: 'A few children have been brought back from Wales; if fares were not so high probably more would have come.' Shoreditch Care Committee Worker states majority of mothers with children evacuated full of praise for treatment of their children. Some in Oxfordshire and some in Cornwall; teachers 'write glowing accounts of wonderful summer holiday'. Hackney: '200 children have had medical examination for Dominions'. Islington: 'Mothers not anxious to send children to Dominions and need reassuring that children will not be whisked away without their consent. Many would like under-fives to be sent into country, especially with elder brothers and sisters. Some grievance where boy and girl of same family are sent to different parts of England, entailing extra postal expense.' Greenwich Metal Works: 'Chamberlain's stock among workers very low.' City: 'Widespread belief that damage done by German bombers much more serious than stated.' Deptford: 'People expect that if things get hot the Government will do something to get them out of it. They always rely on everyone else and take little responsibility themselves. Some dock labourers absorbed in ARP but many unemployed. Others waiting to be called up.' Hendon: 'People disturbed at large number of aliens not interned in district. Do not suspect them of being Fifth Column but their fear of the Gestapo so strong that they are already defeatist and may easily panic.'

WEDNESDAY 3 JULY 1940

In an atmosphere of waiting the public is, in large measure, calm and determined. There are, however, significant pockets of defeatism and growing dissatisfaction on certain questions. One of these causes of uneasiness is the continued controversy over the sounding of sirens. Public opinion is still perplexed about official intentions over air-raid warnings and looks for a strong statement of definite policy. This lack of confidence in warnings is in marked contrast with growing confidence in shelters. There are new examples of the voluntary manning of shelters in the public interest.

There is still a good deal of confusion about what compulsory evacuation from coastal areas will mean and there is evidence that many families have prepared their own schemes of 'crash evacuation'.

In certain areas increasing signs of defence preparations have brought confidence; in others the 'flimsy defences' set up by the LDV receive strong comment.

Yesterday's air raids received more comment than usual. This appears to be due in part to the increasing strain of the general situation and in part to the siren controversy. Behaviour in air raids was excellent.

In many reports we find requests for martial music and other emotional outlets for public feeling.

There is a very strong movement developing against the 'men of Munich'. Further reports on Chamberlain's broadcast show that it had a depressing effect, although it had little influence on the 'anti-Chamberlain movement'.

Waste of paper comes in for a good deal of public comment.

Observers recently returned from tours in the North and in South Wales give stirring accounts of the fine spirit of the people and of their determination to resist to the end.

Points from Regions

The question of sirens is still anxiously discussed. From Nottingham come reports that opinion is about equally divided for and against sounding sirens as early as possible; the view is stressed that factory workers should continue at their posts even as our troops have to do. Cardiff reports that the controversy is still active and, in spite of the Home Secretary's statement, a really definite ruling would be welcome. Newcastle reports considerable public anger at Jarrow where an 'All Clear' signal was followed by bombs one-and-a-half minutes later, just as people were leaving their shelters. In all public places last night there was strong criticism of this as casualties were numerous. Crowds of sightseers after the raid impeded the work of Civil Defence personnel and the Regional Commissioner is issuing a statement on the subject to the public, asking them to be more sensible. At Newcastle enemy aircraft were seen by thousands of people leaving work and no siren was sounded until nearly ten minutes after bombs had been dropped. There was no AA fire and no fighter planes were seen; this led to some public criticism. Reading reports that there is a growing public feeling in favour of taking some risk and having a good night's rest. From Cambridge come reports of public speculation about casualties in the raids on the North East Coast; people are inclined to attribute this to the absence of sirens. In this Region feeling now is favouring the early sounding of sirens; some have expressed the view that the limited sounding has been deliberately adopted to make people think the raids are smaller than they are. Hertfordshire newspapers are at present forced to describe raids in the immediate locality as having occurred in 'south-east England'.

Today ten reports of unfavourable reactions to Chamberlain's speech have been received (from Paddington, Finsbury, Aldgate, Chelsea, Taunton, Chatham, Weedon, Daventry, Bradford, and Tunbridge Wells). No favourable reactions have been reported.

Rumours of parachutists in limited numbers are circulating in Oxford, Rugby (where Henley is named as the site of descent) and Daventry.

NOTTINGHAM (North Midland) Interest in overseas evacuation is considerable, and many regard it as a quid pro quo (the Dominions send us troops, we send them children). Elimination of our Continental allies has produced indifference among large sections of the public to foreign affairs. Norman's speech on war loan received without enthusiasm.

CARDIFF (Wales) Uneasiness over the fate of the French fleet continues. There is some disappointment that we have not yet taken more active measures against Italy. Defences being built in the south part of this Region appear to anticipate attack from the east, and there is some public comment that this indicates that the prospect of invasion from the west is not treated seriously enough.

BELFAST (Northern Ireland) Anticipation of air raids is leading to a public demand for shelters in all urban areas. Only isolated requests for inclusion of Ulster in overseas evacuation scheme.

MANCHESTER (North Western) Some criticisms of the excessive zeal of the LDV are heard.

BRISTOL (South Western) Daylight raids are welcomed by the public as a change from the more disturbing night raids. In many cases office staff have continued work in shelters. On the whole raids are accepted calmly and philosophically though in rural districts some middle-aged people are reported to be jumpy.

READING (Southern) Rumours of places bombed are rife.

TUNBRIDGE WELLS (South Eastern) Increasing coastal defence measures are leading to some anxiety at Dartford and in the Canterbury district. The voluntary evacuation of Thanet has produced a vicious circle and tradesmen are having to leave as there is no more business. Compulsory evacuation is looked upon as a certainty in the near future and the working-class people are anticipating that the Government will have to look after them. Many miners have left the Kent collieries to seek employment in pits in other parts of the country.

LEEDS (North Eastern) Satisfaction is expressed at the recent Government restrictions, e.g. the coastal ban, as indicating a stronger determination to conduct the war with vigour. Requests are being made for a clearer definition of siren policy. There is considerable anxiety in rural parts at the large number of fields which are eminently suitable for landing grounds.

EDINBURGH (Scotland) The flimsy nature of road defences has led to public comment and the alleged absence of our fighters when enemy bombers have been over is also leading to grumbles. Continued favourable reports of Ellen Wilkinson's broadcast are received. The appearance of Spitfires over Aberdeen last night had a heartening effect on the public.

LONDON

Marylebone Road Labour Exchange: 'Big register of English and aliens in Women's Department; some ill-feeling against aliens who are supposed to try and get first pick of jobs.' St Pancras: 'Chief reason for non-evacuation among very poor is that parents cannot afford clothes and shoes needed by children in the country.' Woolwich, Matchless Motor Cycles: 'Big innovation in factory, e.g. introduction of music during working hours, has surprising effect of changing mood of depression to cheerfulness.' Fulham: 'Mothers no longer making enquiries about evacuation of under-fives to country.' Carter Paterson: 'Good response to appeal for Civil Defence and LDV. Each depot organising own LDV; local territorials helping by giving instructions and lending rifles. Firm not yet equipped but has provided own armlets.' Chelsea Housing Estate: 'Ellen Wilkinson's talk appreciated. Tenants making great effort to do something themselves. More salvage collected from one block of flats than ever before. Some children brought back from Surrey; railway fares too high to bring others back from Wales.' Euston: 'Housing Estate Commissioners have supplied fire fighting apparatus to tenants and are arranging demonstrations in using them.' Priestley's stirring broadcast had noticeably cheering effect on merchant-seamen in Red Ensign Club. Business and Professional Women's Club in City of London: 'annoyance of having to rise in the night for air-raid warnings. Most people admitted to extreme tiredness after disturbed nights. Large number of women have now decided to remain in bed until they hear gunfire to prevent loss of energy caused by lack of sleep.'

THURSDAY 4 JULY 1940

There is little change in morale: most people are still waiting with considerable cheerfulness and determination.

1. News of the French fleet has been the chief topic of interest during the morning. Last night rumours gathered and spread on this subject.

2. There is little interest in the Balkan situation. People do not know what to think.

3. Daylight raids were taken very calmly: the siren controversy is less acute. There are many requests for more details of raids over this country or for further explanation about the need for secrecy. Information about raids is very quickly carried by telephone or letter to all parts of the country. The amount of rumour about raids is high.

4. There is some growth of anti-Semitism.

5. The torpedoing of the Arandora Star *is reported to have affected the growing interest in Dominions evacuation for children.*

6. An important cause of complaint is the inability of Labour Exchanges and other bodies to absorb willing labour.

7. A record of overheard conversations yesterday showed that Hitler's failure to begin his invasion on the projected date (2 July) was widely commented on. 'Well he didn't do it this time', 'Don't speak too soon', 'Perhaps the Channel Islands began it', 'We ought to have the flags out — he didn't do it after all', 'You're tempting Providence', 'It won't be over on 15 August either'.

8. The NUR anti-appeasement resolution is a strong topic of conversation.

Points from Regions

News about the French fleet has been received in all Regions with satisfaction and relief, though there is considerable regret that we should have had to take action against some elements of the French fleet. The public are most anxious to learn what are the full gains in ships. It is felt that this strong action gives welcome evidence of Government vigour and decision. Edinburgh records that this impression has been strengthened by the Government's strong reply to Japan about the Burma road.

Favourable reactions to Chamberlain's speech are recorded in Parkstone Quay and Clacton, but unfavourable ones from Marylebone and Sandown, IOW. From Glasgow comes a report that Clydeside workers were greatly angered by a passage in Chamberlain's interview with the American press; this passage was taken to mean that the workers did not start working really hard until the bombs began to fall, and that the workers themselves are primarily responsible for the present lack of supplies.

The siren controversy is now dying down.

Requests for more detailed news of places bombed continue to be received, as many observers feel that the absence of definite news is the greatest cause of the present spate of rumours about bomb damage. Reiteration of the service reasons for the present policy is suggested from some quarters.

NOTTINGHAM (North Midland) From Kettering it is reported that there is some apprehension in connection with Hitler's timetable and the way he has kept to it. Lincoln reports some defeatist talk, taking the form of doubt as to whether we should be worse off under Hitler than at present.

CARDIFF (Wales) First two daylight raid warnings at Cardiff yesterday were taken in an exemplary manner; much haste but no panic. Crowds formed outside public shelters and there was some confusion after the 'All Clear' in the dispersal of the crowds to buses and trams. The presence of the Dutch army in Pembrokeshire is viewed with some distrust, and many of the public doubt their efficiency, and in some cases even their loyalty.

BELFAST (Northern Ireland) Projected voluntary evacuation of Belfast schoolchildren taken calmly. Some public questioning about state of West Coast harbours in Eire as potential enemy submarine bases. Test mobilisation of Defence Volunteers in Antrim and Down produced excellent response.

MANCHESTER (North Western) Supply of arms to LDV has raised spirits. Some criticism of appointment of Lord Milne on ground of age. Many people doubt wisdom of the old men and long for fresh vigorous young minds. Sinking of *Arandora Star* has raised doubts about safety of children being evacuated overseas.

BRISTOL (South Western) In face of day and night raids nerves are becoming steadier. Report from a poor area: 'if you had been in the public shelter here during yesterday's raid you would know why people say Hitler has taken on an impossible task.' Growing demand for heavier air-raid reprisals against Germany. There are requests from 'safe' areas for shelters.

LEEDS (North Eastern) People are becoming increasingly confident in the efficiency of the RAF, and attribute the fewer alarms to the powers of the Fighter Command. Confidence in the services is high but there is still feeling that civil administration could be more vigorous.

EDINBURGH (Scotland) In Glasgow thought of overseas evacuation is deterring people from registering their children for home evacuation, for fear that compulsory overseas evacuation may be adopted once the children have left home.

NEWCASTLE (Northern) Favourable comments on Priestley's broadcast continue to be received. Overseas evacuation very popular in Middlesbrough (over 2,000 applications). Some adverse criticism of damage by bombs being shown on newsreels. Many people are furnishing their shelters as part of their homes. In Tuesday's daylight raid in Newcastle many of advertised public shelters are stated to have been locked and people could not get in.

READING (Southern) Exaggerated rumours of bomb damage are very common. Anxiety is reported in Portsmouth and Southampton at the heavy increase in mercantile losses recently.

BIRMINGHAM (Midland) As a result of bombs being dropped in some areas with a yellow warning only, headmistresses in Wolverhampton have suggested that schools should be privately warned early so that children may be got to safety in good time.

CAMBRIDGE (Eastern) Daylight raids on East Coast were taken extremely calmly though it is felt that the case for sirens is greater during the day than at night. On the whole, however, the public approves of the sparing use of sirens. A curious feature of these raids is the absence of public bitterness towards the raiders. Many working-class people are now sleeping in shelters. Spirit of LDV in East Suffolk reported excellent. Some criticism of placidity of BBC postscripts – timorous and dull.

TUNBRIDGE WELLS (South Eastern) The public in Kent and Sussex were more thrilled than alarmed by yesterday's abortive raiding. Still doubt in Folkestone about situation in connection with compulsory evacuation. Brighton indignant at press story that seafront has been taken over by military.

LONDON

Reports show people less apprehensive of air raids since warning last week. Instructions given about sirens welcomed in last night's talk. Chief anxiety among people who are still trying to decide whether to send their children to the country or not. Hendon Community Association: 'Women tenants objected violently to speaker who talked down to them in phrases such as "looking after the old man". Pride themselves on knowing what to do in an emergency and on relying on themselves in time of danger.' London Professional Women's Club reports members' suspicion that Air Ministry casualty lists are incomplete after talking with RAF men. Lewisham: 'Many enquiries at CABs by refugees from Channel Islands who have become separated from relations. Difficult to get information about these people.' Holland Park: 'Blast- and splinter-proof shelters being erected in side streets. Speculation in neighbourhood as to whether people should go out of their houses at night to take refuge in them.' A certain amount of disquiet is reported from several districts over the non-publication of news heard privately, such as the sinking of a transport or other ships, and damage done in air raids on this country. Brompton: 'Grumbling in neighbourhood because local Labour Exchanges cannot help people to get farm work after broadcast appeal.' Dagenham Labour Exchange states appeals for National Service have resulted in several hundred women applying each week for such work, whereas Exchange can only place 50 to 70 a week. Women go away dissatisfied and annoyed, but Exchange officials are unable to help them further. Most have family ties and cannot move to districts where there might be work for them. Local problem of low morale in Irish quarter of Dagenham where approx. 300 men are at work. Wives very nervous of air raids. People living in small houses near military objectives such as Croydon aerodrome and Woolwich Arsenal anxious as stray bombs are bound to miss their objectives. Westminster COS reports people in locality have excellent communal spirit and are helping to make air-raid shelters attractive. Standard Telephones, New Southgate: 'a growing feeling amongst working-class women that they would be as well off under Hitler as they are now. These women have considerable influence as they run the family and try to make ends meet. Propaganda asked for.'

FRIDAY 5 JULY 1940

The French Fleet action has had a good effect on morale: underlying anxieties have decreased and there is general relief. This sign of aggressive action on our part has been generally welcomed and even the fact that many French sailors lost their lives has been allowed to pass with little comment. There have been indications of apathy during the last week but today confidence and certainty are returning to check the drift in morale.

Raids were taken calmly and there is reassurance over the sounding of sirens. Rumour about raids is still high.

There is some increase in rumours attributed to Haw-Haw: many of these are concerned with coastal evacuation.

Inefficiencies in the mobilisation of man-power and woman-power continue to be the subject of critical comment.

Points from Regions

All Regions express widespread approval at our action against the French fleet. The public feel that no other course was possible and they welcome this evidence of our initiative. Reports on the Prime Minister's and the First Lord's speeches are universally and strongly favourable.

NOTTINGHAM (North Midland) Return of 400 airmen prisoners to Germany has quite discounted any sentimental feeling which may be present about the French. Reports indicate strong feeling that we should continue to take a firm line in our dealings abroad particularly with Japan. Romanian situation is stated to have decreased anti-Russian feeling, and many say we should accept Russian help without scruple. Opinion about America continues hopeful of ultimate and decisive intervention. Farmers who are willing to make fields unsafe for plane landing are asking for a Government lead.

CARDIFF (Wales) Industrial work in factories and mines continues vigorously. The Balkans situation is viewed with indifference by the great mass of the public.

BELFAST (Northern Ireland) De Valera's statement about maintaining and defending Eire's neutrality is regarded by the majority as banging the door on any proposals for a united military command of Ireland. Disappointment in many parts that Ministry of Supply has refused to establish munition factories in Northern Ireland.

MANCHESTER (North Western) Channel Island children who are to be moved from manufacturing towns to country districts do not want to go and the towns do not want children to leave. The people have taken the children to their hearts.

BRISTOL (South Western) Comparative inactivity of past few days has further steadied public attitude towards air raids. Welfare Officers again stress that the most nervous part of the community are women only partially occupied at home. Raids have greatly improved the attitude of people in Taunton Reception Areas to evacuees; the public feel that evacuation is now necessary, and increased billeting allowances have further helped. A bomb in Cornwall has increased enthusiasm for Civil Defence. A false alarm of parachutists at Exeter demonstrated a prompt and efficient reaction by the LDV, and has increased local confidence.

LEEDS (North Eastern) Hull and Keighley Corporations have sacked COs. There is general public satisfaction with the Services but still much dissatisfaction with the Home Front. Salvage campaign is weakened by sight of new steel girders put into buildings not intended for war work. In Leeds there is difficulty in getting men and bricks for building shelters and this has led to an attack on the Building Trades Federation at the City Council. There is still resentment at the appointment of ex-officers rather than experienced rankers as LDV commanders, and working people in factories still feel they are inadequately defended. The public is eager to help but many state they do not find the same spirit of urgency in the authorities.

EDINBURGH (Scotland) French and British troops in Glasgow reported to be fraternising in good spirits. De Valera's speech has renewed anxiety about Eire. Some vague resentment against Lord Craigavon who is regarded as an obstacle to agreement with southern Ireland on joint defence. Sinking of *Arandora Star* has frightened many parents who were in course of registering children for overseas evacuation.

NEWCASTLE (Northern) Lorry drivers are again reported as spreaders of exaggerated air-raid damage rumours.

READING (Southern) Regret tinged with criticism at our giving up of the Channel Islands. Some feel they should have been held at all costs like the Ypres salient in the last war. Some criticisms of the Government attitude in repeatedly urging the public to keep calm; requests for more emphasis on the martial side and for demonstrations of our military strength by parades, processions of tanks, and bands. Flimsy and inadequate road barricades are criticised.

BIRMINGHAM (Midland) Members of Information Committees continue to receive protests about bombs falling during yellow warning. Anxiety about the armament of the LDV continues.

CAMBRIDGE (Eastern) Increasing support for the idea of sounding sirens rather more freely during daylight raids than at night.

TUNBRIDGE WELLS (South Eastern) Requests for a weekly five-minute talk from the Minister of Information. Still some mistrust of news reported. Many state they would always prefer to know the worst.

LONDON

Feeling of satisfaction reported from most districts about action taken over French Navy. 'Regrettable, but impossible to do anything else in circumstances'. 'People glad we have taken initiative at last.' Luxury trade workers in West End losing jobs rapidly. Camden Town Labour Exchange reports situation becoming increasingly difficult as many of such workers live in district. Ranks of unemployed also increased by closing down of East Coast places and people returning to London without work. From Chiswick comes strong criticism of conditions in small factories during black-out. 'Lack of ventilation and smoky atmosphere affects women workers. Canteen arrangements often appear inadequate.' More criticisms of lack of LDV equipment in works and factories, especially of steel helmets. Some factories urgently seek directives as to type of defence arrangements to make and how questions of insurance and workmen's compensation will be settled. Lack of coordination reported between recently set-up Information Committees and bodies such as the COS and CABs. Ealing: Icilma Factory lately put on to confidential Government work. 'Workers, although tired from long hours enthusiastic at doing something important for national effort at last.' Hornchurch: neighbourly scheme in operation for sharing Civil Defence apparatus. Council gives demonstrations and lectures and provides stirrup pumps to those who have attended them. Southall: 'Refugees from Channel Islands have created situation of disquiet in neighbourhood, as they arrived before announcement of demilitarisation of islands had been made, and arrangements were not made to receive them.'

SATURDAY 6 JULY 1940

The French fleet action is still having a good effect on morale, although today many people are wondering what percentage of the French fleet has in fact been saved. There is a declining interest in the news, partly accounted for by an increased interest in invasion, but primarily brought about by bewilderment both about the content and the interpretation of news.

1. The public finds it difficult to understand official reasons for withholding news about air-raid damage, and are dissatisfied with the explanations so far given. There is much private communication of detailed news and many rumours, both of which contribute to public disquiet. There is no doubt that the public would prefer to be told the truth however unpleasant, and an impression is growing that the withholding of unpleasant news is official policy. 'Why don't they tell us? We can take it', is a common expression.

2. There is some growth of anti-French feeling of an indiscriminate kind. Most people condemn the Pétain government, but some say 'We shall be fighting the French soon,' 'We were never real friends with the French'.

3. The Channel Islands evacuation, now becoming more widely known by the distribution of refugees, is the subject of critical and anxious comment. It is even referred to as 'The beginning of the end'; 'inefficient and disheartening'; 'it has the smell of defeat'.

4. Although the internment of aliens has popular support, in intellectual and professional circles the situation has created grave alarm and some defeatism. Letters carry news of this 'breakdown of high principle' to other countries. There is criticism not only of the desirability of internment but of the methods by which it is carried out.

5. There are rumours about the Duke of Windsor; most persistently, that he will be the puppet ruler of a Nazi administration.

6. There are fewer grumbles from the agricultural community.

7. The use of labour and material for non-essential building is strongly criticised in reports from all parts of the country.

8. The fear of 'appeasement' is strong in certain sections of the community, and the movement against certain Ministers is gaining ground. Many letters show that the movement is spreading to those who are not normally politically minded. 'Does the Government realise it is playing with fire?'

9. Reports from all over the country show that morale is high and that the will of the people to prosecute the war is sound. At the same time there is evidence that the 'will to sacrifice and to win' is in constant need of stimulation and guidance. 'The hungry sheep look up and are not fed.'

Points from Regions

NOTTINGHAM (North Midland) Feeling against conscientious objectors growing in Peterborough. From the same town reports of uneasiness that the appeasement Ministers continue in office. Work people express the opinion that some firms are not being given the opportunity to work to capacity (clothing factory and foundry).

BELFAST (Northern Ireland) Great interest shown in announcement of recruiting for two battalions for Home Defence. German propaganda about the British threat to Eire's neutrality is regarded as indicating an early German air invasion. RAF attacks on German naval bases have created great satisfaction.

MANCHESTER (North Western) Indiscriminate internment of all aliens distresses more thoughtful people who regard it as evidence of panic action.

BRISTOL (South Western) Marked increase in neighbourliness in Plymouth as a result of recent events. Suggested that LDVs are the worst offenders in spreading rumours of parachutists. Many Bristol housewives are arranging bedrooms on the ground floor to cope with air-raid alarms. Devonport accepts the damage to the *Scharnhorst* sceptically.

LEEDS (North Eastern) There are more recruits for Doncaster LDV than required. Miners' leaders have had to appeal to young miners not to leave the pits to join up.

EDINBURGH (Scotland) Some resentment felt against the impression given by the Government that as the Channel Isles are strategically unimportant no one should worry about the inhabitants. A Stonehaven report indicates that those associated with Moral Rearmament are saying that there is no need for this country to be at war with Germany and differences could be settled by the application of MR principles.

NEWCASTLE (Northern) In Middlesbrough public shelters are being manned about 11 p.m., particularly by women and children, whether there is a warning or not. Voluntary Wardens and ARP workers are feeling the strain of continued night work.

READING (Southern) Bournemouth is upset by damage to summer season.

BIRMINGHAM (Midland) Coventry reports agitation about the loss of the Channel Isles. Many believed that they are near the British Coast.

CAMBRIDGE (Eastern) The sinking of the *Arandora Star* has caused uneasiness amongst parents planning to send children overseas. Hope is expressed in coastal towns that financial help from the Government will go much further than at present indicated.

TUNBRIDGE WELLS (South Eastern) The Bishop of Chichester and the Mayor of Eastbourne have made statements about evacuation causing alarm in the Eastbourne area. Some belief in Chatham that dockyard workers, waiting for ships to come in for repairs, are short of work.

LONDON

Chief topics of conversation still French Navy and abandonment of Channel Islands. Action over former generally approved; Channel Island policy considered disquieting, especially in districts receiving refugees. More explanation asked for. Churchill's speech had rousing effect, reports many observers. Widespread anxiety about children evacuated to Wales and South West England, combined with no details of raids. Parents disturbed in mind as to whether to bring children back or not. Evidence that deaf people are increasingly apprehensive of raids. Many stay up at night watching the sky. In some districts arrangements are made that someone will be sure to inform them of warnings. Morden: 'Army allowances inadequate. Delay in arrival of special allowances causing annoyance to women concerned. Need in this and other districts for creches or day nurseries to free mothers for war work.' University College Hospital: 'Hospital Almoner encouraging pregnant woman to register for evacuation. Comparatively small response.' Chiswick: 'Two hundred Dutch and Belgian refugees resented by soldiers' wives as many are men of military age. Work should be given them as they are bored and appear ungrateful.' Woolwich Labour Exchange: 'People working twelve hours a day for seven days a week: too busy to be nervous of raids. Large body of married women seeking factory work. Cannot all be absorbed at once.' Tidbrook: 'Neighbours getting together and helping each other with Civil Defence.' Pinner: 'People disturbed by Civil Defence lecture in which statement occurred that if bomb dropped in Wealdstone it would destroy houses in Pinner (four to five miles away). Women combining to buy aeroplane. Fifty have contributed'. Clapham: 'More definite information required as to what arrangements will be made for homeless if bombing is heavy. Rest Centres being set up where people can remain for 48 hours but too few for large population.' St John's Wood: 'Individual has organised small street of 60 houses for fire fighting. Has collected 45 fire fighters, 12 stirrup pumps, and £10 worth of equipment. Scheme working well.' Holloway: 'Interned aliens want useful work; very distressed to think they are useless. Work would strengthen their morale. Women could sew and prepare hospital equipment.' Bermondsey: 'People in neighbourhood anxious about Norwegian sailors who appear to have plenty of money and nothing to do. Spend all day in public houses and then go to West End. Many casual dock labourers out of work. Percentage absorbed into Civil Defence, but do not take readily to regular work. Considerable unemployment amongst women in luxury trades.'

MONDAY 8 JULY TO SATURDAY 13 JULY 1940

On 9 July tea was rationed. Bacon, ham, butter and sugar had been on the ration since January, and meat since March. Now the Ministry of Food announced that all ration-book holders, including children, would henceforth be entitled to 2oz of tea per person per week. At first Home Intelligence reported that 'the majority of the public . . . accept the measure cheerfully' but within a few days it was 'beginning to affect people who find two ounces will not last a week'. This was mainly a working-class grumble, but irritation with rationing was also to be found 'in luxury restaurants such as Harrods. Customers walk out saying they will go elsewhere to get more generous portions of sugar.' The time had come, said the Minister of Food Lord Woolton, for the whole nation to cut out luxuries in preparation for the long siege that lay ahead. From 15 July, he announced, hotels and restaurants would be forbidden to serve more than one main course of meat or fresh fish at every meal. Confectioners had been told to stop icing their cakes. Cooking fats and margarine would be rationed from 22 July.

There were many references in the morale reports to fears of invasion and some speculation that Hitler would seize control of Ireland and turn it into a springboard for an assault on Britain. Eire, under the leadership of Eamon De Valera, was not only neutral but virtually defenceless and could only have been defended by British forces based in Northern Ireland. In an attempt to bring Eire into the war, the War Cabinet had authorised Malcolm MacDonald, the Minister of Health, to visit Dublin for top-secret discussions with De Valera in June 1940. Churchill and the War Cabinet were prepared to make a 'solemn undertaking' in favour of the re-unification of Ireland, in return for the stationing of British forces in the south. De Valera, however, was determined to maintain Irish neutrality and rejected the offer. Under intense pressure from Whitehall the Prime Minister of Northern

Ireland, Lord Craigavon, then made a public offer of cooperation with Eire in the joint defence of Ireland. De Valera replied that a defence policy for the whole of Ireland would only be possible if partition were ended. The Irish question had ended in stalemate once more.

Although 10 July was later officially classifed as the first day of the Battle of Britain, there was little at the time to mark it out as a turning-point in the gradual escalation of the war in the air. It was, however, the day on which Lord Beaverbrook, the Minister of Aircraft Production, issued an appeal to housewives to hand in household items made of aluminium to the local offices of the Women's Voluntary Service. 'We will turn your pots and pans into Spifires and Hurricanes, Blenheims, and Wellingtons,' he assured them. Patriotic housewives responded eagerly at first, handing in kitchen utensils and many other household items. But as Home Intelligence reported, they were quick to notice that articles made of aluminium were still on sale in the shops. The appeal was, in fact, a stunt intended to dramatise the need to accelerate aircraft production: the amount of high-grade aluminium that could be extracted from pots and pans was negligible. There was better news elsewhere. After some doubts about whether the deal would go through, the Packard company in Detroit agreed to manufacture 6,000 aero-engines for the RAF.

On 11 July the Ministry of Information launched a radio, press and poster campaign urging the public to refrain from spreading rumours and join Britain's 'Silent Column'. As a last resort they were asked to inform the police about indiscreet characters like 'Mr Secrecy Hush-Hush', 'Miss Leaky Mouth', or 'Mr Pride in Prophecy'. Morale, Home Intelligence recorded, remained high, but there were many minor complaints and undercurrents of anxiety: 'Society doctor reports many wealthy patients asking for poison prescriptions to take if Germans come.'

MONDAY 8 JULY 1940

General morale is maintained at a high level: from several Regions come reports which state 'Morale, especially in the working classes, has never been higher', 'Factory workers are in high fettle', 'Air raids have in no way affected morale, rather the reverse.' News of aggressive air action has had an important effect in stimulating and maintaining morale. The effect of the French fleet action is still being felt and is referred to frequently as 'the turn of the tide', 'hitting hard'. There is little evidence that the consequences of these actions are fully considered: aggressive actions in themselves bring forth public appreciation and enthusiasm. Verbatims indicate public temper: 'Well, we've shown what we can do', 'That'll give Hitler a surprise for a change.'

In this atmosphere of public confidence and cheerful aggressiveness, the Lord Privy Seal's broadcast reference to 'the coming zero hour' (with its implication that we wait Hitler's pleasure) fell on stony ground.

The public in fact is conscious of 'waiting' less than usual, and although there is plenty of talk of invasion, raids and evacuation, it is dominated by the belief that aggressive action on our part is beginning.

Points from Regions

From several Regions come reports that the obstruction of fields so that enemy planes cannot land is developing on a very small scale only. There is doubt as to the best and simplest form of obstruction, also as to what authority is responsible for advising and ordering steps to be taken.

Our action against the French fleet continues to be a source of satisfaction, and many hope that we will rapidly man the surrendered ships with British crews. An intense anger has been aroused by the treachery of the French airmen who joined in the attack on Gibraltar.

Our continued raids on Germany give people great satisfaction and make them the more willing to put up with the raids in England. Strong hopes are expressed that our attacks by air will be intensified, particularly upon places where preparations for invasion are being made.

J.B. Priestley's broadcast has been everywhere approved.

Nottingham reports that the criticism of the less frequent siren warnings has almost completely died down. Cardiff reports concern in North Wales at the absence of AA defence measures. Bristol reports anxiety at Plymouth inasmuch as people state that a German raider was able to dodge in and out the clouds for over an hour eluding AA fire without a single British plane appearing. Tunbridge Wells reports that children in public playing fields had no idea what to do when the siren was sounded just before lunch on Sunday. They have instructions what to do at school, and when going to and from it, but no instructions for holidays.

Ireland is much discussed as a site of invasion and there is much doubt, especially in Scotland, about the satisfaction expressed by Lord Craigavon. Many in Glasgow and Edinburgh do not share this satisfaction.

The system of volunteer labour for defence work which has been successful at Dundee has produced friction between the voluntary workers and the unemployed.

NOTTINGHAM (North Midland) Demands for vigorous attack on French fleet in German controlled ports.

CARDIFF (Wales) Further reports of criticism of Chamberlain's speech. Repetition of minor items of news all through the day on the wireless continues to be resented.

BELFAST (Northern Ireland) Evacuation of schoolchildren going satisfactorily.

MANCHESTER (North Western) Public feeling towards LDVs improved by their appearance in uniform, but criticism of their manners and activities continues. Non-publication of full casualty rates in air raids is leading to the comment that they must be very heavy.

BRISTOL (South Western) Influential Salisbury people have formed unofficial group to kill gossip and rumours. Complaints that evacuated schoolteachers are not pulling their weight have been received from Devon.

LEEDS (North Eastern) Public continue eager for action rather than speeches.

EDINBURGH (Scotland) Requests are for more instruction on how to prepare children for air raids and how to behave during raids.

NEWCASTLE (Northern) In some areas, owing to absence of sirens, public congregate in streets and watch for dimming of lights in local factories which occurs when yellow warning is received. Unemployed in reserved occupations who are not being called up are reported to be indignant.

READING (Southern) Complaints of inadequate Home Defence measures – e.g. flimsy road defences, fields unobstructed – continue common. Puzzlement that Chamberlain should still be in office is as marked as ever. Some defeatist talk on the lines 'we couldn't be worse off under Hitler' continues to be reported from both towns and villages and an intensification of propaganda on the theme of 'a day of your life under Hitler' is urged. Requests for more stimulating propaganda, particularly in the form of bands and military display, are common.

BIRMINGHAM (Midland) Coventry workers willingly gave up their annual holiday to further war production. Municipal Councils continue to suspend COs.

CAMBRIDGE (Eastern) Voluntary evacuation among the poor in coastal areas has declined following our recent naval successes. They anticipate that compulsory evacuation for them will be organised for them by the Government when necessary. No fear about the efficiency of our armed forces but traces of anxiety lest the country should be divided amongst its leaders as happened in France.

TUNBRIDGE WELLS (South Eastern) The feeling for army bands and martial music grows stronger, and many industrial concerns who have wireless for their employees in the work-rooms reiterate this demand. Publicans are uncertain what to do during air raids. Some stay open, some close, and some close but retain their patrons.

LONDON

West Ham: 'People becoming sceptical of evacuation and some bringing children back. No call for evacuation to Dominions.' Watford: 'Neighbourhood full of troops; excellent spirit everywhere. Publicity given to harm done by civilians moving in France has roused determination to avoid similar occurrence. Excellent women's volunteer services in operation and small local groups organising themselves for fire fighting and community help. Unemployment growing of young girls under seventeen normally employed in Printing Works. Too young for munitions or other women's services.' Chelsea Housing Estate: 'Children arriving back from Suffolk because soldiers are posted there. Parents considering this means area no longer safe although forty-five miles inland. Some taking holidays as usual though few going away for more than a day's outing. Social barriers breaking down on estate owing to shared anxieties and dangers'. Walworth: 'Special National Savings drive supported admirably.' Bethnal Green: 'Big increase in unemployment among cabinet woodworkers and bespoke tailors, causing despondency in families concerned. Labour Exchanges crowded; some tenants moving from homes as they cannot afford the rent.' Some complaints in East End districts that dustmen are selling privately and making profit out of carefully collected tins, bones, paper and other salvage. Housewives angry. Expressions of mistrust among people of differing social circles of published casualty figures and other war news. Details of air-raid damage received in letters circulates as rumour and becomes distorted and magnified.

Action Points

For the information of the authorities concerned the following points have been extracted from the various reports received today by Home Intelligence Division:

MI7. Reports have again been received from Nottingham of anxiety of farmers about the protection of their fields against possible landings from the air. Although an urgent request has been made for obstructions to be set up over as wide an area as possible, this appeal has so far met with only small success.

It is reported from Manchester that the feeling of the public towards the LDV has been 'improved by their appearance in uniform.' Nevertheless the criticism which has already been reported of their behaviour still continues.

In various parts of the country the public is reported as expressing a strong desire for military bands, parades and so forth.

Air Intelligence. The following is an extract from the report received from Manchester: 'If the Air Ministry persists with their new policy not to give the number of dead in air raids, rumour will eventually get out of hand. Already it is being said that casualties must be pretty bad if figures cannot be given.' Criticism on these lines is contained in various other reports.

Home Security. The danger arising from the ignorance of small children of what they should do in air raids is strongly emphasized in the report from Tunbridge Wells which says 'Sirens were sounded in the street just before lunchtime on Sunday, and it was clearly evident that hundreds of children in the streets and playing fields had no idea what to do. It was pitiful to see little groups of very young children so terror-stricken that they could not remember their quickest way home. There was a wild scamper straight from the Common, the children running across the main road with a complete disregard for traffic.' Although instructions have been given on the action the children should take if a warning is given on their way to school or on their way home, there appears to have been no advice given to them about what they should do when playing in the streets or elsewhere.

A different aspect of this problem is touched upon in a report from Scotland which says 'The suggestion has come from various quarters that special broadcasting talks should be given on how parents should prepare children for air raids, and how to behave in the presence of children during raids.'

Newcastle reports that the public in the Eston district wait outside factories in this area, where sirens no longer seem to be sounded, and watch for the dimming of the lights inside which takes place when a yellow warning has been received. 'When this takes place the public enter shelters and the police have great difficulty in convincing them later on that "Cancel Caution" message has been received.'

It is stated in the Bristol report that the Cotswold Bruderhof Movement continues to be 'deeply suspect'.

The Ministry of Labour. Today's Edinburgh report includes the following comment on volunteer labour for defence work. It is said that although this has been successful in the Dundee district it has produced serious friction between volunteers and ordinary unemployed sent by the Labour Exchange to fill sand bags etc.

'Firstly, it is almost impossible to get the unemployed to turn out. The Labour Exchange Manager was asked by the military officer in charge of the work to get 400 men out (contractors having failed to get any), but only a dozen or so turned out the following morning. Secondly, the volunteers working in the evening for an hour or two fill 50 bags, while ordinary casual labourers working all day fill very much less. Thirdly, the labourers themselves are reported to object to the volunteer labour as shortening for them this easy and lucrative employment. Public resentment at the attitude of unemployed labourers is growing.'

Ministry of Supply. It is stated that people in the Hatfield (Herts) district are seriously dissatisfied with the inadequacy of the Borough Council's salvage arrangements. Although the residents in this district are careful to sort out their own refuse it is stated that no proper attempt is made at the Council's yard to separate waste material from that which can be usefully salvaged.

Reports of a different kind but in connection with the same subject have been received from Stepney where it is stated that 'tins, bones, paper etc., carefully saved for the sake of the country, is taken by dustmen to rag-and-bone shops where it is sold for their own profit.' Our informant says that many women of the district are prepared to substantiate this accusation.

TUESDAY 9 JULY 1940

Morale continues high: there are indications that invasion is ceasing to be the terrifying and novel idea that it once was. In coastal areas evidences of preparation make the subject dominant in public and private conversation and there is keen anxiety below a calm surface. In other slightly less vulnerable areas military confidence has been transmitted to the civilian population and, as one observer remarked, 'everyone is so keyed up, I can't think what will happen if Hitler doesn't come after all'. There is still a good deal of questioning about the Government's evacuation plans, although people are satisfied on certain points, and many people have now completed their private plans for 'crash' evacuation. On the whole there is more talk of invasion than of air raids, which everywhere have been taken calmly. There is a considerable increase of public confidence in siren policy.

The threat of invasion brings strongly to the front popular demand for aggressive leadership.

Lord Woolton's broadcast was welcomed as a sign of official determination and direction: the public is in a mood to respond to any call for sacrifice. References to the newly-rationed foods were all amiable. 'Fancy spoiling our nice cup of tea.' 'There'll be nothing to do in the air-raid shelter.' There are only isolated examples of disapproval and hoarding.

There is little interest in the news, and some tendency to over-simplify the war situation, the intricacies of which are beyond public interest and comprehension.

Recent statements about the extent of our defence preparations found a ready response: people are thirsting for information, and any attempt to meet their demand is soon reflected in a decline of public criticism.

Points from Regions

Lord Woolton's announcement of the new rationing restrictions was very well received, except in one Region (Birmingham). Cardiff reports that people are very sorry but more willing to sacrifice than ever; the introduction of the rationing without notice was greatly appreciated. Belfast states that the restriction is accepted as inevitable. Reading stresses the excellence of the broadcast and suggests that it should be made into a pamphlet. Cambridge feels that the hardships will not be unduly heavy and the cheerful way the news was presented made a good impression. Tunbridge Wells states that well-to-do customers are proving most difficult to shopkeepers and are demanding up to 1cwt of tea. The majority of the public, however, accept the measure cheerfully. Bristol reports that the new rationing is accepted willingly by everybody and the great majority of people are ready to put up with still more if necessary.

NOTTINGHAM (North Midland) Duff Cooper's circular letter very well received. Requests for further details of damage we do to Germany on our raids. Villages in Lincolnshire which accommodate AA guns complain because they have no shelters. Further requests for propaganda pointing out to women what life would be like under Hitler.

CARDIFF (Wales) Invasion of Ireland generally anticipated. Some decline in demand for conscription of everything and everybody. Some people are enquiring about possibility of changing paper money into silver in case of emergency.

BELFAST (Northern Ireland) Dissatisfaction that there are still 40,000 workless in Northern Ireland. Good response to recruiting drives for Home Defence battalions. Much discussion of united Ireland defence plan; if De Valera had his way, people say, all Ireland would be neutral, disarmed, and helpless. Britain must therefore either get Eire's consent for entry of British troops to prevent invasion or send in troops without consent.

MANCHESTER (North Western) People on Fylde coast nervous about invasion from Ireland. Packard refusal to make aero-engines is causing uneasiness as to whether all is well concerning our Purchasing Commission. Policy about friendly aliens is causing anxiety.

BRISTOL (South Western) The past fortnight's raids have thoroughly awakened the public in the South West. Cornwall still complains about inadequate local defences. Gloucester is greatly encouraged by the obvious reinforcement of its defences. Plymouth, which has suffered heavily, is standing up to the raids philosophically. There is, however, a good deal of anxiety at the absence of detailed casualty figures. Anti-CO feeling is again increasing, particularly in North Wiltshire.

LEEDS (North Eastern) Simplification of war and news of Britain's armed strength has improved morale, and comments on administrative muddles are rarer than they were. Complaints of lack of details of air-raid casualties are common. Possibility of invasion via Ireland much discussed.

EDINBURGH (Scotland) Small Scottish burghs are confused about the voluntary organisation of labour for defence purposes. There is doubt as to whether they or the county authorities are responsible for obstructing possible landing grounds.

NEWCASTLE (Northern) Private evacuation from Sunderland, Middlesbrough and Scarborough continues. Public confidence has considerably increased since sirens have been sounded promptly in this area for the last few days and ARP personnel have proved very efficient.

READING (Southern) The South Coast is taking its conversion into a Defence Area calmly. Bournemouth people wonder why their liberty to receive visitors is destroyed, while that of Brighton remains. Reading reports irritation with air raid wardens who unnecessarily advertise yellow warnings and worry their neighbours thereby.

BIRMINGHAM (Midland) From Coventry, Stoke, Nuneaton, and Wolverhampton, come demands that members of the former Government still in office should be removed.

CAMBRIDGE (Eastern) Towns not affected by ban on private motorists were greatly confused by announcement in two London papers yesterday that ban covered 'a large part of Norfolk, Suffolk and Essex'. Voluntary evacuation from coastal towns goes on slowly, and there are now some complaints at the cost of keeping two homes going. Ipswich, Bury St Edmunds, and other towns, witnessed aerial battles without sirens. This has led many of the population to spend their nights in Anderson shelters, and women are staying up all night to make sure that their sleeping children are taken to safety if bombs fall but no siren is heard. The need for the 'All Clear' siren after an aerial battle when no warning siren has been sounded is particularly stressed.

TUNBRIDGE WELLS (South Eastern) General satisfaction at the announcement at the size of our defence forces but much comment at appeals for voluntary labour when we still have so many unemployed. Brighton middle-class people are asking whether if they stay put they will lose all their furniture in a rush evacuation, and if so whether it would not be advisable for them to evacuate now.

LONDON

Tea rationing caused surprise but accepted as necessary; poor people wonder how to manage as usual consumption is considerably more than two ounces a week. Acton: 'Feeling very bitter about surrendering Channel Islands without resistance. People feel we may be sold out like the French.' Increase of insularity reported from several quarters. People expressing confidence in being British and having no one left to let us down. Observers worried by non-protection of bicycles left in railway cloak rooms. Demand action. Though relief is general that aliens are watched carefully and apprehended if suspicious, opinion is held that real danger lies among our own people. Some evacuated children writing and asking to be brought back because they have experienced raids. Stepney: 'Soldiers waiting for discharge often experiencing hardship as allowances are delayed. Assistance Board will not accept responsibility until final discharge is through.' Brixton: 'Works closing down; growing unemployment among builders, dockers and other workers unused to being out.' Club leader reports effect of new long hours on juveniles. 'Boys of fifteen now working twelve hours a day showing unmistakable signs of fatigue with grey faces and heavy eyes.' Hendon: 'People arriving from South East Coast – Margate, Ramsgate, etc. – and enquiring at COS offices about money. Some able to get billeting allowance although evacuation was not compulsory. People in district expressing confused ideas about the whole situation.' Although people are still grumbling at not being given more details of air raids, from several sources reports show that Air Marshal Joubert's explanation had a good effect on morale. More confidence in RAF noticed, state observers, since this talk.

WEDNESDAY 10 JULY 1940

There is little change in morale: people are generally cheerful, although in those areas which have been constantly raided there is anxiety and lassitude. There is no diminution in determination.

1. The morale of women in working-class raided areas is being lowered by lack of sleep and by the family responsibilities with which they are burdened.

2. The public is not convinced of the necessity for withholding information about air-raid damage and casualties, and disappointment has been expressed that Sir Hugh Elles devoted so little time to this matter. Districts in which damage has been done cannot understand the official phrase 'damage was slight', and particular suspicion becomes generalised.

3. Reports on the state of feeling among young people show that many have failed to identify themselves with the war, and many are consciously, as well as unconsciously, non-cooperative.

4. Many people feel a need for martial music, processions and bands, and other stimulants of righteous aggressiveness. The sight of Dominion troops in London has been heartening, but there have been many suggestions that opportunities should be found for parades and marches.

5. The Channel Islands evacuation still causes considerable disquiet. The publicity given to the evacuation has left a feeling of defeat and planlessness. Further explanations are needed.

6. A public statement is needed on the withdrawal of savings from banks.

7. A further day's observations have brought to light some complaints about tea rationing, and there appears to be evidence in certain districts that the public bought heavily during the day of the announcement.

8. Reports from those areas considered to be likely of invasion show that the population is confident (if not over-confident) and that preparations ought to be made for situation in which no invasion occurs.

Points from Regions

The siren controversy still continues in those areas subjected to air raids. Cambridge, Bristol and Cardiff report that lack of air-raid warnings is affecting public confidence. The effect of lack of sleep on the nerves of the population, although relatively slight, is becoming apparent.

NOTTINGHAM (North Midland) A group of professional men discussed with concern the serious impression created on the public mind by the accuracy of some of Hitler's forecasts. The view was expressed that some of Hitler's technique should be adopted by us in this respect. 'We shall be no worse off under Hitler' is commonly heard amongst young girls in their teens. New food rationing accepted philosophically.

CARDIFF (Wales) Evidence of preparations for defence creates state of optimism. General feeling that manual workers should be allowed extra rations of tea and butter.

BELFAST (Northern Ireland) Agitation for getting Ulster's unemployed on urgent war work continues. Parents asking for early decision as to possibility of evacuating Ulster children overseas. A number of people are disturbed by Morrison's broadcast statement on the Empire's inferiority to Germany in steel production.

MANCHESTER (North Western) Yesterday's yellow warning during the day rapidly became public property and was acted upon as if it had been a red warning.

BRISTOL (South Western) Real desire of parents in Falmouth to get their children away, although the women mean to stay by their menfolk. Communiques which announce 'a few' or 'several' casualties make the public think that the casualties are very heavy.

LEEDS (North Eastern) Civil Service still causes grumbling on account of administrative slowness. It is widely suggested that Moral Rearmament constitutes a Fifth Column on the ground that the Oxford Group Movement went to those countries where Fifth Columnists have been successful, the leader is a German and the movement is associated with the wealthy, who are potential Fifth Columnists. Absenteeism continues among miners in the Doncaster area.

EDINBURGH (Scotland) Very small working-class pockets in Glasgow still maintain that they would be 'as well off under Hitler'. Grumbles about LDV and ARP have been greatly diminished in the past fortnight. Opinion in the West of Scotland favours a forced occupation of Ireland, preferably by Dominion troops rather than British.

NEWCASTLE (Northern) Still criticism of the failure to utilise more fully the unemployed.

READING (Southern) The Lord Mayor of Portsmouth has moved from his house to live in the Guild Hall in order to encourage the 'stay put' movement. Hotels and boarding houses in Bournemouth and Southsea expect Government compensation following their inclusion in the Southern Defence Area. The reluctance of Packard to manufacture aero-engines is creating anti-American feeling. The impression spreads that the Government is not frank about air-raid casualties.

BIRMINGHAM (Midland) The Government's appeal for volunteers to work on local defences is receiving good response.

CAMBRIDGE (Eastern) Norwich took yesterday's air attack well, though the high proportion of women killed has aroused a feeling of resentment against the present siren policy; had they been sounded many might not have been caught in the streets.

TUNBRIDGE WELLS (South Eastern) Stories are circulating that the Army is underfed, although complaints appear to be directed against poor cooking and bad service rather than against the food. The public think that as sugar is difficult to get, fruit which would normally be used for jam-making should be available at low prices. Irritation at the congratulatory tone of the BBC announcement with regard to low unemployment figures, when there should be no unemployment at all. There is concern about the bridge to the Isle of Sheppey. If destroyed the island would be entirely cut off from food supplies.

LONDON

People calm everywhere in spite of suspecting that air raids are more serious than divulged officially. Tea rationing accepted as necessary sacrifice; working-class women wondering how to manage and many saying: 'My husband will not be able to drink tea as strong as brandy, and the children will have to have milk.' Office staffs are very concerned about the ration. Some leakage of information evidently in Chelsea as several grocers found themselves selling large quantities of tea on Monday. Could not understand reason until after broadcast. Mr Alexander's speech highly approved. Some movement of people into outer London from South and South East Coast. Evacuees being billeted without difficulty. Professional Women's Club considers BBC talks lacking in inspiration. Would like martial music as a change. Many people think Dominion troops should have had proper official welcome. Some foster mothers in West Country writing to parents in London that bombs are dropping all round. This causes anxiety, but parents on the whole loath to bring children back and spoil their holiday. Children evacuated to Brixham and Newton Abbot write home commiserating with parents for having so many raid alarms in London. Red Ensign Club: 'Twenty-nine Estonian seamen just brought in after ship blown up. Grateful for kindness. No feeling against them or other foreign seamen noticed in Club'. Chelsea: 400 Polish refugees just arrived from France, mostly women, adding to several hundred Dutch and Belgian refugees in neighbourhood.

Refugees who have been in Chelsea for some time have very low morale and long to return to their countries. Men and women are separated and only one per cent have been given work. Except for wealthier workers, local people suspicious and unfriendly towards them. No Civil Defence arrangements in being and possibility that they may panic in air raids. Some expression of suspicion in Chelsea that Sir John Anderson has Fascist sympathies and is protecting or releasing Fascists who have been detained. Deptford: 'People still worrying that they have had no news for many weeks of menfolk in Army. Delays of thirteen weeks to six months in some cases in receipt of Old Age and Widows Pensions, causing serious hardships.' Twickenham: 'People still dissatisfied with arrangements for salvage; consider there is slackness in other matters including rendering large playing fields useless for landing grounds.'

THURSDAY 11 JULY 1940

The public is cheerful and there is little change in morale. There is evidence, however, that cheerfulness is superficial: people are disinterested in the general war situation and its international implications, and Hitler's failure to arrive is promoting an apprehensive feeling that 'he must have something very unpleasant in store for us.' Determination to challenge and meet this surprise is widespread, and confidence in the Navy is at a high level. 'The Navy will win the war for us in the end.'

Air raids continue to be taken calmly. In heavily raided areas there is a demand for further reprisals, and aggressive RAF action is strongly applauded. Official policy about the publication of air-raid casualties and damage is not understood and widely resented. Local information about casualties, which are not reflected in official bulletins, has brought suspicion on other official communiques, and on the honesty of official news as a whole.

There is considerable dissatisfaction that the evacuation of children to the Dominions is receiving setbacks. The public is confused and alarmed at this apparent change of policy without detailed explanation.

Comments on the statement that no civilians are to be included in Honours Lists have shown some resentment, and provide indications that although civilians do not necessarily want rewards, they feel themselves to be, or about

to be, in the front line of battle. Honours are a recognition of this fact.
There are other signs that the relationship between the civilian and the
military needs watching.

Points from Regions

NOTTINGHAM (North Midland) Complaints that Nottinghamshire
villages are inadequately protected against bombs. Evacuated children
are in Lowdham, where schools are without shelters. Support in
rural areas for compulsory measures for obstructions on possible
landing grounds. Small response to Regional Commissioner's appeal.
Criticism of inadequate passenger transport facilities in rush hour.

CARDIFF (Wales) Public still uneasy about air-raid warnings. Many
calls for an entirely different 'All Clear' signal. Uneasiness in North
Wales concerning the number of cyclists, presumably on holiday,
with only an Identity Card without photograph as a check. Raid and
casualty rumours still prevalent.

MANCHESTER (North Western) RAF feats cause much satisfaction.
Banning of Fascists approved, but considered overdue. Criticism of
tea rationing; cafes and restaurants provide means of evasion for
those who can pay. Aluminium appeal has caught public fancy, but
people ask why shops are still selling these goods. Butler's broadcast
good, but delivery too 'Foreign Office.'

BRISTOL (South Western) Continued raids on South West Coast
accepted philosophically. Criticism in South Devon and Cornwall that
defences are not as good as they might be. Concern from poorer quarters of raided towns over restoration of damaged property. Government
policy 'in due course' not clear. Torquay complains that some people
appear to be taking no part in war effort and asks for compulsory
service. Also complaints of the inefficiency of the warning system.

LEEDS (North Eastern) Big air battle widely discussed. Irritation
that papers give too much German propaganda from American
sources. Dissatisfaction that road barricades round Doncaster are

made of old cars etc., which could be used as scrap. The barricades are thought to be of little use. Rationing accepted without complaint.

NEWCASTLE (Northern) Possibility of invasion of Ireland widely discussed. Opinion expressed that IRA would give active support to Germany. Prevalent opinion in many centres that time is ripe to abandon voluntary system altogether. People anxiously awaiting a lead. New rationing accepted calmly as part of the war effort.

READING (Southern) Aluminium appeal goes well. Newport Employment Exchange reports reluctance of farm workers to be associated with COs. Suspicion that we are not frank about air-raid casualties linked with continued announcements that German raids here do minimum damage. Demand for fuller news about Mediterranean and Africa.

CAMBRIDGE (Eastern) Siren controversy fully resumed. Lowestoft Town Council in favour of greater freedom, as also the rural communities. Reported that some women reluctant to allow their husbands to go to work so long as present warning system remains.

TUNBRIDGE WELLS (South Eastern) Growing confidence in ability of RAF to defend the country. Rumours of unnecessarily high wages being paid to youths on defence work by contractors.

BIRMINGHAM (Midland) Perturbation that bombs drop during yellow warnings. Many people in recently bombed areas spend early hours of the night in shelters. Warwick reports concern that the removal of place names is not sufficiently thorough. Controversy at Coventry over retention of COs in municipal services.

BELFAST (Northern Ireland) RAF successes yesterday strengthened confidence. Satisfaction at banning British Union. IRA activities cause strong feeling against anything savouring of Fifth Column.

EDINBURGH (Scotland) Anxiety about Ireland and disbelief in ability to defend itself against invasion. Prevalence of drunkenness in Glasgow at weekends causes comment. Some scepticism as to reported ineffectiveness of German raids. Suppression of British Union welcomed. Absence of news of shipping losses adversely commented on in Glasgow circles which know such losses have occurred.

LONDON

People disturbed to find aluminium still sold in shops when they go to buy enamel to replace pots and pans given to the Government. This reported from Mill Hill, Victoria, and Kensington. Discontent expressed at differences between soldiers' allowances and high pay of men in some reserved occupations; equality of sacrifice asked for. Children still returning from raided areas. Hoxton reports some brought home from South Wales after sending letters to parents saying they were nervous from so many warnings. 'These returned children look well,' states observer, 'and show no sign of nerves'. Twenty-seven children from same school returned in last five days from Radstock. Many people fear wholesale coming back to London before long. Stepney: 'owing to growing unemployment in district there is considerable depression. Typical remarks are: "fares going up, food going up, no work and no money coming in. It's a nice world!"' Announcements in press that Government may not be able to send children overseas causing anxiety and annoyance. Dissatisfaction at red tape and trouble over getting all particulars finished to send children away. Suspicion voiced that publicity has been given to scheme for ulterior motives. This may have bad effect on morale among disappointed middle and upper classes and still more among working classes who think that only rich children have got away early. Working class hardly aware of existence of New British Broadcasting Station, but roughly 10% of middle class with powerful sets occasionally listen from curiosity. 'Haw-Haw listening has gone down since news became very serious,' state many observers in different districts. Some women who listen remark: 'we get our news first from German stations as long as Germany is winning the war.' Harrow: 'lack of rifles among local LDV causing disquiet and lack of confidence; factories still not armed'. Hammersmith: 'friction over local Civil Defence personnel'. Willesden: 'proposed Government scheme to set up small creches has induced people to start them voluntarily. Women anxious their small children should be cared for while they are at work.' Poplar:

'children having to go long distances to school because own schools are closed. Many parents refusing to let them go so far afield. Responsible people anxious that law of compulsory education should in this manner be allowed to slide.'

FRIDAY 12 JULY 1940

There is little change in morale. Cheerfulness continues. There is increasing confidence in the RAF and in Civilian Defence measures.

Air raids were taken calmly although reports from certain districts show that after raids there is some measure of civilian evacuation. The siren controversy continues strongly in certain districts. There is public criticism of the withholding of detailed casualty lists.

The publicity given to brick and concrete domestic shelters has produced misunderstanding and criticism among Local Authorities, because shortage of labour and materials is well known.

The rationing of tea is being criticised in working-class districts.

The appeal for domestic aluminium, after meeting with an enthusiastic response, is now being criticised because of the stores of aluminium freely on sale in shops.

Points from Regions

Desire for removal of appeasement members of Cabinet reported from Godalming, Middlesbrough, Wadebridge, Newquay, Lincoln and Cambridge; report from Northampton states that feeling is dying down. Duff Cooper's broadcast generally well received, but opinion expressed in Manchester that it was 'too ineffectual' to do us good in the United States.

NOTTINGHAM (North Midland) Conduct of public in shelters at Grimsby admirable. Recent official warnings about imminent invasion said to have been overdone. Impatience reported of men in middle twenties who have not been called up. Satisfaction expressed in Grimsby at Duff Cooper's second letter.

CARDIFF (Wales) Will to win increased by experience of air raids. Many optimistic that Russia will be helpful to us in her own time. Rumours of result of air raids still rife.

MANCHESTER (North Western) RAF successes a tonic. First enthusiasm of aluminium damped by large stocks of articles for sale. Adverse comment on railway conditions for troops.

BRISTOL (South Western) People generally in good heart. A complaint from Wiltshire that tea rationing affects the cup made after an air raid. Preparations for defence have heartening effect. Morale in Falmouth low and many people have left recently.

LEEDS (North Eastern) Air raids have improved morale. Criticism: 'Why has Government not controlled aluminium producers more successfully?'

READING (Southern) Raid on southern city has entirely failed to shake morale. Civil Defence functioned well.

BIRMINGHAM (Midland) Disquiet that isolated raiding planes have dropped bombs although there had not been even the yellow warning. Plea from Coventry that notification of yellow warning be sent to schools to get the children into shelters. Wolverhampton reports some dissatisfaction about tea ration.

CAMBRIDGE (Eastern) Growth of feeling that time is ripe for Britain to take aggressive action. Surprise in Norwich at air-raid warnings when bombs have not fallen, after appreciating the restricted siren policy at night time. Approval of Prime Minister's appeal to Civil Service.

TUNBRIDGE WELLS (South Eastern) Fear that Ireland may be another Norway, only with more serious consequences. Increasing demands for military bands. Reported from Canterbury that soldiers are becoming restive because of curtailment of leave facilities.

NEWCASTLE (Northern) Noticeable absence of grumbling. Conduct of public in air raids steadily improving. Criticism exists with regard to provision of shelters. Reports from Blaydon and Stanley areas of undercurrent of dissatisfaction amongst miners, on grounds that unemployment amongst miners and closing of pits should not be tolerated.

BELFAST (Northern Ireland) Leading advocates of united defence plan now admit that Eire neutral is an insuperable obstacle. Craigavon's statement is regarded as clearing the air. Continued demand for scheme to get unemployed into work.

EDINBURGH (Scotland) Observers report that people in Glasgow are pessimistic though not defeatist. In Scotstoun and other places workers are being paid off whilst systematic overtime is still worked. In some places people are discounting the possibility of invasion. Reported that holiday-makers are apprehensive that the powers of police and LDV might be used against them.

LONDON

General morale high; people cheerful and optimistic on the whole. London considered by many too well protected to be raided; others think this complacency dangerous. Exaggeration of damage done by bombers in country districts of which details are sent in letters and passed on from person to person. Suburban districts such as Southgate reported uninterested in national issues. Anxiety expressed over Ireland. Complaints received that BBC is stressing events of last war: 'we are inclined to rest on our laurels too much'. Intelligent observer considers isolated cases of defeatism most dangerous, e.g. people who consistently believe bad news and mistrust good news have depressing effect and no argument will move them. If they were made to look ridiculous, suggests observer, they might be cured. Positive ideas and plans for post-war world asked for by thinking middle class. Tea rationing beginning to affect people who find two ounces will not last a week. Elderly women asking for three ounces as they need the stimulation of tea several times a day. Duff Cooper's speech considered excellent by many people; but some afraid they will be closely watched and unable to talk at all. Areas taking in South and South East Coast refugees have adequate preparations for them. Woolwich factory reports wireless and gramophone music have greatly increased workers' cheerfulness: 'staff working busily and happily in spite of long hours and do not seem unduly tired. This is proved by freedom from serious accidents'. Marylebone: 'rumour among women that sons are being asked to volunteer as parachutists in case of invasion; mothers strongly advise them not to as they think it is "absolute butchery"'. Some feeling among poorer people who buy from small local shops that prices are not strictly controlled, is reported in West End. Downham: 'parents of evacuated children cannot see them now as they are too far away; suggest that mayor or other important person in borough should visit children and bring back news'. Richmond: 'strong resentment among parents of four hundred children registered for Dominions. Opinions held: "the Government should not have publicised scheme until sure of children going; if ships can take interned aliens, surely it is more important to take children."' More complaints from several districts that people are buying aluminium in shops for themselves. Shepherd's Bush: 'one thousand French convalescent soldiers in White City; need news, amusements and amenities'.

SATURDAY 13 JULY 1940

There is little change in morale: there is an optimistic temper. People frequently say that RAF successes and aggressive air action over Germany make them feel confident and cheerful.

In some Regions there is evidence of relaxation: 'Down here we are resting on our oars.' In some cases this lull appears to promote an increase of criticism of the Government. There are also signs that the strain of the past few weeks is having an effect on continuous effort.

News from abroad continues to arouse little interest. Even the French situation is not a strong topic of conversation. There is a growing feeling of 'isolationism'.

Although the public response to the appeal for aluminium has been good, there are still criticisms of the Government's failure to use its compulsory powers.

Points from Regions

In spite of explanations, criticism continues that aluminium articles are still on sale. It is pointed out from Reading that this situation suggests inadequate Government planning, and this mistrust tends to affect other Government schemes. Dissatisfaction is widely expressed at the postponement of the overseas evacuation scheme. Comment is 'occasionally heard' in Newcastle that now rich children have been safely evacuated the scheme is dropped when it comes to the turn of the poor. Educated circles in Reading suggest that without careful explanations the United States may be annoyed after their many offers of hospitality.

NOTTINGHAM (North Midland) Considerable exasperation over Eire's attitude. It is felt that the press pays too little attention to the area in British hands throughout the world, as compared with area conquered by Germany on Continent. Nottingham reports cases of friendly aliens, left free by tribunals, who have been victimized by fellow employees.

CARDIFF (Wales) General attitude of crowds in shelters during daylight warnings cheerful and optimistic. Civil Defence services in many districts commended. Disappointment that Italian Navy still eludes ours. Hooper's and Sinclair's broadcasts well received.

MANCHESTER (North Western) Optimism grows as time passes and invasion does not occur.

BRISTOL (South Western) Postponement of invasion has done much to relieve anxiety. Impression common that our recent activities 'have given Hitler something to think about'. Small minority still wonder if conditions under Hitler would be worse. Exciting nature of air battles has led to slackening of precaution in coastal regions. Bath complains that the day after the recent appeal for defence work volunteers, Post Office officials were ill-informed of the scheme. Newquay refers to its 'ghastly' state of unpreparedness, as do other towns. Strengthening of defences in Penzance has had heartening effect.

LEEDS (North Eastern) Hull standing up well to daily raids and disturbed nights. Barnsley reports healthy attitude to the war. Committee of men and management set up in Doncaster to stop absenteeism among young miners. Dissatisfaction at inadequate watch on roads near coastal zone. Complaints of wasteful work, such as road mending, still in progress.

NEWCASTLE (Northern) Durham reports men listening more frequently to Haw-Haw to secure details of raids on England. In some quarters people show less inclination to obey air-raid alarms and only get out of bed on hearing planes or gun fire. Satisfaction at increased supplies for LDV. Anti-Chamberlain comment shows signs of increase.

READING (Southern) Comparative lull has brought increase in criticism of Government. Criticism that appeals for LDVs and aluminium were badly presented.

BIRMINGHAM (Midland) Dissatisfaction from Stafford and Sutton Coldfield about equipment and control of LDV. Coventry reports that evacuees from coastal areas are too loose-tongued about incidents in their areas. Reported that air-raid wardens too frequently pass on yellow warnings to the public.

CAMBRIDGE (Eastern) Evidence that people are accommodating themselves well to new restrictions, although the elderly undoubtedly feel the strain of the situation. Slight apprehension at news of imposition of curfew in certain northern coastal areas. Spirit of younger people remains keen. Evidence of conscious reticence in matters likely to help enemy. Packard's agreement to produce aeroengines created satisfaction.

TUNBRIDGE WELLS (South Eastern) After expecting blitzkrieg for eleven days Kent and Sussex people are beginning to relax, though many realise Hitler wants to create this attitude. Efforts to arouse sense of responsibility in men drafted to Sheerness for defence work has met with limited success, and removal from their families affects their outlook. Hooper's talk well received in Tunbridge Wells.

BELFAST (Northern Ireland) Success of RAF offensive attacks thought to cause Hitler's hesitation to invade Britain. Pétain's activities viewed with mild contempt. Silent Column campaign approved but suggestion to place 'chatter boxes' in clubs and hotels regarded as childish. Country folk visiting Belfast circulate stories of military occupation of farms. Much interest aroused in scheme to give Civil Defence lectures in cinemas.

EDINBURGH (Scotland) Air raid which caused civilian casualties in Greenock has not adversely affected morale. Glasgow observers stress difficulty of taking interest in war as there has been no evidence of military activity in the city since the outbreak. Complaints that broadcasts describing defence preparations make no mention of Scotland. Glasgow shopkeepers who are opening their shops on Fair Monday complain that those in nearby towns do not propose to do so. Bombed towns still produce usual rumours.

LONDON

Morale remains the same; people growing less apprehensive of invasion, but determined as ever to win the war. Complaints that national appeals are made before machinery exists to deal with them. This irritates people and has been the case with appeals for women's work; motor mechanics for aeroplane work; need for aluminium and now for smaller matters such as buying and storing of coke and acquiring of stirrup pumps – neither of the latter available to enquirers. Some cases of hardship reported among people evacuated to London from coastal areas: removers charging double normal rate, while people left in Defence Areas afraid to wait until ordered to move with one suitcase as they cannot afford new furniture. French soldiers and sailors appearing in West End public houses; observers report new spirit of comradeship between them and British springing up and open expression of feeling that we are all fighting now for democracy and know who our enemies really are. Society doctor reports many wealthy patients asking for poison prescriptions to take if Germans come. Irritation about rationing among well-to-do circles shows itself in luxury restaurants such as Harrods. Customers walk out saying they will go elsewhere to get more generous portions of sugar. Some expression of opinion in middle-class intellectual circles that it is hypocritical to talk about fighting Naziism and treat refugees harshly. Croydon: 'Servicemen complaining they must pay full postal rates in England, whereas in France their postage was free. Another grievance is that cigarettes given free in France are not given in England.' Honor Oak Estate: observer reporting lack of neighbourliness now gratified to find WVS starting housewives' service and coordinating people's activities; this improving morale greatly. More appreciation of Duff Cooper's speech and reports that anti-rumour campaign already having effect; people in buses and other public places discouraging gossip.

MONDAY 15 JULY TO SATURDAY 20 JULY 1940

While the RAF carried out daylight raids on the barges the Germans were assembling in Belgium and Holland for a prospective invasion, the Luftwaffe launched a series of massed attacks on coastal shipping. On 14 July an air battle over the straits of Dover was witnessed by the BBC's Charles Gardner, who recorded a live commentary in the style of a sports reporter at the climax of an exciting game ('Oh boy – I've never seen anything so good as this'). Broadcast on the nine o' clock news, his report received a mixed reception. On the basis of 300 interviews in London, Home Intelligence concluded that 'a considerable majority spoke enthusiastically of the broadcast', but women in particular reacted against the treatment of war as a game and 'his callous Oxford accent made it worse.'

A broadcast by Churchill that same evening won 'universal approval', but the government in general was the subject of many complaints. Discontent over siren policy was vocal and persistent, and, as in previous weeks, Home Intelligence reported an abiding lack of trust in official news sources and strong criticism of the government's refusal to allow the press to publish details of the location of air raids or the numbers killed. At a time when a number of wealthy people, including Duff Cooper, were privately arranging to send their children overseas, the postponement of plans for a state-assisted scheme to evacuate children to the Dominions gave rise to 'sharp recrimination against the rich'. There was much resentment too of the 'Silent Column' campaign. Coinciding with a wave of prosecutions of members of the public for spreading 'alarm and despondency' by word of mouth, it looked ominously like a deliberate attack on free speech. 'Many people think that grumbling is in the British tradition,' Home Intelligence warned. Popular sympathy was aroused by the case of a 74-year-old Bristol man who was sent to prison for a week for telling a neighbour that he had it on the authority of a high official in freemasonry that the swastika would be flying over the House of Commons in a month's time.

Among the more politically conscious concern for civil liberty was intensified by the introduction of government legislation which provided for special courts to exercise summary jurisdiction over civilians in 'war zones' in the event of an invasion. The public, Home Intelligence reported, was in the main confused or indifferent, but a working man on a tram – a successor, perhaps, to 'the man on the Clapham omnibus' – remarked: 'If we are not shot by the Germans we are evidently going to be shot by our own people.' These war-zone courts were of course never put into practice. The government, meanwhile, acted to assuage concerns over civil liberty. Sir John Anderson stepped in to remit many of the fines and sentences imposed on those convicted of spreading alarm and despondency, and Churchill himself called a halt to the 'Silent Column' campaign. Speaking in the House of Commons on 23 July he admitted that it had been a mistake and 'has therefore passed into what is called, in the United States, innocuous desuetude'.

On 18 July the Prime Minister announced the closure for a period of three months of the Burma Road, the main supply route for the forces of nationalist China in the war against the invading Japanese. The decision, taken in response to Japanese demands, was criticised in political circles as an act of appeasement akin to Munich. Another discouraging if minor episode was the capture by the Italians of Moyale, a British outpost on the frontier between Kenya and Abyssinia.

MONDAY 15 JULY 1940

There is little change in morale: people are cheerful. Reports show that there is some slackening in the intensification of effort, and that people are beginning to think that 'Hitler will not come after all'.

Air raids continue to be taken without panic. A careful investigation in a raided area showed:

(a) There is still uncertainty about siren policy.

(b) The bringing down of raiders in the area has a psychological effect immensely greater than the military advantage gained.

(c) Most people have become 'shelter conscious' and in the case of many women this feeling is in danger of being exaggerated.

(d) As yet there is little anger against the German raiders, especially among women. Casualties are regarded fatalistically and damage accepted philosophically.

(e) Most working-class women are convinced that children are as safe in vulnerable areas as anywhere else.

A small survey of reaction to Charles Gardner's broadcast description of the Channel air battle (London, 300 interviews) showed that nearly 50% heard the broadcast, and that many who had not listened to it had heard about it. A considerable majority spoke enthusiastically of the broadcast. Of those who did not like it many were women whose comments showed that they did not think war was a game. 'A battle isn't a Boat Race'. 'His callous Oxford accent made it worse.' 'It might have been a football match: I don't like football commentaries.' It is evident, however, that the broadcast created a high degree of interest. Highly emotional arguments were put forward on both sides and the broadcast is a topic of conversation today.

Points from Regions

Reports from all Regions agree that the Premier's speech last night won universal approval, and the assurance that there will be no peace discussion was welcome and heartening. A typical comment from Bristol is 'that's the sort of thing we want and he's the fellow we can follow'. Reference to 1942 elicits much comment. Reading RIO reports more spontaneous messages of commendation than after any other important speech.

CARDIFF (Wales) The public in the south of the Region is acclimatised to warnings and raids, but in the north concern is felt about insufficiency of public refuges and AA defences. Still many complaints that the 'All Clear' too closely resembles the warning signal. Previous peace movement enthusiasts are beginning to show pugnacity under the stress of bombing. Some anxiety expressed whether we are not broadcasting too much information to the enemy, e.g. how to counteract invasion.

MANCHESTER (North Western) Public is beginning to wonder what is happening in North Africa and strategic retreats and the apologetic air of some of our statements causes disquiet. Many people wonder whether it is unpatriotic to take holidays.

BRISTOL (South Western) Marksmanship of Bristol AA batteries thought to be poor. More people receiving news of air-raid damage with the detachment they previously showed to road fatalities. Anxiety in Devon and Cornwall has been partly allayed by the obvious speed-up of defence. Suggestions persist that railway officials are a source of rumour.

LEEDS (North Eastern) Determination still strong. Usual complaints received against unnecessary motoring, building, etc.

NEWCASTLE (Northern) The experience of air raids seems to have given people steadiness and there has been a lessening of anxiety during the past week. Satisfaction is expressed at the steps taken to counter rumour-mongering. Many people are still puzzled that aluminium articles should continue to be on sale after the recent appeal.

READING (Southern) Home Defence measures on the South Coast are welcome despite the restrictions they involve. Disquiet is caused by the fact that political leaders should ask the country to stand fast against invasion, and yet evacuate their children in spite of the example of the King and Queen.

CAMBRIDGE (Eastern) The air-raid siren policy is not discussed with same intensity as during the past few days, but there is a tendency to attribute the frequent sounding of sirens at night at Norwich as a mild attempt by the Fighter Command to 'get their own back on the population for complaining of the absence of sirens'.

TUNBRIDGE WELLS (South Eastern) Criticism constantly received of the wording of official statements. An announcement that the Germans have made a statement 'which was a lie' would be better understood than 'which was entirely disproved.'

Evacuation from Chatham has affected many tradesmen.

BIRMINGHAM (Midland) Recent bombing attacks on Germany, and British fighters chasing raiders away successfully is a tonic to people who have experienced raiding planes during the past fortnight. Leamington urges that motor cyclists be incorporated in local defence.

BELFAST (Northern Ireland) Intense indignation at IRA outrage which destroyed Ministry of Food's stores. Some dissatisfaction over butter and margarine rationing among artisans' wives. Recruiting campaign for Home Defence battalion is being intensified.

EDINBURGH (Scotland) Failure to sound siren in Aberdeen during Friday's air raids has aroused intense feeling, and the Chief Constable who is in charge of Civil Defence is being booed in the streets. There is evidence, however, that opinion is almost equally divided between support of, and opposition to, the no-siren policy. There is a strong expectation of intensified air raids in the near future. Adverse comments that Duff Cooper has evacuated his son to America. Many thousands of new ration books have not yet been issued and in some places shopkeepers are taking the risk of supplying housewives for whom they can vouch without ration books.

LONDON

Churchill's talk much appreciated. Reports today show people cheerful and confident in consequence. Priestley's talk liked by majority. Chelsea: 'widespread indignation that rich people have gone to America with children while Government scheme has been postponed; great satisfaction expressed that Princesses have not been sent'. Some disapproval at wealthy people riding in cars on Sundays; waste of petrol grumbled at. Observers at yesterday's march of French volunteers remarked that there should have been more pageantry and a band to encourage the Frenchmen; great friendliness shown by English crowd and some cheering. More complaints from soldiers at cost of tobacco and cigarettes in England after getting them free in France. Watford: 'aliens arriving in district after leaving Defence Area; most are unemployed and English residents are inclined to be suspicious of them.' Expression of feeling among intelligent people that there should be greater discipline everywhere and that severe measures would be accepted as a relief. Albert Docks: some thousands of unemployed dock workers in district as port is half closed. Men classed as being in reserved occupation and cannot get other local work. Statement asked for as to whether these dockers will be needed in Port of London or should apply for work elsewhere. Bethnal Green: 'few complaints about tea rationing but extravagance of some people brought to light; e.g. one family of three using quarter of pound a day. Real hardship where different members of family work on shifts as fresh pots of tea must be brewed for meals at different times.' Office workers providing own tea complain they will be hard hit. Walham Green: 'two hundred women receiving unemployment pay between 11.00 and 11.30 a.m. one day last week'. Large number of women recently thrown out of work in neighbourhood. Much criticism of Government heard during this time by women, and references to Bevin's recent appeal. Typical remarks from poorer women:

'the Germans find plenty of work for their women' and 'our Government don't trouble about unemployment'.

TUESDAY 16 JULY 1940

There is little change in morale.

1. Further comments on Gardner's broadcast confirm yesterday's impression that the majority who listened approved of this presentation. There are protests from women and local press correspondents on the subject.

2. Evidence suggests that, although the siren controversy continues acutely, the public in raided areas is becoming acclimatised to air raids. Damage is accepted philosophically. Absence of detailed information is resented, and is one of the causes of rumour. On the other hand many people fear that the mention of localities, except in the vaguest terms, would endanger evacuated children.

3. There is increasing confidence in Civil Defence services, the RAF and the Navy.

4. Prosecutions for 'defeatist' talk are beginning to be a topic of conversation. Many people think that grumbling is in the British tradition, and there is nervousness at the way the Act may be interpreted.

5. The internment of aliens is still causing dismay in certain circles, and rumours circulate that all aliens will be evacuated, without notice, to the Dominions. There is distress and bitterness among the friends and relatives of interned aliens. At the same time it should be understood that internment of aliens has popular support.

6. There is great disappointment at the postponement of the plan for evacuating children to the Dominions. There was initial resistance among the public to sending children abroad; vigorous publicity overcame that resistance, and the results of a statistical survey showed that the parents of approximately 1,000,000 children were prepared for them to go. The effect of a reversal of policy has promoted sharp recrimination against the rich, whose children were enabled to sail. But a kindly attitude is brought to light: 'Rich children won't miss their parents so much – they're accustomed to travelling.' The psychological effect of the scheme and its publicity has been bad.

7. There is evidence that the 'Silent Column' campaign, although receiving public response, is not having a desirable psychological effect. Social workers and observers report increasing suspicion and unneighbourliness.

8. Anti-Chamberlain feeling continues to grow.

Points from Regions

Reports continue to confirm the widespread approval of the Premier's speech on Sunday night.

NOTTINGHAM (North Midland) Report from Grimsby that rumours of compulsory evacuation from towns on South and East Coast cause apprehension to residents.

Absence of definite news concerning air-raid casualties is generating gossip. Doubts are widely expressed as to whether Air Ministry bulletins give the truth and the whole truth. A Grimsby businessman has had 700 copies of Duff Cooper's 'Letter' made and circulated. Several requests for New British Broadcasting Station to be jammed received from Leicester.

CARDIFF (Wales) Great cleavage of opinion prevails regarding siren warnings. Groups for working stirrup-pumps, etc., increasing, with a consequent growth of confidence. The rise in wages is affecting institutions, hospitals, etc., which cannot afford to compete for domestic staff.

MANCHESTER (North Western) Prosecutions for careless talk are causing some anxiety, and it is suggested that there is no outlet for healthy grumbling. People are asking if there is something of importance they do not know about the Moyale situation. Friendly treatment of French soldiers causes some jealousy amongst British troops who are under active service conditions.

BRISTOL (South Western) Reports from Falmouth say that people are beginning to realise that they have to put up with raids and tension is eased. Dorset reports some uneasiness that there may be compulsory evacuation in the coastal regions. Swanage complains of lack of public shelters. Exeter citizens are demanding the camouflage of petrol storage tanks following a reported German claim that these had been damaged. Cornwall concerned that additional filters for civilian respirators have not been fitted.

LEEDS (North Eastern) Confidence increasing in LDV following further issues of rifles. One report states that Government's refusal to give enough facts makes people think there is something in the background it dares not reveal, and in this way it is responsible for spreading speculative talk. Some uneasiness at the news of fires at three paper mills sharing a Government contract for war material. Workers at these factories are eager for a military guard or rifles for their own use.

NEWCASTLE (Northern) Many comments received on the extent to which yellow warnings become known to the civilian population. Rural areas complain about Ministry of Supply's delay in stating price to be paid for last wool clip, and delay in payment.

READING (Southern) Warnings and air raids are losing some of their terror, and in the areas affected population is becoming accustomed to take shelter rapidly and calmly. Many believe that high losses inflicted on the enemy by RAF may cause Hitler to pause. Aluminium appeal still causes confusion. Prospect of increased taxation of small incomes causes anxiety.

BIRMINGHAM (Midland) Public beginning to wonder whether Hitler will not adopt a policy of blockade rather than of sudden attack. Walsall, Wednesbury and Worcester Town Councils have decided to dismiss CO employees.

CAMBRIDGE (Eastern) Suggested that the announcement by radio or press of Hitler's programme in relation to dates tends to impress women, in particular, with the inevitability of Hitler's successes. Evacuation from the coast line continues, but the public is confused between the 'stay put' injunction to the South Coast and the 'please leave' injunction to the East Coast.

TUNBRIDGE WELLS (South Eastern) Confusion over evacuation continues, with demand for more explicit instructions. Anti-gossip campaign and heavy penalties imposed on rumour-mongers is having effect.

BELFAST (Northern Ireland) Speculation about delayed invasion. Unofficial announcement that Purchase Tax is to be confined to luxuries gives satisfaction to artisan population.

EDINBURGH (Scotland) Renewal of mild complaint about our supposed inactivity in Africa and the Mediterranean. Official and press presentation of Moyale withdrawal as either insignificant or masterly receives hostile criticism.

LONDON

Feeling of confidence increasing, largely due to fact that nothing serious has happened yet. Some people thinking tide has turned and beginning to grow complacent. 'Hitler daren't come to London' is typical working-class comment expressing this view. Reference in Churchill's speech to defending every street in London has drawn comment: 'we shall not be sold out as the French were by their Government.' Dismay expressed by relatives and friends at rumours that interned aliens will be sent to Canada without appeal or second tribunal. Intellectual circles uneasy at arbitrary treatment of refugees; e.g. several Italians who lived for years in England taken on *Arandora Star* without trial; remaining Italians bitter at apparent injustice. Police action seems on whole to have been as considerate as possible; Italian families helping each other. Contact in Chelsea writes: 'extreme right-wing opinion still considers Russia more dangerous enemy than Germany; Franco considered hero in spite of German and Italian sympathies as he saved Spain from Communism.' Some anti-Semitism discovered in different districts which might become aggressive on provocation. More expressions of irritation at absence of casualty figures and opinion that exaggerated numbers will fly round as rumour if details of raids are not given. Greenwich: 'more publicity should be given to offer of American Seamen's Union to man boat without wages to take children to US. Statement asked for that Government will stay here and not go overseas; this feeling linked with fact that upper-class children have arrived in America. Antagonistic sentiment rising against rich people in consequence.' Harrow: 'disappointment that there is no war work for women in spite of appeals. Growing unemployment among luxury-trade West End workers; majority unprepared to move to other districts for work.' Complaints that newspaper vendors are chalking up defeatist placards in West End. Manager of branch of Big Five Bank considers wrong impression given by newspaper reports that people leaving Channel Islands were refused money at banks. Fears publication of such statements might cause mistrust of security of banks. Confusion over billeting reported in districts taking evacuated people from coastal areas; householders afraid they will have penniless people on their hands. Complaints from several quarters that tea rationing is particularly hard on old age pensioners.

WEDNESDAY 17 JULY 1940

Morale is high: people are cheerful but critical.

1. Invasion date *(Friday). This prediction largely spread by means of prominent press publicity is a dominant topic of conversation. Evidence shows that many people are seriously alarmed (evidence that domestic and commercial plans have been changed). Many messages have come from those holding responsible positions protesting against the publicity given to the statement. The legend of Hitler's 'invincibility' is a continuous factor in popular psychology.*

2. Prosecutions for 'defeatist talk' widely criticised. Informed circles are nervous at the way in which the Act may be interpreted: working-class people feel suspicious and afraid. 'Oh I don't know. Best to pass no opinion these days. You might get hung'. 'We are fighting for freedom but losing what freedom we've got'. 'I'm afraid to open my mouth'.

The case of the 'poor old man of 74' prosecuted for saying he thought Hitler would win is the subject of much comment: it is frequently called 'a miscarriage of justice', 'what we're all in for'. The clerical campanologist has also aroused much ill-informed sympathy.

3. The public at large is not much concerned by the problem of press censorship.

4. The Ministry's 'Silent Column' campaign is being criticised. 'It is spreading suspicion and unhappiness'. 'If we can't talk what can we do?' 'It's all very well for them to say "Don't talk". I'd like to see them trying it themselves'. 'Look at the newspapers. Why don't they tell them to shut up?' 'Stifling criticism. That's what it is.'

There is no doubt that there is an effort being made to obey instructions not to talk and the effect of this effort is bringing depression and suspicion. This is not as yet a widespread result but the prognosis is not good.

5. The public has not yet reacted strongly to news about the new War Zone Emergency Courts. Preliminary reports, however, show that criticism is much stronger in London and the East than in the Midlands and West, where it is clear people do not consider themselves candidates for the courts. There is some significance in this verbatim: 'It's just like DORA in the last war – once you've got it you can't get rid of it. They always say it's an emergency'. Other people approve the new machinery without enthusiasm.

A detailed report will be submitted tomorrow.

6. There is a good deal of criticism that salvage schemes are not being conducted with sufficient enterprise and energy.

7. Two wishful thinking rumours:

    (i)   that Oswald Mosley is to be sent to Canada.
    (ii) that some of the dud bombs dropped in this country were found to contain sand with messages of greeting from Czechoslovakia.

There will be no report on Friday, 19 July.

Points from Regions

NOTTINGHAM (North Midland) Growing criticism of lack of details published about air-raid casualties. General agreement that air-raid warnings should not be sounded for lone raiders. Widespread view that many Local Authorities are not providing facilities for collecting and separating waste. Reports that teachers are concerned about instructions to keep children in school and not to transfer them to shelters if bombs are dropping near.

CARDIFF (Wales) Common belief that fewer air raids during last two days represents lull before the storm. A little trouble has been caused in industry on account of inadequacy of warnings of air raids in which casualties have occurred. Dissatisfaction in Pwllheli because local aerodrome was bombed the day assurances were given in the House that all aerodromes were well defended.

MANCHESTER (North Western) Sentences inflicted for gloom or despondency talk affect ordinary folk who are becoming afraid to open their mouths.

BRISTOL (South Western) Reports say that if present policy of with-holding air-raid details continues, all news will be regarded with mistrust. The effect of extra sleep due to the lull in air activity is noticeable. Weston-super-Mare complains of lack of shelters. Following vague reports that 'a south coast town' has been bombed, billeting officers state that parents are travelling to Weston to find out for themselves whether it is safe for their children.

NEWCASTLE (Northern) Some parents are perturbed that the date of evacuation of children from places mentioned by name by BBC tells the enemy when stations will be exceptionally crowded. Despite public denials rumours suggest that certain Ministers favour a stale-mate peace arrangement now under consideration. Reports received of discontent of soldiers through boredom.

LEEDS (North Eastern) Criticism of authority still common and one observer reports that 'many people think that those at the top don't believe in the freedom they talk about.' Suggested that anti-rumour campaign, now considered successful, should not be further developed to the point that people become afraid of each other.

READING (Southern) Evidence accumulates from centres which have been bombed that one of the best sedatives is the knowledge that Germany is being bombed more heavily. Demand for illumination of the African situation continues. Signs that Churchill's reference to the defence of London combined with the news that members of the Government have sent their children to US causes anxiety as to whether we can defend ourselves as well as is officially intimated. Bournemouth hotel-keepers are planning joint demand for Government assistance.

CAMBRIDGE (Eastern) Some speculation regarding Hitler's next move and some nervousness concerning the application of powers given to authorities by the new EPA.

TUNBRIDGE WELLS (South Eastern) Employers in Maidstone area critical of call-up arrangements, due to instances of older and more experienced men being enlisted while younger men are kept waiting. Annoyance caused by announcements in popular press that Hitler will invade Britain on Friday. It is pointed out that a private citizen making such a statement could be liable to imprisonment.

BIRMINGHAM (Midland) Renewed complaints that yellow warnings are passed on to public by air wardens. Recurrence of Haw-Haw rumours in Wolverhampton area.

BELFAST (Northern Ireland) Feeling that danger of invasion has receded a little but that preparations must not relax. Emergency budget viewed rather gloomily by income-tax classes.

EDINBURGH (Scotland) Enemy aeroplanes have passed over Clydebank twice in last three weeks, and although held by searchlights met no AA opposition. Communist propaganda, which is effective among the intellectual young artisans, is making full play of this evidence of unpreparedness as well as with the slackness of important workshops and shipyards, where overtime is being worked even when there is not sufficient work to do; the moral drawn is that this Government is not really determined to fight Hitler. Drunkenness is prevalent in Clydebank mainly among war workers previously unemployed for long periods.

LONDON

Mixed reactions to new War Zone Emergency Courts Bill. Majority agree it may be necessary. Many criticise the manner in which it has been introduced and some are highly suspicious of it. Failure of overseas evacuation scheme still rousing resentment and disappointment. Working class grumbling at MPs and families going to America. Observer reports evidence that idleness and unemployment are having a mischievous effect on juveniles; court cases believed to be small fraction of those undetected as police are taken up with other duties. Willesden reports uneasiness among mothers of evacuated children over lack of news about bombed places. Suggestion made that teacher should send postcard to local CAB after raid to say all is well. Parents could enquire at bureau for such news. People wishing to visit friends in Defence Area uncertain as to whether they will reach destination as railway officials cannot tell them. Explicit instructions asked for. Talk of possible peace proposals in papers today brings reaction from several quarters that there will be trouble if there is any suggestion of accepting them. Prosecutions for careless talking and anti-rumour campaign causing considerable uneasiness and criticism. Many people think that prosecutions cause more dismay and depression than talk itself. Younger people, especially men, express fear that free criticism is being lost. Strong representations that talk in press about Hitler planning to invade Britain on Friday is the kind of rumour-mongering that the public is now supposed to suppress.

THURSDAY 18 JULY 1940

There is little change in morale.

1. *The public has still not reacted strongly to the War Zone Emergency Courts. It is not a topic of general conversation and outside London and certain areas in the defence zones people are disinterested on the grounds that they are unlikely to be affected by the courts. Many people have had their attention drawn to the problem by accounts of agitation in the House and by press headlines. There is more response than yesterday but one is impressed by the delayed reaction. On the other hand professional opinion is strongly affected and left-wing and working-class circles express concern. A field study showed that although people said they understood the proposed new machinery in fact they did not do so. Approximately one-third of those questioned expressed vague approval, one-third detached disapproval, a statistical minority were strongly antagonistic and the rest held no opinion.*

   It was evident that there is a good deal of popular confusion about recent legislation. Many thought that the new courts were to try those accused of defeatist talk and rumour. Overheard conversations record a number of cynical and semi-humorous references to 'jugging for grousing'; most of the comments, however, show that war legislation is regarded as unpleasant but inevitable.

2. *There are a number of rumours about the coming 'peace offensive'.*

3. *There is still a good deal of soreness about the 'aluminium muddle'.*

4. *The urban public is beginning to regard a food shortage and possibly a famine as a danger as great as that of invasion.*

5. *Middle-class women responding to Bevin's appeal have been very disappointed to find that machinery does not yet exist for absorbing weekend labour.*

   There will be no report on Friday, 19 July.

Points from Regions

Reports from most Regions agree that the majority of the public neither understands nor is greatly interested in the new 'War Zone Courts' Bill. The need for a simple explanation is voiced from Scotland, Reading and Tunbridge Wells. Little comment is aroused in Ireland, in view of the examples of IRA activities which point to the need for wide powers. While it is generally agreed that special courts with such powers are needed in the war zone, anxiety about the scope of the Bill is reported among the 'educated classes' and the more thoughtful workers in many areas. From Scotland, Leeds, Newcastle and Bristol comes criticism that the power of life and death should be placed in the hands of one person, without appeal. Reading reports it is felt that 'the proposed law smacks too strongly of Fascism'. Cambridge reports some fear that it will be hard to get rid of this measure when times are less critical. West Country legal circles consider the Bill places too much power in the hands of the military. Professional classes in Nottingham are stated to regard it as 'rather hysterical', and the absence of a court of appeal is talked of as 'shocking' and 'a copy of the worst practices of the Nazis'. Educated circles in Cardiff express satisfaction that Members of the House are safe-guarding public interests.

NOTTINGHAM (North Midland) Letters from towns alleged to have suffered air-raid damage confirm the truth of many such rumours, and increase suspicion of the official version. Members of the armed forces are said to be a chief source of rumour. Indifference to the war noticeable in the mining area.

CARDIFF (Wales) Great concern is felt that we have succumbed to Japanese pressure, which may harm our relations with Russia and America. Resentment is expressed at drastic action taken against apparently trivial rumour offences.

MANCHESTER (North Western) Housewives pleased with new scheme for butter and margarine.

BRISTOL (South Western) Distrust of Silent Column on grounds that most people will soon be afraid to say anything. Confidence increasing in Cornwall due to improved local defences. Reports from Bristol of shop-lifting by people sheltering in shops during air raids.

LEEDS (North Eastern) Much popular resentment against post-ponement of sea evacuation.

NEWCASTLE (Northern) Complaints of insufficient equipment for Civil Defence casualty services. Further requests for military bands, parades, etc.

READING (Southern) Appeal for voluntary labour for Home Defence measures launched last week has failed dismally, and is ascribed to the vague and casual way in which the appeal was launched.

BIRMINGHAM (Midland) The Ministry's campaign against chatter is helping to diminish rumour.

CAMBRIDGE (Eastern) Criticism of lack of strict discipline in LDV from some quarters. Feeling that American Government should offer protective transport.

TUNBRIDGE WELLS (South Eastern) Criticism that Priestley's informative talk or his visit to Margate does not conform to the anti-gossip campaign.

BELFAST (Northern Ireland) A growing volume of opinion that enemy talk of invasion is prelude to peace offensive. Rumour in Belfast that there is a food shortage in Britain.

EDINBURGH (Scotland) The news of the agreement to block the Burma Road causes disquiet as it may affect our relations with US and Russia, and a few comments that 'the Munich men are at it again' are heard.

LONDON

People asking questions uneasily about Italy, Japan and the war in Africa. Opinion expressed that we should put weaker Axis partner out of court first. News considered misleading. 'Why are we told we have lost one little fort in Africa after another and then comforted by phrase: "we retired according to plan"? This savours too much of Flanders retreat.' More questions agitating public mind: 'are we going to give way to Japan all along the line?' and 'are we leaving China to her fate?' Many people feeling nervous about anti-gossip campaign and state they are afraid to open their mouths. From other quarters people are said to be discounting rumour and are quite cheerful. Some criticisms of sensational press presentation of Sir John Anderson's War Zone Courts Bill. Simple explanations would ease people's minds about this and such remarks as 'if we are not shot by the Germans we are evidently going to be shot by our own people' made in tram by working man reading newspaper would be silenced. Identity Cards thought by many people to need photographs to provide true safeguard. Some need in working-class districts for creches in which mothers can leave babies and young children when working in factories. Neighbourly scheme introduced in North St Pancras to bring women on housing estate together reported successful; improving spirit of neighbourhood. Morale of middle-class wives left alone all day in suburbs considered by many lower than that of other people; more need for local schemes. In some poorer districts, reports observer, idea is gaining ground that it is useless to save money, as if district is bombed savings will be lost. Also reported that many of these people think in vague terms of 'thousands of aeroplanes descending upon them and causing irreparable destruction.'

SATURDAY 20 JULY 1940

Morale is high. But a generalisation made two months ago is still true: 'The whiter the collar, the less the assurance'.

1. *Reactions to the expected 'peace' speech: 'Hitler speaks — in vain'. On the whole people have treated the speech less seriously than the press have done. People laughed and jeered.*

2. *The lack of exciting events combined with nervous tension has provided an opportunity for people to criticise Government policy. Although there is a good deal of ignorance about Far Eastern affairs, the closing of the Burma Road is resented. 'I'm not too sure about this Burma Road business — but if what I think is true, then I wish I was a Chinaman, they do seem to know what they're fighting for. We're fighting for freedom — are we? Whose freedom? Only ours by the look of it, and let everyone else go to hell'. 'I don't like the news from China — mind you, I don't understand it really'.*

    The retreat from Moyale is similarly castigated: 'Another successful withdrawal!'

    The Channel Islands have by no means been forgotten. Scattered refugees keep the story alive.

    CORB, aluminium and tea are discussed with resentment.

3. *Most serious cause of tension are the prosecutions for defeatist talk and for spreading rumours. There is alarm at the coincidence of measures which appear to be aimed at the freedom of the civilian. The civilian is beginning to feel, and has been encouraged to feel, that he is in the front line; at the same time attempts apparently are being made to undermine his status. The following verbatims are typical:*

> *'Of course I think rumour's a bad thing but I find myself defending it now that people are being prosecuted'.*
> *'I feel really angry. It's the Gestapo over here'. 'They can prevent us talking but they can't prevent us thinking'.*
> *'Those two men who were fined £5 each for leaving their jobs for half an hour. I think it's scandalous. £5 for just a half hour'. 'I see they're*

> *tightening up the factory laws. Good thing too. Poor devils working*
> *12 hours a day – can't possibly do their best'.*

'*This Silent Column campaign is a backhand. Although I agree that people*
shouldn't say dangerous things, this makes you feel you daren't say
anything'. 'It takes the heart out of you, doesn't it?'

It is clear that the public has been taken by surprise. The new legislation
is unintelligible and the need for further explanation and previous expla-
nation is emphasised in many of our reports.

Points from Regions

Reports of the reception of Hitler's speech show that for the most
part public opinion follows that of the newspapers. In Cardiff it is
said that the speech represents 'an underlying fear in Hitler's mind'
and 'it is merely laughed at' in Leeds. Bristol considers it has little
effect on the war, and only slight reaction has been apparent in
Birmingham, Leeds and Belfast. It is suggested that this is because
the speech followed anticipated lines.

NOTTINGHAM (North Midland) Premier's speech still spoken of
with enthusiasm. Dissatisfaction with Lincolnshire War Agricultural
Committee on the grounds that full use is not being made of land
and that there are too many vested interests. The idea persists that
the recent earthquake was really a catastrophic explosion.

CARDIFF (Wales) New arrivals to the Dutch Army in the Western
Counties are effectively spreading news of the deadliness of British
bombers. Some criticism about new air-raid casualty policy, and
disappointment, but many agree that reticence is unavoidable.

MANCHESTER (North Western) Adverse comment persists on the
evacuation of the children of prominent persons. It is increasingly being
said that the scrap muddle is spreading from aluminium to other things.

BRISTOL (South Western) Growing support for the view that now
civilians should be treated as members of the Forces, and civilian

casualties issued in the same way. Modification of 'War Zone Courts' meets principal criticisms. Bath reports casual conduct on account of continued alarms without visible damage. Complaints again from Plymouth of lack of coordination of sirens.

LEEDS (North Eastern) Defensive stage of war has caused some apathy among younger people. Morale is lowest in Bridlington and other towns where livelihood of many has disappeared. Many consider Silent Column publicity overdone. Many sections express the view that we are not trying to win Russia's friendship, which we need.

NEWCASTLE (Northern) Present lull is creating some nervous tension. Rumours largely diminished, but perturbation exists owing to increase of prosecutions for careless talk. Many urge aggressive action against Italy.

BIRMINGHAM (Midland) No undue alarm about new War Courts, which are considered the best way to deal with Fifth Column activities. Dissatisfaction over smallness of tea ration.

READING (Southern) Appointment of new C-in-C. Home Forces has tended to crystallise suspicion voiced recently that all is not well with Home Defence and more vigour is required. Silent Column is considered too negative. Monthly publication of air-raid casualties well received on the whole.

CAMBRIDGE (Eastern) Another unheralded raid on Norwich has revived the siren controversy. Reaction is anger against 'incompetence somewhere' rather than fear. Feeling of expectancy yesterday among some sections of public due to prophecies of invasion.

TUNBRIDGE WELLS (South Eastern) Commented that Sir Alan Brooke's nickname 'Wizard' is unfortunately like that bestowed on Gamelin. Criticism that BBC broadcasters are highly educated and speak with 'posh' accents, and the use of 'ordinary people' is suggested. Women in Medway towns complain against authorities for failing to sound air-raid warnings when bombs were dropped in Gillingham area on Thursday.

BELFAST (Northern Ireland) Recruiting drive in country districts gaining momentum.

EDINBURGH (Scotland) Premier's statement has not dispelled uneasiness about closing the Burma Road although majority are willing to take the Premier's lead. Growing agreement that Silent Column campaign is being carried too far. Many middle-class people are asking 'why didn't we consult the Soviet?' and doubts about a Far Eastern Munich are freely expressed.

LONDON

People express apprehension at possibility of misuse of War Zone Courts, while at same time considering them necessary evils in extreme circumstances. Tea rationing hitting poorer classes very hard; some comment made on difference between soldiers' generous rations and those of Civil Defence workers who should have same privileges. Bethnal Green reports misgivings still present among parents of evacuated children in Wales, especially when people visualise children living in South Wales industrial area. Idea current that: 'Hitler is out to destroy the children; as soon as they reach a place bombs drop, and when he sank the *Arandora Star* he really meant to get the children going to Canada.' Report that Indian community in London is depressed and unenthusiastic about war. Although anti-Nazi in feeling is not pro-British and is not involved in national effort nor made to feel it has vital part to play; asks for more Indian news. Convictions for rumour-spreading causing uneasiness. Considerable anti-Chamberlainism, weakening confidence in Government, still reported. Some expressions of dismay received at press suggestion that Priestley's and Charles Gardner's talks should be censored. People returning from Defence Area calm and philosophic on whole; this having good effect on people who have not yet experienced bombing. Much grumbling about food and food prices reported from World's End, Chelsea. Women stating bread and potatoes all they can give men now as bacon, fish, eggs, vegetables and all but a little meat far too expensive; most using tinned foods. From Brixton comes evidence of latent anti-Semitic feeling. Criticism of Eden for slowness in call-up and admiration for Stafford Cripps expressed in

Walham Green. Interest in Cripps mission to Russia in spite of soft pedalling in news. Complaints from Lewisham that dustmen have to sort rubbish at depot, wasting precious time. Some concern expressed at danger of smells and flies in food collection.

MONDAY 22 JULY TO
SATURDAY 27 JULY 1940

The Luftwaffe continued its attacks on coastal shipping, accompanied by scattered raids across England, Scotland and Wales. Home Intelligence assessed reactions to the announcement that 336 civilians had been killed in raids in the month beginning 18 June and reported widespread complaints about the condition of public air-raid shelters.

Addressing the Reichstag on 19 July Hitler had made what he called 'an appeal to reason and common sense' and urged the British to make peace. It was a belligerent, menacing speech that according to Home Intelligence made little impression on the general public. Britain's rejection of Hitler's 'peace offer' was delivered by the Foreign Secretary, Lord Halifax, in a broadcast on 22 July. A fox-hunting high churchman known in political circles as 'the holy fox', Halifax described the war as 'a crusade for Christianity', but Home Intelligence reported that the 'high moral tone' of his speech was 'above the heads of a large section of the public'.

More comprehensible, but no less heavily criticised, were the budget proposals announced by the Chancellor of the Exchequer, Sir Kingsley Wood, in the third wartime budget on 23 July. The standard rate of income tax was raised from 7s 6d (37.5p) in the pound to 8s 6d (42.5p). Rates of surtax and estate duty were increased along with duties on wine, beer and tobacco, and purchase tax, a new form of tax which had first been announced in April, was imposed at a rate of 33.3 per cent on 'luxury' items. In peacetime tax increases were usually unpopular but the main criticism levelled at Kingsley Wood – a close pre-war ally of Chamberlain – was that he had failed to go far enough. In London, Home Intelligence concluded, 'intelligent opinion calls it "Compromise Budget" and remembers that Sir Kingsley Wood is one of the "Old Gang"'.

Home Intelligence had often noted the strength of opposition in professional and intellectual circles to the wholesale and indiscriminate internment of enemy aliens. On 23 July Sir John Anderson announced a review and relaxation of the policy of internment, but there was evidently a time-lag before the new regulations were translated into practice. On 25 July it was reported that there was dismay in Stepney 'at sudden internment of class C alien men and still more at internment of alien men living in London since before last war; petition sent by both Gentiles and Jews'.

The belated release of the news of the sinking of the troopship *Lancastria* highlighted one of the problems involved in censorship. The ship, in peacetime a Cunard White Star liner, was evacuating British troops and civilians from the port of St Nazaire when it was bombed and sunk on 17 June with the loss of over 4,000 lives. Although the news was withheld, there were many survivors who spread word of the tragedy on their return to Britain and it had also been reported on German radio. 'The release of the news without adequate explanation has produced criticism and general suspicion,' Home Intelligence recorded.

By the end of the week Mary Adams's department was embroiled in the controversy over 'Cooper's Snoopers' (see p. xv). 'The work of Home Intelligence,' noted the report for 27 July, 'has been considerably dislocated by the present press campaign.'

MONDAY 22 JULY 1940

Morale is high: people are cheerful and determined.

1. References to Hitler's 'peace' speech have practically disappeared from public conversation.

2. The spirit of people in raided districts is admirable. Our reports, however, all contain reference to
   the siren controversy
   the shelter-conscious attitude of the working-class population
   the need for making shelters warm and damp-proof in preparation for
       the winter
   the efficiency of the Civil Defence services

3. The population is in no need of exhortation either to be cheerful or calm: there is need of explanation. Recent legislation has taken people by surprise and there has been insufficient warning of coming instructions and regulations. Verbatims illustrate this: 'There's too much talking at people nowadays', 'We're not jittery; I suppose they are', 'If only they'd explain a bit more there wouldn't be so much resentment'. The Ministry of Information is not popular – partly because its functions and activities are not understood.

4. The Silent Column campaign continues to be widely criticised in spite of official assurances. The relationship between the campaign and prosecutions for defeatist talk and rumours is considered sinister.

5. The victimisation of Conscientious Objectors and treatment of aliens continues to provoke anger and suspicion in intellectual circles.

6. Certain campaigns which have aroused public annoyance, e.g. aluminium, brick and concrete shelters, salvage, recruitment of female labour, have been inadequately organised and the public has been quick to recognise this general defect.

Points from Regions

Although reports from Belfast and Cambridge state that Nicolson's speech has removed some of the misapprehension about the Silent Column campaign, and Newcastle feels that it is now set in proper perspective, there is criticism from Reading that 'the Government does not trust the people as much as it ought to.' Both Tunbridge Wells and Cardiff complain that the military are the worst offenders 'against whom no disciplinary action appears to be taken.' In Scotland people are asking why the campaign was called 'the Silent Column'. In Bristol some people are complaining that together with the new war courts our regime is becoming dangerously akin to the one we are fighting.

NOTTINGHAM (North Midland) Road defences are much appreciated. Belief that Italy is vulnerable to sea and air attack. Complaint that rural schools should provide adequate shelters and that the police do not always take seriously reports of lighting infringements. Government publicity is considered too 'wordy', and so little read.

CARDIFF (Wales) Closing the Burma Road has revived resentment against the appeasement group in the Government. Criticism that many shops, in turning out customers and locking doors during air raids, cause congestion in the streets.

MANCHESTER (North Western) General Smuts's address welcomed. Some women shocked by month's casualties and feel that announcement should be in smaller doses. Some bitterness about COs registered on Ministry of Labour's evidence.

BRISTOL (South Western) Morale still high in Bristol and Plymouth, particularly among working class. Increased strengthening of defences having good effect on morale. Return of children to evacuated areas causing some concern. Suggested that gossip about dates of invasion has had an adverse effect.

LEEDS (North Eastern) Apathy said to be growing in South Yorkshire mining areas. Priestley's talk last night received special praise. More people now saying that 'they are being talked *at* too much'.

NEWCASTLE (Northern) Hitler's speech generally regarded as a confession of weakness and intended for internal consumption. Complaints about the marked difference in the meat ration allowed to troops and heavy industrial workers. Reports from Scarborough on serious effect of defence regulations on shopkeepers, etc. who feel they are facing ruin.

READING (Southern) Defeatism decreasing although still existing in isolated pockets among white collars and workers. Paragraph in Minister's letter of 19 July dealing with evacuation caused criticism and confusion.

BIRMINGHAM (Midland) Smuts broadcast is a topic of conversation in Midlands. Criticism that it is not necessary to say who is going to read BBC bulletins, and complaints of repetition and dullness. 'All they want is the news.' Strong demand from Walsall and West Bromwich for more military bands.

CAMBRIDGE (Eastern) German occupation of most of the Continent has caused less interest in the fate of individual countries under Nazi rule. Feeling that a more aggressive policy should be launched, encouraged by week-end speeches.

TUNBRIDGE WELLS (South Eastern) Concern that agreement with Japan is having a bad influence on our relations with US and USSR. Internment of distinguished refugees causes anxiety in intellectual circles as to whether best use is being made of potential allies. Adverse comment on the number of Jews of military age suffering from heart trouble and varicose veins.

BELFAST (Northern Ireland) State of preparedness prevails in spite of raids. Anti-gossip week generally welcomed. Morale high.

EDINBURGH (Scotland) Uneasiness about absence of air-raid warnings reported from Glasgow. Stories of food for France from Red

Cross sources raises queries on efficacy of blockade. Account of six Hurricanes routing eighty enemy planes in fifteen minutes received with scepticism. Smuts's speech well received.

LONDON

People cheerful and optimistic at weekend when Hitler failed to invade Britain on Friday as threatened. General feeling now that war will last a long time as invasion cannot succeed and we shall then settle down to hammering away at Germany by RAF. Strong resentment still felt among all classes at Silent Column campaign and at police prosecutions for spreading rumour, which are considered 'ridiculous'. MOI becoming unpopular again; much of this feeling directed against the Minister. Indignation expressed at what people say to be 'a policy which is turning us into a nation of spies.' Labour Party candidates meeting agreed that prosecutions for idle talking were upsetting public morale seriously. People in new positions of minor authority accused of officiousness and bullying manner, reminiscent some say 'of the early days of the Nazis.' Statement issued by Ministry on Saturday has helped to relieve public to some extent, but harm has gone too deep to be so quickly cured. Need for creches in factory area considered imperative by observers. Brixton reports food waste and clean paper mixed with other rubbish; local people take little trouble to separate it as authorities have not given strong lead. West Indian and West African communities of London nervous of German attack on West Africa since capitulation of France; question whether large well-equipped native force is trained to act with British fleet against German thrust from north. Most coloured people reported anxious to pull weight in war effort; unable to, except in St Pancras where twenty are ARP wardens. Some dismissals because of colour. Grievance that students of Aggrey House who volunteered for Civil Defence at beginning of war not yet made use of. Strong feeling in Barnet that Belgian refugees, given hospitality and money, are ungrateful and uncooperative.

TUESDAY 23 JULY 1940

Morale is high. People are fully behind the war effort although small pockets of defeatism confined to certain localities, age groups or social groups are still present. The last week has been one of public criticism however and the stock of the Government has fallen. The various causes of this criticism have already been noted:

> *Prosecutions and heavy sentences for defeatist talk*
> *Capitulation over the Burma Road*
> *Confusion over certain Government instructions, e.g. Stay Put, Siren policy.*
> *The press campaign against the internment of aliens.*
> *Tea rationing (among the working classes)*
> *Silent Column campaign*
> *The 'postponement' of seavacuation*

There is confidence in the armed forces (particularly in the Navy and RAF) but less confidence in the Administration.

Reactions to the Foreign Secretary's broadcast are best seen in verbatims: 'Too much like a bishop', 'Depressing', 'Disappointing', 'Unsatisfactory', 'What about the Burma Road?', 'A statesman has to be a fighter these days', 'He didn't explain anything', 'Very nice and gentlemanly', 'Old-fashioned diplomacy', 'Too much like the Chamberlain days', 'It was a dull speech: I switched off', 'I liked the high moral tone', 'It's no use treating a mad dog like that'.

Many people failed to react to the broadcast at all and there was little attempt to relate the reply to Hitler's speech.

From various areas come reports that there is a drift in opinion towards disbelief in invasion.

Points from Regions

Reports indicate that the high moral tone of Halifax's speech has given satisfaction to the upper classes although above the heads of a large section of the public. From Cambridge comes the criticism that it was 'an excellent sermon, but lacking the directness which the situation demands', and a working-class comment from Bristol is: 'any Bishop could have done as much from his pulpit'. Little enthusiasm has been noticed in South Wales, and Tunbridge Wells criticises the speech as 'too devotional and containing little new', although praised as sincere and determined. The religious note found acceptance among all religious creeds in Belfast, but Reading reports that it has served to crystallise a vague feeling that a more offensive diplomatic attitude should be adopted to rally to our cause all world opinion which would not favour a German victory.

NORTHERN (Newcastle) Phrases like 'strategic withdrawal' in communiques are in danger of becoming standing jokes. People appear to understand better the reason for the siren policy. Adverse comment on visibility of prominent light-coloured buildings thought to provide good landmarks, and camouflage is urged.

NORTH-EASTERN (Leeds) Misgiving aroused by prosecution of prominent South Yorkshire Councillor, the basis of the charge apparently being his strong criticism of Chamberlain for our unpreparedness, and as a traitor. This is contrasted with Halifax's 'we shall not stop fighting till freedom for ourselves and others is secured'. Continuance of voluntary censorship evokes favourable comment. Unemployed in NE coastal area are contrasting their plight with munition workers' wages. Miners complain that new house cellars have only 5-cwt capacity, and coal storage for winter is impossible.

NORTH-MIDLAND (Nottingham) Leicester night workers resent siren policy on grounds that wives and children will not have enough time to take shelter. Many people in rural areas feel that truth is suppressed in news bulletins in order to maintain morale. Evidence that long distance transport workers are source of rumours.

EASTERN (Cambridge) Campaign against careless talk still creating misapprehension and absence of neighbourliness. Confusion over rents and rates in coastal zones.

SOUTHERN (Reading) Stock of Ministry of Information continues to slump in the Region, and explanation of Ministry's functions required.

SOUTH-WESTERN (Bristol) Misapprehension about Silent Column persists. Concern in Somerset about number of flat fields containing no obstacles. Soldiers in Wiltshire district express hostility against CO parson arrested for breach of the peace. Complaints of condition of children recently evacuated to Cornwall. Reported that people are listening less to Haw-Haw.

WALES (Cardiff) Lack of shelters in North Wales causes anxiety. More people staying in bed during raid warnings, which occur almost nightly. Although most people are willing to accept totalitarian methods to combat Hitler, proposed censorship and prosecutions have created feeling that complete totalitarianism is neither desirable nor necessary.

MIDLAND (Birmingham) Recurrence of uneasiness that members of late Government are still in this one. Good response to appeals for funds to provide aeroplanes. Many retired workers returning to Coventry factories.

NORTH-WESTERN (Manchester) Attitude in disbelief in Blitzkrieg growing. Cost of brick shelters arouses some criticism. Success of stirrup pumps creates a desire for their greater availability.

SCOTLAND (Edinburgh) Some nervousness displayed by Aberdeen shipyard and dockyard workers in anticipation of danger, but disappears when danger arrives. Suggested that sounds of British and German planes should be broadcast.

SOUTH-EASTERN (Tunbridge Wells) Pointed out that case of man fined for saying 'this is a capitalist war in defence of dividends' contrasts with freedom of *Daily Worker*. Examples of careless talk by soldiers constantly received. Tradesmen along Kent and Sussex coast worried about their position and it seems that the public has taken the announcement that evacuees from Defence Areas are relieved of rates and other liabilities as an indication that they need not pay tradesmen's debts.

NORTHERN IRELAND (Belfast) Much speculation about significance of mining approaches to Irish Sea and Bristol Channel. Employers of labour asking for increasing quantities of anti-gossip slips for wage packets. General praise for prowess of RAF continues.

LONDON

Lord Halifax's talk made little impression. Silent Column campaign still drawing vigorous protests from all classes and though Ministry's statement has improved matters Gestapo idea is widespread. Non-defeatist majority of working class afraid that Government's anti-defeatist propaganda shows nervousness. Publication of air-raid casualty numbers for past month has shocked people; although they wish to know of casualties they express surprise at their extent. Improvement in reporting details of air raids commented on by many observers. Pleasure expressed at more indications in recent talks of what we are really fighting for. Surbiton reports local people interested in 'a kind of smoke screen set up each evening when the moon is bright'. Silvertown factory recently installed loudspeakers in canteen as workers complained they could get no news between 7 a.m. and 6 p.m.; this found to work admirably. South London housing estates stated to present special problem of loneliness and isolation. Ask for Ministry vans to dispense news and music as housewives inclined to be dispirited and miss neighbourliness of East End. Lambeth conference of business men and women reports difficulty of communicating with Government departments when offering facilities for factory supplies. Hounslow women busy with voluntary work, but many disappointed after applying for sugar ration to make jam to find fruit prices prohibitive; feel all prices should be strictly controlled.

WEDNESDAY 24 JULY 1940

The lull in events is reflected in morale. People are calm, not highly interested in the wider implications of the war, critical of the Government's home policy but fundamentally cooperative in all measures which are believed to indicate a vigorous war policy. Defence measures are approved and are giving increasing confidence. Factory employees are working at high pressure although there are signs of fatigue because of long hours and few holidays.

People were expecting much greater Budget demands and the blow, when it came, seemed gentle. There was some criticism that the Chancellor did not go far enough, that the Budget was too conventional and that further demands must be made quite soon. There is some working-class criticism about the taxes on beer and cheap entertainment; others refer to the 'appeasement Budget' and mark up the Chancellor's past associations. On the whole, however, the reaction has been negative.

There is general appreciation of the Prime Minister's frankness over the Silent Column campaign but little attempt to 'name the culprit'. As usual the Ministry of Information is considered the chief offender and the relationship of the Ministry with prosecutions for defeatist talk has been freely canvassed. The Government is considered to have shown signs of grace by its response to public feeling both about these prosecutions, about the Silent Column and about aliens. An analysis of verbatims shows that there is more talk about these matters than about the Budget.

During the last few days observers have been reporting on the way in which the public took the publication of the monthly air-raid casualty figures. The great majority of people were surprised and disturbed at the figures.

(Local example of good morale: air-raid warning received in cinema with cheers.)

Points from Regions

The general reaction to the Budget is cheerful resignation, due to expectation of more severe taxation. From many Regions criticism is received that the Budget does not go far enough: 'it is better to skin us right out now than build up a burden to be carried later', comes from Bristol, and a Reading comment is that 'for most people it might have been worse, but from a national point of view it might have been better.' The collection of income tax at source is approved for the most part as it is considered easier to meet the tax that way.

NORTHERN (Newcastle) Comment that County Councils and Local Authorities are not adjusting finances to meet the situation. Tendency persists among some industrial classes to stay awake at night in anticipation of air raids. Problem of boots and shoes for poor children is causing some anxiety.

NORTH-EASTERN (Leeds) Confidence in military and LDV increasing. Morale improved in Bridlington and coast defences have increased confidence generally. Traders and boarding-house keepers depressed at slowness of Government to help in seaside towns. Scarborough upset that 2,000 evacuated children remain although people are invited to leave.

NORTH-MIDLAND (Nottingham) Vivid contrast of basis of Halifax's appeal thought effective. Scarcity and price of eggs subject of much comment. Figures of people killed in raids came as a shock to some in view of official bulletins minimising damage and casualties. Villagers in vicinity of aerodromes feel they are neglected in the matter of shelters.

EASTERN (Cambridge) Re-examination of sentences for careless talk has alleviated anxiety. Increased speculation on the possibility of assistance from USSR. Approval of move to sponsor leadership of Haile Selassie.

SOUTHERN (Reading) Report of drift back to complacency in rural and urban areas, although no sign of unwillingness to accept sacrifice. Film of children arriving in USA hissed in Winchester.

SOUTH-WESTERN (Bristol) Premier's statement on the Silent Column well received. Report that in Devon villages women feel they should have their sons and husbands at home because any peace could not be worse than war.

WALES (Cardiff) Increasing numbers not seeking shelter during night raids. Dorothy Thompson's broadcast appreciated by many. Regret expressed in some quarters that compulsory savings have not been imposed.

NORTH-WESTERN (Manchester) Plans to revise treatment of friendly aliens and sentences for defeatist talk has done much to reassure public opinion, and Premier's statement on Silent Column welcomed.

SCOTLAND (Edinburgh) Question of chief interest to people on East and West Coast is 'Where are our fighters and AA guns?'; and complaints of absence of opposition have increased on Clydeside. A rumour in Edinburgh last night said that the best guns had been transferred to England, and as a result faith in our defences is becoming undermined.

NORTHERN IRELAND (Belfast) Admiralty announcement of destroyer strength has encouraged public. Premier's statement on Silent Column caused surprise in some quarters.

SOUTH-EASTERN (Tunbridge Wells) Public asking why the price of soft fruits is so high. Reported that 'Go to it' slogan is now resulting in decreased output through fatigue.

LONDON

Reactions to Budget: relief at its leniency coupled with an uneasy belief that it did not go far enough to carry the tremendous burdens of expenditure needed to win the war. Intelligent opinion calls it 'Compromise Budget' and remembers that Sir Kingsley Wood is one of the 'Old Gang'. Army people wish beer and tobacco could be duty free for troops. Pleasure expressed by professional people and those in contact with refugees at Sir John Anderson's new policy. Stepney reports hardships connected with interned aliens among Jewish community where several old people were arrested. These cases have produced a sense of injustice disproportionate to their number. Some defeatist talk concerned chiefly with fallacy of saving reported from Kensington. MOI films popular with public in GB cinema Chelsea, reports observer. Dangerous gossip films made greatest impression; Priestley's film liked by all classes and evacuation film least popular: criticism 'that film was less real than the others and the mother too condescending'. Some people dubious about the veracity of air-raid casualty numbers. 'No resentment but belief expressed that actual numbers are far greater'. Scarcity of eggs chief topic of discussion in markets of poor districts – comparison made with Germany's one egg a week ration. Communal pig tub placed in Chelsea garden; has proved such success that second has been added. More resentment expressed that sugar for jam making was released too late for cheap soft fruit, and fruit prices soared when sugar finally became available. Some people disturbed at slack observance of black-out in Chelsea. Great enthusiasm for war among very poor reported in Shoreditch and, in spite of hardships, no grumbling about food. Borough Council has opened depots for salvage in two localities. French soldiers billeted in White City reported more cheerful since facilities for seeing French films have been open to them. Dorothy Thompson's talk appreciated; people state they are glad to be in touch with America again and have missed Gram Swing. Willesden has admitted seventy refugees as honorary members of Social Centre; new spirit of friendliness grown up between them and English members.

THURSDAY 25 JULY 1940

There is little change in morale: people are cheerful and determined. 'There is nothing wrong with the morale of the man in the street' is a common observation in our reports.

Beaverbrook's vigorous broadcast was generally appreciated and favourable comments on Dorothy Thompson's broadcast continue to be received.

Middle-class opinion waits for the Government to implement the promises given about defeatist talk prosecutions, aliens policy and the war zone courts.

Good reports continue to be received about the conduct of the public during air raids.

Reports from factories show how great is the political ignorance and un-responsiveness of many young women workers.

Points from Regions

Comments that the Budget is too timid come from Leeds, Cardiff and Reading, and that it does not face up to the problem of increased expenditure in munitions and supply, from Manchester. A Bristol reaction is that 'we're going to win, so pay we must', but there is a feeling in Scotland that the new tobacco tax will be hard on serving soldiers.

Six Regions report that Beaverbrook's broadcast was very welcome. His newsy style is contrasted favourably with drearier broadcasts, and the report of progress was comforting. Newcastle says it has created greater determination.

NORTHERN (Newcastle) Several centres suggest that permanent assistants should be appointed to clean and ventilate public shelters in constant use. Criticism in industrial centres of tea ration.

NORTH-EASTERN (Leeds) Coastal areas not yet bombed seem to fear air raids more than invasion. South Yorkshire coalfield feels Premier is curbed by Conservative Party machine. Leeds Co-op. Party have moved resolution demanding removal of 'appeasers' from Government. Feeling in Bridlington-Hull areas that farmers should be compelled to put obstacles in flat fields.

NORTH-MIDLAND (Nottingham) Relief at Premier's statement on sentences for careless talk. Criticism in organised labour of selection of LDV officers. Demand for sanitary arrangements where shelters are much in use, and for more village shelters. Dorothy Thompson's broadcast much appreciated.

EASTERN (Cambridge) Plight of coastal towns becomes increasingly acute, and tradesmen badly affected. Opinion expressed that Hitler's invasion plans may be postponed until he has secured oil supplies. Tendency towards false sense of security seems likely to grow.

SOUTHERN (Reading) Some anxiety on broader aspects of Government policy due to press articles demanding aggressive ideological lead. Restlessness among non-politically minded manifests itself as demand for offensive action. Abandonment of Silent Column has stemmed criticism against Government. Suggestion that Dorothy Thompson's broadcast should be issued as a leaflet.

SOUTH-WESTERN (Bristol) Freedom from raids having good effect on people's nerves. The homeless in Plymouth, due to raids, taking the troubles in good part. Strong element of disaffection reported from Forest of Dean. General satisfaction at review of gossip sentences and internment of aliens. Complaints of flooding in Anderson shelters.

WALES (Cardiff) News that a plane has been brought down off Welsh Coast has had excellent effect. General approval of MPs seeking safeguards for citizens in new war court legislation. Heavy manual workers feel they deserve consideration in tea rationing. Insular indifference to Balkan situation.

MIDLAND (Birmingham) Criticism that a month is too long between air casualty announcements. Marked attention throughout the area to the position of COs. Communists trying to work through 'the League of Reconciliation.' Wide appreciation of Dorothy Thompson's broadcast.

NORTH-WESTERN (Manchester) Evidence that indifference to news about air raids and a false sense of security are growing. More talk of holidays. Some consider the Chancellor of the Exchequer afraid of labour.

SCOTLAND (Edinburgh) Further complaints from Montrose and Peterhead that enemy bombers are coming over unchallenged by sirens or fighters. Anderson's war courts still little understood. Complaints of delay in getting shelters from Peterhead and Kincardine. Few complaints about tea ration. Dorothy Thompson's broadcast popular.

SOUTH-EASTERN (Tunbridge Wells) Belated announcement of loss of *Lancastria* increases mistrust in Government news, and some people have stopped listening to bulletins. Annoyance that BBC refers to 'Herr' Hitler and 'Signor' Mussolini. Report that Local Authorities have made no provision to help cases of hardship in Hastings due to evacuation order.

NORTHERN IRELAND (Belfast) More authentic news asked for, in view of rumours of enemy activities round the coast. Premier's Silent

Column statement puzzled many, coming in middle of Ulster's anti-gossip week. Some nervousness about coal supplies. Aluminium collection still going forward under Government stimulus.

LONDON

Unemployment growing in many districts owing to closing down of luxury trades. New depressed areas springing up and munitions factories insufficient to absorb idle workers. Chief problem: women who cannot leave districts because of family ties to seek work elsewhere. Budget considered by City 'indeterminate' and business men complain that they cannot formulate plans. Wealthy people with big obligations badly hit; making desperate efforts to keep workers employed in spite of reduced business; capital tied up and assets becoming liabilities. Opinion expressed in City that business recovery after war will be very slow. Silent Column campaign 'completely answered by PM in House' conclude many people. New comments made on descriptions of convoy air raids. 'Why should we send only a few fighters to meet forty or fifty German planes? If we sent more the destruction of enemy aircraft would be greater; begin to wonder if we have enough aeroplanes to meet such attacks.' Lord Beaverbrook's talk has drawn favourable comments; people appreciate his 'virility'. Dorothy Thompson's talk still praised today and suggestions made that it should be translated and used in foreign broadcasts. Great need expressed for music and marching songs to give people stimulation and outlet for their feelings. Stepney Evening Institutes report local dismay at sudden internment of class C alien men and still more at internment of alien born men living in London since before last war; petition sent by both Gentiles and Jews. Educational plight of Stepney reported; emergency schools providing half time education now open but attendance slight. Children having to cross dangerous Commercial Road to attend school being kept at home. Ignorance reported among people in Deptford and Greenwich areas of conditions in country, especially in Wales where children are evacuated.

FRIDAY 26 JULY 1940

Morale is still high and people are cheerful.

1. *The campaign against the Ministry of Information continues in the press. An enquiry designed to test the amount of public feeling roused by the Silent Column campaign showed that in one large aircraft factory less than 10% of the employees had heard of the campaign; in a specimen village less than 5% of the population had heard of the campaign. On the other hand the prosecutions for defeatist talk are a general topic of conversation and a large proportion of the public have been affected by rumours, fears and criticisms.*

2. *Siren policy is still much commented upon and in certain areas, e.g. Edinburgh, widely criticised.*

3. *The long-delayed announcement about the* Lancastria *has had a bad effect upon morale. The loss of the* Lancastria *was generally known in certain districts and the news had been heard in German wireless programmes. The release of the news without adequate explanation has produced criticism and general suspicion.*

4. *From many districts come complaints that important official forms are written in incomprehensible language. Official instructions of this kind are often re-written for general understanding. There is also a good deal of criticism of the waste of paper involved in the wide distribution of certain official forms, e.g. transport returns.*

5. *Sir Philip Joubert's broadcast was widely appreciated. His accents are friendly yet determined and there is evidence that the public has increasing confidence in his authority.*

There is a growing feeling that too many campaigns take the form of unconstructive prohibitions (Don't gossip, Don't spend, Don't waste, Don't listen to enemy broadcasts).

Points from Regions

The withholding of the news of the *Lancastria* is the subject of much adverse criticism. The story was known in Plymouth through survivors, and a rumour that 3,000 men had been lost with her was prevalent in Leeds three weeks ago. Fears that other bad news is withheld are reported from Tunbridge Wells and Manchester, and the fact that the news was only released after publication in an American paper gives rise to the feeling that it would otherwise have been withheld longer. One comment is: 'that the mass of the people has proved itself steady, and should not be treated as children.'

NORTHERN (Newcastle) Many complaints about Means Test for supplementary Old Age Pensions. In one centre older men are acting as unofficial scouts to watch for ARP workers being called out for yellow warnings, and then warn other inhabitants who go to shelters. Miners express satisfaction at scheme for sharing British coal market.

NORTH-EASTERN (Leeds) Morale good. Feeling that 'more is happening in the war than is revealed.' Adverse comments because farmers in the Region have not made bare strips in their wheat fields as a safeguard against fire.

NORTH-MIDLAND (Nottingham) Munition workers are feeling the strain of long hours, but little grumbling is heard. Ex-servicemen concerned about danger of giving ammunition to inexperienced Home Guards. People asking why waste materials cannot be given direct to Government, instead of through dealers. Mixed feeling expressed about siren policy. Complaints from county areas of shortage of shelters and contex filters for gas masks.

EASTERN (Cambridge) Reports of more determined attitude of women in contrast to a month ago. Although all doubts about Silent Column are not removed there is evidence that it has checked irresponsible talk. Feeling that Hitler has postponed invasion till Rumanian oil problem is solved, gains ground.

SOUTHERN (Reading) Depression following collapse of France has disappeared. Propaganda about 'island fortress' has caught on, but Gen. de Gaulle has not, and there appears to be little discrimination between the French Government and the people. On sea coast intensification of attacks on convoys evokes anxiety as to justification of German claims.

SOUTH-WESTERN (Bristol) Morale well-maintained. Public has taken Budget 'in its stride'. Hitler's speech still a subject of discussion, although his feeler is rejected. Cirencester reports that few people took cover during recent dog fight. Complaints of coal supply delays from Trowbridge. Bombs dropping on an estate which rumour says Goebbels intends to inhabit have greatly increased the rumour.

WALES (Cardiff) Invasion anticipated, and confidence in defences and desire to end suspense are expressed. News that over twenty planes were intercepted and shot down on their way to Wales has caused a great deal of satisfaction. Workmen want to know whether to work on if asked to continue when sirens have sounded. Rumours of lack of coordination between ground defences and fighters in Chepstow area, and of discontent among French sailors in Liverpool.

NORTH-WESTERN (Manchester) Public paying more attention to inadequacy of soldiers' pay and minor concessions are advocated. Position of French sailors in Liverpool area complicated by *Meknès* incident.

SCOTLAND (Edinburgh) Concern about lack of drainage in air-raid shelters, and complaints about lack of opposition to enemy aircraft are common in the West. Adverse comment about apologetic explanation in BBC news of lack of troops on Libyan frontier.

SOUTH-EASTERN (Tunbridge Wells) Careless talk noticed among workmen constructing buildings for Government use. Bitter complaints about prices of soft fruits, and opinion is held that speculators are responsible; hope is expressed that plum prices will be controlled. Joubert's refutation that enemy planes can be distinguished by engine note considered a good feature of his talk.

NORTHERN IRELAND (Belfast) Wide belief that recent bank outrages are the work of IRA seeking money for Fifth Column activities. Announcement of Eden's inspection of Northern Ireland defences gives satisfaction. Boothby's statement on feeding stuffs welcomed by Ulster farmers. Continued confidence in RAF superiority.

MIDLAND (Birmingham) Campaigns offering the public opportunity of buying fighter planes received good support, as does the collection of aluminium. Criticism from country areas that too many tramps are allowed on the road in present circumstances.

LONDON

News of *Lancastria* sinking makes people ask if many more of our ships have not been sunk. Women with free time on hand would like to do voluntary war work but find it difficult to get as hours are limited. Mothers of large families quite content that their work is of national importance. Mitcham factory reports workers speaking less freely than usual; if war is mentioned everyone very careful of what they say. Servicemen accused on all sides of giving away too much information about regiments and stations; civilians disturbed and try to prevent them talking. Unemployment problem in docks growing. MOI film 'Women and Munitions' rousing storms of protest by women in Woolwich and surrounding districts who cannot get munition work and want it badly. Labour Exchange Manager inundated with deputations, telephone calls and visits from angry women. Arsenal having just reduced overtime, women needed still less than before. Hackney women arranging to take in each other's families if blocks of flats are hit; less neighbourliness shown in streets of private houses. Some anti-Semitism revealed in district; feeling expressed that Jewish people 'get more of everything than Gentiles'. Problem of clothes chief trouble to mothers of evacuated children in East End. Mill Hill reports excellent morale in district but several nervous people not sleeping as afraid every aeroplane overhead is German. Considerable wishful thinking about European famine reported among middle class. North Kensington parents interested in scheme for compulsory physical training for children from fourteen to eighteen; communal kitchen in district proving great success. From Bethnal Green come complaints of people smoking in air-raid shelters; suggest atmosphere would be unbearable in long raid and especially bad for children. Shelter amenities on local housing estate still unprovided; causing ill feeling. Epsom reports Canadian soldiers acquiring sense of grievance over delay in getting home letters. Air Marshal Joubert's talk received very favourably.

SATURDAY 27 JULY 1940

The people are cheerful and there is some risk of complacency. There is little nervous tension about the prospect of invasion and there are indications that many people are beginning to believe that 'Hitler's plans have gone awry'. Some observers report that the press is thought to be 'keeping up the idea of invasion as a newspaper stunt'. There are reports too that Hitler's speech is considered 'a sign of weakness'. These tendencies are signs of over-optimism to which careful attention should be paid.

NB. The work of Home Intelligence has been considerably dislocated by the present press campaign and in consequence the daily analyses of reports has of necessity been much curtailed.

Points from Regions

Criticism of the withholding of the news about *Lancastria* continues.

Relations between military and civilians are stated to be improving steadily in several Regions (Newcastle, Nottingham, Reading, Edinburgh). Reading states that the ubiquity of uniform has excellent effect on civilian morale and that people are becoming accustomed to the inevitable dislocation which the presence of the military causes. There are minor grievances about the roughness of the Canadians and lack of helpfulness on the part of the military to the LDV. In Aberdeen church-goers are developing a scheme of private hospitality to soldiers.

Complaints about the condition of shelters are reported from Newcastle, Nottingham and Bristol; Anderson shelters are becoming waterlogged and public shelters put to improper uses. The need for organised cleaning of public shelters is stressed.

Satisfaction at the amendments to the regulations on the new war courts is reported from two Regions.

NORTHERN (Newcastle) Increasing public agreement with postponement of overseas evacuation, thanks to recent news of sinking of passenger ships.

NORTH-EASTERN (Leeds) In spite of Joubert's explanations many people still claim to be able to tell a German plane by its broken note. Lord Harewood's remark that 'our morale will be upset if we become aware that the Government is not telling us the truth' has met with much approval. Dissatisfaction reported on coast where men on defence work are earning £9 a week while soldiers get 14/-. Liability of evacuees from Jersey for military service is discussed in Huddersfield, as they are believed to be exempted.

NORTH-MIDLAND (Nottingham) Criticism that tea rationing affects poor far more than rich is common. Price of fresh fruit and shortage of eggs causing annoyance. Many parents express relief that decision about overseas evacuation has been taken out of their hands.

EASTERN (Cambridge) Constant repetition of identical or similar news in BBC bulletins continues to be criticised. Requests that detailed descriptions of aerial dog-fights should be placed at end of news. Some demand for a detached weekly review of the war situation.

SOUTHERN (Reading) Complaints from Aldershot that Army building contracts are going to firms from London and elsewhere not in the area.

SOUTH-WESTERN (Bristol) In spite of last night's aerial activity morale continues high. Growing feeling of confidence in RAF. Sightseeing prevalent in Cheltenham during recent daylight raid. Requests in Chippenham for contex filters and shelters.

WALES (Cardiff) Interest increasing in events in Balkans. Many hope Russian and Turkish interests will soon conflict with those of Germany to our advantage. Satisfaction at additional American embargoes.

MIDLAND (Birmingham) Reports indicate much discussion of the likelihood of a blockade war rather than an invasion, and this is causing a false sense of security. Bus company is appealing for staggering working hours at factories so that it may continue to carry its ever increasing number of passengers.

NORTH-WESTERN (Manchester) Suggestion of daily one minute's silence is received unfavourably. Many people sceptical about 'masses of planes' from USA. They still read of six Hurricanes fighting eighty Messerschmitts and say 'let the facts speak; we are not interested in paper planes.' Profiteering over soft fruit is believed by many housewives to be occurring.

SCOTLAND (Edinburgh) Continued praise of Beaverbrook's broadcast; his accent made a pleasing change from that of the usual BBC speaker.

SOUTH-EASTERN (Tunbridge Wells) There is confusion over the Government's attitude towards holidays. Those engaged in war work understand there will be no holidays for them, yet many officials are apparently to get their annual leave with pay. This strikes many people as unfair.

NORTHERN IRELAND (Belfast) Report of attack on convoy by German aircraft off Ulster Coast has stimulated interest in war.

LONDON

Women increasingly disgruntled at lack of employment, particularly in munitions factories. Much comment about sinking of *Lancastria*. More definite news wanted about air raids. Private information often exaggerates damage done and official attitude does not allay anxiety caused in this way. Much comment about allowances of all kinds. Soldiers' wives' allowances not based on present cost of living figures. Some soldiers said to be throwing up promotion because extra pay, instead of benefiting their wives, is deducted from special grant. Allowance for aliens compares favourably with Public Assistance and allowance for soldiers' children. Anti-Chamberlain feeling still strong in some areas. Cheap milk scheme not yet fully understood.

MONDAY 29 JULY TO SATURDAY 3 AUGUST 1940

The week began with the launch by the Minister of Supply, Herbert Morrison, of a National Salvage Campaign directed mainly at house-wives. 'There are war weapons in your household waste,' a press advertisement declared. 'Every scrap counts, so save every scrap – of paper, metal, bone. Keep them separate and put them by the dustbin every collection day.' The campaign, according to Home Intelligence, was well received, but the public continued to complain about siren policy, the suppression of the news of the sinking of the *Lancastria* and the inadequacy of the tea ration. Another grievance was the high price of fresh fruit, which many housewives wanted for jam-making, but on a more cheerful note the release of pickled eggs was said to have given 'satisfaction to densely populated areas'. From Mayfair an observer reported that the communal pig bucket was proving to be a great success.

Although war industry was expanding and unemployment falling, the contraction of peacetime activities was causing hardship in places. In coastal resorts like Bournemouth or Scarborough hotel and catering businesses were facing bankruptcy, and it was reported that London solicitors were a 'new depressed community'. There was also some indication that the Communist Party, which had isolated itself by opposing the war, was attracting support through the exploitation of class grievances. 'Although there is a high degree of national unity about the prosecution of the war,' Home Intelligence recorded on 3 August, 'the poorer sections of the community are outspoken in their belief that sacrifices are unequal.' In parts of London there were signs of a revival of anti-Semitism directed against German and Polish Jews, though the internment of long-established Italian residents was now condemned as unjust.

On 30 July eighty German bombers and fighters made a daylight attack on the port of Dover, and seventeen German aircraft were shot down. The decision to relax the censorship rules and allow the location of the raid to be published was widely welcomed.

While the daily reports still began with the statement that morale was holding steady, this seemed increasingly superfluous. 'A most reliable observer,' Home Intelligence noted on 29 July, 'at the end of a tour through many parts of England, says "People don't want exhortation to be cheerful: they are cheerful. They don't want to be told to be good: they are as cooperative as they can be. What they want is information and explanation with lots of jam by way of music, processions, flags, songs and all the rest."'

MONDAY 29 JULY 1940

There is little change in general morale. The tendencies to over-optimism which have been already commented upon are still in evidence and should be most carefully considered. The present lull which has given rise to these reactions has been used by the press for unconstructive criticism and attacks upon leadership. These attacks upon leaders have produced some confusion in the popular mind and if they continue there are indications that they will lead to increasing bewilderment. Press criticism of the Minister of Information is only reflected to a very slight degree in our daily record of verbatims and overheard conversations. The feeling against Chamberlain is also not as strong as it was. At the same time, however, there are more over-heard comments on 'the inefficiency of the Government', on 'doubtful leadership', on 'bickerings in the Government'. From the point of view of national unity these are undesirable signs.

The meetings which the Communists held during the weekend were extremely well-attended and in Hyde Park the attendances were the best recorded since the beginning of the war. In Newcastle successful Communist demonstrations demanding better ARP shelters, etc. were held. It is impor-tant to record that the new 'non-Party' attitude which the Communists are adopting is striking a note which is likely to find response. At the same time, it is important to observe that Communist support for the 'Men of Munich Must Go' campaign has brought about the withdrawal of more moderate sympathy.

The withholding of news about the Lancastria *has had a most undesir-able effect and continues to be widely commented upon.*

A most reliable observer, at the end of a tour through many parts of England, says 'People don't want exhortation to be cheerful: they are cheerful. They don't want to be told to be good: they are as cooperative as they can be. What they want is information and explanation with lots of jam by way of music, processions, flags, songs and all the rest'. This sums up many other reports.

Points from Regions

NORTHERN (Newcastle) Complaints from heavy industrial centres about the tea ration. Voluntary shelter stewards appointed in Middlesbrough and has resulted in more comfortable conditions. Decrease in employment in coal mining is causing demand for coal storage campaign to be pressed.

NORTH-EASTERN (Leeds) Feeling expressed against the Secret Session. Further restrictions of freedom of speech and criticism would be unpopular. Budget appears to be universally accepted. Yorkshire coastal resorts impatient for the Government to institute a scheme of assistance.

NORTH-MIDLAND (Nottingham) Appreciation of re-broadcast of Dorothy Thompson's talk. Alterations in internment policy well received. Some concern still expressed over new War Courts. Dissatisfaction in some villages over selection of local Home Guard commandants. Farmers' wives anxious about tea ration for harvest period when farmworkers drink large quantities.

EASTERN (Cambridge) Public becoming more accustomed to wartime conditions. Imposition of curfew in coastal zone has not caused undue alarm. Scepticism regarding Air Ministry communiques on results of German raids. Financial difficulties of families of those serving with the Forces are creating some anxiety. Scheme of private patrol in Bury St Edmunds for warning householders of impending raids not welcomed by local Civil Defence.

SOUTHERN (Reading) Morale high, although some complacency due to the failure of invasion to materialise. South Coast Defence Area settling down and Bournemouth facing a ruined summer season well in expectation of concessions similar to those made to Brighton. Some discontent in Reading at increase in soft fruit prices.

SOUTH-WESTERN (Bristol) Increased defence measures in Barnstaple are improving morale, and a frequent sight of fighters over Stroud has a heartening effect. Reports show that the Region is singularly free from rumours. The Housewives Service is being taken up enthusiastically by WVS. Cheaper beer and tobacco for the Forces would be welcomed.

WALES (Cardiff) Civil Defence services are alert, but it is feared that prolonged waiting may cause relaxation of vigilance. In many districts siren policy causes frequent cessation of work and lack of sleep at times when there is no visible or audible enemy action. Application of Purchase Tax to books generally condemned.

MIDLAND (Birmingham) Large section of opinion thinks there will be no attempted invasion. Representation from Wellington that beer and tobacco concessions should be made to men in the Forces. Herefordshire County Council gives CO employees alternative of continuing at private's pay or leave of absence without pay for duration.

NORTH-WESTERN (Manchester) Morale in Manchester-Salford area excellent after last night's raid. Little rumour, but some papers are trying to work up a story of 'public anxiety' because no alarms were given.

SCOTLAND (Edinburgh) Expectation of invasion has decreased due to widespread preparations for defence. Priestley's broadcast widely approved. Some speculation about immediate developments in the Near East.

SOUTH-EASTERN (Tunbridge Wells) Criticism of delay and presentation of the news of the *Lancastria* still received. Hopes expressed that concessions in tobacco prices will be made to soldiers. The scheme for buying aircraft components is appealing to the public.

NORTHERN IRELAND (Belfast) Puzzlement over denial of reports of attack on convoy off Ulster Coast, as gunfire was rumoured. Renewed demand for Government munition factory to be established on account of surplus labour. Criticism of awkward position of public shelters in Belfast. Business houses complain of excessive postal delays due to censorship.

LONDON

Evidence from many quarters that people are resenting too much exhortation to be cheerful. They say in East End 'We have got our tails up – why do they keep on telling us to put them up!' News of *Lancastria* sinking still causing uneasiness; people fear that though we hear of RAF losses we are not getting news of shipping losses. Suspicions voiced that they are extremely serious. General opinion in City that Budget is too lenient: 'Traders in great difficulties to meet obligations while ordinary citizens can still afford luxuries; income tax should have been 10/- in the £.' Many people suggest bicycle licence. Business and Professional Women's Club meeting unanimously approve the deduction of income tax at source. London solicitors make new depressed community; though extremely hard hit are reported to be stoical and confident in outcome of war. Sense of injustice reported among British citizens in districts where Italians ran small businesses at summary internment of people they had known for many years. Many are looking after Italian children whose parents had been interned without tribunal. Resentment in parts of City where fur and mantle trades congregate at alien Jews unabsorbed into national service and free to make money. Responsible observers fear growing anti-Semitism if young men between twenty and thirty five are not conscripted to work on land or some other form of national service where they cannot make profits. Most of these are German and Polish Jews. Whitechapel reports children streaming back from Reception Areas and parents taking on debts to pay fares. West Ham complains of growing lack of discipline among local children. Factory Defence Scheme now working well, states supervisor of large London concern, who before complained bitterly at lack of organisation. Consequent increase of confidence and cheerfulness among volunteers and workers. Younger ARP wardens reported to fear jobs not justified and consider they should be freed for Home Defence while older men take their places. Chief food grumbles over weekend shortage of vegetables and high prices of fruit. Priestley's postscript warmly appreciated.

TUESDAY 30 JULY 1940

Morale remains steady.

There is a good deal of satisfaction at the publication of the name of the place where yesterday's raid took place (Dover).

There is confidence in Civil Defence measures but the siren policy is the subject of continued criticism in certain areas.

Mr Ogilvie's broadcast was commented upon favourably in many reports.

Points from Regions

Three Regions report great satisfaction that Dover was disclosed as the town which was the object of yesterday's air raid, and hope is expressed that this practice will be continued.

NORTHERN (Newcastle) Complaints received of absence of sirens in early morning raid on Monday, when two women were killed who had quick access to shelters which remained intact. Favourable comments on Dorothy Thompson's broadcast. Complaints of prices of fruit and vegetables, although growers complain they cannot always get rid of supplies.

NORTH-EASTERN (Leeds) Morale good and few complaints heard. Anti-Japanese feeling getting stronger and pro-Russian opinion growing. Local agitation at Wetherby on account of uncamouflaged paper factory which is said to be good guide for enemy aircraft to new armament factory opposite.

NORTH-MIDLAND (Nottingham) Evidence that Silent Column campaign has had good effect. General desire for better relations with Russia. Both Germany and USA are said to have better wireless news than us, and there is general desire to know as much as possible of what is happening. Some lack of faith felt in the French people. Little interest shown in personalities of military leaders.

EASTERN (Cambridge) An air raid early today in Norwich involving casualties in the working-class quarter has caused criticism at the absence of sirens, which would have enabled victims to reach safety. The holding back of news of the *Lancastria* has caused distrust. General confidence in our defences, but local criticism of neglect of road barriers.

SOUTHERN (Reading) Reports of speed with which rumour grows about local and distant bombings due to lack of precise news. Opinions expressed that Britain should demonstrate she is fighting not only to preserve the Empire, but for a community of interest for the peoples of Europe, to counteract creation of Hitler's 'New Europe'.

SOUTH-WESTERN (Bristol) Morale high and people taking sporadic air raids well. Many feel Hitler has changed his invasion plans. Reports from Cornwall show that presence of soldiers is putting people in good heart. Rumour and gossip quiet. Complaints of coal shortage from Truro and Exeter. Requests from Falmouth that shelters can be made available from evacuated areas.

WALES (Cardiff) Morale excellent. It is surmised that the time draws near when we shall attack again with an army abroad. Beaverbrook's statistics and confidence have had heartening effect. Release of pickled eggs gives satisfaction to densely populated areas. Tea ration still unpopular with heavy workers. Protests still reported against inclusion of books in Purchase Tax.

MIDLAND (Birmingham) Defeat of German attack on Dover caused great satisfaction and confidence in RAF to deal with any attempted air invasion. Coventry, Wednesbury and other towns report keenness of women to cooperate in salvage schemes.

NORTH-WESTERN (Manchester) Business circles alarmed at speed with which Japan has exploited our weakness in closing the Burma Road. Public has little knowledge of army administration, but feels the new Committee has plenty to do.

SCOTLAND (Edinburgh) Interest in Irish question greatly decreased. View held that we shall receive some assistance from Russia at some future date. Re-broadcast of Dorothy Thompson's talk popular.

SOUTH-EASTERN (Tunbridge Wells) News of Dover air battle has had heartening effect, especially in other coastal towns. Opinion widely held that Hitler has changed his plans. Rye and Winchelsea beach dwellers, who have had to evacuate at short notice for military reasons, were outside special areas scheme and there is no central authority to ensure their welfare.

NORTHERN IRELAND (Belfast) Keen interest in Ogilvie's broadcast, due to his Northern Ireland associations. Some concern over friction with Japan. Enemy activity against British ports interpreted as indication that invasion is postponed.

LONDON

Mention of name in Dover air battle has roused great interest and expressions of satisfaction. This is reported from many districts and classes of people, and several wonder whether it means change of policy with regard to bulletins of air raids in places which would not give away valuable information to the enemy. Implication that such change of policy would be warmly welcomed. Ogilvie's talk appreciated by all listeners reporting today. Kensington need reported for statement about post-war aims and conditions of living. Prominent members of sporting community express concern at Germany's statement of post-war aims in Europe as compared with our lack of constructive policy. Reduction of working hours approved from health viewpoint in districts such as Woolwich where fatigue forced workers gradually to reduce hours, even before Bevin's statement. Complaints of exploitation by removal firms of evacuees from coastal areas reported from Lewisham. Refugees in Brixton include Dutch, Polish and Belgian; Dutch and Polish grateful for what is done for them but Flemish ungrateful and unwilling to take jobs. Islington reports Belgian refugees under misapprehension that allowances are paid as a right by Belgian Government and afraid that if they take work these allowances will be stopped. Local jealousy reported among British who would like jobs that Belgians are encouraged to take. Observer in Mayfair reports communal pig bucket great success.

WEDNESDAY 31 JULY 1940

There is little change in morale today, and the press campaigns against the Secret Session and certain Ministers have aroused relatively little public interest. The press reports from foreign sources of troops massing across the Channel have aroused rather more interest, but even this is limited.

The arrest of the British subjects in Japan has been considerably talked of, and three Regions record a public demand for strong action. Such remarks as 'We should never have given way on the Burma Road question', 'That's what comes of trying to appease the Japanese', are mentioned as typical.

Sir John Anderson's short talk on ARP last night was generally appreciated. Its simplicity and terseness were welcomed and it was described as 'a good refresher course on household ARP'. His reference to gas has produced many enquiries about contex filters in those areas where filters have not yet been fitted.

The proposed modifications in the tea ration have been received with 'general thankfulness'. Several Regions report that the tea ration has affected the public as a whole more than any other food ration introduced so far.

Points from Regions

NORTHERN (Newcastle) Interest reported in Balkan situation, and desire to know what British action is being taken. Absence of sirens has caused many protests, and some older people are not going to bed till daylight. There is a rumour in Newcastle that air-raid warnings will not be given even to wardens.

NORTH-EASTERN (Leeds) Morale still high. Some evidence that Secret Session is unpopular with the public.

NORTH-MIDLAND (Nottingham) The withholding of news of the *Lancastria* still gives rise to critical comments. It is widely urged that soft fruit prices should be controlled. Overtime among workers is causing strain and absenteeism. Many villages complain of delay in receiving contex filters. Dissatisfaction from Leicestershire that Army casualty lists get unduly large headlines in several leading papers.

Persistent conviction that recent earth tremor was an explosion due to enemy action.

EASTERN (Cambridge) Resentment still felt in Norwich owing to absence of sirens yesterday. Evacuation from coastal towns slackening, and many who have left believe that they are free from rent and rates.

SOUTHERN (Reading) Demands from Guildford, Portsmouth, and High Wycombe for more detailed news of German air raids on Britain, and that the BBC news should be made more interesting. Evidence that Haw-Haw's following is diminishing, but the German news still attracts listeners.

SOUTH-WESTERN (Bristol) Morale remains high. People still affected by the withholding of news of the *Lancastria*, and wonder what else is kept back. Complaint from Minehead that potential holiday-makers have the impression that South West resorts are dangerous areas.

WALES (Cardiff) Continued night warnings have caused much tiredness. Criticism that the only news of our shipping losses is from German communiques. Reports confirm that troops are the worst offenders in discussing military matters in public.

MIDLAND (Birmingham) Houses of Pacifists stoned in Coventry, where City Council has decided not to discharge COs. Demand in Small Heath (Birmingham) that Home Guard should be decentralised on the basis of street units. Transport organisations claim that they will be unable to cope with winter traffic unless munition workers' hours are staggered.

NORTH-WESTERN (Manchester) Some disappointment that Premier does not intend to answer Hitler, as Halifax was considered inadequate. Swiss reports of troops massing for invasion of Britain has had unsettling effect on many.

SCOTLAND (Edinburgh) Irritation at alarmist chalking 'Invasion imminent?' by news-boys in Edinburgh. Still slight mistrust of RAF successes. Parents of evacuated children worried because they are receiving fewer letters; this is due to high postage expenses and to the children taking the injunction against careless talk so seriously.

SOUTH-EASTERN (Tunbridge Wells) High morale in Dover area following Monday's raid and satisfaction expressed with Civil Defence services. Public respond promptly to sirens in towns which have not yet been bombed.* Budget increases faced cheerfully. In country districts many who have grown more food are now left with a surplus. Belief in Maidstone that an invasion attempt was made during Monday's raid on Dover.

NORTHERN IRELAND (Belfast) Opinion that invasion is postponed is modified by reports of troops massing on French Coast. Business-men welcome Dalton's statement on tightening the blockade. Criticism of large numbers of unemployed in Ulster. New ration of supplies for home textile trade caused disappointment among manufacturers.

LONDON

On the whole morale remains good, though some people continue to wonder how Britain can win. A certain amount of discontent persists amongst women because of small army allowance; this may ultimately affect their morale. Feeling against foreign refugees growing in some districts. Foreign troops in Chelsea mistrusted as people think 'they are eating our food and they get the rifles our Home Guard should have'. Comment about the scarcity of eggs – even hospitals have difficulty in getting them. Delay in news about *Lancastria* still causing resentment and announcement that SS *Liverpool* had not been lost caused some people to listen to Haw-Haw to obtain more correct version. Resentment still felt amongst women not able to obtain munitions work in London area. Comments that in poor localities certain food bought in small quantities is charged at proportionately higher rate than large quantities. After announce-ment had been made that extra sugar was obtainable for jam making it was found that grocers did not have the extra sugar to sell; fruit

* Editors' note: see subsequent erratum in report for 15 August.

which had already been bought to make jam was thus wasted. Some
Finchley refugees would like to do odd jobs, even a few hours weekly.
Labour Exchange officials disapprove even though British workers
would not take such jobs. Few cases reported in this district of
victimisation of British subjects bearing foreign names.

THURSDAY 1 AUGUST 1940

*No change in morale. There are signs, however, that a feeling of compla-
cency is beginning to grow up in some quarters. This is shown in a fairly
widely expressed belief that invasion may be indefinitely delayed. Coupled
with this development are indications of wishful thinking about the possibilities of aid from Russia, hostility to which country is seldom expressed.*

*A tendency to scepticism is still noticeable in opinions about news. This
is partly attributable to the way in which it is put over by the BBC. There
are criticisms of war talks on the ground that there are too many, and that
these are sometimes 'depressing instead of reassuring.' 'The BBC news bulletins
still minimise our reverses.'*

*The prevailing uncertainty about the siren policy is still reflected in a few
Regions, though anxiety on this score seems to be lessening. A slight increase
is shown in other worries, among which are the wage anomalies of certain
skilled workers, and the uneven working of the salvage scheme. Most of these
problems, however, seem to be of local rather than national significance.*

Points from Regions

NORTHERN (Newcastle) Belief in German invasion diminishing.
Reports show that Russia's assistance in the war will be welcomed
by many who do not like the social system of USSR. Complaints
about wage anomalies increasing among skilled craftsmen. Situation
in Scarborough serious where many small businesses are faced with
bankruptcy, largely due to the evacuation of the well-to-do.

NORTH-EASTERN (Leeds) People in raided areas are adjusting themselves well to the raids. Many fishermen whose vessels have been

requisitioned by the authorities resent not being allowed to serve on them. Official explanation of removal of road obstructions generally accepted. South Yorkshire reports that practical munition work is popular in Technical Schools.

NORTH-MIDLAND (Nottingham) Indications that all sections of public would welcome Russia as an enemy of Germany, if not as an ally of Britain. Scepticism with regard to official news is widespread. General feeling Budget is not nearly drastic enough. Grumbling in Rutland at insufficient number of shelters. Excellence of Beaverbrook's and Dorothy Thompson's broadcasts still discussed.

EASTERN (Cambridge) Siren controversy continues unabated in Norwich. Reference in Anderson's talk to the possibility of being sprayed by gas has caused some alarm in Chelmsford area. Complaints that there are too many war talks, and that they depress, instead of reassuring.

SOUTHERN (Reading) Complacency in some districts because anticipated German attack has not materialised. Complaints among middle classes over continued failure to mobilise man-power. General feeling that BBC news bulletins still minimise our reverses.

SOUTH-WESTERN (Bristol) Morale still remains high. People are now used to nightly visits from raiders and take to their shelters as a matter of course. Reports that the working class is pleased with steps taken to deal with the 'hard-core' of unemployment.

WALES (Cardiff) Occasional bombs have been dropped in agricultural districts in mid-Wales, causing little damage, and the general reaction is one of pride that these areas are now 'in the show'. Some disappointment that direct action against Italy has not been taken this summer due to scepticism of the standard of Italian forces. The Secret Session has aroused little public interest.

MIDLAND (Birmingham) The practice of dropping flares from aeroplanes is causing concern in Herefordshire, especially among women. Cancellation of August Bank Holiday received with equanimity.

Midland towns are responding well to Government's appeal to save and salvage.

NORTH-WESTERN (Manchester) Women worried by hint of check up on sugar used for jam, as many have kept some hoping for cheaper fruit prices. Criticism of waste of material likely to result from removal of road barriers. Hustle to complete elaborate barrier system in Liverpool has attracted much attention. Some uneasiness about US ban on export of aviation spirit.

SCOTLAND (Edinburgh) The new registration scheme for Glasgow dockers will help to ease matters, as Glasgow is the only large port in which this scheme is not yet operating.

SOUTH-EASTERN (Tunbridge Wells) Indignation at absence of sirens especially for raid on Sheerness on Tuesday of last week. Though morale is good, many do not go to bed or else sleep fully clothed. Voluntary evacuation continues from Dover area, but a number who left some weeks ago have now returned. All large hotels in Eastbourne have closed down, and few boarding houses are doing any business.

NORTHERN IRELAND (Belfast) People unperturbed by reported plans of immediate invasion. Belfast pleased with the performance of the *Alcantara*, which was built and lengthened there. A few evacuated children have been brought home from Reception Areas.

FRIDAY 2 AUGUST 1940

There is little change in morale: there is cheerfulness and increasing confidence in our defences.

Although there are indications of some slight over-complacency among certain sections of the community, there is also evidence that the dangers of 'a false lull' are beginning to be appreciated.

Interest in the international aspects of the war has revived a little by the publication of Molotov's speech and conversations show that many people are vaguely disappointed both by the general tone of the speech and by the references to this country. Evidently there has been a good deal of wishful thinking among people who are not politically minded: Russia has been thought of as a potential ally or at any rate as a factor not likely to operate to our disfavour.

There has been a good deal of popular satisfaction at the revision of the defeatist talk sentences, although there is little evidence that people at large are greatly concerned about the curtailment of civil liberties. Many factory workers are fatigued and working long hours: there is more concern about conditions of work and prices than about libertarian principles. On the other hand professional classes are considerably disturbed by the regulations of recent months and by the curtailment of liberties which appears to threaten.

The treatment of COs is another subject which is causing concern to professional opinion.

A report on anti-Chamberlain feeling still shows a high percentage of people who think that Mr Chamberlain should not be in the Cabinet, but sentiment is not as strong as it was and it is noticed that more people are saying they have no opinion and that more people make evasive replies.

The withholding of the news about the Lancastria is having a noticeable effect on people's belief in 'official news'. Comments show increasing scepticism.

Note: contact with several agencies using interview methods shows that there have been no increased difficulties or untoward incidents. The man in the street has not been touched by the press campaign.

Attached is a copy of the German leaflet dropped over this country last night.*

Points from Regions

Four Regions report disappointment in Molotov's speech. A comment from Wales is that it indicates a prolonged war, and from Scotland comes the criticism that 'inspired' press articles had anticipated a change in Russian policy. It is realised that Russia is playing her own game.

* Editors' note: no leaflet was found attached to this report.

NORTHERN (Newcastle) Some complaints of differing interpretations by officials of the conditions governing entry into defence zone. Delay in announcing the loss of the *Lancastria* has weakened belief in the news, and reports show a tendency to listen more frequently to German broadcasts. Strong complaints from shipbuilding industry about new purple warning regulation, as danger from accident is thought to be greater than from bombs. Problem of cold tea for harvest workers causes anxiety in rural areas.

NORTH-EASTERN (Leeds) Morale and confidence unchanged. Bevin's remarks on COs appreciated, also Lord Portsea's speech on the Channel Isles, as many evacuees from there are now in this Region. Opinion in Leeds not unfavourable to Manchester's scheme of blackout curfew for children. Royal visit to Hull revealed no diminution of loyalty to the Crown.

NORTH-MIDLAND (Nottingham) In Grimsby where naval losses are known almost immediately delay in official announcements is shaking public confidence. Interest in BBC bulletins has decreased on account of repetition. People are not taking shelter in Grimsby during AA gunfire, due to curiosity. In raided areas enemy action has stiffened morale. Obstruction of fields against landing aircraft has been intensified by farmers.

EASTERN (Cambridge) Need for declaration of a clear policy with regard to sirens is regarded as urgent in Norwich; there is faith in the shelters, but no opportunity for using them. The release of the town's name for publication has aroused mixed feelings, and it is felt that there is a case for publishing the casualty roll. The apparent absence of RAF and AA protection over Norwich is causing disquiet.

SOUTH-WESTERN (Bristol) News of leaflets dropping in Somerset spread quickly, and the public were eager to secure them as souvenirs. Complaints from Bristol of lack of buses for troops in out-of-the-way camps and that there is chafing at present inactivity, especially among Dominion troops. Siren controversy persists in Trowbridge. Coal shortage still acute in Trowbridge, Truro and Exeter.

WALES (Cardiff) Reported machine-gunning of Norwich has aroused resentment. Many believe invasion postponed till events will give Germany hope of consolidating on part of our coast or on Eire.

MIDLAND (Birmingham) Morale of women in bombed rural areas excellent. Criticism from Nuneaton that midnight passes for Polish airmen sometimes cause scenes after closing time.

NORTH-WESTERN (Manchester) Mention of names of towns bombed, and visited by royalty, has caused satisfaction. Eager enquiries as to whether enemy leaflets were dropped in this Region. Disappointment that so little has been done to stop internment of anti-Hitler aliens.

SCOTLAND (Edinburgh) Concern in Edinburgh that Polish and Czech officers have no official club, and from Glasgow comes comment on the plight of Polish officers and men, and their families, who are depending on public assistance. Private efforts are being made to assist them.

SOUTH-EASTERN (Tunbridge Wells) Some criticism of prominence in press to Stimson's statement that we may be defeated in thirty days, as likely to spread despondency and alarm.

NORTHERN IRELAND (Belfast) Favourable comments on specific mention of Dover and Norwich in air-raid bulletin. Macmillan's statement for full employment of industrial capacity on war requirements received with satisfaction.

LONDON

Several people express opinion that attack on Ministry of Information is a press stunt. More politically minded people antagonistic, expressing fear that democratic methods are being superseded. Average person not affected. German leaflet dropping aroused interest. Suspicions voiced that there is something in leaflet not revealed in reports of Hitler's speech as leaflets were so quickly collected. Suggested publication of text of leaflet in press. Lack of discipline among children in most districts increasingly noticeable; attributed by responsible observer to absence of fathers on National Service. Morale of Belgian refugees lower than others as they have no Government here to give them a lead. Allowances vary in different Boroughs. 'Mightier Yet' posters most effective yet produced by Ministry. Romford people disturbed by fact of enemy planes circling for about two hours over-head without British planes; might feel happier if warnings were given when enemy planes above. Some poor people do not know suitable person to countersign application forms for new milk scheme. Milk retailers are found to be uncooperative about milk scheme as it creates additional work; this keeps some people from making applications. Charlton people would like some form of lighting during black-out; feel that rationing is necessary and no one feeling the pinch except for sugar. Finsbury report that morale is excellent but strain showing physically – complaints of overwork and tiredness.

SATURDAY 3 AUGUST 1940

Morale is high.

There is a growing confidence in the defences of 'our island fortress', and although there is at present no danger of a 'Maginot line' mentality this is a possibility which publicists should not overlook.

The idea of a fully comprehensive salvage scheme is readily accepted, and there is willing cooperation on the part of housewives; at the same time interviews show that householders are sceptical about the success of official schemes and critical of the present position.

Reports show that many workers are in doubt about holidays. Should they take family holidays if possible? Where is it desirable to go? Is it really Government policy to encourage holidays lasting a week or more?

Indifference about international affairs continues.

Although there is a high degree of national unity about the prosecution of the war, the poorer sections of the community are outspoken in their belief that sacrifices are unequal. Although the family income of many industrial commu-nities has increased, it is clear that certain regulations and restrictions strongly affect the working classes. Practical difficulties, e.g. long hours, high prices, tea rations, are frequently spoken of in illustration of inequality of sacrifice demanded.

Points from Regions

Three Regions report general satisfaction at Lord Beaverbrook's inclusion in the War Cabinet. Hope is expressed in Manchester that he will displace Chamberlain, and anxiety lest aeroplane production may suffer.

NORTHERN (Newcastle) Many sources report satisfaction at the modification in treatment of refugees. Criticism received of the removal of road barricades, which in some cases has decreased the feeling of protection. Local troop manoeuvres gave rise to a rumour that immediate invasion was anticipated.

NORTH-EASTERN (Leeds) It is generally expected any day the war will take a more serious turn and people are prepared for it. Many protests against the high prices of fruit, and growers complain they get no return.

NORTH-MIDLAND (Nottingham) Belated news of losses still criticised, although there is praise for the Admiralty communique explaining differences between our tonnage losses and German claims. General agreement that a tobacco concession should be made to the Armed Forces and many consider free travel warrants should be given to troops who have to go long journeys for leave. Some demand from householders for a more uniform policy of billeting evacuees. Leicester reports difficulty in disposing of surplus allotment produce.

EASTERN (Cambridge) Hitler's leaflets regarded as a sign of weakness on his part. Publication of full series of RAF raids has favourably impressed the public; some quarters suggest an explanation might be given as to why our machines are superior. Molotov's speech considered a setback for us, and there is a growing feeling for a stronger attitude towards Japan. Siren policy still criticised in Norwich. Encouraging reports of high morale received from a bombed East Anglian village.

SOUTHERN (Reading) Reports show that the public is confused over the point at issue in the press attack on the MOI. Many towns complain they see less of their MPs than in peace time.

SOUTH-WESTERN (Bristol) Air activity continues, and lack of co-ordination in sounding sirens is commented upon. Alleged lack of AA protection in Penzance. Plymouth hopes references to 'a town in the South West' will be abolished, as visitors from London expect to find it in ruins. Bristol reports need for instructions on how to prevent flooding of Anderson shelters.

WALES (Cardiff) Continuous air raids, although causing lack of sleep, have stiffened morale. Doubts as to whether we are doing as well in North Africa as BBC and press make out. Reported project to arrest Japanese as reprisals welcomed.

SCOTLAND (Edinburgh) Hitler's leaflet has reassured people of the accuracy of the press reported speech; some criticism of the action of the Chief Constable in collecting them. Slight recurrence of invasion talk. The sounding of sirens in Tayport after a bomb had exploded has caused renewed, although milder, complaints.

SOUTH-EASTERN (Tunbridge Wells) More people inclined to stay in bed while raids are in progress. Many regard criticism of MOI as a newspaper stunt, and there is an idea that the Ministry's title suggests giving information as its chief function.

NORTHERN IRELAND (Belfast) Ulster Farmers' Union to lodge protest against low prices to be paid to potato growers for next two months. Further evacuation of children being planned from Belfast. The courage of the gunners of the *Highlander* is praised by the seafaring-community.

LONDON

Allowances for wives of serving men still quoted as causing hard-ship and resentment in all districts especially compared with civilian wages. Growing unemployment in Watford where printing industry is turning off hundreds of workers, making people express fear of coming winter and its hardships. Some women reported to be agitating about proposal to introduce vitamin B into white bread, saying it will be doped; instead would prefer wholemeal bread such as rich can buy. Seavacuation considered 'a muddle'; women asking for clear statement of present position. Fear that Nazi propaganda blaming Britain for possible famine in Europe may not be sufficiently countered, especially in conquered countries. Boys between fourteen and nineteen finding difficulty in getting training as firms know they will lose them when old enough for army; club leaders being called up; a responsible observer feels that some scheme is urgently needed to absorb these young people. Chiswick complains that children are destructive in neighbourhood and breaking windows. Suggestion that parents should be encouraged to teach children how to use leisure time constructively. Woolwich reports women's register of unemployed increased by 450 last week because of MOI munitions film. Southall: milk scheme well organised. Clapham reports mistrust of 'house visitors' but most contacts volunteer that in their opinion criticism of Social Survey is largely press stunt. Walworth Evening Institute states students saying 'we never listen to Haw-Haw now – he is not nearly as funny as he was'. Lack of condensed milk new hardship among very poor in district as they cannot afford fresh. Townswomen's Guilds report housewives delighted at prospect of increased tea ration. Islington: some pessimism has been noticed among Civil Defence personnel due, observer states, to long idle hours in canteens and recreation rooms. People complaining of waiting many hours in Exchanges in Brixton and Tooting for PRD payment as officials are seriously overworked. Soho: 'gossip that more prominent Fascists are free while inoffensive waiters and other workers interned. Many tales of discontent voiced about *Arandora Star*'.

MONDAY 5 AUGUST TO SATURDAY 10 AUGUST 1940

'At the moment the war is somewhat in the background,' observed Home Intelligence on 7 August. After the seismic events of May and June, and the blood-curdling threats which had accompanied Hitler's 'peace offer', no invasion had taken place and there was something of a lull in hostilities. There was still some scepticism about the official figures for British and German losses in the air, which always seemed to show that Fighter Command was victorious, but popular confidence in the defensive capacities of the RAF was growing. Far away in the horn of Africa Italian troops were invading British Somaliland, an event that Home Intelligence reported as briefly causing some unease: 'people everywhere want to hear that we are taking the initiative, but instead we are once more on the defensive, this time against the despised Italians.' In Chelsea, it was reported the following day, the 'intelligentsia' were 'almost defeatist in consequence'.

On 2 August German aircraft had dropped leaflets containing an English translation of Hitler's Reichstag speech over the south of England. 'There is evidence,' Home Intelligence recorded, 'that the public is dissatisfied at the actions of the police (and wardens) in collecting the German leaflets ... These would be valued as souvenirs and many people declare that they would like to read with their own eyes what was written in the leaflets.' There was also 'some interest', the Cambridge regional office noted, in the plea for a compromise peace made by Richard Stokes, the Labour MP for Ipswich. Hitler had declared that Germany was fighting to create a New European Order. This raised the question of what the British were fighting for, a topic of some significance for the propaganda war in which the Ministry of Information itself was engaged. The regional office in Reading reported a 'growing local demand that Government should formulate a peace aims programme for Europe. Even unimaginative Slough Information Committee has voiced this.'

August the 3rd marked the beginning of the Bank Holiday weekend, and Home Intelligence remarked on the large holiday crowds, but on Bank Holiday Monday itself most factories and offices worked a normal day. So did Home Intelligence, which reported with an almost audible sigh of relief that the press campaign against 'Cooper's Snoopers' had made scarcely any impression on the public. On the home front more generally there were problems: 'The Prime Minister's leadership is unchallenged but evidence suggests that there is no such close identification between the people and the Government as a whole.'

One of the few Whitehall departments to win the confidence of the public was the Ministry of Food under Lord Woolton. The Ministry's cookery tips, broadcast over the radio in the *Kitchen Front* programme, were much appreciated by housewives, and Woolton's decision to make the wasting of food a criminal offence was generally well received. On a more critical note, women in 'certain London districts' were disturbed by the proposal to introduce Vitamin B into white bread: 'wholemeal bread as supplied to the upper classes would meet the case.'

The wholesale internment of enemy aliens, a policy which had yet to be reversed in spite of promises of a more liberal approach, remained a black mark against the government. 'Hardship reported in East London,' noted the daily report on 7 August, 'on account of the internment of aliens, leaving families practically destitute; some internees resident in this country for over forty years, many infirm and old, deserving of better treatment.'

MONDAY 5 AUGUST 1940

There is little change in morale which continues to be high.

The Prime Minister's message (on invasion) was warmly welcomed by those in positions of responsibility and reports indicate that his warning was not without effect. Nevertheless there are many who say that, taking into account the popular view that 'Invasion is off', the warning was not personal enough nor strong enough.

There were large holiday crowds over the weekend but there is still a good deal of confusion about the official attitude to holidays.

Mr Duff Cooper's broadcast was on the whole favourably received but there are signs that the continued press campaign has made people less ready to accept what he says uncritically. This attitude has not developed far and many people suggest that it might not have developed at all if he had been broadcasting regularly. From direct and indirect questioning it is clear that a large number of people disapprove of the press campaign against the Minister even though they have been influenced by it. At the street level 'Cooper's Snoopers' have scarcely made any impression: most people, especially in the provinces, have little idea of what the fuss has all been about. The whole controversy has been well above the head of the man in the street. Reports show that a majority of those who had any opinions about the 'snoopers' were in favour of them; those who were against them frequently had distorted ideas of their functions. 'Snooping under the bed' and 'Spying through the keyhole' were reported hallucinations.

The granting of increased Old Age Pensions is a cause of satisfaction (although minor pension grievances still remain in this field). Nevertheless there is evidence that the concession has been insufficiently publicised.

The siren controversy continues.

Points from Regions

For the time being, it is proposed to give points from only six Regions each day, so that these points will cover two-day periods, instead of one-day periods. If, however, events of importance occur in any Region a daily report will be given from that Region.

The Prime Minister's warning against complacency towards the threat of invasion has been widely welcomed. Newcastle reports that it has checked undue complacency in several quarters. Bristol regards it as very necessary as many people were refusing to think about the black side. It is also stressed that the statement will help to 'show the enemy that we have not gone to sleep.' Northern Ireland regards it as timely, as public expectation of invasion had definitely receded. Nottingham states that general opinion is that invasion threats will have to materialise before Hitler's boasts are taken seriously. 'The time has passed when the population could be frightened by the threat of invasion.'

NORTHERN (Newcastle) There are requests from Scarborough that some form of assistance should be arranged for middle-class people who are seriously hit by the Defence Regulations. The continued success of the RAF as shown by official communiques is leading to a little scepticism, and there are requests for explanation of the RAF's qualitative superiority. Flooding of air-raid shelters continues to be complained about. There are complaints of 'excessive' poetry reading in wireless programmes.

NORTH-MIDLAND (Nottingham) Limitation of siren sounding popular in Chesterfield. Rural areas without sirens ask for advice as to their conduct when town sirens are heard in the distance. Many still claim to be able to distinguish German from British planes by their sound. Deduction of income tax at source popular. Many people suggest COs should receive only army pay plus allowances and some people would welcome same rates of pay for factory workers. High fruit prices are still cause for complaint.

SOUTH-WESTERN (Bristol) The arrest of Japanese in England is popular with the public. No grumbles about the absence of Bank Holiday. Holiday resorts on the Bristol Channel coast complain about the mention of the Bristol Channel in Home Security bulletins and say that their trade thereby being ruined. Devonians still think they can identify enemy planes by their sound.

MIDLAND (Birmingham) Although munition workers continue busy over Bank Holiday there is a good deal of criticism; complaints from several centres say that workers feel overtired and that more good would be done by relaxation of the regulation than by rigid observation of the non-stop working plans. Some people in country districts think currency notes may depreciate and silver hoarding is being reported. The need for staggering hours of work in factories so as to ease the burden of transport undertakings is acute.

SCOTLAND (Edinburgh) The siren controversy is in full swing once again as bombs have preceded sirens on three consecutive nights. At the same time the public are not upset by the bomb explosions and many prefer to avoid the suspense of waiting after the sirens have sounded. There is some public feeling that the AA defences of Edinburgh are not as strong as they should be.

NORTHERN IRELAND (Belfast) Birchall's broadcast 'mercilessly trouncing Hitler' keenly appreciated. Sinclair's clear exposure of Nazi exaggeration of British shipping losses highly praised. Public attitude summed up thus: 'facts are the best propaganda'. Few people said to be listening to Haw-Haw, Italian news in English or New British Broadcasting Station. Anti-war propaganda by Communists in Belfast is having little effect. Some complaint that recruiting drive has given results below expectations.

LONDON

Morale is on the whole quite good and there is almost an apathetic feeling growing up amongst some people; they feel that the danger of invasion is growing less and that the war probably won't last very long. No feeling of panic or alarm even in districts where bombs have been dropped and damage caused. Amongst the more thinking section of the population there is a growing feeling that some really constructive policy for the future should now be formulated. Appeals to people's courage unnecessary; invigorating and homely talks like Mr Hackett's more effective. Still many complaints about hardships caused by inadequate allowances to soldiers' families; similar cases very often treated differently. Discontent amongst evacuees from

Margate living in Hanworth about their allowance relative to that given to foreign refugees. Less feeling against refugees; in some districts they are able to get work thus creating a much better spirit among the refugees themselves. Interest in the news seems if anything to be decreasing; one day seems very like another. Preference is expressed for BBC rather than press reports. Fulham reported that the women in the district seem to be much happier now over having sent the children out of London. Shopping is proving a little difficult in some districts and queues for eggs have been noticed. These can now be procured for 2/-, but 3/- a dozen was being asked for fresh eggs. Very little grumbling is heard about food difficulties.

TUESDAY 6 AUGUST 1940

Morale is high.

The Prime Minister's message about invasion continues to be discussed: people in authority emphasise its timeliness and except in remote and rural areas there is some evidence which shows that the public has taken note of the warning.

There are many in authority who feel that the present lull should have been used (and might still be used) for a clear statement of a constructive peace policy on our part. Some of our reports show that there are members of the public who would like to be given an opportunity of reading for themselves the German leaflet giving Hitler's speech in full, and thus assuring themselves that nothing had been hidden from them. They are under the impression that definite 'peace terms' have been put forward by Hitler.

The Prime Minister's leadership is unchallenged but evidence suggests that there is no such close identification between the people and the Government as a whole. There are comments which suggest that the people are not fully informed about Government policy and they do not consider themselves closely in touch with it. Grumbling at personal discomforts and wartime dislocations is low but there is vague and somewhat bewildered criticism of Government activity. Reports show that press criticisms have confused the public mind without disturbing it seriously. Verbatims show this: 'I suppose there's something behind it all', 'There's something hidden but I don't know what it is', 'I wish there were a few more like Winston', 'Does the Government know what it's doing?' At the same time there is confidence in the armed forces, especially in the Navy and the Air Force, and there is evidence of increasing satisfaction at the state of our land defences.

The siren controversy continues. From various Regions come reports showing concern that people do not take cover in daylight raids, and there is some evidence that taking cover is ceasing to have the sanction of public opinion.

Points from Regions

The regional reports continue to endorse the value of the Prime Minister's warning against complacency about invasion, and some suggest that this complacency is still not yet removed. Leeds says the warning is timely. Cambridge states that there is danger that the warning has not been fully driven home; over-optimism is still general except in parts where bombing has been heavy. Reading welcomed the statement as an antidote to the growing unimaginative complacency, adding that the complacency is not yet destroyed. Many people argue that we are now so well prepared that Hitler will hardly dare to attack, and the Dover success has encouraged hopes that our air defence will be able to deal with the enemy.

NORTH-EASTERN (Leeds) Plans to make Home Guard a second line army are popular. Many people anticipate a 'blitzkrieg' next weekend. Confusion about who is to ring church bells in the event of invasion is still prevalent. Many reports of dissatisfaction with local leadership of Home Guard. Shop assistants who had to work over Bank Holiday are upset because many large munition works in the Region closed down.

EASTERN (Cambridge) Some friction reported between hosts and evacuees in Reception Areas. High morale of women in villages which have been bombed is reported.

SOUTHERN (Reading) Reports suggest that best stimulus to public opinion would be news of offensive action against the enemy in addition to bombing. This feeling is most marked in places where Dominion troops are restlessly kicking their heels. There is a growing demand for the announcement of a progressive and constructive peace policy on our part. Some little speculation on how we are to win if Japan enters war against us.

WALES (Cardiff) Increasing public confidence in power of the RAF to deal with night bombers. Duff Cooper's broadcast commented on very favourably as also is his last news letter. Growing anti-Japanese feeling and satisfaction at arrests of Japanese. Hopes expressed that Japan's attitude may lead America into the war before Christmas. Some uneasiness that French Colonies will in due course be used as bases for operations against us. There is a growing public desire among the more thoughtful classes for a Government post-war plan for Europe, to counteract Hitler's campaign for a new order in Europe. The rumour situation is much improved.

NORTH-WESTERN (Manchester) Our firmer attitude to Japan is popular in Lancashire. Some grim amusement that the United States are having to deal with sabotage and strong hatred of Lindbergh. Considerable depression at unemployment figures and many wonder whether we cannot learn from Germany how to make proper use of man-power. Priestley considered best broadcaster yet and many regret that he should clash with the popular item 'Hi Gang' in the Forces' programme.

SOUTH-EASTERN (Tunbridge Wells) Dissatisfaction in villages in Defence Areas that police permission is not always granted for relatives to visit them while Londoners enter areas by cycle on by-roads and are not stopped.

WEDNESDAY 7 AUGUST 1940

Good weather and holiday spirit have made a valuable contribution to continued cheerfulness. Fatigue has been lessened.

The announcement of prosecutions for food waste has been well received and many reports comment on the sympathetic way in which it was put across to the public and commend the way in which the authorities apparently thought it wise to take the public into their confidence. There is a general willingness on the part of housewives to cooperate in salvage schemes; at the same time there is strong criticism of high fruit prices and the waste which this must bring. There is also continuous criticism of waste of paper by Government authorities and other bodies. (Advertisements come in for special comment).

The siren controversy continues. There is further evidence that people are not taking cover in daylight raids and that those who are left in strongly vulnerable areas tend to regard themselves as 'too tough to take cover'. Reports from Ipswich suggest that quite a number of people have been adversely affected by continuous alarms.

Special attention is drawn to reports from Scotland which show that suspicion has been strongly roused of the truthfulness of official bulletins. Penicuik was bombed last night and the news soon spread; nevertheless the 8 o'clock news bulletin this morning stated

'There is no news of any enemy air attacks on this country last night. Agency reports speak of aircraft, believed to be enemy, having been heard over South-west England and Wales, but so far there is no indication of bombs having been dropped'.

This bulletin roused strong criticism.

There is evidence that the public is dissatisfied at the action of the police (and wardens) in collecting the German leaflets dropped on this country. These would be valued as souvenirs and many people declare they would like to read with their own eyes what was written in the leaflets. It has been suggested that reproductions of the leaflets should be made for circulation, and this would satisfy those who are dissatisfied as well as convincing opinion abroad of our sincerity.

Points from Regions

NORTHERN (Newcastle) Full public discussion of invasion in course of past four weeks has converted nervous heartiness into genuine confidence. Demands for aggressive action against Italians. Several quarters report Ministry of Food propaganda is having excellent results; many women are passing war-time cookery hints heard over wireless around among their friends. Still some anxiety about food distribution during invasion and requests for explanatory propaganda.

Buses continue a most common place for gossip and rumours in country districts.

NORTH-MIDLAND (Nottingham) Northamptonshire has taken air raids well. Suggestions received that ARP officials should give instruction on ARP matters based on the technical experiences of recent raids. In Nottingham many feel householders still need instruction on dealing with incendiary bombs. Birchall's broadcast popular. Balloon barrage film enthusiastically received, but MOI film on Food thought ineffective. Rutland complains at high pay of munition workers as compared with Service pay.

Invasion fears definitely diminished; general impression is that danger is now remote. General slackness of public and Forces reported in Grimsby, and martial music suggested as a remedy.

SOUTH-WESTERN (Bristol) No anxiety at Italian invasion of Somaliland. Prospect of invasion of Britain faced calmly. Surprise and a little anxiety in Dorset that there have been no raids for a week. Stronger hatred of Germans in Dorset than elsewhere in Region attributed to low machine-gunning attacks in this county. Anti-waste measures regarded as an obvious necessity. Local censorship on Irish mail reveals general morale high with great confidence in Prime Minister; cancellation of holidays philosophically accepted; letters also show some complaints about absence of sirens, and a growing tendency to stay in bed after sirens have sounded.

MIDLAND (Birmingham) People continue calmly confident. Rural areas in Herefordshire report perturbation at number of planes heard overhead at night. Public still doubtful as to whether they should tell strangers the way and whether they should demand to see their Identity Cards first. Criticism that BBC announcers change the tones of their voices too obviously when dealing with bad news or enemy stupidity.

SCOTLAND (Edinburgh) Satisfaction at reaction of Japanese to Britain's stronger line. Growing disquiet in academic and professional circles at treatment of friendly aliens. Some suspicion reported that Government regards Nazism as enemy of Britain rather than enemy of freedom. News of bombing of Penicuik is being passed round by word of mouth thus tending to heighten distrust of RAF bulletins since morning news stated there was no air activity during the night. Keen appreciation of Duff Cooper's broadcast in spite of criticism in press correspondence columns. Glasgow postal censorship on Irish mail reports morale very good; comments on high prices and unemployment in Glasgow; Irish soldiers in West of Scotland reported contented. Ministry of Food's advertisements with recipes widely appreciated by many housewives.

NORTHERN IRELAND (Belfast) No nervousness at invasion threats. General comment: 'enemy troops may land, but Hitler will be sorry he sent them.' Some concern at invasion of Somaliland and at extent of British shipping losses. Several sources report belief that air-raid damage in England is much bigger than communiques admit. Increased contributions to British Exchequer by Ulster approved by majority. Ministry of Food order for preventing waste generally approved. Parents urging school holidays in Ulster should be extended to middle of September in view of invasion threats.

LONDON

People everywhere reported to be in excellent spirits and quite cheerful. At the moment the war is somewhat in the background; those who can are trying to get holidays. It is felt that reminders like Mr Churchill's message are needed from time to time to counteract complacency. Too much stress laid on the need for bolstering up morale – 'leave us alone and we will be all right'. Very little comment about the war in Africa though some people rather uneasy about the situation; feel that we have not made sufficient preparation despite the time at our disposal. Willesden reports growing antipathy towards refugees – mostly Belgian in this area. Some children still being brought back from Reception Areas on very slight pretext. Some discontent among professional nurses over amount earned by Voluntary Auxiliaries with little training. Grievances still reported about inadequacy of army allowances and unsympathetic treatment at Assistance Board Offices. Discontent also over women's employment and brusque treatment at Labour Exchanges. Some grumbling over billeting rates for evacuees from coast compared with refugees' allowances. Confusion over siren reported from outlying areas: people with children worried when bombardment starts without warning, also when raid is over and no 'All Clear' is given; this means people spend more time in shelters than is necessary. News given out about our air activities, although spectacular and wholly admirable, loses effect by similarity of reports. Bitter feeling still reported amongst young men who volunteered for Army not yet called up and unable to get employment. Hardship reported in East London on account of the internment of aliens, leaving families practically destitute; some internees resident in this country for over forty years, many infirm and old, deserving of better treatment. Salvage scheme now fully inaugurated in most districts and people enthusiastic; also 'Digging for Victory' in suburban areas. Women in certain London districts agitated about proposal to introduce vitamin B into white bread – say that wholemeal bread as supplied to upper classes would meet the case. One London factory with 400 men in Home Guard still without uniforms and rifles.

THURSDAY 8 AUGUST 1940

Morale is high and people are cheerful.

The man in the street, although not particularly concerned or informed about Somaliland, is somewhat shocked to discover that we are on the defensive against the 'despised Italians' (position summarised overleaf).

Many people are disposed to take a holiday this week and criticism is therefore at a lower level. Nevertheless, housewives protest strongly at high fruit prices, and there is a pretty widespread feeling that cigarette prices should be reduced for Home Forces.

The effect of the Prime Minister's warning about invasion is wearing off and many people are more apprehensive of a long and dreary winter than of immediate invasion.

Points from Regions

The news from British Somaliland has excited varying amounts of interest. From Leeds it is reported that the subject is not talked about very much, though it is thought to be the beginning of a general attack on this country and the Empire. Manchester reports that the man in the street is prepared to write off British Somaliland if the defence of Egypt requires all our forces, but adds the comment 'it looks bad'. Cambridge reports some disappointment at the news and satisfaction that the phrase 'strategic withdrawal' has been avoided. Reading reports some uneasiness; people everywhere want to hear that we are taking the initiative, but instead we are once more on the defensive, this time against the despised Italians. Cardiff records some disappointment at our temporary set-back in Africa, particularly so because anti-Italian feeling is strong throughout South Wales. From Tunbridge Wells comes the report that the public are wondering if they have been told the whole truth; if we have had a bad reverse they want to know as quickly as possible; many think that Italy is much stronger than we were led to believe when she first entered the war.

NORTH-EASTERN (Leeds) More people anticipating invasion, but popular feeling is that Germans will not get beyond the coast. Sheffield Corporation has decided by a vote of forty-seven to thirty-nine not to sack their CO employees; Doncaster has taken the opposite course by a vote of sixteen to eleven. Coastal zone ban on Yorkshire Coast reported to be working satisfactorily. Some criticism of Greenwood's speech; view expressed that there are too many committees and too little action in absorbing man-power and woman-power.

EASTERN (Cambridge) Siren controversy active in Norwich and Romford. Chief Constable of Isle of Ely suggests names of German prisoners should be included in our news to Germany. Some interest continues in Mr Stokes's plea for a negotiated peace. Financial difficulties of coastal dwellers still in evidence.

SOUTHERN (Reading) Growing local demand that Government should formulate a peace aims programme for Europe. Even unimaginative

Slough Information Committee has voiced this. All classes regard threat of invasion with some complacency. Need stressed for authoritative statement explaining implications of collapse of France in relation to African campaigns.

WALES (Cardiff) Eccentricity of sirens now generally accepted. Concern at lack of air-raid shelters for schools in Reception Areas. Great satisfaction in Welsh reading circles at possibility of withdrawal of Purchase Tax from books. Acrimonious discussion about position of municipal employees who are COs. Principality pleased at makeshift wireless Eisteddfod.

NORTH-WESTERN (Manchester) Increasing feeling that concessions to troops over cigarettes, postage and transport should be introduced as soon as possible. Anomalies of soldiers' pay also a matter of growing adverse comment.

SOUTH-EASTERN (Tunbridge Wells) Daylight raid warnings not treated seriously enough by public. Suggestion made that shopkeepers should not admit public during raids. Fruit prices still a very common cause of complaint as people see trees heavily laden and cannot understand why prices are so high. Crowborough residents protesting at employment of labourers imported from Eire for local defence work, when many Britons are unemployed. Many believe that there is wastage of food going on in Army camps.

FRIDAY 9 AUGUST 1940

There is very little to report.

Fear of invasion is low in those parts of the country remote from the Eastern Coasts.

Interest in the African situation is negligible.

There is satisfaction at the increases of pay for the men of the armed forces.

Points from Regions

The news of the RAF successes yesterday has produced general satisfaction in the South-Western and Midland Regions. Scotland records cheerful comment, but some people are wondering whether our losses in ships and planes do not outweigh the German losses. There is general satisfaction that the Germans state that they have lost only two planes. Belfast records great admiration and enthusiasm at the result of the air battle.

NORTHERN (Newcastle) While the full meaning of the Viceroy's statement about India is not clearly understood, reports express general appreciation of it; there is feeling that it should strengthen the loyalty of India and also have an effect on American public opinion. Bevin's statement about transference of labour welcomed; farmers are criticised for refusing to define their labour requirements for harvesting; unless this is done satisfactory transfer of unemployed is impossible. 'Stay put' pamphlet generally welcomed, though a more aggressive tone in this and other statements about invasion would be popular. It is suggested that de Gaulle should announce his intention of subjecting the present French government to trial in due course. Some anxiety among poor whose wages have not increased at effect of increases in prices of clothes.

NORTH-MIDLAND (Nottingham) Royal visit to Derby created greatest enthusiasm both in town and surrounding country, although advance news of it was only passed round by word of mouth the previous evening. Some discontent reported at our lack of aggressive action against Italy. Employers and workers both want a definite lead from the Government on the subject of holidays; some workers have now been given holidays while in other factories the original no holidays decision remains unaltered.

SOUTH-WESTERN (Bristol) Events in Somaliland are not arousing much interest though the more intelligent minority are stated to be worried about the possible effects on our communications with Red Sea and Suez. Exeter is stated to be very far from dismayed that it was raided two nights ago. This undercurrent of satisfaction is said to be associated with a feeling that the city has 'grown up'. Areas which have not yet received contex filters for gas masks are once again asking for them, as evacuees who arrive already possess them. People are stated to be quite unmoved by Hitler's peace terms leaflet.

MIDLAND (Birmingham) Many complaints received by RIO's office because bombs dropped in Birmingham causing one fatality last night nearly an hour before sirens were sounded. Birmingham people also complaining about shortage of eggs. Magistrates reported to be taking a more severe view of black-out offences and some are considering prison without the option of a fine.

SCOTLAND (Edinburgh) News from Somaliland provoking mildly critical comment: 'Why is it always a case of small British forces fighting heroically against great odds?' Reports show that for past ten days many have been asking for strong action against Italy; news of strategic retreat is doubly unwelcome. Comments have also been received that good news from the air is usually a preparation for bad news in other spheres. Many believe that Italy has transported a large number of soldiers to Libya in spite of our Mediterranean blockade. On Clydebank over-confidence is reported about invasion. On East Coast, however, invasion is expected but this is not causing alarm. Siren controversy continues, but official policy is gaining ground. Edinburgh postal censorship on Irish mail confirms this. In Edinburgh area feeling is growing at absence of our fighters when raiders are over, and an official explanation is requested. Edinburgh postal censorship reports morale as shown in letters to be excellent. Soldiers wives writing 'very bravely'.

NORTHERN IRELAND (Belfast) Still some uneasiness about our shipping losses. Complaints in Londonderry at excessive testing of air-raid sirens. Farmers complain at low potato prices fixed by Ministry of Food.

LONDON

Morale on the whole quite good but in some of the poorer districts people rather unhappy and worried about making ends meet especially where husband on service and evacuated children always needing new clothes. Some misapprehension expressed in various quarters about situation in Somaliland. In Chelsea, intelligentsia said to be almost defeatist in consequence. London business men yesterday also depressed about it. Morale of well-off Jewish refugees said to be low – reputed to be extremely selfish. Suspicion in some quarters about official news because of delay over *Accra*; doubts also expressed about numbers of our aircraft lost. People in financial circles and big business wonder how to meet their commitments; still feel Budget too indeterminate, don't know what policy to adopt. People in doubt about the powers of the Home Guard especially those not in uniform. Resentment said to be growing amongst soldiers' wives and older men over munition workers' earnings. Belgian refugees in Hackney, Stoke Newington and Hampstead all express desire for work; observer in Hampstead afraid that idleness will have bad effect on their morale. Possible need for special Belgian Legion. Shortage of eggs still felt. Reported from Bethnal Green that small businesses suffering because of lack of supplies. Approval expressed about broadcast talk on Tuesday night by 'The Armstrongs'; felt to be an excellent medium for getting across points of everyday interest and vital importance but would be more effective if moral less obvious. Morale of French soldiers and sailors at White City said to be bad because of enforced idleness.

SATURDAY 10 AUGUST 1940

Morale remains high although reports from certain Regions show that people are 'resting on their oars'.

Interviews show that the Somaliland situation is beginning to arouse interest: people think it is more important than they did at first. This opinion is associated with a suspicion that 'there is more behind it than meets the eye'. This attitude has been reported on many times. There is evidence that it arises, in part, from a lack of news interpretation. *Verbatims illustrate this problem:* '*I suppose those out-of-the-way places are really quite important*', '*Is it Africa or India they're after now?*', '*Thank God it wasn't a strategic withdrawal this time – although I suppose there's not much difference anyhow*', '*I wish I knew what it all meant*', '*Does it mean the Suez Canal will be closed?*'

This ignorance and bewilderment leads to suspicion of news sources on the one hand and on the other to an increasing feeling of isolationism. The fact that many people are relieved to be fighting alone and are anxious to curtail our responsibilities illustrates one point of view; the other is shown by the doubt which increasingly falls on official news. Our air losses are constantly compared with those of Germany and since German communiques are widely heard or read in this country people are at a loss to understand the reasons for our disproportionate losses. Without interpretation and explanation vague suspicions grow. The recent publication of the recent comparative table of air losses brought many comments illustrating this: '*I thought the losses were about 5 to 1, not 2 to 1*', '*It's not as favourable as I thought*', '*I wish I felt sure that we always told the truth*'.

Informed opinion considers that the White Paper on the internment of aliens is unsatisfactory.

There is a growing demand in certain circles for a statement on 'peace aims' although at present there is no evidence that this demand is general among the people as a whole.

Points from Regions

Interest in the possibilities of invasion is becoming less marked. Opinions about the significance of the campaign in Africa vary; there are some misgivings about the trend of events reported in the last few days. The disparity between our own claims and those of the Germans in connection with aircraft losses continues to be a matter for fairly widespread speculation.

NORTH-EASTERN (Leeds) Little interest seems to have been aroused by the Somaliland battle, but it is said that the public in Huddersfield are sceptical of 'the customary explanation that the military reverse is one that does not matter'. There is said to be an increasing demand that peace aims should be stated in terms complementary to the war policy. This feeling is reflected with some emphasis in the local press.

EASTERN (Cambridge) 'There is still a tendency for people to express perplexity at the big difference between our planes and those of the German Command. When German communiques claim equally overwhelming successes many people suspect that our own communiques are drawn up on a similar principle. There is a general desire for a convincing explanation why our own aircraft are so strikingly superior.' There are more complaints about the way in which applicants at Labour Exchanges are treated by the Exchange clerks.

SOUTHERN (Reading) Some misgiving is felt about the efficiency of certain of the Government's war activities and about the mobilisation of man-power. 'The indiscriminate internment of refugees, especially of men who might be of assistance to this country, has caused unfavourable comments. The rise in unemployment, together with the inadequate use of administrative and technical talent, is again the subject of discussion.'

WALES (Cardiff) Some uneasiness is felt about the situation in Africa. The activity there, 'coupled with the German effort to intensify the blockade against us, is giving rise to a fairly common belief that invasion has been relegated to the background.' At the same time, it is widely stated 'that we must steel ourselves to meet very much heavier night bombing.' The withdrawal of our troops from Shanghai has aroused little comment.

NORTH-WESTERN (Manchester) There is still some worry about air-raid alarms, chiefly from country districts where little damage has been done, but curiosity seems to outweigh apprehension. The police yesterday had to prevent charabanc trips to one of the bombed areas. It is suggested that the French war guilt trials should be given the fullest publicity, 'as final evidence of the character of the Vichy Government.'

SOUTH-EASTERN (Tunbridge Wells) The claims of Brighton, Hastings, and other Sussex Coast towns for a fixed curfew hour are being considered by the Regional Commissioner and the military. It is said that the area and the duration of the curfew are likely to be revised and it is the hope of applicants that this revision will last until the end of September. There seems to be some confusion about the authorities who are to be obeyed during invasion or bombardment, and complaints are made that the 'Stay where you are' leaflet does not give sufficiently explicit instructions. It tells people not to take orders except from soldiers, police, Home Guard, or ARP authorities, 'but it is commonly believed that only the military and police can legally control the movements of people during invasion or bombardment,' and at other times have the power to do so only in Defence Areas.

MONDAY 12 AUGUST TO SATURDAY 17 AUGUST 1940

Home Intelligence returned, at the start of the week, to the theme of popular mistrust of the news media. Following the great air battle over the Channel on 8 August, a photograph in the press had appeared to show five enemy aircraft shot down in flames and plunging head-long towards the sea. The Air Ministry, however, subsequently put out a statement explaining that it was not an official photograph, and that no such incident had been reported by RAF pilots. The photo, in other words, was a fake, or as one anonymous member of the public was quoted as saying: 'There's some dirty work going on somewhere.'

The story was soon forgotten but another controversy was to have more long-lasting consequences. Gracie Fields, the most popular female entertainer in Britain, had recently left for Canada with her husband Monty Banks, a film producer. Banks, who was Italian, would have been interned as an enemy alien if he had remained in Britain after Italy's declaration of war. In the House of Commons a Labour MP alleged that Banks was a fascist, and that he and Gracie had been allowed to take thousands of pounds worth of jewellery out of the country at a time when government regulations restricted everyone to a travel allowance of £10. The press repeated the allegations, but in the end the details proved less damaging to Gracie Fields's repu-tation than the simple fact that she had left Britain in its hour of maximum danger. Although she returned to Britain in 1941, subse-quently travelled thousands of miles entertaining British troops around the world, and staged a successful comeback after the war, she could never quite erase a lingering question mark over her actions in 1940.

After the military disasters of May and June the daily reports were beginning to reflect a more optimistic view of the progress of the war. The news from Somaliland, where the Italians continued to advance, was eclipsed by the 'Battle for Britain', as Home Intelligence called it: the Churchillian phrase 'Battle of Britain' had yet to catch on. August the 13th, to which the Luftwaffe gave the code-name *Adlertag*, or 'Eagle Day', marked a ratcheting up of the German air assault with a day-long sequence of massed attacks on targets in the south-east of England. An even larger air battle, in which the Luftwaffe mounted simultaneous attacks on Tyneside and the south of England, was fought two days later. 'Confidence and cheerfulness prevail,' ran the report for 16 August. 'Intensified raids are everywhere received with calmness, the results with jubilation.' Almost every account Home Intelligence received of the public's response to air raids suggested that morale was holding up strongly. More than that, the almost daily reports of Fighter Command's victories, and the spectacle of great air battles fought out in full view of civilians on the ground, were generating a sense of euphoria. 'The fact that this Region bore the brunt of yesterday's air attacks,' reported the regional office in Tunbridge Wells on 17 August, 'has heightened rather than lowered morale, and people are exhilarated by the feeling that they are now in the front line.' The BBC reported miners cheering on slag-heaps as they watched the air battle. According to the Edinburgh regional office, Scots were eager to join in: 'Many people in Scotland are now waiting impatiently "for their turn to come, and a first glimpse of a Spitfire chasing a Dornier".'

There was, however, no shortage of minor complaints and anxieties. From Driffield in Yorkshire resentment was reported at the burial with full military honours of a Nazi airman. Eggs were in short supply in the South East and many women living in hotels in Kensington were said to be prone to depression. But Home Intelligence no longer warned of pockets of defeatism. 'Streamers already being made privately in East End to celebrate victory,' it was noted on 14 August, 'and remarks made that "it will only be a matter now of a few months".'

MONDAY 12 AUGUST 1940

There is little to add to Saturday's report except further confirmation of the suspicion of news sources which continues to develop. Over the weekend the public showed great interest in the 'faked photograph' episode and verbatims illustrate the strong suspicion and criticism which were shown as the story became elaborated: 'Fancy taking the trouble to deny it on the wireless: there's some dirty work going on somewhere.', 'Faking photographs – just another example of what's going on behind the scenes.', 'What is the truth? You never can tell nowadays.' Many comments bitterly critical of the press were reported; others were contemptuous of 'censorship', 'officialdom'. The rights and wrongs of the story were clearly not appreciated. This added to the general bewilderment. The prominence given to the story by the BBC made the public feel that there was something very important behind this. The net result has been to strike another blow at public confidence.

Another subject in which the public has been at variance with the press is the prominence which has been given to the affairs of Gracie Fields. BBC Listener Research has shown that Gracie Fields's popularity in her own field is unrivalled and she has become highly thought of as an individual as well as an artiste. At the beginning of press publicity (which not only recorded questions in the House but gave editorial and news comment) public opinion was favourable to Gracie. It refused to think ill of her and attributed any possible evil to her Italian husband. As the press continued to comment on the affair, however, public opinion, although not strongly antagonistic to her, has now become much more critical than it was. Reports show that people feel much of the story is hidden and that an absent person has not had a chance of defending herself.

There is considerable jubilation about our successes in the Channel air battles although there is some evidence that people feel that our planes are being lost for purely defensive reasons.

Points from Regions

The present phase of the war, in which we appear to be waiting for the enemy to take the initiative, is causing widespread opinion that offensive action should be undertaken, particularly against the Italian Navy and factories, the continental ports now in German hands, and in North Africa. Fear is expressed at the loss of prestige we shall suffer in the eyes of the natives if territory is given up in British Somaliland.

NORTHERN (Newcastle) The Corporations of Newcastle, Middlesbrough, and Darlington have adopted resolutions concerning the employment of COs, and many individuals consider that if COs were paid an equivalent rate to that received in the Army there would be less public irritation on this score. An increase in comradeship and mutual helpfulness has been apparent as the result of air raids. Comparison between road and raid casualties does not meet with universal approval, and it is suggested that the real comparison is between weekly and monthly figures of air-raid casualties. There is intense interest in the rate of aircraft production and it is suggested that information on our race to reach equality with Germany would be welcomed. Complaints that in some areas with few shelters school shelters are not open to the public after school hours.

NORTH-MIDLAND (Nottingham) Spitfire funds have reawakened enthusiasm 'to do something for the nation.' An explanation of apparent British apathy in the Mediterranean would be welcomed. Some criticism in Nottingham and Northants at the inadequacy and late release of reports of aerial activities, and a feeling that insufficient is told about the major raids on Great Britain. The decision to tax food in small tins is causing hardship in small families; many people wonder why there is a shortage of treacle and the egg shortage is a cause of complaint. In Chesterfield it is thought that workers might buy more Savings Certificates, but many of them think they cannot withdraw their investments at short notice, and hesitate to buy, for fear their present wages may not continue. General demand that fresh news should be read at the beginning of BBC news bulletins.

SOUTH-WESTERN (Bristol) Air raids and reports of damage are the main topics of conversation. Reports from Truro and Taunton indicate that people have faced the bombing well, and, in the event of invasion, would now play their part far better than two months ago. As a result of the Portland and Weymouth raid a number of women and children have left, and the demand for shelters, permission to erect which has already been granted, is strong. A fund has been started to help those affected by damage, which was in the poorer quarter of the town, and morale generally is high. The new order making the western counties a Protected Area is welcomed, and surprise is expressed that this step has not been taken before.

MIDLAND (Birmingham) Satisfaction that an increase in pay is granted to the army. Long hours are causing fatigue to workers and employers complain of absenteeism; this is partly due to the uncertain instructions about Bank Holiday. There is some grumbling about the absence of air-raid warnings, repetition in BBC news bulletins, and the comparison between the pay of soldiers and munition workers' wages.

SCOTLAND (Edinburgh) Sunday's air battle has strengthened confidence in our air defences and diminished local discontent at the apparent impunity of lone enemy raiders over central Scotland and the Clyde, which are not challenged by our fighters; this local discontent may become serious if there are more undefended air raids and no official explanation is forthcoming. The broadcast talk by George Anderson of SS *Highlander* was greatly appreciated. Complaints from Glasgow amongst teachers about neglected education, and from West Highland districts about food shortage caused by delay in censoring parcels. Gordon Highlanders in the extreme north of Scotland find routine boring, and want to be parashots.

NORTHERN IRELAND (Belfast) Satisfaction expressed at heavy losses inflicted on the enemy in Sunday's air battle, and hope that we shall be able to replace planes faster than we lose them. Widespread speculation concerning the cause of explosion which shook houses in coastal towns early this morning; one report states that an aeroplane without lights flew over the town shortly after the explosion. As a result of public criticism, Belfast ARP services are to be reorganised.

LONDON

Everything continues fairly quiet and practically normal in the London area. Domestic problems are of greater moment than war news. Unemployment amongst women still growing in some districts as manufacture of non-essentials decreases. Jubilation over air battles. RAF highly praised in all quarters – results having a heartening effect. News from Africa carefully watched by more thinking section of population; some feel that a Government statement about the situation might help. Comments about bad effect of loudspeakers throughout the day in districts where many people working at night. Much comment still about children not attending school and a growing lack of discipline – even trained Social Workers finding them more difficult to manage than a year ago: irregular life having bad mental effect on children. Chelsea reports school attendance almost normal. Strong criticism that time and money spent on upholding morale in this country not really needed. Reports from most districts that salvage campaign being carried out successfully. 'Stay Put' leaflet considered good.

TUESDAY 13 AUGUST 1940

There is very little to add to the reports of the last few days. Morale is still high and the fact that many people are taking a few days holiday has reduced criticism. At the same time this leisure has given people more time to read the press and to review the situation: this fact brings strongly to light requests for explanation and news interpretation. It may also have contributed to the increased criticism of the press (and of news sources) which is evident in our reports. However, there are more indications that the public is ignorant and uncertain than that it is highly critical. Public confidence in the outcome of the war is still strong and has not yet been much affected by these perplexities. Reports from remote and rural areas show that many people there are insufficiently conscious of the gravity of the situation and that the war is by no means the main topic of conversation. On the other hand, observers report that people in intensely raided areas are beginning to feel the strain.

An investigation is being conducted into the attitude of the public towards the 'blockade of Europe'. An interim report shows that the great majority of people are, at the present time, *unmoved by the prospect of starving populations and express realistic views about Nazi propaganda on this subject. It will be important to check any change in public opinion during the coming months.*

Points from Regions

Reports from raided areas show that morale remains high, and the raids have had a stiffening effect. In South Wales continued increased air activity and its successful results has consolidated confidence in the RAF and created encouragement for the future.

NORTH-EASTERN (Leeds) Despite recent raids, most people believe soldiers who were in France, who say we have little idea what an air raid means. Postal censorship reports on letters from this Region to Eire show that morale is very high. There is criticism in Driffield at the burial of a German airman with full military honours and ostentation in contrast to the recent quiet burial of a soldier who died as a result of the Dunkirk action. The naming of places recently bombed is much appreciated. There is a demand from Huddersfield that the Union Jack should be more in evidence.

EASTERN (Cambridge) There are complaints in Norwich that those whose houses were damaged in recent raids have not been provided by the Local Authority with alternative accommodation to which they consider themselves entitled. There is optimism in rural districts at the success in harvesting grain crops despite the potential menace of incendiary bombs. A tour in the rural areas of Bedfordshire has shown the existence of a demand in smaller villages for adequate protective equipment for ARP workers. There is some scepticism concerning communiques describing air-raid damage, and it is noticed that both British and German communiques disclaim the successes of enemy attack. A number of complaints have been received of profiteering by catering establishments.

SOUTHERN (Reading) Public is uneasy that Italians are being allowed to keep the initiative in Africa, and in view of former withdrawals a lack of confidence is felt in our military machine. The rise in unemployment figures also needs explanation if the feeling that there is still something wrong with the Government, in spite of the Premier's leadership, is not to gain ground. The suppression of place names in connection with Friday's running fight is criticised.

WALES (Cardiff) People of all classes are snatching a few days holiday, although mostly staying at home or taking day trips. Opinion is strong that the blockade must be rigorously pursued. There is concern at the decreasing amount of work available in coal mining districts. Some disappointment at the lack of naval activity in the Mediterranean. Many are confident that Russia's interests will compel her to check German influence in the Balkans. Some complaints from troops at the lack of uniformity and regularity of leave.

NORTH-WESTERN (Manchester) Although the public does not believe it is told the whole truth, there is confidence that we can beat a blitzkrieg. Warm discussion goes on in Merseyside of siren policy, where bombs have dropped without warning. Hope is expressed that the Premier will use the anniversary of the outbreak of war to make a speech on the new order we intend to establish.

SOUTH-EASTERN (Tunbridge Wells) When sirens sounded yesterday in Tunbridge Wells the public behaved as stupidly as on previous occasions, despite strongly worded articles in local press; wardens attempting to get people to cover were jeered at, and it seems evident that parents have told children to come home if a warning is given when they are on the streets. Wearisome repetition of news items by BBC is causing annoyance. Now that Eastbourne is in a Defence Area, laundries are only working two or three days a week: female employees sent a round robin to the Minister of Supply asking to be given work of national importance for the rest of the week.

He is reported to have said he cannot make use of their services and this has caused some bitterness among them.

WEDNESDAY 14 AUGUST 1940

Morale is high: there is general satisfaction over the results of raids over our ports. There are some indications that people are beginning to believe that these intensified raids are preliminaries to a more general attack or invasion. On the other hand verbatims show a scepticism founded on previous false alarms, e.g. 'News. I never listen to it. When the Germans come over I'll start thinking about invasion.'

Every day provides us with some further evidence of people's doubts about news: formulae repeatedly come in for criticism; any explanation which throws light on the background situation is welcomed. Technical descriptions, i.e. those which give the reader or listener some sense of control over the situation, are well liked and eye-witness accounts, whose authenticity can be guaranteed, are approved.

Morale in heavily raided districts is relatively undisturbed. There is increasing confidence in Civil Defence services. A working-class woman is reported to have said: 'Look here. I've lost everything. Not even a cup and saucer left. But I've still got my hearing and my eyesight. And my life. So I mustn't grumble.'

Further reports on the attitude of the public towards the 'blockade of Europe' show that humanitarian scruples are not troubling the public conscience. There are some expressions of sympathy with the Belgians (particularly) and the Norwegians. A statistically negligible number of people are against the blockade. Many people spoken to seemed aware of the implications of Nazi propaganda on the subject.

Points from Regions

NORTHERN (Newcastle) The system of air-raid warnings is a main topic of conversation, and on account of the increase in these complaints are growing about the hours of full time ARP workers, for whom a 12-hour shift is a fairly regular occurrence. Further concessions in the tea ration are hoped for. The stopping of supplies of cement to Local Authorities which urgently require it for shelters is the subject of many complaints.

NORTH-MIDLAND (Nottingham) There is a genuine dread of the black-out in approaching winter months. Reports show a desire for more explanatory accounts of air battles, and contrast is made between the flippant tone of the BBC announcer stating that casualties were slight and no material damage was done after a raid, and information received by post from residents of raided areas. There is general keenness to salvage waste materials. From Derby comes a demand for cheap milk for old age pensioners, a substitute for the wailing siren which tends to shock, and complaints of waste in the erection of road barriers which were almost immediately taken down.

SOUTH-WESTERN (Bristol) Recent RAF successes are commented on with jubilation. There is a feeling that we have insufficient troops in Somaliland. Favourable comment has been received on the accuracy of bulletins describing the damage in Weymouth and Portland. Exeter and Swindon reacted excellently to their first daylight raid, and streets were quickly cleared. Renewal of night raids over Bristol is causing loss of sleep. The question is still asked why German bombers can fly over the city without being disturbed, but it is felt that on account of the good work of our fighters recently the public will put up with sleepiness. Employers are not satisfied with Anderson's statement of their liabilities if workmen are injured or killed while working during air raids.

MIDLAND (Birmingham) People whose houses were demolished in last night's raid are showing a splendid spirit, although there is uneasiness regarding the sounding of warnings. There is some concern also that although civilian casualties in air raids are given as trivial, the monthly total comes as a shock. Some anxiety is reported about the position in Somaliland, and impatience expressed at our attitude towards Japan. Farmers are complaining of damage caused by foxes in cornfields.

SCOTLAND (Edinburgh) RAF successes are warmly praised everywhere, and our official figures of German and British plane losses are not questioned, although many believe that damage is minimised. An insurance firm reports many enquiries about insurance and compensation by the Government for property destroyed or damaged in air raids. Shortage of equipment has halted recruiting for the Home Guard in some districts, and some units are discontented with the lack of development in the training system. In many quarters it is felt that amenities for the troops should be supplemented by private hospitality, especially in small towns.

NORTHERN IRELAND (Belfast) There is great local interest in the export trade drive, but the linen industry, anxious to increase production, is greatly hampered by flax shortage which has thrown many out of work. Satisfaction expressed that books and newspapers are exempt from Purchase Tax. British air successes are enthusiastically praised. Many watch the press for signs of internal trouble in France. The *Belfast Telegraph* Spitfire Fund, opened a few days ago, has already received the requisite £5,000.

LONDON

Morale high in all reports. News of air battles stimulating. This exhilaration offsets disappointment that Italian territory not attacked and fears expressed in intellectual circles at our apparent weakness in Africa. Excuses made for our reverses in the Italian campaign cause annoyance to many people, especially businessmen with connections in towns like Kassala who feel insulted when it is given out that 'Kassala is a small unimportant village'. Strong opinions heard on all sides that propaganda exhorting us to be courageous is not only unnecessary but impertinent. Personal fear of air raids on London diminishing with RAF coastal successes. Tougher belligerent feeling is spreading. Working people resent number of private cars on roads using valuable petrol; express opinion that voluntary workers with labels on cars are more self-important than valuable to the community. Business and Professional Women's Club meeting unanimously expressed approval of Social Survey. Low income people glad to be questioned, report several observers, and even express gratification that Government wants to know what they think because 'this is a people's war'. Streamers already being made privately in East End to celebrate victory and remarks made that 'it will only be a matter now of a few months'. Urgent need for nursery centres in Deptford to relieve working women during day is reported. Willesden CAB has collected 150 signatures of women who would gladly avail themselves of such facilities. Harrow reports many coastal evacuees in district; although suffering severe financial loss and anxiously seeking work these people are in good spirits and glad to sleep at night after continuous raids. Kensington reports many women living in hotels inclined to depression and gossip for lack of useful occupation. Need for social club where women can discuss problems in neighbourly fashion reported on Westminster Housing Estates. Clubs of this type now organised have greatly improved morale of similar estates in St Pancras. Complaints still received at hardships caused by delay in allowances to soldiers' wives coming through. Finchley reports bitterness of British born subjects of unnaturalised parents at not being able to get Government work through Labour Exchanges.

THURSDAY 15 AUGUST 1940

There is little change in morale which continues to be high. Intensified raids have been taken with calmness and courage. At the same time there is further evidence of casualties being caused because people did not take cover.

There are many enquiries about the most effective methods of securing protection against flying glass. Many people feel that they are not being given the benefit of previous experience and ask for local demonstrations of various protective measures.

The siren controversy continues: some reports show acute anxiety as well as anger at the non-sounding of sirens. There still appears to be a great deal of uncertainty about official policy. Many people feel that the methods adopted are purely empirical.

News continues to come in for a good deal of criticism: people complain about the relative slowness with which facts are released as well as about the reiteration of formulae ('Serious but not Critical', 'Agency messages report').

Eden's broadcast was well received and praised for the indications which it gave of 'offensive action'. Women particularly commented favourably on the speech.

Points from Regions

From both Tunbridge Wells and the Holesworthy area of Suffolk come reports of people refusing to take cover when sirens have sounded, and treating the warnings with contempt. The fact that the bus service continues to operate in Tunbridge Wells is one reason for this attitude. Warnings for sporadic raiders in South Wales are now so frequent that carelessness becomes daily more apparent, and the majority of casualties in Portsmouth, Gosport and Southampton was among people who did not take shelter.

NORTH-EASTERN (Leeds) Morale is higher than at any time previously in Hull, particularly among the working class, and the increased efficiency of the Home Guard has improved morale in Barnsley. The exodus from the coast has slackened, and some people are returning to it from the West Riding. The finding of parachutes has not had a disturbing effect. Resentment is expressed in Sowerby at attempts to represent the Somaliland situation in a more favourable light than is considered justified. It is reported from Driffield that if there is a repetition of the funeral of the Nazi airman with full military honours, it may provoke hostile demonstrations. There is still confusion on the safeguarding of windows from blast, and strips of paper are still being put up on windows.

EASTERN (Cambridge) Reports from coastal areas suggest a slight stiffening of attitude towards the war. RAF exploits continue to arouse intense satisfaction. The discovery of shell fragments apparently fired from the French Coast has caused a deep impression, although no alarm. There is some grumbling by members of the Forces over delay in getting leave. Anxiety is still felt for men of the 7th Battalion Royal Norfolk regiment, which was in the Dunkirk evacuation. Eden's broadcast was generally approved. The air-raid siren controversy continues in the Romford area. Scheme has been approved in Chelmsford for the purpose of providing mutual relief in the event of air-raid damage. The question of appointing women police is still raised from time to time in various localities.

SOUTHERN (Reading) The air battle in the South has stimulated the whole Region and to a great extent smothered anxiety over Somaliland. Stories of the bravery and coolness of inhabitants of the bombed towns have spread rapidly. Some observers consider that our air successes are being unduly magnified in that they give the impression that we are mastering the full force of aerial blitzkrieg. After the raids, families in the poorer quarters who have their dwellings destroyed are in urgent need of comfort and advice, and it is difficult for police or Civil Defence personnel to supply these demands on account of their special duties.

WALES (Cardiff) Many of the more careful are now furnishing their shelters and those who can afford it are making provision to keep out the wet. Recent Air Force victories have been loudly praised, and even the few sceptics confess that the published results are better than their wildest expectations. Eden's speech received very well and the forecast of initiative and aggression on our part has been welcomed. Slowness of our authorities in releasing news, compared with the German and Italian authorities, is the cause of some grumbling. The bombing of North Italy has caused great satisfaction. Hoover's food ship proposals are still decried. The printing trade is gradually reaching the depths of depression.

NORTH-WESTERN (Manchester) Eden's speech criticised as too long, and containing too many propaganda cliches, but prospects of our taking the offensive are welcomed. The use of 'serious but not critical' in connection with Somaliland is thought inapt, as the public remember it in connection with France. Raids on Italy give widespread satisfaction.

SOUTH-EASTERN (Tunbridge Wells) There is a shortage of eggs, and poorer families have had none for a week; preserved eggs are not to be obtained. A local Non-Conformist minister with Pacifist leanings has had his windows broken and peace notices removed, and his printer will not produce his monthly magazine unless it is submitted to censorship.

ERRATUM: Points from Regions, 31.7.40., South-Eastern. Line 3 should read: public *do not* respond promptly to sirens in towns which have not yet been bombed.

FRIDAY 16 AUGUST 1940

Confidence and cheerfulness prevail. Intensified raids are everywhere received with calmness, the results with jubilation. At the same time there is continued criticism of the siren policy.

Observations made during the warnings in London showed that many people did not take shelter but continued their normal activities. Many left shelters after a few minutes although today more people stayed in shelters for a longer time. Dominant feeling was annoyance and boredom (outside Croydon). In Croydon there is a good deal of criticism that the sirens were not sounded until too late. (Further details contained in London report – over).

Observers report that taking shelter and obedience to ARP instructions is much more in evidence in middle-class areas than in working-class districts. It is noticed that after warnings or raids conversation is greatly stimulated, and it has been suggested that this provides an opportunity and occasion for 'talking points'.

Reproduction of Lord Trenchard's suggestions in the Penny Press brought many enthusiastic comments. The idea is one which is in accord with public sentiment at the moment.

The passing of 'August 15th' is reported to have had a tonic effect and there is evidence that the date had become well planted in people's minds. One report says the bandying about of dates has had a lowering effect on morale.

Interest in the Somaliland campaign has been obscured by the 'Battle for Britain'. There are, however, a number of anxious references to 'what lies behind the scenes in Africa'.

Joubert's broadcast had many favourable comments and several reports enquire why he does not broadcast more frequently.

There have been references to the Swinton Committee in today's reports. There is general confusion about the subject but the result of the publicity has been to stimulate the suspicion which has been remarked upon so often. 'I wonder what lies behind it all'.

Many examples have reached us of recent propaganda by Moral

Rearmament: the card headed 'Morale' which has been sent to many Local Authorities is creating a certain amount of suspicion that local officials being made a vehicle for this propaganda.

Points from Regions

News of RAF punishment to enemy raiders continues to have a stimulating effect on public opinion, and more than counteracts the effects of disturbed nights in raided areas. Complaints about unopposed raids from Scotland have decreased.

NORTHERN (Newcastle) The fact that fighters on night patrol are more in evidence has caused satisfaction. Eden's speech was well received. Many complaints are received of the freedom with which soldiers discuss the work they are engaged upon.

NORTH-MIDLAND (Nottingham) Confidence prevails. Suggestions are still being made that there should be a statement on the Government's aims after the war. Approval of broadcasts by Dr Wood, George Hicks and Harcourt Johnstone. The rationing of raw materials for manufacture is a matter of serious concern for those engaged in hosiery, boot and shoe manufacture; it will almost certainly cause short time and employees are already apprehensive about continued employment in the late autumn. Lincoln reports a strong feeling that sentimentalism must be combated with regard to Hoover's proposal to feed Europe.

SOUTH-WESTERN (Bristol) Intense interest in the air war over-shadows the fighting in Somaliland, but a report says that people are prepared for 'a strategic withdrawal'. In Exeter the passing of August 15th without fulfilment of prophecies has had a tonic effect. Complacency is not so evident and the possibility of land invasion uppermost in most people's minds. The heavy raids on Germany are popular in Plymouth, and the public think we shall hit back very hard now without waiting for the enemy to take the initiative. Criticism of alleged muddle of air-raid warning at Crediton.

MIDLAND (Birmingham) Morale unaffected by enemy raids but renewed criticism of the delay in issuing siren warnings; last night casualties had been caused before the sirens sounded. There has been a recurrence of localised parachutist rumours due to the finding of German parachutes, but it is not affecting public steadiness. There are some complaints from Nuneaton that the rising cost of living is affecting people with fixed incomes.

SCOTLAND (Edinburgh) Many people in Scotland are now waiting impatiently 'for their turn to come, and a first glimpse of a Spitfire chasing a Dornier.' The news of invasion by parachutists in Ayrshire (as it was thought) caused considerable excitement, but no sign of fear. Rumour has it that the parachute plane came from Ireland, and this brought a renewal of speculation about the Ireland menace. There is a growing impression that 'we get the truth but not the whole truth' in the news. There is some evidence of a growing disquiet about the situation in Somaliland, and anti-Italian feeling seems to be even deeper than anti-German feeling. Both men and women are being paid off in Singers Works at Clydebank and they are told this is due to the capitulation of France; there is a strong demand that Singers should go into war work at once. Many recommendations are coming in asking that the public should be persuaded or compelled to carry gas masks. Many people are uneasy about surface shelters in school playgrounds which are practically white and would make an excellent target.

NORTHERN IRELAND (Belfast) Some quarters think that the reported losses of British aircraft do not include planes that may be destroyed on the ground. It is felt that a decisive Italian victory in Somaliland would seriously damage British prestige. There is continued criticism of high unemployment in Ulster, and a more dynamic policy by the Northern Ireland Government is demanded. Farmers will be badly hit by the prohibition of the sale of cream, as much is exported.

LONDON

Croydon reports morale excellent during and after raid. Many comments, however, that casualties could have been avoided if sirens had been sounded before bombs dropped. Factories in district stopping work anyway at time of raid so that warnings would not have prevented valuable production. Observer reports workers leaving damaged factory looked shaken but not panicky. Everybody in district helping people affected by raids; excavation still going on. Surrounding districts such as Mitcham, Romford, Lambeth and Carshalton excited by raid; many people watched it instead of going to shelter. Criticisms today by factory workers in these districts at absence of siren warning. Apprehension reported among old age pensioners in Romford who live close to each other and alone in small bungalows: 'afraid to sleep at night in case of raid with no alarm'. Carshalton reports crowds of children 'thrilled by spectacle of air raid; not nervous at all'. Reaction to warnings in other parts of London various. Four people in one Kensington bus panicked at siren; other reports show many people running to shelters and then leaving them before 'All Clear' was sounded. Complacency about no air raids on London vanishing, but people on the whole are excited rather than apprehensive. Much satisfaction expressed at descriptions of how German plane losses are counted, especially talk by Air Marshal Joubert. These descriptions are making people believe almost completely in the authenticity of news of German losses. Observer listening to public broadcast outside shop describes audience laughing scornfully at German reports of losses and terrible damage to Southern England. Expressions of opinion overheard that German propaganda has overstepped the mark. More bitterness reported against Italy than Germany and keen desire to attack Italy herself. News of Italian raid very welcome. At same time, sympathetic attitude towards Italians long resident in England reported from many districts. Hampstead states need for including refugees in national effort growing urgent. Belgians especially becoming thoroughly depressed; lack of work lowering their morale. Willesden reports difficulties of mothers asked to visit evacuated children when ill because of lack of funds. Townswomen's Guilds report jam-making going strong in suburban districts.

SATURDAY 17 AUGUST 1940

Intensified raids have not affected morale; rather the reverse: confidence is increased, opinion is stiffer and there is a feeling of growing exhilaration. The spirit of the people in raided areas is excellent.

Both press and wireless describe with apparent approval the behaviour of air-raid spectators, e.g. 'bus is grand-stand' (Daily Telegraph), 'miners cheering on slag-heaps as they watch air battle' (BBC News). From these reports a confusing picture arises: official shelter policy contradicts the sanction given by press and wireless.

People are slightly less critical of the news and rumours are much less in evidence. This is partly due to the naming of bombed places and to the demonstrations which have been provided of the falsity of German communiques.

Air battles are obscuring other topics; there is, however, a strong undercurrent of anxiety about Africa, and an increasing interest in American affairs.

Points from Regions

News of air activities remains the predominant topic of conversation, and the air battles are everywhere regarded as encouraging victories. The attitude towards the war is stiffening, and there is less tendency to compare it with a sporting event. Villages in which German planes have been brought down are proud of this slender association with the exploits of the RAF, and the general feeling in raided areas is that 'we can take it'.

NORTH-EASTERN (Leeds) The Somaliland war is not arousing much interest. The only criticism of news is that our reports of damage to Germany by RAF raids seem exaggerated when compared with reports of damage done here. A number of people quote Col. Knox's reported speech that 'we are not getting the truth because warring nations only reveal such information as they desire.' There is criticism from Don Valley that the police and military, in collecting German leaflets and preventing their circulation, have led people to say there is something in them which the Government does not want people to know. Complaints from Wharfedale of inadequate transport for soldiers and munition workers.

EASTERN (Cambridge) The public has behaved in an exemplary manner when taking to shelters, but the frequency of warnings in some cases produces an attitude of indifference. There is general belief that damage to property is heavier than is admitted, and there is a similar attitude towards shipping losses. Now London has been attacked there is a feeling that the RAF should raid military objectives in Berlin. The public are somewhat puzzled over the situation in Africa. Anxiety over trading losses continues in coastal areas, and some dissatisfaction because multiple shops are able to keep open while many local tradesmen have closed down. Criticism has been expressed in West Norfolk at the practice of private enterprises collecting scrap material in rivalry with Local Authorities.

SOUTHERN (Reading) Conversation centres far more on accounts of raiders being seen to crash than on harrowing tales of damage or casualties. Confidence and cheerfulness are noticeable everywhere, and the punishment inflicted on raiders appears more than to counteract the damage they do. In some circles there are comments on American reaction to the air raids as evidence of somewhat scrappy reports in our press. There has been a surprising decrease in rumours. Discussion at the more intimate types of public meetings largely centres on the need for a clearer definition of our peace aims and post-war reconstruction.

WALES (Cardiff) Reaction to bombing is invariably one of anger and firmer determination, particularly where casualties occur. Results of air battles are anxiously awaited. In some areas, crowds which remain to watch and cheer air battles have been the cause of great anxiety to Civil Defence workers, and they deprecate the condoning of this attitude by the press and BBC. Our efforts on land since the beginning of the war are being compared unfavourably with those on the sea and in the air.

NORTH-WESTERN (Manchester) German communiques are losing credence as their claims extend to places in which individuals can personally check their falsity. The general view is that things are working up to a crisis, but confidence is high. Disappointment expressed that Joubert should think the public not properly appreciative of the heroic action of the RAF, when in fact admiration is unbounded. The Lancashire business community is concerned about German propaganda in South America alleging that cotton mills have been wrecked, and the industry in a chaotic condition; hope is expressed that adequate counter measures are being taken.

SOUTH-EASTERN (Tunbridge Wells) The fact that this Region bore the brunt of yesterday's air attacks has heightened rather than lowered morale, and people are exhilarated by the feeling that they are now in the front line. Behaviour of both public and Civil Defence workers was admirable at Northfleet, which suffered heavily as most of the bombs fell in a congested area. Most people still cannot understand why names of towns are sometimes given in announcements, and at other times only a vague reference is made. A shortage of labour for hop picking is expected.

LONDON

Morale in all districts excellent even where considerable damage done by raids. In places where warning is given but no raids have taken place people are calm; they take shelter when siren goes but stand at doors to see what is happening. Epsom doctor says: 'Morale good, discretion bad. People don't realise how quickly danger may shift from one point to another – they should be told more of the risks they run, this especially in regard to children'. Malden reports much damage done and dislocation in the district but public services being restored as quickly as possible. No panic noticeable and everyone anxious to help those whose homes and property have been destroyed. The spirit is wonderful. Feel that local registers should be set up everywhere to deal with problems of homeless people. Reported from South London that a statement by a responsible official that gas bombs had been dropped caused confusion and alarm. Comment received from Stoke Newington that it would be better if buses went to nearest open space or square; if they are hit there is danger of fire from petrol. Feeling in London business circles that war effort will be greatly interfered with if everyone takes cover when sirens go; action should be left to individual judgment. Still confusion about sirens and opening up of public shelters. People now realise London not immune from air raids. Confidence has increased since more details given about raids and magnificence of RAF. Anderson shelters now proving their worth. Bitter feeling amongst soldiers in Bethnal Green sent home on convalescent leave without pay after being wounded at Dunkirk: wife's allowance insufficient to provide for invalid husband and credit no longer given for goods in East End. Feeling amongst London exporters that trade is being stifled: difficulty in obtaining export permits, cannot send goods abroad until payment received from country of destination. Comment from Woolwich about Mr Eden's speech – felt to be unfortunate that a Cabinet Minister when referring to our ultimate victory should have spoken of the 'odds' being in our favour.

MONDAY 19 AUGUST TO SATURDAY 24 AUGUST 1940

By the third week of August the Battle of Britain was moving further inland. With the aim of delivering a knock-out blow to the RAF, the massed attacks of the Luftwaffe were increasingly directed against the airfields and fighter stations of Air Vice-Marshal Park's 11 Group ringed around London. The capital itself was not yet a major target but as the daily reports show it was already subject to occasional raids. Croydon and Wimbledon were bombed on 18–19 August, Slough, Richmond Park and Dulwich on 24–25th.

After a major air battle on 18 August the Air Ministry claimed that the Luftwaffe had lost 152 aircraft, the RAF 22. For the period between 1 August and 17 August German losses were put at 675, British losses as 191. Although the figures published at the time often overestimated the number of enemy aircraft destroyed, they were broadly correct in the sense that Fighter Command was indeed getting the better of the enemy. 'The continued success of the RAF still overshadows all other topics of conversation,' Home Intelligence reported on 19 August. The damage which events at Dunkirk had so unfairly inflicted on the reputation of the RAF was now forgotten and the airmen were the heroes of the hour. Churchill himself set the seal on their fame in a speech in the House of Commons on 20 August: 'Never in the field of human conflict was so much owed by so many to so few.' The withdrawal of British forces from Somaliland, announced the previous day, was said to have caused disappointment over the damage to British prestige, but the effect appears to have been short-lived. On 22 August the Manchester region reported: 'Somaliland is almost forgotten already'.

Surprisingly, in view of the fact that it had been such a contentious issue over the past two months, siren policy was still confused and confusing. In Birmingham, frustration over repeated delays in the issue of warnings had led to the formation of voluntary street patrols which alerted residents when aircraft were heard overhead. In London, however, Home Intelligence recorded that many were 'standing in the open to watch what is going on, betraying a falsely fatalistic and don't care attitude.' So much publicity was given to a raid on Eastbourne by a single German plane that 'twenty-nine coaches arrived from London to see the damage'. On a more positive note air raids were said to be giving rise to a new sense of neighbourliness.

In the United States former President Herbert Hoover had recently issued an appeal to Britain to enter into an agreement with Germany to provide for the distribution of food to the peoples of the occupied countries. Millions, Hoover warned, were faced with the threat of starvation. As their part of the agreement, however, the British would have to lift the naval blockade on food supplies to Europe, and trust the Nazis to see that they were fairly distributed. The findings of the Wartime Social Survey left no doubt that public opinion was over-whelmingly in favour of continuing the blockade: the people's war, as it was fast becoming, allowed for no half measures.

The daily report from London on 21 August drew attention to a social problem that was to cause much anxious comment during the war years: the disruption of family life and a loss of parental control over children. Evacuated children were still drifting back to London but many schools had closed, others could only offer a part-time education, and some parents were failing to send their children to school at all. 'It is felt,' Home Intelligence recorded, 'that discipline and home life in evacuation areas have practically disappeared: even quite young children forming themselves into bands of hooligans.'

MONDAY 19 AUGUST 1940

The events of the weekend have not affected morale: there is increasing confidence and determination and a growing excitement which shows itself almost as exhilaration. In raided areas there is confidence in Civil Defence services and a growing neighbourliness. There appears to be a deliberate attempt to restrict alarmist rumours and there are many indications of controlled behaviour. Grossly exaggerated stories are rare.

The siren controversy continues.

Opinion in certain circles is highly critical of the delay in liberating news for America and there is much speculation about the reasons for this tardiness.

There is more evidence of the distribution of Moral Rearmament propaganda.

Mr Duff Cooper's Saturday broadcast received a certain amount of criticism, mainly for his 'contemptuous references' to invasion. Many people complain that the speech was overshadowed by the Canadian broadcast which followed.

Points from Regions

Reports show that the population remains steady, and air raids are faced with calmness and fortitude. The continued success of the RAF still overshadows all other topics of conversation, and great confidence is expressed in our airmen. Growing confusion as to the official policy in regard to the sounding of sirens is noted, and there are further complaints that sirens are not sounded, and that they are being sounded after planes are heard and the 'All Clear' given before the raiders have left.

NORTHERN (Newcastle) Many instances are reported of people watching dog fights, and cheering our fighters. Previous doubts as to the credibility of news bulletins referring to RAF successes and air-raid casualties have been dispelled by more detailed broadcasts, and the successes of local fighter squadrons and slight damage caused by bombs. Some dissatisfaction among farmers in Morpeth area who criticise some instructions they receive on the ground that many of their fields are unsuitable for the purposes required.

NORTH-MIDLAND (Nottingham) The more detailed accounts of raids on this country are welcomed, and it is suggested from Grimsby that there will be less ground for alarm if casualty totals are given daily. A general feeling prevails that the full blockade should be maintained, and there is concern about Hoover's proposal to send food to occupied countries. Troops in Lincolnshire are dissatisfied at being in villages or private parks, and suffering from boredom while waiting for invasion to materialise. Further evidence that an increase in the tea ration would be welcomed by small householders. Complaints from parents and friends of serving men about non-delivery of parcels and postal orders. The erection of field obstructions has been suspended after Attlee's statement that the responsibility has been transferred to the Military Authorities.

SOUTH-WESTERN (Bristol) Some doubt is expressed about the Somaliland campaign and there is a feeling that Italy has gained a moral advantage because we have allowed her to take the initiative, but the news of the naval and air action against Libya has caused satisfaction. Despite lengthy night warnings, Bristol is carrying on as usual. In Exeter the view is held that bombs were dropped recently through bedroom lights being switched on as soon as householders were awakened by sirens. It is reported from Bath that regret is expressed that the French news sheet is not to be issued, as stories are heard of French troops who are wounded, or stranded in England, and feel cut off. Explanation of the care with which claims of successes against enemy aircraft are checked has done much to strengthen confidence in our communiques.

MIDLAND (Birmingham) In several districts of Birmingham unofficial street patrols have been formed due to complaints about delay in the sounding of raid warnings; these patrols notify residents when aeroplane engines are heard. Some factory workers are complaining that they are not paid for time spent in shelters. In outlying parts of the Region black-out stipulations are not well observed, and motorists do not always immobilise unattended cars. Prosecutions are being made against people attempting to obtain rationed food from Ireland.

SCOTLAND (Edinburgh) There is a demand for further bombing of Italian towns, and the belief that injury to Italy will have a great moral effect. Eden's and Morrison's speeches forecasting offensive action are welcomed. Some people object to the way in which the bombardment of London has been glossed over as a mere incident. Complaints are prevalent about the unsanitary conditions of public air-raid shelters. Unemployed men starting at some armament factories are finding difficulty in making ends meet because they receive their first pay at the end of the second week. It is rumoured that reserved jobs are being found for professional footballers, and this is part of a slight but general ill-feeling against those in reserved occupations.

NORTHERN IRELAND (Belfast) The three main topics of conversation are the destruction of further numbers of enemy planes, the German announcement of the mining of the Irish Sea and North Channel, and the German note to the Eire Government regarding blockade. Anxiety is expressed about the attitude of the Eire Government if Germany should try to enforce harsh conditions in return for facilities for shipping and that De Valera may be driven to make terms detrimental to British interests. Duff Cooper's broadcast appreciated, although some listeners did not like his invitation to Hitler to get on with the invasion. Enthusiasm for the Ulster Spitfire fund continues unabated. Businessmen are pleased that censorship of incoming letters will shortly be carried out in Belfast, as there have been many delays under existing arrangements. There is a growing interest in the references of American public men to the war situation as affecting Britain.

LONDON

Chief emotion among people suffering raids in all districts extreme anger and wish for reprisals, especially on Berlin. Morale extremely high, although nervousness shows itself in self-conscious joking and occasionally in nonchalant attitude of not hurrying to shelter. Too many people, especially men, are standing in the open to watch what is going on, betraying a falsely fatalistic and don't care attitude. Pride among Civil Defence workers high at being under fire and at efficiency of organisation proved. Young volunteers, unused to sights of physical violence, showing remarkable coolness on handling terrible HE casualties. Neighbourliness proving able to cope with all homeless people; Wimbledon and other suburban districts being particularly good in this respect. Praise in the Maldens of help and consideration of wardens who visited Anderson shelters to see how people were getting on. Appreciation of visits of high officials several hours after raid took place expressed by people – as recognition of their heroism, tragedies and efficiency by authority encouraging. Considered opinion has it that any propaganda to increase people's courage at this time would be irritating beyond measure. Confusion reported in Piccadilly after crowd had made for large Swan & Edgar's shelter to find it was closed on Sundays. Elderly people started panicking and it took several minutes for policemen to disperse crowds to other shelters. Large crowd, particularly of children, at Zoo calm when sirens went on Sunday afternoon. Too many for tunnel shelters and at first some bewilderment as to know where to go instead. Need for more large notices of over-flow shelters and officials to direct people to them as panic might easily take place on crowded Sundays if bombs were actually falling. The Minister's speech criticised as being dangerous and invitation to Hitler to come here considered to have been accepted. West Ham reports falling attendance of children at classes and societies since air-raid alarms; some parents afraid to allow children to go far from home. Severe criticism of BBC's feature in 9 p.m. news after Croydon bombing; e.g. interviewing by Edward Ward of people who had experienced raid. Considered bad propaganda as interviewer 'sounded patronizing and people over-excited and either callous or flippant.' Appreciation of Sunday night's postscript about Merchant Navy.

TUESDAY 20 AUGUST 1940

Morale remains high: there is confidence and cheerfulness.

Lull on the home front has allowed the public time to comment on the Somaliland withdrawal. Preliminary reports show that the outcome was expected; nevertheless people feel that British prestige is weakened. They are amazed that the 'despised Italians' were capable of such rapid success. 'Fed up' might be used to describe reaction. Observers report many comments on the way in which the affair has been progressively described. 'We should have recognised the danger signals: first silence, then inadequate news, then hints that the place wasn't worth defending, then the successful strategic withdrawal'. 'Why weren't we told what to expect at the beginning? We're not children'. 'Fancy, the Wops, it's disgusting.' 'I suppose it means that we've lost the Suez Canal.' Many people, however, are reported to be saying that 'Winston will explain everything'.

There is little comment on the new powers of the Regional Defence Commissioners. The public does not understand what these powers are. Nor are the Commissioners themselves well known.

The siren controversy continues.

Points from Regions

All reports show that morale remains consistently high, and despite the short lull in air activity, the tonic effect of recent successes is still apparent. The news of the withdrawal from Somaliland has had a mixed reception.

NORTH-EASTERN (Leeds) Sheffield, Rotherham, and Penistone received their first raid by bombers last night, and reports show confidence is unshaken. The variation in the number of enemy machines claimed to have been brought down by our Air Force in different newspapers has a disturbing effect in Barnsley. The new powers of the Regional Commissioners appear to be little understood. The serious effect of the war on enrolments for technical and evening classes for the coming winter has been reported from several quarters, and there is a feeling that the Government should take steps to make attendance compulsory. Young solicitors in military service who have to jettison their professional skill and maintain a family on private's pay compare their position unfavourably with members of the medical and dental professions who get the financial benefit of a commissioned rank. Sarcastic comment is reported from Skipton at the number of cars used for joy-riding during week-ends.

EASTERN (Cambridge) There is much fatigue in places where sirens have been sounded freely at night time and growing indications of indifference to warnings; there has also been difficulty over the crowding of sightseers to inspect damage. The general public seems to have taken the withdrawal from British Somaliland philosophically, although there is some disquiet in more thoughtful circles over the situation in the Mediterranean. The sound of heavy gunfire during the night off the Norfolk Coast set up mild speculation concerning a possible attempt at invasion, but this did not reach serious proportions.

SOUTHERN (Reading) The main subject of conversation is still the achievements of the RAF, and a feeling that 'at any rate, we have won the first round.' The siren controversy still goes on. Duff Cooper's broadcast has received more adverse criticism than any previous speech, particularly his invitation to Hitler to invade us. Many people feel we have lost an opportunity to convey to America our confidence in ultimate victory through the happenings of last week, and it is felt that the deciding factor in Japan's attitude towards this country will be whether they consider Germany can defeat us in a short space of time.

WALES (Cardiff) Unlucky salvos of bombs on Cardiff and Swansea when guns were not firing and few searchlights were to be seen has strengthened belief that the aerial defence of the Region has been weakened to supplement defence of the South East Coast, and created a sense of grievance. The result of Anderson's investigation regarding siren warnings as a result of the Croydon raid is expectantly awaited. The occasional omission of Wales in communiques dealing with air raids, or the mention of South Wales only when districts in the north should be included, have led to a certain lack of confidence in communiques and news. Opinion is still strong that the blockade must be relentlessly pursued. The evacuation of Somaliland, although anticipated, has caused disappointment. Many evacuated children are so settled in North Wales that difficulty is anticipated when they have to be sent home.

NORTH-WESTERN (Manchester) The Somaliland evacuation is poorly received, as the contemptuous references to Italy are remembered, and attempts to minimise evacuation do not go down well. Men in the Forces liked the line of self-assurance in Duff Cooper's broadcast, but civilians think this is overdone and in bad taste. Stephenson's revelation that all is not well with our ship-building is talked about, and there is a feeling that, despite their energy, both Bevin and Morrison could further speed up their efforts. Confidence is high and there is no sign of 'jitters'.

SOUTH-EASTERN (Tunbridge Wells) The growing number of enemy machines brought down on the coast near Worthing has had a tonic effect on the district. Sunday's raids in which 140 German planes could be seen have made the public more anxious to take cover when sirens sound. There is a grievance in Eastbourne that so much publicity was given to damage caused by a single Nazi plane on Friday. It is reported from Brighton that twenty-nine coaches arrived from London to see the damage, and the question is asked as to who organises the trips. Residents in South Coast towns affected through these becoming part of the Defence Area feel that the Government has offered little hope of financial relief.

WEDNESDAY 21 AUGUST 1940

Morale continues high.

The Prime Minister's speech was received extremely well, according to all reports. From Northern Ireland comes the comment that it is the most forceful and heartening he has yet made. Newcastle reports that it has created a strong feeling of confidence. Two Bristol verbatim reports are as follows: 'Everyone feels now that, come what will, we are top dogs; the past week has shown that we shall win no matter what slight doubts there were before.'

'Bristol has implicit trust in Churchill. If he says things are all right Bristol people know they are all right; if he says they are bad, they know they are bad.' From Scotland comes the report that the three points which interested people most were, first the reference to the Russian Air Force as perhaps immobilising a large part of the German air fleet, secondly the hint that the war might not last as long as was formerly expected, and thirdly the reference to closer relations with the USA. People in Scotland still seem reluctant to face up to the prospect of a long war, and the air successes of last week have strengthened the hope that the war may end quickly. There is no evidence that the Prime Minister's references to the food blockade have produced any antagonism or disagreement.

Comment on the Somaliland evacuation is still limited and regional reports suggest that its impact is not great.

The siren controversy continues heatedly.

Points from Regions

As usual the Prime Minister's speech yesterday has been received very well, and created a strong feeling of confidence. References to the Russian Air Force & closer relations with USA are particularly noted, and many consider this to be the most heartening speech the Premier has yet made.

NORTHERN (Newcastle) There is considerable public discussion on the sounding of sirens and in some towns people are losing all faith in the present policy and going to shelters immediately aircraft are heard. Reports from Stockton-on-Tees show that requests by employers for workmen in key positions to continue during raids has met with good response. Criticism is reported from several quarters that after concrete defence structures have been completed with all haste there is considerable waste of time and money making alterations which should have been foreseen. The evacuation of Somaliland is a disappointment, but has not caused despondency.

NORTH-MIDLAND (Nottingham) The stimulating effect of RAF successes is still apparent. Approval is still being expressed of the more informative accounts of air raids on this country, but a criticism from Leicester is that there has been no disclosure of the number of RAF machines destroyed on the ground. Very few operatives in Leicester factories are carrying gas masks, and it is felt that nothing short of a gas attack would induce people to carry their masks. There is still a tendency to 'watch the fun' during air raids. Arrangements for giving raid warnings are still misunderstood. Comparatively little interest is shown in African operations, but there is disappointment at the need for withdrawal from Somaliland.

SOUTH-WESTERN (Bristol) Weston-super-Mare reports a feeling that the Premier was a little too optimistic. There is strong feeling that the blockade of Europe should continue. The Somaliland evacuation has had little effect on public opinion, as it was anticipated, and little importance attached to it. Dissatisfaction in Exeter because there are apparently no protective fighters or AA guns, and the siren policy is a chief topic of conversation.

MIDLAND (Birmingham) Serious complaints come from all parts of the Region that bombs drop before sirens have been sounded, and the feeling is that people should be afforded an opportunity to get to shelter. Railway signalmen in Lichfield feel strongly their lack of protection against flying glass and splinters. There is a feeling that an attack on Italy would probably shorten the war, and that to allow her even local successes will increase Italian morale at our expense.

SCOTLAND (Edinburgh) People seem still reluctant to face up to the prospect of a long war and the air success of last week has strengthened the hope that it may finish quickly. The Somaliland withdrawal has occasioned little comment in Clydebank, although freely discussed in Aberdeen. There is still a general impression amongst Clydeside shipyard and munition workers that the yards and shops have not yet properly 'got down to it'. The position is better than it was, but not good enough to convince workers that Morrison's remarks in his recent speech applied to Clydeside.

NORTHERN IRELAND (Belfast) There is considerable speculation concerning the German plane which crashed in Co. Kerry. More than 2,000 Ulster men have registered under the order affecting men with engineering experience, including two MPs. Complaints are made of absence of news from London when Berlin was supplying the world with running commentaries on air attacks.

LONDON

Reports from all areas show morale to be excellent. Recent air-raid alarms proved that confidence has greatly increased since the beginning of the war and people showing more neighbourliness towards each other. Citizens' Advice Bureaux and similar offices which were besieged by anxious people after first alarms in September were practically empty after last week's raids. Many people did not take shelter when the siren went; even men in uniform in Kensington Gardens took no notice and civilians are inclined to follow their example. Confusion still exists as to what people should do when siren goes; some employers grudge wasting time and don't encourage their staff to take shelter. Street shelters in Paddington and Bayswater without roofs owing to shortage of material. Doubt is still expressed about the accuracy of German air losses. Evacuated children still returning to London. Many areas, particularly East End, view with gravity lack of full schooling facilities for children especially those under eight. It is felt that discipline and home life in evacuation areas have practically disappeared: even quite young children forming themselves into bands of hooligans. Hoxton and Shoreditch parents, normally not anxious about education, want full time schooling restored as they are unable to control their children. Hackney and Stoke Newington where class of parents is better realise children are growing up without sufficient education. It is difficult to prosecute parents for not sending children to school and bad parents are taking advantage of this. It is felt that the progress of twenty-five years has been broken down in one. Some bitter feeling expressed about the giving up of Somaliland and French held to be responsible; no anxiety expressed about general situation in Middle East so long as the White Ensign is still flying. Churchill's speech yesterday, particularly his reference to the RAF, thought to be completely right – epitomises the feeling of the country. Letters from internees in Isle of Man show conditions to be good.

THURSDAY 22 AUGUST 1940

1. During the four days August 16th – 20th (i.e. before the Prime Minister made his statement) the Wartime Social Survey asked the question:

'What do you think of our food blockade of German-controlled countries?'

with the result:

Approval	Qualified Approval	Disapproval	No Opinion
82%	1%	3%	14%

Percentage of men approving   90
Percentage of women approving   72
(because greater percentage of women had no opinion)

An analysis of the arguments put forward by those who disapproved showed that some objected on humane grounds, others from self-interest (disease from famine areas will spread to England).

Those who expressed qualified approval were generally sceptical about the success of our blockade (upper and middle-class reaction).

About 60% of those expressing approval did so on grounds of 'absolute necessity', 'could not do otherwise' etc.

The subject will be continuously studied and a further analysis of the replies is being made.

2. There was considerable disappointment that Sir John Anderson did not make a full statement of policy yesterday. Most people appear to have expected it.

Therefore the siren controversy continues unabated.

3. Further criticism of Mr Duff Cooper's last broadcast is coming to light. There are more strongly unfavourable than favourable references in our reports. There is a small minority strongly in favour.

4. There is a good deal of annoyance and some anger at 'misleading official statements about casualties and damage'. People in a damaged area cannot understand the use of phrases like 'little material damage', 'Few casualties', and although morale remains high, this subject represents a definite point of tension and dissatisfaction.

Points from Regions

Reports from raided areas show that morale remains very high, and seems to rise in proportion to the number of raids, about which most people are philosophical, and not unduly worried.

The aftermath of the Premier's speech is confidence, and his remark about the Russian Air Force has given rise to a good deal of speculation.

NORTH-EASTERN (Leeds) Comment on the Air Minister's broadcast reflects the confidence of the man in the street in the progress of the war. Complaints regarding the sounding of sirens continue to be received, principally from Rotherham which was recently bombed. Keen dissatisfaction was expressed at the Hebden Bridge Local Elementary Education Committee at the inadequate air-raid accommodation for schools.

EASTERN (Cambridge) An exception to calm behaviour in air raids has been at Ramsey, Hunts., where, after a warning, twenty mothers went to the local school to demand their children. Some comment has been aroused in Lowestoft that BBC news bulletins made no reference to the fact that six people were killed as a result of direct hits on shelters. The appearance of RAF fighters was heartening. Absence of warnings in the Chelmsford area has caused nervousness and renewed demand for private shelters. A rumour has gained currency in the same area that troops, engaged on anti-invasion manoeuvres on the coast, were unable to cope with the emergency. Many fields in West Norfolk are still not obstructed against enemy aircraft.

SOUTHERN (Reading) There is some danger that people may mistake the Premier's optimism in ultimate victory for a feeling that it is already in sight, and more thoughtful people realise that hard times are ahead and that we may suffer reverses in different parts of the world. The siren controversy still continues, especially in the smaller towns.

WALES (Cardiff) Daylight raids without warnings leave a sense of grievance, and Anderson's explanation of the Croydon incident caused disappointment. Speculation is widespread concerning the lull in daylight raids. Raids on military objectives in Italy cause great satisfaction. The Air Minister's broadcast had a mixed reception.

NORTH-WESTERN (Manchester) Somaliland is almost forgotten already, but there is some puzzlement about the Balkan situation. Air Minister's talk approved, but some people fear we may exaggerate Nazi losses by too much manipulation of figures. Opinion is sharply divided on the Home Guard, and many think officers and better discipline are needed. Manchester is receiving many stories about air-raid damage to other Midland cities.

SOUTH-EASTERN (Tunbridge Wells) Complaints have been received from a number of villages because they have no sirens, and in country districts where there is perhaps not even a village Constable there is a feeling that wardens should have more authority. Lorry drivers say that they cannot hear sirens above the noise of their engines; sometimes drive into towns being raided without realising it. There is discontent among bus drivers and conductors at not being allowed to stop their buses in raids, as some had narrow escapes last Sunday. Country dwellers say the supply of sugar for jam making is considerably delayed. Reference in the press and by the public to the 'All Clear' instead of 'Raiders Passed' lead many Civil Defence workers to believe that if gas is used in air raids, people will remove their masks when the 'Raiders Passed' is sounded.

FRIDAY 23 AUGUST 1940

Morale continues high.

The lull in air activity has produced a decrease in interest in the news. At the same time in many areas the question of the sounding of sirens is being heatedly discussed; the volume of this controversy is by no means apparent from a study of the daily press. Large numbers of people throughout the country have now had practical experience of hearing sirens sometime after the arrival of enemy planes and the onset of bombing and AA fire (as happened in London last night). Reports show that the public faith in the sirens has considerably diminished, and in some places private warning systems organised by individual enterprise are functioning.

There are many signs that the Prime Minister's reference to 'an offensive' has been widely welcomed.

Points from Regions

Reports still stress the beneficial effect of the Premier's speech and Morrison's broadcast last night was also well received. The present siren policy is still causing discontent, and there are further instances of bombs dropping before the warning is sounded. Evidence is still accumulating that the public supports the decision that the blockade should not be raised. Reprisals on Berlin are asked for in view of the bombing of London, and news of action against the Italian fleet is eagerly awaited.

NORTHERN (Newcastle) Morale remains steady and recent events have increased confidence. The belief is widely held that any food sent to Europe to relieve hardship would certainly be diverted to German use. With the increase of attacks on industrial towns and London, many are stating that we have been too squeamish in the past and should return with interest methods used by the enemy. The new allowance for Workmen's Compensation has caused satisfaction.

NORTH-MIDLAND (Nottingham) Opinion has hardened in the last few weeks, and in some of the raided areas inhabitants are more angry than fearful. A report shows that most people believe official figures of German air losses. In Grimsby bombs dropped just after a train entered the station and it is suspected that enemy planes followed the train; it is suggested that trains might be stopped in populated areas after the warning had sounded. Criticism of Duff Cooper's last broadcast that it was somewhat too boastful has been expressed. Housewives in the Lincoln area have been reassured by the Ministry of Food's promise to take action against 'rings'.

SOUTH-WESTERN (Bristol) The Premier's reference to the time when we shall take the offensive has had a cheering effect. In raided areas neighbourliness shows itself in offers of help to those affected by the raids. Annoyance is felt that whereas Trowbridge has had eighty warnings, Melksham, which is four miles away, but under different control, has only been disturbed six times. Exaggerated accounts of damage to the aircraft factory in last night's raids are circulating in Bristol. A report from Camborne shows that the effect of whistling bombs has failed to shake morale, and many regard it as another instance of 'Hitler's bark being worse than his bite.' In Camborne and Redruth communal schemes for picking blackberries and making jam are in operation. Rumour in Exeter that the local squadron secured most victories in last Sunday's air battle makes many think that the proximity of a champion squadron adds to Exeter's vulnerability.

MIDLAND (Birmingham) Continued criticism about the lack of sirens before bomb dropping, and some sort of intermediate warning is suggested. In several towns unofficial listening posts have been set up. There are serious complaints from several centres of a shortage of coal, although the areas are close to the South Staffordshire coalfield, and with ample rail and canal facilities. Requests have been received for weekly casualty lists.

SCOTLAND (Edinburgh) The shelling of Dover has caused no consternation, and it is felt unlikely to afford the enemy much success, but more press comment on its impracticability would reassure the public. Press comments convey the impression that Japan is becoming more dangerous, and there is a strong feeling that we ought to do something about it. The release of members of the Anarchists Federation, found not guilty of charges against them, has disappointed many who knew the men were working actively against the prosecution of the war in Glasgow.

NORTHERN IRELAND (Belfast) Position on the Egyptian border is being watched with some uneasiness. Anger at the disclosure that 800 French planes are being placed at the disposal of the enemy, and the action of the Vichy Government is denounced as base treachery. There is no evidence of a sentimental view of the blockade. Much interest is aroused in the announcement that the Ministry of Supply is making a new survey of Ulster's deposits of iron ore and bauxite. Ulster's Spitfire fund has reached £30,000.

LONDON

Widespread indignation today at German planes appearing over London and dropping bombs without hindrance or siren warnings for eighteen or nineteen minutes. Sir John Anderson's statement of siren policy has not cleared up situation in opinion of general public. Surprised comment reported from many people that searchlights caught and held enemy planes magnificently in their beams, but that no fighters or anti-aircraft guns were there to render them harmless. People rushing in crowds to scene of disaster before police can rope off area. Demands from responsible people that police or Home Guard should be more ruthless in preventing sight-seeing crowd from gathering both for their own sakes as area may still be dangerous, and for the sake of Civil Defence workers and actual sufferers. Reaction of housewives with houses destroyed at first thankfulness for own safety, then anxiety about future. Common questions: 'Who will pay for this damage? Where shall we live now? How shall I get my rations as my book is lost?' Rumours still current about high casualty figures in weekend raids, especially Croydon; disappointment expressed that LIC boards have not carried details of local damage. Children playing in streets in poorer districts reported to run home, even if half a mile away when sirens go off; this causes confusion and entails dangerous risks. Non-attendance at emergency schools serious problem in certain districts. Petty pilfering, especially of fruit and vegetables in abandoned gardens, rife. Parents no longer insisting on children keeping law of compulsory education. In many cases mother goes out to work and leaves older children in charge of younger. Consequent evils: lowering of educational standards and neglect of medical attention leading to increase of scabies and nose, throat and teeth trouble. Suburban people reported to dread rigours of winter more than poorer people as have larger houses to heat. All however express hope that Government will set up coal depots in each Borough. Offensive spirit stated to outweigh defensive and people anxious everywhere for us to attack. Disappointment over Somaliland turning to belief that we shall 'get our own back when the time comes'. WVS praised highly in many districts. Towns-women's Guilds enthusiastically doing National Service by turning all available fruit into jam. Peckham reports enthusiastic reception of 700 to 800 Belgian, French and Polish refugees changing to suspicion and resentment at number of able bodied men hanging about. All districts report widespread return of evacuated children.

SATURDAY 24 AUGUST 1940

(Owing to raid warning, interruption, front page is omitted)

Points from Regions

From several Regions come complaints of the failure to sound sirens, coupled with a widespread public belief that there is at times consid-erable delay in putting ground defences into action. The RIO at Leeds reports that there have been several complaints from Rotherham that no balloons were up in the immediate vicinity during last Monday's 11 p.m. air raid. The public believe that the absence of the balloons enabled the raider to dive down to his objective. One bomb exploded near a grounded balloon. As there were no warnings, furnaces were actually being tapped at the moment of the raid, and coke ovens in the neighbourhood were lighting up. The RIO at Cambridge reports that the siren controversy continues. The RIO at Reading states that there is widespread criticism about sirens. The public understand that too frequent warnings cause general upheaval, but they are not entirely satisfied by Sir John Anderson's statement. He reports that there is a divergence of prac-tice between different towns, and that on three occasions bombs have been dropped at Southampton without warnings being given. It is felt that if bombs have dropped without warning, the 'Raiders Passed' should be given in due course even though no initial warning has been sounded; otherwise people remain too long in their shelters or, alternatively, come out too soon. The RIO at Tunbridge Wells states that in residential areas in his Region the public favour frequent rather than infrequent sounding of sirens. On Thursday night a plane was over the town on and off from midnight to 4 a.m., but it was not till 4 a.m. that the siren sounded. Many of the public believe that the plane was German and they are critical because although it was clearly caught by the searchlights there was no fighter or AA opposition.

NORTH-EASTERN (Leeds) Hit and run raids on Bridlington are stated to have caused many people to leave the town; people are asking why it is still a Reception Area. MOI meeting on air tactics on Tuesday night at Rotherham (following raid mentioned above) was best attended meeting in the town for many years. Raid at Stockbridge caused no panic and Civil Defence services are reported to have worked smoothly and efficiently.

EASTERN (Cambridge) Recent spell of cold weather has turned people's minds towards the approaching winter, and many are thinking apprehensively of the black-out. Considerable fatigue is reported in areas where there have been frequent night raid warnings; night workers in particular find these very trying. Posthumous award of VC to member of Royal Norfolk Regiment has caused keen satisfaction in the county.

SOUTHERN (Reading) Morale unaffected by air raids, but much criticism of sirens. Better educated people are anxious about whether we are adequately counteracting the barrage of anti-British propaganda which is being used on France by the Germans. There is also some misgiving in these quarters about our propaganda in the Near East, the United States, and other neutral countries.

WALES (Cardiff) Criticism that this Region is not always mentioned in air-raid communiques when it should be is increasing. Many believe that our news is true only 'insofar as it goes'. There is, however, general credence of the RAF and enemy plane losses. The attacks on Channel convoys have led to suggestions that the western ports should be developed still more and used to their maximal capacity.

This point is also raised by sailors and their relatives, where ships sail direct to the East Coast from abroad. The more thoughtful sections of the public approve of the milder attitude towards enemy aliens, though even they usually qualify their approval by saying that every case must be investigated as thoroughly as possible. The Prime Minister's speech has led many to believe that Russia will be before long a thorn in Germany's flesh, even if there is no open war between the two. Troops in the Region are reported to be very appreciative of efforts made for their entertainment and comfort.

NORTH-WESTERN (Manchester) Bevin's new 'idle-workers' scheme is helping to allay the concern which many have felt at war production firms (including even aircraft firms) who lay off skilled workers from time to time. News of our new types of RAF planes has heartened people. Public stated to be expecting RAF figures unreservedly and suggestion is made that any further attempts to convince people of their authenticity will savour of us suggesting too much. Some puzzlement at attacks on convoys on East Coast, as many believe that almost all our trade is now diverted to West Coast. As details of internment camps become known, there is growing feeling about our treatment of anti-Nazi aliens. Discontent reported from Blackpool because Polish airmen there are believed to be getting better pay than RAF.

SOUTH-EASTERN (Tunbridge Wells) Soldiers on leave are stated to be ignoring air-raid sirens. This bad example is quickly followed by civilians.

MONDAY 26 AUGUST TO SATURDAY 31 AUGUST 1940

'The success of local campaigns for Spitfires has been remarkable,' the Newcastle regional office reported on 26 August. With the support of a propaganda campaign led by Lord Beaverbrook, movements had sprung up in many parts of Britain and the British Empire to collect funds for the 'purchase' of Spitfires, Hurricanes or other military aircraft, which were then named after the donor with an inscription on the fuselage of the plane. Many of the funds were run by local authorities, others by companies, others again by private individuals. The Conservative MP Garfield Weston, a Canadian businessman, donated £100,000. A Mrs Dorothy Clark of Sheffield started a 'Dorothy' Spitfire fund to which all Dorothys in Great Britain were invited to contribute. The Durham miners sent a cheque for £10,000 and the poor, or many of them, contributed their pennies. The fund-raising campaign was arguably good for morale by giving people a sense of participation in the war, but as the government did not need the money, and the planes would have been built in any case, it had more to do with patriotic emotion than with aircraft production. As Home Intelligence reported from Edinburgh, there was some dissent: 'The Lord Provost of Glasgow's refusal to sponsor the Spitfire fund has gained considerable support on the grounds that it is the Government's job to provide the planes.'

The Home Intelligence reports were dominated by the war in the air to the exclusion of almost everything else. The Luftwaffe launched major attacks on ports and airfields in the south on the 24th, 26th, 28th and 30th and on the 24th bombs were dropped on central London in daylight for the first time. As the weeks passed the civilian death toll increased, the monthly Civil Defence reports submitted to the War Cabinet estimating that 304 people were killed in the month ending 7 August, and more than 1,000 between 7 August and 1 September.

Night bombing was also intensifying with up to 200 towns and villages bombed in a single night, and practically the whole of Britain covered by a 'purple' warning. London was under a 'red' warning on most nights and many people were spending the hours of darkness in an Anderson shelter at the bottom of the garden, or one of the public shelters erected for people without a garden. 'Lack of sleep beginning to tell on people in all districts', noted the London report on 31 August, 'showing itself in paleness and lassitude of children and irritability of grown-ups. This is particularly true of poorer quarters where crowded conditions prevail and public shelters are packed and noisy at night. Unhygienic and unsanitary conditions reported in large buildings used as shelters in Bethnal Green, City etc. where hundreds of people of mixed ages and sexes congregate with bedding and remain all night. Shelters not designed for mass sleeping.' Meanwhile complaints over the unreliability of air-raid warnings were as loud and persistent as ever.

On 25 August the RAF bombed Berlin for the first time. 'There is a definite and noticeable increase in the demand for recriminatory measures and some anger at reports that our aircraft have returned with their bombs from Germany,' the daily summary noted on 27 August. 'There is still an inadequate realisation of the importance of targets. There is quite a strong demand for retaliation on civilians. At the same time, in our judgment, there is as yet no great anger against the Germans.'

MONDAY 26 AUGUST 1940

No general report today.

Points from Regions

Reports indicate that morale is maintained at a high level, and there is a continued increase in our ability to secure ultimate victory. The offensive and defensive exploits of the RAF are almost entirely responsible for the present outlook and in particular the bombing of Berlin has caused great satisfaction.

NORTHERN (Newcastle) Reports show strong support for the official policy on the food blockade. There now seems some uncertainty amongst the public on the advisability of mentioning towns by name in air-raid reports due to anxiety of relations of residents. The success of local campaigns for Spitfires has been remarkable. The broadcasts of the British Workers Challenge Station are regarded in several small towns as poor in quality, and the language irritating. Approbation expressed about several of the Ministry of Information's films.

NORTH-MIDLAND (Nottingham) Despite disinterest in African affairs, there is continued evidence of disappointment over Somaliland campaign. Too many people continue to go into the streets in Chesterfield during the period of air-raid warnings. Anderson's announcement on warnings has caused misgiving in certain quarters, particularly as on Friday purple warnings were received half-an-hour after bombs were dropped. A number of rumours about damage to Croydon is prevalent, and casualties are said to be high. Renewed demands for fresh news to be given at the beginning of BBC bulletins. In Chesterfield cheap milk for children over five would be welcomed, and there is evidence that the sugar ration for jam is being abused.

SOUTH-WESTERN (Bristol) A noticeable improvement of morale in Barnstaple is apparent. Reports are received of dissatisfaction over 'strategic withdrawals' and people ask when we are going to make an attack. The necessity for continuing the food blockade is appreciated. Exaggerated accounts of air-raid damage are widespread.

MIDLAND (Birmingham) The air-raid warning controversy continues, and in Birmingham questions are asked about the fact that raiders are apparently allowed to hover for long periods without apparent challenge.

SCOTLAND (Edinburgh) Wide expression of approval on the bombing of Berlin. The Premier's statement on the blockade has found ready acceptance. The Lord Provost of Glasgow's refusal to sponsor the Spitfire fund has gained considerable support on the grounds that it is the Government's job to provide planes. Press comments on the congestion in Glasgow Harbour are that 'it is an invitation to the Germans to come over.' Considerable complaints about interference by German broadcasts with Home Service programmes, particularly after 10 p.m.

NORTHERN IRELAND (Belfast) Great admiration for the way in which the British are taking German raids, and detailed reports of damage are regarded as a sign of British confidence. Announcement that food rationing scheme is to be overhauled is welcomed, as the difficulties of retailers in disposing of surplus stock has been the subject of comment in both press and Parliament.

LONDON

London has come through a weekend of extensive raids with courage and calmness. Croydon proper extremely resentful that after one hour's warning 'Raiders Passed' signal sent them back to bed only to have bombs dropped on them in ten minutes time with considerable damage and loss of life. Responsible local official states public has lost all confidence in warning system and this loss of confidence is spreading to other branches of Civil Defence. Most districts remarked on fact of raiders returning after warning ceased on

Saturday night. East-Enders experiencing screaming bomb for first time expressed great fear but did not panic. Those in shelters remained, although they said it sounded as if the bomb was falling right on top of them. Still far too many people go sight-seeing after first ten minutes in shelters. No absentees today from large Silvertown factory in spite of employees' sleepless nights and experience of bombs. Local people impressed by vigour and efficiency of fire fighting at docks. Delayed action bombs causing apprehension in these areas. Exaggerated rumours of casualties and damage rife. Shoreditch: 'large crowds gathered today to see raid damage; show no resentment at being kept at safe distance by cordon and police. People tired today but very excited; nine out of ten overheard conversations concerned bombing. Although women will not go far from home they are carrying on their normal occupations.' Muddle reported in Stepney Green over people rendered homeless by bombs; matter was taken in hand by authorities. Tooting reports people still careless about showing lights. Stepney people using new brick shelters in streets. Those with Anderson shelters now arranging them to spend night in. East Ham has recruited 10,500 volunteers for Mutual Aid for Good Neighbours Association to provide in each street supplementary system to Civil Defence. Watford reports considerable hardship locally among people who cannot pay their rent because of war time financial stress. Maltese refugees in Kensington hotel appear to be bored and aimless. Do not seem to make full use of adjacent park to take their babies in.

TUESDAY 27 AUGUST 1940

Air raids dominate thought and conversation. Determination has not weakened but our reports show a definite increase in apprehension. This appears to be caused by:

1. An increasing lack of confidence in sirens. Many are reported to be saying 'They don't mean anything: a bomb's just as likely to drop after the All Clear'. They are beginning to prefer to rely on their own diagnosis of an approaching raid and to sleep in shelters rather than risk a false All Clear.

The siren situation is beginning to create restlessness and in those people not urgently occupied a sense of being on the 'qui vive'.

2. Women with children are beginning to show strain.

3. The inconsistency of regulations leads to irritation, e.g. in some places no one is allowed to leave until the raid is over, in others they are free to do so.

4. There is still a good deal of uncertainty about transport facilities at night.

5. There are complaints about the conditions in public shelters, e.g. insufficient seats.

6. The realisation that night raids may persist throughout the winter is bringing despondency.

Superficially people are cheerful and it should be remarked that there are many complaints of people ignoring shelter instructions. At the same time a large number of people took shelter for the whole of last night's raid.

There are certain specific rumours about air-raid damage and casualties, e.g. the 300 girls killed in the Croydon scent factory, but on the whole people are speaking with control about raids.

Reports from cinemas show that audiences have taken the warnings calmly, that they generally stay until the end and do not panic. There has been no noticeable decline in attendances.

There is a definite and noticeable increase in the demand for recriminatory measures and some anger at reports that our aircraft have returned with their bombs from Germany. There is still an inadequate realisation of the importance of targets. There is quite a strong demand for retaliation on civilians. At the same time, in our judgment, there is yet no great anger against the Germans. There is as much bitterness about sirens. A condition of affairs exists, however, in which anger against the Germans may grow rapidly. It is important that this emotion should be canalised and should not be allowed to attach itself to what is considered to be a major grievance at home: siren policy.

Points from Regions

Criticism of the present siren policy continues. Several reports indicate that people in raided towns consider they are inadequately safeguarded by AA defences. There is also a growing feeling that reprisals should be taken for deliberate German attacks on non-military objectives and the machine-gunning of civilians, and the fact that our bombers bring back their loads if unable to locate the enemy target is not well received in towns subjected to German attempts at demoralisation.

NORTH-EASTERN (Leeds) Bombs causing fatal casualties fell two hours after 'Raiders Passed' had sounded. The first serious raids in the West Riding have raised rather than lowered morale. Communiques on air-raid damage are not believed by many who live in bombed areas. Inhabitants of Bridlington complain that the town has no AA guns, and it has suffered severe damage. Many comments are received from isolated rural areas in the Yorkshire dales about inadequate black-out precautions, where lights can be seen for miles.

EASTERN (Cambridge) Monday's raid on Cambridge increased controversy over the siren policy, and there is bewilderment at the absence of AA defence and fighters. There is a tendency for people to remain in their doorways watching for air battles during alarms. There appears to be a general feeling that the Germans do greater damage by sporadic raids rather than by mass attacks. The apparent ease with which RAF stations are attacked has caused some surprise, especially among those who learn of the effects at first hand.

SOUTHERN (Reading) Although the Region has had a large share of raids there is no sign that morale has been affected. It is likely that too frequent reiteration that civilian bombing is of no significance will not be believed, and it has been pointed out that Holland was compelled to surrender largely through the threat to repeat the bombing of Rotterdam at Utrecht. Recent restrictions imposed on public meetings are likely to cause dissatisfaction.

WALES (Cardiff) The bombing of military objectives in the suburbs of Berlin has met with unanimous approval, and there is widespread criticism that our planes should bring back their bombs if unable to locate a definite target. The effect of recent speeches by Ministers is still apparent in the feeling of confidence which is prevalent. Many still hope for offensive naval operations against Italy soon. The evacuation of Somaliland still rankles despite the official explanation. There is a large influx into cinemas when daylight warnings are sounded, and on account of the length of recent warnings and loss of transport comment is frequently overheard that entertainment must be enjoyed within walking distance of home, and at an early hour. The slow methods of public shelter construction in North Wales are the object of much criticism.

NORTH-WESTERN (Manchester) Much interest is aroused by our raids over Berlin, and there is a feeling that we should have no scruples about bombing civilians there. Criticism is growing over what the public considers to be attempts to gloss over damage to this country, and the use of such phrases as 'a few deaths', etc. New posters boosting the contribution of the railways to the war effort has intensified feeling against higher fares.

SOUTH-EASTERN (Tunbridge Wells) The people of Gillingham are not going to shelter at the sound of guns. During night raids public shelters have been little used and most people appear to have kept awake with lights burning almost all night. The public seems prepared for similar enemy action in the future, with the hope that Berlin inhabitants are undergoing the same experiences. Voluntary Civil Defence workers would like a press appeal to employers to allow staff so engaged to arrive late for work in the morning when they have been on duty after midnight. Destinations chalked by railway workers on waggons containing war materials are believed to make valuable information available for the enemy.

WEDNESDAY 28 AUGUST 1940

Morale is much the same today although a good many people in the London area are suffering from the effects of loss of sleep as the result of the raids during the last few nights.

There has been no noticeable increase in the number of people carrying gas masks, and the fear of invasion seems to have receded.

The air war remains the chief topic of conversation and the optimistic faith in the RAF is still the highest common factor of conversation. There are, however, complaints that we are not doing enough in the way of bombing Berlin objectives, and there is a demand that Berlin should be bombed yet more heavily.

Points from Regions

There is no perceptible change in morale, which remains high, although the effect of loss of sleep is noticeable in some areas. Exaggerated accounts of damage to various parts of Great Britain as a result of air raids are once again appearing.

NORTHERN (Newcastle) There are increasing complaints of the burden placed on those whose income is just too large to be eligible for a free shelter. In view of the fact that the rural population cannot provide so many Home Guards as the urban, and consequently the more frequent periods of night duty for each Guard, it is suggested that the towns might arrange for some of their members to serve the surrounding countryside. Some indication that the approaching long winter nights are being viewed with apprehension.

NORTH-MIDLAND (Nottingham) Raids in Leicestershire have stiffened morale, and all those concerned with Civil Defence have responded well. With the exception of the Prime Minister's speech, recent utterances by other Ministers are not considered to have made an effective contribution to morale. Members of HM Forces and Civil Defence are guilty of much indiscreet talk. In Leicester the guarding of air-raid damage by troops with fixed bayonets is considered 'unnecessary and likely to cause resentment.' There is further evidence of public indifference to the need for carrying gas masks.

SOUTH-WESTERN (Bristol) War in the air excludes almost all other topics; there is strong demand for the bombing of Berlin and offensive action against Italy, and the latest naval reports have been well received. The need for continuing the blockade is emphasised. Bristol inhabitants are becoming so accustomed to raids that they are little inclined to seek shelter when warnings are sounded. Some concern in Plymouth that an enemy plane was able to circle for several hours without a fighter appearing. People consider that the prospects of invasion are receding. There are rumours of supposed air-raid damage.

MIDLAND (Birmingham) The Lord Mayor of Birmingham has inaugurated a Spitfire fund. It has been suggested that unless country schools can be provided with shelters, the authorities should be given warning of raids so that the children can be sent home.

SCOTLAND (Edinburgh) Few among academic and professional people seem satisfied with the presentation of news, and in particular with the way in which that of the week-end raids was broadcast. There is much exaggerated talk of damage, and photographs in the papers serve to increase the impression of the harm done. There is some nervousness in the Shetlands, due to the fact that these islands are nearer than the rest of Great Britain to Norway, where invasion preparations are said to be in progress; there are also rumours that several mail planes have been shot down, which produces a feeling of isolation, and there are rumours of Fifth Columnists in the labour camps. Interference with the Home Service programme is reported from Fife and Angus.

NORTHERN IRELAND (Belfast) The extension of the British air offensive over Germany and Italy is welcomed. The German claim that bombs on Wexford villages were not dropped by German planes was anticipated in Ulster, and the Eire Government's statement accepted. *Belfast Telegraph* Spitfire Fund expected to reach enough for a squadron today.

LONDON

Observer spending nights in public shelters in poor crowded districts states glare of electric light and noisy manner of some adults upsets children who cry and fray people's nerves. Many come with inadequate protection against cold and concrete floors. Harrow official describes cheerfulness of destitute awaiting money after raids. Great neighbourliness evident. Many sightseers to scenes of damage causing extra work for police. Greenwich contact reports: 'congregations of people without shelter at either end of river subway, which is closed during air raids; women in shelters singing to drown noise of HE bombs; men standing outside shelters but big bang hurried them inside; tram men refuse to drive during raids – general opinion expressed that communications should cease during raids, and night facilities be available afterwards to convey marooned people home from central London.' Members of West End Evening Institute regret economic wastefulness of refugee internments, and failure to make use of 'propaganda potential' of Anti-Nazis and Anti-Fascists; light BBC programmes often beneath intelligence and taste of listeners. Richmond factory girls holding raffles for Spitfire fund. Malden raid evoking many new orders for air-raid shelters. Mitcham: fears that UAB allowances to destitute after raid not sufficient to eliminate financial worry. Complaints that Croydon land suitable for allotments still unused. Reported pilfering from Enfield shelters. Also tendency to crowd doorways of shelters, preventing free ventilation. Complaints about shabby Underground advertisements and spaces that could be used for gay propaganda paintings. Stanmore contact reports that a local hospital has inadequate shelters and staff not fully protected for duties during air raids; local troops could dig additional trench shelters; many children in wards could be evacuated to less vulnerable area. Some station canteens inadequately stocked to supply crowds caught by raids. Shelter rest rooms needed in many large munition factories to help combat fatigue and strain. Hackney contact reports: appreciation of Hilton's talks; belief that US may yet enter war; worry at increased costs of gas and electricity.

THURSDAY 29 AUGUST 1940

There is no noticeable decline in morale although in London particularly there is some depression mainly brought by lack of sleep. At the same time more people are taking active steps to make their shelters into sleeping places, and when this is done they are calmer and more cheerful. There is a slight increase in the number of people taking shelter and a considerable proportion spent the whole of last night's warning period in public or private shelters.

There is general confidence in Civil Defence services although there is no diminution in public uneasiness about sirens (see over).

There is a noticeable increase, particularly in the South, in the number of people who say they expect a gas attack. A special study made recently showed that approximately 10% of the population of the areas investigated expected an invasion, about 10% expected that the Germans would, as an alternative, intensify air raids over this country and 4% thought there would be gas attacks. The percentage of those carrying gas masks, however, shows little change, although more people carry them in a place which has recently been bombed.

Exaggerated stories of damage and casualties appear to have increased slightly.

In heavily raided places there is bewilderment and some anger at official descriptions of the damage.

Interest in the international situation is much less: there is practically no general interest in the state of affairs in the Balkans.

Points from Regions

The siren policy is still causing widespread and adverse criticism. In Manchester last night, the 'Raiders Passed' was sounded long before bombing had ceased, whereas the night before bombs did not begin to drop until after the signal. The particularly long periods during which Norwich has been under red warnings, interrupted by brief intervals of 'Raiders Passed', causes much comment and the absence of sirens when bombs have fallen in Cambridge is also criticised. Opinion is expressed on all sides in the Southern area that warnings are inadequate, although the need for a minimum number is realised.

NORTH-EASTERN (Leeds) Morale is high, particularly where damage is slight, but in some parts of the Region there is a feeling that worse damage cannot be prevented. There is widespread appreciation at the decision of the Regional Commissioner to sound the local 'Raiders Passed' when bombs have been dropped with no warning preceding. Exaggerated rumours of casualties are quickly spread. Complaints against the proposed resumption of racing continue to be made. In intellectual circles there is a belief that a clear post-war policy would incline America and Russia more to our war effort.

EASTERN (Cambridge) Warnings are being taken calmly and there is evidence that private shelters are being used rather than public shelters. Some confusion exists over transport arrangements, as in some areas buses do not run during the alarm. Many sleep regularly in shelters. In view of raid warnings just before the end of school hours, some schools are reported to advocate a daily session from 9 to 1 p.m.

SOUTHERN (Reading) Stories of attacks on Birmingham, Coventry and Portsmouth cause some nervousness as do the repercussions of the sporadic bombings to which the Region has been subjected. Reports from Newbury state that labourers employed on bombed aerodromes begin to show nervousness and in Oxford a number of workpeople have left their jobs in a locality which has been bombed. Generally speaking, morale appears to be best in those places which have been heavily bombed.

WALES (Cardiff) It is becoming known that a large number of bombs dropped at night fall in open spaces wide of any objective, and at the same time the official bulletins of our night raids on Germany are believed. The broadcast by the Minister of Pensions on compensation was much appreciated. There is a recurrence of complaints of the lack of Welsh programmes. Agreement is being reached by mutual arrangement in the mining industry on the question of lost time due to raids. Many civilians are confident of their ability to distinguish the German from the British engine beat. The attacks on Italy and Libya cause great satisfaction.

NORTH-WESTERN (Manchester) A private lookout system is growing as a result of the warning problem. The fact that bombers found targets on a dark night with low clouds, and that there appears no way of counteracting prolonged raids by single machines, is much commented on. There is a demand for more localisation of warnings.

SOUTH-EASTERN (Tunbridge Wells) Air raids in this Region are now frequently followed by the rumour that gas has been used; this may be due to respirator drills by Civil Defence personnel. Shopkeepers report that daylight raids at lunch-time or after have caused women to shop earlier in the morning. Anxiety is still being caused through lack of news of men reported missing after Dunkirk. There is grumbling over the time taken for special army allowances for high rent and medical fees to come through.

FRIDAY 30 AUGUST 1940

In London particularly people are more cheerful today.

Many people anticipating night raids went to shelters early and slept there all night. In Stepney, for example, there were queues outside shelters at 6 p.m. 'We might as well prepare for the worst'.

Although there is no noticeable decline in morale, collected verbatims show many remarks like these: 'Well it can't go on like this for years', 'Some one ought to show common-sense and stop it', 'No one can contemplate six months of this', 'This sort of thing is lunacy'.

Our reports clearly indicate that morale is higher in the provinces (particularly where warnings and raids have been experienced for some time) than in London (where in some districts people have shown considerable apprehension during the last few days).

In the provinces there are a number of exaggerated rumours about the raids over London. There is also some slight resentment at the way in which London air-raid news has been starred. This is due in part to the fact that many provincial towns, unlike London, have not been named.

There is a general increase in rumours and exaggerated statements about air-raid damage. Rumours about gas attacks are common: some of them can be traced to the false alarms about gas given recently.

The prominence given by the press to the behaviour of the King and Queen and the Prime Minister during air raids (not taking shelter) has caused many people to enquire what is the official policy.

Points from Regions

NORTHERN (Newcastle) The recent intensification of raids has made no change in morale. The problem of loss of sleep is becoming increasingly acute, and in many quarters a definite lead for the public on how to adjust habits to recover sleep is urged. Owing to the comparative silence of AA guns lately there is a rumour that AA guns have been diverted to the South in view of the supposed greater need there.

NORTH-MIDLAND (Nottingham) There is an increase of feeling that we are not hearing the whole truth about damage to industrial plant, and there are rumours both of damage and of heavy casualties. The offensive action against Italy has caused satisfaction. There are less people carrying gas masks than three months ago in Grimsby. There is also a protest from Grimsby that the BBC unduly magnifies the raids on London when other parts of the country have also suffered badly. Reported from Lincoln that many farm-workers listen to Haw-Haw, although chiefly for amusement.

SOUTH-WESTERN (Bristol) Air attacks on this country and on Germany monopolise public conversation. People are standing up well to continuous bombing. Sirens are again the subject of complaint in Glastonbury and Trowbridge, and in the former town, where no bombs have yet fallen, people run into the streets when the sirens sound to see what is happening. Lack of shelters is reported from Tiverton. 400 people have left the Scilly Isles this morning due to air attacks, and the population feels that the defences of the Islands have been neglected. There is a rumour in Bristol that gas mask parades are being held in Berlin, and it is reasoned that the Nazis are preparing to make gas attacks.

SCOTLAND (Edinburgh) The absence of specific news of damage in the South is causing the public to exaggerate the amount considered to have been done. Annoyance is expressed that Berlin is not being bombed as is London. The public is surprised to learn that we have guns on the South Coast capable of bombarding France which have not been used for fear of upsetting the French. The publicity given to a committee to explore the use of Glasgow as a port more fully is considered a direct invitation to the Germans to pay more attention to Glasgow. There is resentment that the railway companies should be considering an increase of fares. There is criticism against the announcement of the resumption of horse racing; it is felt that the feeding stock for horses should be used for poultry which is being killed off.

NORTHERN IRELAND (Belfast) Curiosity aroused by hints in press of preparations of counter strokes against Germany. Little comment on German apology to Eire for bombing the *Kerry Head*. Interference with Home Service programme reported during 8 a.m. and 9 p.m. news.

MIDLAND (Birmingham) The bombing of Berlin has caused great satisfaction. Following recent raids on Birmingham there is considerable discussion as to the adequacy of the city's defences, and it is felt that the interception by fighter aircraft must be possible at some point along the raiders' route. There has been an increase in the amount of rumour following the recent raids, suggesting in Coventry that Birmingham has been heavily damaged and vice versa, and quite untrue.

LONDON

People reported to be prepared for anything provided Germany is raided too. Some questioning of absence of gunfire and fighting when raiders approach, especially after reports that RAF bombers faced 250 miles of severe AA barrage on way to Berlin. London glad not to be disturbed by warnings even though planes heard. Beckenham upset by bombs with casualties and no sirens. Jewish mothers in East End keep calm though highly strung; still attending needlework and cookery classes. Comment that fewer German planes brought down lately. East Ham: 'complaints of unhygienic conditions of salvage put out long before collection. Keepers complaining of experiencing difficulty in clearing parks of children especially as unable to blow whistles. Shift workers disturbed during day by noisy children playing in streets'. Angel: 'part of shelter divided off for sleeping, but unfortunately sleepers disturbed by conscientious marshal asking periodically if everyone is all right.' In many districts complaints that men stand about outside shelters or on balconies smoking during raids; when activity comes close they dive into shelters startling occupants who are unaware of nearness of danger. Some quarrelling reported among tired women in housing estate shelters. Old people living in top floor flats of estates get flustered and take long time to reach shelters. Chelsea: 'occupants of shelters disturbed by colourful running commentary on raid by wardens'. Complaints that lights of torches and car lamps often too bright during raids.

SATURDAY 31 AUGUST 1940

Points from Regions

Air raids in the Regions continue to be borne patiently and without panic. Some Regions report that each morning the public are agreeably surprised to find that so little damage has been done. The effects of lack of sleep are beginning to make themselves shown in many parts. There is resentment at the 'excessive' publicity given to raids on London by the national press and jealousy is reported from Southampton, Portsmouth and other places. Requests for a uniform policy for omnibuses in air raids have been received. People on cross country journeys complain that they are made to get out of their buses in outlying parts and are anxious about what will happen in the winter.

The Regional Information Officer at Reading points out that the evidence of strain as a result of raids appears to be a matter of personal temperament rather than locality. He suggests six lines of argument which may be used to counteract these effects:

1. The patriotic: 'We must be British and stick it; men in the Forces have to put up with worse than this'.

2. The statistical: comparison with road casualties, the area of England and so on.

3. The retaliatory: 'worse things are happening to Germany'.

4. The fatalistic: 'If a bomb's got my name on it, it will get me.'

5. The shame argument: 'We should be ashamed of ourselves for behaving like this.'

6. The stubbornness attitude: 'If the Germans think this is going to [get] us down, they will be disappointed.'

He goes on to say that semi-facetious comment, such as tales of old ladies of eighty-three who say they would not miss it for worlds, is not appreciated.

Fear of invasion appears to be on the wane and reports from Cardiff and Leeds stress this.

NORTH-EASTERN (Leeds) A feeling of stalemate in the war is reported to be noticeable. Hull, which has had long raids on six successive nights, reports that people are 'as cheerful and optimistic as ever' though evidence of lack of sleep is marked. Morale of 300 homeless people in Sheffield stated to be remarkably high. Serious concern expressed about education in raided areas; in Bridlington schools are reported to have closed because of sparse attendance of children after sleepless nights. Announcement of new siren policy eagerly awaited.

EASTERN (Cambridge) Almost entire Region is now getting plenty of ARP practice. Main reaction is grumbling at interruption of work. Press in Region reported to be refusing advertisements of the 'lonely soldier' type. Decision of French Colonies in Africa to join de Gaulle considered by many as good for prestige.

SOUTHERN (Reading) Fears expressed that many pictures of air-raid damage in press may produce a distorted impression not only at home but abroad. Criticism of our propaganda abroad persists, and suggestions in American press that we are 'only hanging on by the skin of our teeth' are taken to mean that our propaganda there is ineffective. Educated people are anxious also about our propaganda in the Near East and Far East, as they feel that the attitude of Greece, Turkey and Japan depends very much on what we can put across in the direction of making them believe in our ultimate victory.

WALES (Cardiff) Bombing of military objectives in Berlin widely approved, and many suggest that a little inaccurate bombing would not be out of place there. Much annoyance caused because London figures largely in the air-raid news while names of provincial towns are still strictly censored. Requests received that individual accounts of pilots' exploits should be placed at end of news, instead of middle. Farmers actually satisfied with quality and quantity of this year's harvest. Continued hopes expressed that we will soon be more aggressive both in Italy and Africa.

NORTH-WESTERN (Manchester) Users of Anderson shelters are reported to be most serious victims of lack of sleep. Satisfaction expressed at attitude of French African Colonies. Requests received that more should be done to 'get across' de Gaulle's personality to the public. Some quarters expect Cabinet changes during the recess, and hope that the PM will drop 'passengers' from both sides of the House.

SOUTH-EASTERN (Tunbridge Wells) Disregard of black-out regulations by both civilians and military are reported. Criticisms of public shelters cover the following points: litter and filth not cleared away; smoking general in some shelters; scaremongering by wardens; and lack of supervision inside shelters.

LONDON

Lack of sleep beginning to tell on people in all districts, showing itself in paleness and lassitude of children and irritability of grown-ups. This is particularly true of poorer quarters where crowded conditions prevail and public shelters are packed and noisy at night. Unhygienic and insanitary conditions reported in large buildings used as shelters in Bethnal Green, City etc. where hundreds of people of mixed ages and sexes congregate with bedding and remain all night. Shelters not designed for mass sleeping, and responsible people fear serious consequences of impaired health and possible epidemics. School on housing estate in South East London has few attendances because of broken nights and head teacher states that children who come are heavy eyed and white. On some estates, shelter marshals run public shelters and organise community singing and games of darts in public spirited manner successfully murdering sleep.

MONDAY 2 SEPTEMBER TO SATURDAY 7 SEPTEMBER 1940

The first week of September brought some good news. On 2 September the Children's Overseas Reception Board revealed that all 320 children were safely back in Britain after the ship on which they had been crossing the Atlantic to Canada had been torpedoed. The ship had not sunk and the children had been rescued by a nearby destroyer. 'There is profound relief that the children from the torpedoed evacuee ship are safe,' reported the Scottish regional office. Seventy-six of the children were from Scotland and 'it appears to be taken for granted that most of the children . . . will carry on with their plans as a matter of course.'

On 3 September, the first anniversary of Britain's declaration of war, the British and American governments announced the destroyers-for-bases agreement whereby the United States transferred fifty ageing destroyers to the Royal Navy in return for a 99-year lease of British bases in the Caribbean and the North Atlantic. 'In some quarters,' Home Intelligence noted, 'this has led to a certain amount of optimistic thinking that this may be a sign of the USA's imminent intervention on our side.'

Meanwhile the Luftwaffe continued to range far and wide, attacking airfields and fighter stations by day, and ports and industrial areas by day and night. As yet the loss of life and the damage inflicted were comparatively light. Churchill told the House of Commons on 5 September that 800 houses had been destroyed or damaged beyond repair by air raids in August. As the night raids intensified, however, the main problem for people in the areas affected was how to obtain a good night's sleep. Some, as Home Intelligence reported, slept on the ground floor of their homes. Others turned their Anderson shelter into a temporary bedroom which, it was claimed, could sleep four people comfortably, but not six: one Anderson shelter in Lewisham was said to hold eleven people sleeping in two tiers.

In London, it was recorded on 2 September, there were queues of people with bedding forming outside the public shelters by 9 p.m. Four days later Home Intelligence noted that sanitary arrangements were in many cases inadequate and the atmosphere foul. 'In several districts cases of blatant immorality in shelters are reported; this upsets other occupants of shelters and will deter them from using the shelters again.' The habit of improvising makeshift shelters was also growing: 'In crowded districts such as Stepney, Bethnal Green, Southwark, Paddington, St Pancras etc. people using large tunnels, subways or cellars where conditions from hygienic point of view are far from desirable. Companionship cheers these people and they state they prefer discomfort and overcrowding together and a feeling of safety to staying at home in bed.'

In the raided areas, Home Intelligence noted, morale remained high and 'it may be some indication of the improved condition of morale that drunkenness has decreased considerably during the past week.' Ironically the report for 7 September noted resentment in the Regions at the excessive publicity given to raids on London, a consequence of the fact that Air Ministry communiques rarely gave the names of provincial towns when they were bombed. The report must have been completed a few hours, or even perhaps a few minutes, before the opening of the blitz on London.

MONDAY 2 SEPTEMBER 1940

Points from Regions

Despite the activities of German raiders, all reports confirm the steadiness and fortitude of the population.

NORTHERN (Newcastle) Although loss of sleep is causing fatigue, many are adjusting their hours of rest by going to bed earlier, and are transferring bedrooms to the ground floor. The policy of stopping buses during raids is causing criticism amongst workers who have to walk home after a heavy day's work. Rumours of alleged damage and casualties after air raids are increasing in Stockton-on-Tees.

NORTH-MIDLAND (Nottingham) Bombs have fallen in many parts of the Region, but those chiefly affected have shown great courage and cheerfulness. Complaint of inadequate defence comes from the Beeston and Chilwell area, where casualties and much damage occurred; fighter planes did not appear and it is alleged that all available guns were not in action. There is divided opinion in the Region on the siren policy; in Northampton it is believed that without a warning Civil Defence services may not be mobilised; there is lack of confidence in Chesterfield due to bombs falling after 'Raiders Passed'. In the latter town there is a tendency to stampede in the streets when the warning is heard, and reluctance to obey wardens. The 'slight damage' formula of official communiques is regarded in many quarters as an understatement, and it is suggested that casualty totals should be published each fortnight.

SOUTH-WESTERN (Bristol) Reports from Bristol, Exeter, Weston-super-Mare and Salisbury, all of which have been bombed recently, show that morale has not been affected. In the Saturday raid on Salisbury many refused to take cover, and the fire services were hampered by people flocking to see where incendiary bombs dropped. Complaints from Barnstaple that contex filters have not been fitted to gas masks, following the arrival of evacuee children with respirators complete. Londoners living in Bath consider that too much is made of damage to London. It is also commented that victims of damage receive no compensation for consequential expenses 'which hits the middle classes, with fixed incomes and obligations, very hard.'

SCOTLAND (Edinburgh) There is profound relief that the children from the torpedoed evacuee ship are safe. Seventy-six Scottish children from towns other than Glasgow and Edinburgh are among the evacuees, and the chief escort officer reports that practically all the children will want to go back to Canada. Some alarm has been created on recent occasions by gunfire practice, and it has been suggested that the public might receive previous notice in some way. Exaggeration of casualties and damage done by raiders in England is still widespread, and the story is circulating in Edinburgh that 300 were killed in the Croydon raids; there have been comparatively few raids in Scotland and people tend to compensate their comparative isolation by exaggerating stories received in letters from the South.

NORTHERN IRELAND (Belfast) Bitter resentment is felt at the sinking of the evacuee ship bound for Canada. There is speculation about the possibility of a curfew for the winter months in Northern Ireland. The concession to the linen trade contained in the new flax order is welcome here. Criticism is expressed by the farming communities about the new prices for cattle and pigs, and it is expected that the Ulster Farmers' Union will make a strong protest to the Ministry of Food.

MIDLAND (Birmingham) Midland industrialists are concerned about the effect on production of the constant night raids, and some consider there should be more active interception of enemy planes proceeding to the area. Altered factory hours are helping to meet the situation and many workers are insisting that they shall be allowed to carry on during raids, their chief concern being that their wives and families shall get due warning. There are demands for increased tea ration in many industrial towns.

LONDON

From many districts it is reported that people start queueing with bedding outside public shelters about 9 p.m. One West Ham shelter with particularly good amenities is said to have attracted people from distance – even owners of Anderson shelters. West Ham observer reports: 'Some mothers with young children do not undress and fear to sleep in case they miss siren; people who have experienced bombs falling in same road help to cheer others and seem less nervous than residents at some distance from damaged area.' Reported mistrust of public street shelters among several Tooting residents owing to rumour of occupants being trapped in a Brixton shelter. South East London observer reports: 'Many people go to shelters now at first sound of gunfire and planes even if siren not yet sounded; wardens and shelter marshals very helpful and friendly; it is found that four can sleep comfortably in Anderson shelter, whilst six cannot arrange themselves for sleeping.' Woolwich observer reports that many people feel no warning necessary when only solitary raider is near. Observer in Stepney reports splendid courage and calmness during bombing on Saturday night and ARP services 'magnificent'; some disgust that sirens were not sounded in time. Observer reports annoyance of passengers held up by night raids at inability of transport workers to say which routes available after raid damage. East Ham resident reports nervousness after Friday night's raid and less confidence in Anderson shelters owing to fatal casualties in shelters nearby; often unable to hear raiders approaching owing to sound of steam trains.

TUESDAY 3 SEPTEMBER 1940

People today are more cheerful than any day since air-raid warnings became so frequent. This appears to be due to adjustments about sleeping arrangements, and many people slept soundly through last night's raid in the London area. Sleeping downstairs and in shelters is becoming a routine in many parts of the country. In a few localities, the siren question is once more much discussed, but the controversy is no longer general. There are still reports of complaints in certain towns, which have been vigorously bombed, that there is no evidence of searchlight, AA, or fighter activity. In such places the feeling of resentment against the enemy is mixed with a feeling of dissatisfaction against our own defences. Generally speaking, however, there is the strongest satisfaction with the work of the RAF and AA defence, and for the first time reports indicate that really strong feelings directed against the raiders are appearing.

The satisfaction which follows all news of our air attacks on Germany is coupled with the hope, and even the anticipation, that aggressive military action may soon be undertaken by our forces in the Near East.

All reports indicate that there is great confidence in our Civil Defence services, though there are still grumbles at the lack of Anderson and other shelters in areas originally thought to be safe but now found to be vulnerable.

Rumours of exaggerated air-raid damage are still circulating and these appear to be mainly due to letter writers who wish to impress their friends.

Thanks to the drought, the beginnings of a milk shortage are reported from the Southern Region, and this may become serious.

Points from Regions

NORTH-EASTERN (Leeds) The biggest raid to date in the West Riding has left morale high, and Civil Defence personnel are more confident after successfully facing their first trial. The small number killed has increased confidence in shelters, but there is much dissatisfaction on the subject of sirens and AA defence; in Bradford people ask 'Why have we no Spitfires?' There is a new and widespread rumour that fires have preceded raids, thus guiding the enemy to their targets.

EASTERN (Cambridge) Some anxiety is caused by the way in which air battle losses are reported, and many go to bed believing our losses to be higher in proportion to those of the enemy than finally transpires. Satisfaction is expressed that where raiding has been heaviest, voluntary services have worked smoothly and efficiently. In Luton, after a severe first raid, bombs fell before the warning, which has caused criticism of Local Authorities, although morale remains high.

SOUTHERN (Reading) Enthusiasm for the numerous Spitfire funds shows the temper of the people, in spite of the rise in cost of living, shortages of various commodities, and the ever present threat of air attacks. Milk is a new problem, and some dairymen have had to restrict supplies as the drought has brought down yields of the herds; stocks of winter foodstuffs are now being used and this will aggravate milk shortage later.

WALES (Cardiff) People in the Swansea district are depressed by damage and casualties of recent raids, but although their defences and the siren system are the subject of criticism, morale is high. The sinking of the liner taking evacuee children abroad has caused indignation, and increased the uncertainty in the minds of parents as to the advisability of sending children abroad. Complaints are received from North Wales that broadcast reception has lately been very bad after 9 p.m. Exaggerated rumours of air-raid deaths in Swansea were prevalent in both Cardiff and Newport.

NORTH-WESTERN (Manchester) After a quiet Sunday and Monday night those in industrial areas are refreshed and cheerful. Many now sleep downstairs or in shelters, and few people are to be seen in the streets after 9 p.m. Renewed interest in evacuation in the poorer districts of Liverpool. Daily figures of Nazi planes destroyed watched with interest and accepted. Evidence of discontent over Means Test in relation to Old Age Pensions supplementary allowance.

SOUTH-EASTERN (Tunbridge Wells) The fixed curfew hour has caused general satisfaction in the areas concerned, as have the new boundaries which are marked by main roads. It is felt that the siren is sounded for too long at night, particularly the piercing note 'Raiders Passed', which seems to awaken everyone. Complaints from the Crowborough district that those who have gone there from bombed seaside towns are being charged exorbitantly for board and lodging.

WEDNESDAY 4 SEPTEMBER 1940

The public is still in a comparatively cheerful state of mind. The continued successes of the RAF both at home and abroad account largely for this feeling, but it has been much helped by the announcement about the acquisition of American destroyers. In some quarters this has led to a certain amount of optimistic thinking that this may be a sign of the USA's imminent inter-vention on our side.

There are further signs that the feeling of bitterness against the enemy is becoming more directly associated with Nazi airmen, though this is not always apparent, as might have been expected, in areas which have suffered the worst raid damage.

The public particularly in London continues to adjust its sleeping habits satisfactorily to the altered conditions brought about by continuous raiding. Although in those areas which have been most heavily bombed, there is natu-rally a certain amount of nervousness particularly on the part of women with children. The resistance of the public is on the whole extraordinarily good. It may be some indication of the improved condition of morale that drunkenness has decreased considerably during the past week.

There is some criticism, mostly from people of moderate means, of the Government's plans for compensation for damage to property and businesses.

Mr Eden's speech, although received with mild approval, does not seem to have aroused much interest anywhere.

Points from Regions

NORTHERN (Newcastle) Evidence that regular raids are creating some bitterness against the enemy. The problem of help for people of moderate means whose houses and furniture have been damaged by air raids is coming to the front, and Government schemes are thought to be inadequate. The raids on Berlin are welcomed. Fuller accounts of damage done by our raids on Germany are requested. Complaints are received of the hours of duty of Civil Defence workers, who, after a twelve hours spell, are called back to long waiting during warnings. Adverse comment is heard of the promi-nence given to raids on London.

NORTH-MIDLAND (Nottingham) In occasionally raided areas it is noticed that elderly people are calmer than their families. In raided villages the inhabitants are showing fortitude and common-sense. In places where factory owners are not obliged to provide shelters, streets are filled with workers after warnings are sounded. Complaint from Chesterfield that clean salvage is not being kept separate from garbage. Miners ready to go on night shifts who notice pit-head lights are extinguished, as is the practice during purple warnings, are returning home.

SOUTH-WESTERN (Bristol) In spite of great night activity recently there are no signs of defeatism. The transfer of American destroyers ranks with air raids as the chief topic of conversation, and it is felt that America cannot withdraw if we need future help. As a result of last night's raid in Weston-super-Mare, people showed more inclination to take cover during this morning's warning. The visit by the Regional Commissioner to the Scilly Isles has had a beneficial effect in Cornwall. Exaggerated stories of air-raid damage are still widespread.

MIDLAND (Birmingham) The continuance of heavy raids has induced the more timorous to go to country districts adjoining the towns during the danger hours at night. The transfer of destroyers has caused much satisfaction. Many people in Coventry have made application for shelters and demand greatly exceeds supply. Many public shelters in the Midlands are being misused by people who take in to them cumbersome articles such as perambulators, thereby reducing accommodation for other people.

SCOTLAND (Edinburgh) There is great satisfaction everywhere on account of the addition to our naval strength from America, and much optimistic talk on the probable date of America's entry into the war. It appears to be taken for granted that most of the children in the torpedoed ship will carry on with their plans as a matter of course. Commercial travellers and others returning from bombed areas are saying how calm and unruffled the people are. Eden's reference to the continued possibility of German invasion has had a salutory effect. Rapid developments are taking place in Edinburgh to provide hospitality for members of the armed forces.

NORTHERN IRELAND (Belfast) Enthusiastic welcome for the Anglo-American agreement. Ulster farmers are to join with British and Scottish Unions in an appeal against new price levels for agricultural produce. Criticism of incorrect broadcast on Tuesday to the effect that a bomb had exploded in a crowded shelter in Belfast. Disappointment that the scheme for acceptance and transport of books and magazines for members of the services without postage does not apply to Northern Ireland.

LONDON

West End cinemas attended normally during day but tendency marked for people to go home before 9 o'clock as expect night warning to take place about that time. In bombed districts cinemas' attendances have fallen. Greenwich contact reports morale greatly improved since exciting air battle plainly visible last Saturday. Before this, people nervous and on edge since dropping of HE bombs nearby, but since air battle tension has gone and they are quiet and calm. In most districts chief problem is sleep and shelters at night. In crowded districts such as Stepney, Bethnal Green, Southwark, Paddington, St Pancras etc. people using large tunnels, subways or cellars where conditions from hygienic point of view are far from desirable. Companionship cheers these people and they state they prefer discomfort and overcrowding together and a feeling of safety to staying at home in bed. In districts where Anderson shelters are common, such as Lewisham, people adapting them for sleeping but damp, lack of air and overcrowding make them unsuitable. One Anderson shelter in district is reported to hold eleven people sleeping in two tiers. Hampstead reports people now sleeping under stairs but those with children tend instead to use public shelters. High praise in this district for Civil Defence services. Reports from East Ham vary on local morale. One contact states people extremely nervous; other reports state that though district has had bad time people are 'behaving splendidly and act in orderly fashion.' Officials in district trying to persuade people to get good nights' sleep by staying at home on ground floor instead of going out to uncomfortable shelters. West Ham reports misgivings among some householders re-housed after homes have been demolished in houses with higher rents than they are used to or able to pay. Grumbling among workers at railway terminus in London suburb when caught by raids and unable to make tea as gas mains are turned off.

THURSDAY 5 SEPTEMBER 1940

In the face of continued bombing morale remains high.

Guidance on sleeping arrangements in shelters is urgently needed, especially in the East End of London, where bombing damage makes the population only too ready to use their shelters to the full (this does not, however, apply to factory workers on duty, the majority of whom like to carry on until danger is near). The noise of bombs and the AA barrage makes sleep in shelters an extremely difficult matter, apart altogether from the problem of crowding people together in a small space.

Hitler's speech is generally regarded as 'encouraging'. The public read into it that the work of the RAF and the blockade are taking effect.

Demands for, and satisfaction at, reprisals continue.

There are reports of dissatisfaction at the present education situation, and the requisitioning of schools for non-scholastic purposes is criticised.

While various small intellectual groups are still asking for a definition of war aims, there is evidence that the great bulk of the population are satisfied with the present situation and are prepared to leave this matter until victory is in sight or attained.

A Haw-Haw rumour alleging that he threatened damage to a certain street is reported from Leeds, the first for a considerable time.

Points from Regions

NORTH-EASTERN (Leeds) Confidence remains high. Many people are now asking 'Is it possible to defeat the lone raider?' There is some feeling that the flashes from trolley trams during air raids act as a guide to enemy aircraft. Rumours are current in Sheffield of high casualties in London and heavy damage in Manchester due to recent raids.

EASTERN (Cambridge) Hitler's recent sneers and threats are regarded as evidence that he is feeling the effect of our blockade and raids by the RAF. The transfer of American destroyers is still the chief topic of conversation. The rising number of Spitfire funds in the Region indicates the admiration and gratitude that is felt for the RAF, although doubt is sometimes expressed as to whether the voluntary subscriptions should not be devoted to benevolent funds.

SOUTHERN (Reading) Hitler's speech and press comments on it have encouraged people generally. Determination is as strong as ever, but in those places heavily bombed there is some sign of strain, a symptom of which is the dissatisfaction with the present system of warnings. It is felt in Aldershot that in any case 'Raiders Passed' should be given, even if the raiders are not announced. From Poole and Basingstoke come complaints of lack of sleep. There is also anxiety as to winter raid conditions, although there is a continuance of the demand for more shelters. In some places our news of air raids is beginning to be questioned, and there is an increase of rumour due to the absence of specific information about raids; this may be on account of comparisons between official communiques, and stories of damage and casualties which spread across the country.

WALES (Cardiff) Some discontent is in evidence because the number of civilian casualties resulting from raids is withheld. The transfer of American destroyers has caused much satisfaction. There is a growing tendency to evacuate school-children situated near dock districts subjected to bombing.

NORTH-WESTERN (Manchester) The main reaction to Hitler's speech is encouragement that he is feeling the blockade, and the hope that if any 'cities are to be razed' we shall do likewise.

FRIDAY 6 SEPTEMBER 1940

The public continue to take the bombing in good heart. In London last night's alarm was talked of jokingly for the most part, and fewer people complain of tiredness today; more are sleeping through the night alarms.

There is general satisfaction at the Prime Minister's announcement that something is to be done about the sirens, and the details are awaited eagerly.

An increasingly fatalistic attitude towards the effect of bombing is reported, and this appears to be coupled with a high state of morale. In the East End the searchlights rather than the sirens are now taken as a sign for going to the shelters. Cooperation and friendliness in public shelters are reported to be increasing, but there are many complaints about 'insanitary messes' in shelters, and improper behaviour of various varieties is causing distress among the more respectable elements of the community.

During the six days August 23–28 the Wartime Social Survey investigated the popularity of our different broadcast speakers. In 551 interviews, the number of times the names of specific speakers were mentioned was as follows:*

Churchill 166, Eden 76, Duff Cooper 62,
John Hilton 42, Onlooker 21, Swinton 18,
Morrison 17, Joubert 14, Bevin 14, Sinclair 14,
King Hall 12, Mais 11, Beaverbrook 10.
Some 46 other names were mentioned.

In response to a specific question on Duff Cooper's talks 58% approved of them (of whom 28% expressed enthusiastic approval), 19% disapproved, 16% did not hear them, and 7% held no opinion. A similar question about J. B. Priestley's talks showed 52% approving, 2% disapproving, 43% not hearing them, and 3% expressing no opinion.

---

* Editors' note: see subsequent *Corrigendum* in report for 7 September.

Points from Regions

NORTHERN (Newcastle) The Prime Minister's speech has been warmly welcomed, and in particular his reference to the revision of the siren policy. Complaints have been received of the showing of lights by the military when billeted in empty houses etc. AA ammunition which is thought to be a new and improved type is much discussed and welcomed. Protests have been received against the action of the Northumberland Education Committee in insisting on the normal hours of school after warnings the previous night, in view of the loss of sleep which is said to be seriously affecting children.

NORTH-MIDLAND (Nottingham) Residents in bombed areas of Nottinghamshire are said to be 'not unduly afraid'. Many people are asking for a quicker and more complete news service of RAF activity. There is still dissatisfaction with such statements as 'casualties small' and 'little material damage', and more people are said to listen to German broadcasts to discover the names of places which have been bombed. The opinion is expressed in Rutland that we should retaliate for German indiscriminate bombing. In Grimsby it is felt that too much emphasis is placed on the age of the American destroyers, and too little on the uses to which they can be put. There are a number of instances of people who have not had news of relatives serving in the Near East since May, and some anxiety is being caused.

SOUTH-WESTERN (Bristol) Air raids are the chief topic of conversation. The Prime Minister's reference to the siren question was welcomed. It is reported from Plymouth that morale is 'wonderfully good' and that womenfolk are getting hardened to raids and warnings. During the first warning at Taunton people acted calmly and went to cover without delay.

SCOTLAND (Edinburgh) In Glasgow it is reported that Hitler's speech aroused a high degree of optimism, as it was felt that 'he must be badly rattled to talk like that'. The Premier's speech was warmly approved. Travellers returning from the Orkneys report that there is popular discontent over the high rates of pay for labourers on Government work; this criticism is freely expressed by both rural workers and soldiers. There are complaints in Stirlingshire among the troops that as all halls and empty shops have been taken over by military authorities, they have nowhere to go, and local inhabitants are doing very little for them.

NORTHERN IRELAND (Belfast) The Premier's forecast of a more determined onslaught on Britain is expected to materialise, but there is less talk now of the invasion of Britain through Eire. In view of recent outrages attributed to IRA the Northern Ireland Ministry of Public Security is considering what remedial action can be taken.

MIDLAND (Birmingham) There is perturbation about the behaviour of a section of the public when night warnings have been sounded; many people are taking a lot of paraphernalia into the shelters, and there are complaints of people settling down for the night, and of flashing of torches. There are requests for air-raid news on a county basis in order that people may be kept more fully informed.

LONDON

The Prime Minister's speech was welcomed. The siren policy is still a controversial subject; most Londoners seem to approve the idea of a preliminary 'stand-by' siren with a further warning to indicate immediate danger. However there is a small school of thought who wish for no sirens. The problem of night sleeping in shelters is the greatest concern of observers, particularly in the poor and crowded districts. Sanitary arrangements in many cases are inadequate: the atmosphere becomes very foul: there are increasing numbers of cases of colds and septic throats especially among children and it is feared that there may be epidemics. In several districts cases of blatant immorality in shelters are reported; this upsets other occupants of shelters and will deter them from using the shelters again. Much distress is reported among school teachers at the fall in school attendances as they feel that their work of years is being completely undone. Woolwich observer notes great excitement and satisfaction at hearing guns in action during day battle and disappointment that they did not fire during the night; also people who have lost everything are cheerful and willing to put up with any discomfort provided Germany is getting her share of raids. Observer in Mayfair has heard many complaints that luxury hotels and wealthy houses do not seem to be strictly dealt with when lights show during blackout. Observers feel that more organisation needed, following 'Raiders Passed' signal, to form crowds into queues at stations and bus stops that have not been in operation during the raid period; suggestion that motorists might relieve situation by giving lifts. Silvertown observer remarked on wonderful spirit of people rendered homeless by raids; fears ill effects from continued sleeplessness due to noise of guns and bombs in docks area.

SATURDAY 7 SEPTEMBER 1940

Morale is unchanged.

Reactions to the Prime Minister's last speech can now be summarised. On the whole it aroused less interest than his previous speeches, though it was well-liked. The parts which created the greatest interest were his references to sirens and to the number of houses demolished. The casualty figures have caused little comment. The siren question is still much discussed as reports from Leeds, Manchester and Wales indicate today. There is surprise that only 800 houses have been totally demolished, as many people thought that 1,000 houses were destroyed at Ramsgate alone. There appears to be confusion between damage and destruction.

There is evidence to show that night raids cause far more upset to people than daylight raids.

There are still requests for clearer instructions to bus drivers in rural areas about what they are to do in air-raid warnings.

Regional complaints that London receives excessive publicity for its raids, both in the press and on the wireless, while important provincial towns have to hide their identity even from themselves, are still reported.

Local Information Committees and others associated with the work of the Ministry of Information contrast the lack of publicity given to the positive aspects of the Ministry's work with that given to the work of the Ministries of Food, Home Security etc.

Corrigendum: *yesterday's daily report on morale should contain the word 'favourably' after the word 'mentioned' in line 4 of paragraph 4, page 1.*

Points from Regions

NORTH-EASTERN (Leeds) Morale and confidence are unchanged throughout the Region, although there is some anxiety about the effects on health of the serious loss of sleep which has lately been suffered. Siren policy continues to be 'a very general topic of conversation'.

EASTERN (Cambridge) Morale is high, and owing to the fact that the Region is now fully accustomed to air-raid warnings, and because raids themselves have lately been less frequent, there is less feeling of anxiety. There are some complaints about the amount of working time which is lost through warnings. Traffic conditions, east and west across Norfolk, are reported as being very difficult when raids have occurred in that area; this refers particularly to bus services.

SOUTHERN (Reading) Although 'nerves are somewhat frayed by the constant movement of enemy planes', the public continues to be in a fairly cheerful frame of mind. There is some divergence of opinion about the attitude which the public should take towards the sounding of sirens. Whereas the Southampton LIC 'stresses the necessity for people not to jump up and seek shelter directly the sirens go', Totton Sub-Committee 'thinks that people should be educated to pay more attention to warnings'.

WALES (Cardiff) There is no change in the feelings of the public, upon whom the war of nerves 'is having little effect.' There has been 'a wonderful reaction' to the Prime Minister's speech.

NORTH-WESTERN (Manchester) There is evidence that the public in this Region is concerned rather more than it is elsewhere about air raids. 'Morale is seriously threatened on Merseyside', where employers are anxious because night work is seriously hampered through warnings and by the fact that workers engaged on it are tired by daytime raids.

SOUTH-EASTERN (Tunbridge Wells) In spite of continuous raids 'morale remains at a high level throughout the Region'. There are some complaints from Eastbourne at the ban on visitors, 'and if the Local Authorities were told why it is not possible to give them facilities which are granted to Brighton, it would help to do away with this grievance'.

MONDAY 9 SEPTEMBER TO SATURDAY 14 SEPTEMBER 1940

On the afternoon of 7 September Londoners were enjoying the glorious sunshine when 350 enemy aircraft appeared overhead and began to drop incendiaries and high explosives on the London docks, which exploded into flame. After a mighty air battle with squadrons of Hurricanes and Spitfires they withdrew, but a second wave arrived over the city after nightfall and, guided by the fires that were still raging, began a series of attacks on the East End that continued into the small hours. Stepney, Whitechapel, Poplar, Shoreditch, West Ham and Bermondsey were all hard hit. That same evening the code-word 'Cromwell' was issued putting Home Forces in the south and east of England on immediate readiness for invasion.

Hitler and Göring had changed tactics and decided that henceforth London should be the Luftwaffe's principal target, though raids on other parts of Britain continued. The raids of 7 September marked the beginning of a sustained assault on the capital that was to run for 76 consecutive nights, excepting only 2 November. The primary aim was to attack targets of economic and military importance rather than civilians, but the spreading of terror was an additional bonus. During the first night of the London blitz 430 people were killed. During the month of September as a whole, 6,600 died, of whom 5,500 were in the London area. Many thousands more had their homes destroyed.

The authorities had long feared an attempt by Germany to launch a knock-out blow against London, but there were two features of the blitz they failed to foresee. Having assumed that most of the victims would be killed, they had made too little provision for the homeless, who were herded into hastily improvised 'rest centres' where conditions were often squalid. And having assumed that air raids would usually take place in daylight, they had failed to design or provide shelters in which people could spend the night. The deficiencies of Civil Defence preparations were cruelly exposed during the first days of the London blitz and the Home Intelligence reports reflect some of the darker aspects of the experience behind the propaganda image of the ever-cheerful, resolute cockney.

'In Dockside areas,' the London report for 9 September noted, 'the population is showing visible signs of nerve cracking from constant ordeals. Old women and mothers are undermining morale of young women and men by their extreme nervousness and lack of resilience.' Already women and children were fleeing the East End, sometimes with very little idea of where they were heading. 'Families in the Deptford area,' Home Intelligence reported on 10 September, 'are making for the hopfields of Kent, taking with them such of their belongings as they can carry, while those further west are making for the main line stations, though without any other apparent object than "to get away from it all."' For three nights running a school in West Ham was full to bursting point with the homeless. On the third night, in spite of repeated warnings to the Whitehall authorities that it was bound to be a target, it was bombed and the occupants killed.

Morale, however, received an enormous boost on the night of 11 September when London's anti-aircraft defences, recently reinforced, blazed away at enemy aircraft amid a crescendo of gunfire. Two days later a dive-bomber attacked Buckingham Palace providing a public relations triumph for George VI and Queen Elizabeth, who were in residence at the time. The civilian population, it was stated, were 'in the front line'. Now the King and Queen were in the front line too.

The Blitz is often said to have generated a warm community spirit, a verdict the Home Intelligence reports confirm – up to a point. The report for 13 September detected 'noticeable friendliness everywhere among all classes and types of people. Everybody is trying to help everybody else – except motorists who are rousing angry bitterness at not offering lifts with empty cars to long queues of tired workers. Even when Home Guard asked motorists to give lifts in Balham to stranded workers they refused. Misuse of public shelters in Wandsworth reported; people push in with bedding and prevent strangers from getting a place.'

Another sign of stress was a revival of the anti-Jewish prejudices which Oswald Mosley and the British Union of Fascists had exploited in the 1930s. 'A certain amount of anti-Semitism in the East End still persists,' Home Intelligence recorded on 11 September, 'but this is not so much on account of a marked difference in conduct between Jews and Cockneys, but because the latter, seeking a scapegoat as an outlet for emotional disturbances, pick on the traditional and nearest one.'

MONDAY 9 SEPTEMBER 1940

In the areas which have been most heavily raided there has been little sign of panic and none of defeatism, but rather of bitterness and increased determination to 'see it through'. There is widespread and deeply felt apprehension, which is apparent mostly in the London Dock area, of a continuation of raids, and much anxiety about the chaos in domestic affairs which has resulted from the activities of the last few nights.

As far as the East End is concerned, this is beginning to show itself in an aimless evacuation to what are believed to be safer places, e.g. the St James's Park shelters and Paddington Station. It appears that this exodus is caused by greater fear than the actual circumstances justify, and it might be a good thing if loud speaker vans, giving encouragement and instructions, could circulate in the streets. There is at present very little official reassurance being given to the public, and it is to some extent this lack of guidance which is causing them to leave their homes. There seems evidence that unless some immediate steps of this sort are taken to check this movement, it is likely to grow.

Men working in factories in the East End are encouraging their wives and families in this haphazard escape, but express their own willingness to stay and face further raids if they can be sure that their relations are in comparative safety.

Owing to the behaviour of the Jews, particularly in the East End where they are said to show too great a keenness to save their own skins and too little consideration for other people, there are signs of anti-Semitic trouble. It is believed locally that this situation may at any moment become extremely serious. This is put forward as an additional reason for a planned dispersal of East End families to be carried out with all speed.

Unsatisfactory reports about shelter conditions continue to be received. Those in the London area and in Birmingham show a state of affairs which from the point of view of health alone is highly undesirable. The practice of carrying bedding, prams, etc. into shelters causes much indignation among people who are thus denied accommodation.

Although it seems to be fairly well understood that for security reasons it is not possible to give many details about the activities of the RAF and

AA units, there is a good deal of comment on what are believed in some places to be inadequate precautions, though the gallantry of both the RAF and the AA crews continues to receive great praise.

There is continued criticism of the BBC's method of announcing casualties and raid details. Special exception was taken to Charles Gardner's broadcast on Saturday, and it is suggested that what is wanted by the public in its present frame of mind is the kind of encouragement which can only be given by a real working-class man who has himself been through the worst of the recent raids.

Points from Regions

NORTHERN (Newcastle) Reports from many centres indicate that enemy news bulletins are receiving progressively less attention. Exaggerated rumours of damage due to raids are still widespread. There is much interest in the speed of our aircraft production, and further facts are eagerly awaited.

NORTH-MIDLAND (Nottingham) The impression of Hitler's speech is that it was 'that of a frustrated criminal'. There is a complaint from Chesterfield that details of the damage to Ramsgate should not have been delayed until the Premier's speech. In Grimsby it is suggested that daily reports of damage and casualties would be less alarming than monthly reports. It is felt in Rutland that householders who have had evacuees since war broke out are now tired of them, and would welcome a shuffle round to other householders. Complaints have been received that the fixed price for plum jam is excessive.

SOUTH-WESTERN (Bristol) Rumours of invasion are rife in the Region today following the ringing of church bells and the calling out of the Home Guard. The raid on London has been appreciated as serious, and it is realised that though casualties were high, they were not more than was to be expected from a severe attack. It is reported from Plymouth that people consider the BBC tends to gloss over damage by enemy aircraft.

MIDLAND (Birmingham) There are reports from Birmingham, Wolverhampton and Black Country towns that householders are going to public shelters and taking their bedding with them. It is 'getting round' that many middle-class people leave Birmingham at night by road and sleep in country districts, and many more are doing this at weekends; this is causing some annoyance among the working class.

NORTHERN IRELAND (Belfast) Some surprise is felt at the extensive casualties and damage in London due to raids, and although bearing in mind the devastation wrought by the RAF in Germany, it is being asked whether the British defences are as effective as has been supposed. It is felt that an invasion of South East England may soon be attempted. There are reports of airmen talking freely about Belfast defences. Householders in provincial areas with whom evacuated children are billeted complain that they have to buy clothes for them, and that the parents do not realise their responsibilities.

LONDON

Strongest feeling one of shock amongst all classes and in all districts as people have lulled themselves into a state of false security saying: 'London is the safest place', and 'they'll never get through the London defences'. No signs of defeatism except among small section of elderly women in 'front line' such as East Ham who cannot stand constant bombing. Districts sustaining only one or two shocks soon rally, but in Dockside areas the population is showing visible signs of nerve cracking from constant ordeals. Old women and mothers are undermining morale of young women and men by their extreme nervousness and lack of resilience. Men state they cannot sleep because they must keep up the morale of their families and express strong desire to get families away from danger areas. Families clinging together, however, and any suggestions of sending children away without mothers and elderly relations considered without enthusiasm. People beginning to trek away from Stepney and other Dockside areas in families and small groups. Many encountered in City today with suitcases or belongings. Some make for Paddington without any idea of their destination. All Dockland people afraid large fires will attract German raiders each night and queue up long before dusk to get places in large underground shelters. Many expressions of bitterness at apparent impossibility of stopping German raiders doing what they like and opinion that Anti-Aircraft gunfire is astonishingly small. This latter point is bewildering and frightening people more than anything else. Lack of sleep already showing signs of undermining morale and working capacity of population. Young black-coated workers in City depressed about news from Africa and express the hope that we can take the offensive there. There is urgent need in Rest Centres for people rendered homeless for toys, etc. for the children, and workers are needed to organise games.

TUESDAY 10 SEPTEMBER 1940

Morale remains unchanged today. Voluntary and unplanned evacuation of East End families continues, and although it is largely confined to women and children, some men are also going. Families in the Deptford area are making for the hopfields in Kent, taking with them such of their belongings as they can carry, while those further west are making for the main line stations, though without any other apparent object than 'to get away from it all'. There is, however, little evidence that these efforts to escape are due to defeatist feelings, but are simply because the people are thoroughly frightened.

Now that they are beginning to feel, and are being referred to, as 'soldiers in the front line', everything should be done to encourage this opinion of themselves. It would undoubtedly help if the public were made to feel that their friends and relations had died for their country, in the same sense as if they were soldiers, sailors or airmen. It might be a small but extremely telling point if, for instance, the dead were buried with Union Jacks on their coffins, or if the Services were represented at their funerals. Attentions of this kind would undoubtedly mean much at the moment.

Among other suggestions that have been made for the alleviation of the difficulties of those in the bombed areas is that field service postcards for civilians should be issued in the areas which have suffered the worst damage, so that the poor can inform their distant relatives of their safety and thus avoid overloading the telegram and telephone services.

The need for mobile canteens in bombed areas is urgent. Certain voluntary societies are already doing their best to provide these facilities, but are quite unable to cope with the immense demands which are made upon them.

The foregoing conclusions naturally reflect the conditions in the London area more than elsewhere, and today's reports from Regions show that their spirits also are steady and confident. Much sympathy is felt with London's sufferings, but confidence is everywhere expressed in the ability of the metropolitan population to stand up to what they are going through.

Points from Regions

NORTH-EASTERN (Leeds) Morale and confidence are unchanged. Keen interest is centred on events in London. Many people feel there should be a curfew in large towns, and a curfew on motoring also has been suggested. There has been a considerable increase in absenteeism at the pits in Rother Valley, and there is much local feeling about the need for better shelters for miners' families, which may explain the increased number of absentees. A report from Ecclesfield states that there is much feeling that communal brick shelters, which are to replace Anderson shelters, do not afford the same protection as steel.

EASTERN (Cambridge) Raids on London are the chief topic of conversation. There is a growing feeling that severe reprisals should be taken on Berlin, although the intensity of this feeling diminishes in proportion to the distance from London.

SOUTHERN (Reading) The view is commonly expressed that the only way to stop the Germans is to bomb Berlin even more extensively than they bomb London. Rumours due to Saturday night's invasion alarm have decreased. The sound of the tocsin brought people out into the streets. People are disconcerted by the late arrival of daily papers, and the revival of the mid-morning BBC news is suggested to meet this need.

WALES (Cardiff) The comparative quietness of the last three days in this Region has left everyone refreshed. The progress of attacks on the Thames Estuary has been watched with anxiety. The continued success of our fighters and the nightly activity of our bombers have raised hopes very high. South Wales coalpits are now mostly working short-time, and there is disappointment that the effort to secure distribution to home markets to fill gaps caused by the loss of continental trade has so far been unsuccessful. Delays in publication, and the nebulous character of our reports on raids on this country, are encouraging increasing numbers to tune in to German stations.

NORTH-WESTERN (Manchester) A peaceful night has strengthened the spirit of those who grumbled at the supposed lack of defences. There is a general feeling that if London can stick it, so can Manchester. There is a query from Salford as to why national leaders do not speak to the public at the present time. There is depression in St Helens through the closing down of a colliery employing more than 1,000 hands.

SOUTH-EASTERN (Tunbridge Wells) Lorry drivers are coming into the Region with harrowing tales of damage and panic in London. Morale is extremely high in the Region, and everyone is full of praise for the RAF. People are still going out into the streets to witness thrilling dog-fights overhead. Residents of Shoreham Beach Bungalow Town were recently ordered to leave by Military Authorities, and it seems that distress has been caused as many of the bungalows were built as an investment by elderly people, and it is reported that no provision has been made to look after them.

LONDON

Exodus from East End growing rapidly. Taxi drivers report taking party after party to Euston and Paddington with belongings. Hundreds of people leaving Deptford for Kent. Increased tension everywhere and when siren goes people run madly for shelter with white faces. Contact spending night in West Ham reports loyalty and confidence in ultimate issue unquenched but nerves worn down to fine point. Conditions of living now almost impossible and great feeling in

Dockside areas of living on island surrounded by fire and destruction. Urgent necessity of removing women and children and old and crippled people today is reported from all sources – official and unofficial. Extreme nervousness of people rendered homeless at being herded together in local schools with inadequate shelters. West Ham school filled to bursting point from Saturday night onwards blown up by HE bomb with many casualties. This has caused great shock in district. People angry at inadequacy of compensation of wrecked and burnt-out houses; grumbling and dissatisfaction openly voiced, states Deptford contact. Civil Defence services receiving much praise but growing exceedingly tired in heavily bombed areas. Class feeling growing because of worse destruction in working-class areas; anti-Semitism growing in districts where large proportion of Jews reside owing to their taking places in public shelters early in the day. People in target areas living in shelters; women emerging for short time to do shopping and bolting back again. Many reported going into tubes to shelter in spite of instructions to contrary. Dismay and wonder at apparent inadequacy of London defences reported from most districts especially in East End, and intense disgust at hospital bombing. Districts less regularly bombed, such as Lewisham and Chelsea, report great neighbourly feeling. Bermondsey Citizens' Advice Bureau inundated with mothers and young children, hysterical and asking to be removed from district. Reports from Woolwich and Eltham that people are saying our searchlights are being used to guide German planes at night – suspicion of Fifth Column activity. Gravesend seriously disturbed that bombs are dropped without warning as planes pass over; London sirens go and then the sirens at Gravesend; when the 'All Clear' goes they know that they will get more bombs dropped on the planes' return journey. People feel that Gravesend is not given adequate consideration by the authorities.

WEDNESDAY 11 SEPTEMBER 1940

Reports now received make it possible to assess critically the effects of continued bombing in the East End. Morale is rather more strained than the newspapers suggest, whereas the damage to property seems to be less than is reported by them. The pictures of devastation and accounts of destruction weaken the resolve of people to stay put.

Organised evacuation is necessarily a slow business but is proceeding uninterruptedly. Voluntary evacuation also continues fairly steadily, though there is a tendency for those who work in badly-affected districts to evacuate themselves during the night and to return in the daytime.

Factors which contribute to the strain on morale are, of course, as much psychological as material. Listening tension (e.g. anticipation of planes and bombs) is one to which little official notice has been paid. Few people are using ear pads or understand that the diminution of noise can do much to lessen their state of anxiety. Nor does there seem to have been enough encouragement for people to try and sleep as and when they can. The fear, mostly among men, that they may lose their jobs, as has already happened in many cases in the Silvertown district, is an added anxiety, and if it were possible for some reassurance to be given that speedy efforts will be made to find other work for them this would undoubtedly have a good effect.

The need for mobile canteens is still urgent, as is the necessity for providing a hot meal every day for families evacuated from their homes.

An increase is reported in the number of people listening to Haw-Haw and rumours, mostly exaggerated accounts of raid damage and casualties, have also increased considerably.

A certain amount of anti-Semitism in the East End still persists, but this is not so much on account of a marked difference in conduct between Jews and Cockneys, but because the latter, seeking a scapegoat as an outlet for emotional disturbances, pick on the traditional and nearest one. Though many Jewish people regularly congregate and sleep in the public shelters, so also do many of the Gentiles, nor is there any evidence to show that one or other predominates among those who have evacuated themselves voluntarily through fear or hysteria.

Reports from the Regions show that their attention is directed mainly towards London's sufferings and consequently their own troubles are to some extent diminished. Shelter problems are common to many districts as are also the various types and causes of anxiety associated with raids. There is, however, no sign of morale weakening, or that powers of resistance and determination are deteriorating.

Points from Regions

NORTHERN (Newcastle) Inability to obtain the necessary material for the completion of shelters and their protection against damp is causing public dissatisfaction; the habit of sleeping in shelters is growing and anxiety is expressed by Local Authorities with regard to the danger of epidemics with the approach of bad weather. The lighting of road blocks is reported in many cases to be unsatisfactory. It is suggested that when enemy 'planes are overhead people are opening their doors to go to shelter, and many shafts of light are shown at critical moments.

NORTH-MIDLAND (Nottingham) A report from Nottingham rural areas shows no weakening of morale, and defeatism which was apparent earlier in the war is disappearing. It is suggested that lights on railways near centres of population should be masked with cowls. Complaints are general that public shelters are being abused by a few people. There is loss of interest in salvage in some villages because dumps have not been collected. The schemes of insurance against property damage have caused widespread interest.

SOUTH-WESTERN (Bristol) The new siren recommendations are widely approved. There is a demand for the continued bombing of Berlin. Evacuees from London are spreading exaggerated stories of London raids. People in Exeter were much impressed by the keenness of the Home Guard to get to grips with the reported invaders during the weekend. There is a current rumour in Bristol that sirens will not sound during the day, and it is reported that women are keeping their children away from school on this account.

MIDLAND (Birmingham) The apparent absence of fighter planes against night raiders is still worrying many people. Local air raids are causing a crop of rumours as to the places and amount of damage caused.

SCOTLAND (Edinburgh) People are watching what is happening in London and forgetting their own grievances. Considerable talk among the Home Guard in the West about the call-out over the weekend is reported, and some say they will refuse to 'turn out on a fool's errand again.' People are quite uncertain as to what they are supposed to do when they hear church bells. The opinion is held in Montrose that the Military Authorities should release a suitable hall for entertaining the troops.

NORTHERN IRELAND (Belfast) Much indignation is felt at the indiscriminate bombing of London, and a consequent satisfaction at the success of RAF raids on Germany, and keen interest in news of the new incendiary weapon. The demand continues for more war industries to absorb the 70,000 unemployed. Farmers continue to protest against reductions in pork and beef prices, and the low prices generally allowed for agricultural produce.

THURSDAY 12 SEPTEMBER 1940

In London particularly morale is high: people are much more cheerful today.

The dominating topic of conversation today is the anti-aircraft barrage of last night. This greatly stimulated morale: in public shelters people cheered and conversation shows that the noise brought a shock of positive pleasure. It made people feel that 'all the time we had a wonderful trick up our sleeves ready to play when the moment came'.

The increased noise kept people awake but tiredness is offset by the stimulus which has been created.

The Prime Minister's speech was well received but not so enthusiastically as usual. The speech was admired for its plain speaking, but there is evidence that many people, having convinced themselves that invasion is 'off', disliked being reminded of it again. Some people remarked that he sounded 'tired'. In Wales people were surprised that Wales was omitted as a possible point of invasion. The speech nowhere created alarm.

There is still a good deal of unplanned evacuation from London, and there is evidence that small batches of refugees arriving without money at provincial stations are creating anxiety and some alarm. There are exaggerated stories of the damage to London circulating in the provinces. These reports are partly due to the stories told by these refugees, but there is also evidence that Haw-Haw rumours have greatly increased.

A reliable observer just returned to London from the North reports that press and radio have given an account of London damage which has an exaggerated effect. Many people appear to think that London is 'in flames'. There is great sympathy for London and on the whole a belief that 'London will see it through'.

Attached are two reports from London for 11 and 12 September.

Points from Regions

NORTH-EASTERN (Leeds) There is intense sympathy with London and a general confidence that the capital will stand up to the present strain. The way in which the King and Queen freely visited the bombed areas is the subject of much favourable comment. Many people still believe that the civilian population in Germany should be bombed. The new warning system for factories is welcomed amongst men and women are pleased that the sirens are still to be sounded.

EASTERN (Cambridge) News of evacuation plans for Colchester and Ipswich has spread to towns outside the new evacuation area, and there is some speculation as to whether Norwich and other towns are to be included. A rumour gained currency along the Essex and Herts. border to the effect that parachutists had descended; this was apparently due to puffs of smoke being seen from AA guns.

WALES (Cardiff) Morale is still very good. Interest still centres on action in the Thames Estuary and London and news is awaited with anxiety. Widespread sympathy is expressed for those in congested areas. The continued bombing of Berlin is a source of general satisfaction. Opinion is widespread that more details of provincial bombing should be released. The procedure for obtaining relief in respect of raid damage is becoming more generally known but there are complaints that official assessment of damage is based on figures below the present cost of replacement. Stirrup pumps are now in great demand following 'self-help' propaganda, but they are extremely difficult to obtain. Little interest is evinced by news from Italy and Africa due to events at home.

NORTH-WESTERN (Manchester) Shortage of shelters is a predominant topic at the moment, and many people realise that they should have planned their protection sooner. Authorities everywhere are pushing on with schemes for erection of shelters, and the sight of bricks and mortar is having a good effect. There was a feeling of anger when it was learned that Buckingham Palace had been bombed.

SOUTH-EASTERN (Tunbridge Wells) In view of the fact that the heavy raids on London indicate that the war is entering a new stage, some people believe that it will be over soon with an Allied victory. There is a complaint from Brighton of lack of synchronisation in sounding 'Raiders Passed'. There is still some grumbling over the fact that RAF bombers sometimes return from Germany without unloading their bombs.

LONDON

Morale high in most districts in spite of damage and casualties. Pessimism reported among businessmen owing to discovery that weather conditions suit German bombers. People worried about possible further breakdown of public utility services and its effect on a population used to 'all modern conveniences.' Traffic difficulties in city causing great irritation and nervous exhaustion among workers travelling in overcrowded trains. City contacts suggest working hours might be staggered or clerks allowed to work half week as little business is transacted. Crowds of sightseers might also be discouraged. Lewisham reports overcrowding of Rest Centres and people growing extremely tired from lack of sleep; workers complaining they cannot concentrate in day time. Latter condition also reported by brain workers who complain particularly of noise and talk in large shelters, especially in blocks of luxury flats, by people who have little work to do by day. Wish expressed that noise and talk in shelters could be branded as 'Fifth Column' activities. Reports from East End show people to be evacuating themselves from heavily bombed areas. In Isle of Dogs those who cannot evacuate themselves reported to be growing angry with authorities, stating they have been forgotten and are on an island which may at any moment be cut off and ringed with fire. Many shelters in district too badly damaged for use; gas and electricity are cut off; there is little water – all this has led to talk today of marching to West End to commandeer hotels and clubs. This type of talk reported also from Stepney, but in lesser degree. Bermondsey reports women and children, old people and invalids impatient to escape to less vulnerable area. Class bitterness expressed there and in Fulham by some individuals. Bermondsey Rest Centres overcrowded, with many people there since Saturday night. People in these centres nervous of remaining there as local school used for same purpose was badly bombed last week. Re-billeting is proceeding.

11 September

LONDON

Morale has jumped to new level of confidence and cheerfulness since tremendous AA barrage. This is true of every district contacted, including East End and areas badly hit yesterday such as Woolwich and Lewisham. 'We'll give them hell now' is a typical working-class comment today. City far more cheerful and less crowded with sightseers than yesterday. Kensington people rendered homeless in night joking when taken in by neighbours. In spite of little sleep, factory workers are turning up as usual and working well; employers reported to be very accommodating about time. Traffic dislocations causing delay and annoyance; people passing in empty cars are much grumbled at by queues of workers waiting for buses who would like to be offered lifts. Unofficial walk-out from dock areas still going on; people from Greenwich reported to be taking buses to Bromley from where they hope to go to the West; others going to Bucks and Herts. A few have any but vaguest ideas as to where they are going and how they will fare there. Many people taking rugs and cushions from poor districts to spend nights in West End shelters: fear of great Dockside fires appears to be chief motivating force. Stoke Newington and other boroughs not close to docks report most people 'sticking to their homes' as long as they can. Re-billeting of homeless people proceeding, but many Rest Centres still overcrowded. As they are not provided with shelters adequate for number of people in them are rousing apprehension in districts such as Bermondsey as two Rest

Centres have been bombed with great loss of life. Stoke Newington now reported to be fitting public shelters with bunks for children.

12 September

FRIDAY 13 SEPTEMBER 1940

In London the anti-aircraft barrage continues to stimulate morale. People are sleeping better in spite of increased noise, and reports show there is an increased feeling of security based on the psychological knowledge that we are hitting back.

People living near guns are suffering from serious lack of sleep: a number of interviews made round one gun in West London showed that people were getting much less sleep than others a few hundred yards away. Very few used ear plugs, and many of those interviewed were still relying on deck chairs instead of mattresses. There is little complaint about lack of sleep, mainly because of the new exhilaration created by the barrage. Nevertheless this serious loss of sleep needs watching.

There is a growth of anger against the Germans and growing demands for 'reprisals on civilians'.

Reports continue to show a great increase in rumours about damage and casualties ('They say the casualties are really ten times bigger than we are told').

Motorists do not appear to give lifts willingly and there is considerable criticism of 'the rich in their cars'.

Points from Regions

SOUTHERN (Reading) The Prime Minister's speech has been received 'with approbation and quiet confidence'. There are some signs of a recrudescence of Fifth Columnist rumours, some of which are attributed to Haw-Haw. Exaggeration of the casualties on a recent raid on Southampton gives rise to a suggestion that the BBC should give a reminder that gossip about air-raid damage 'can be just as dangerous as the spreading of totally unfounded rumours'.

NORTH-MIDLAND (Nottingham) Leicestershire IC has received 'urgent representations' about the delay in supplying the Civil Defence services with uniform and equipment. The Nottingham IC would like an explanation of the variation of the Ministry of Labour Gazette's cost of living index. The decrease of two points during August seems to be doubted.

SOUTH-WESTERN (Bristol) Mr Churchill's speech has had 'a stimulating effect'. A demand for reprisal raids on Berlin is made in various parts of the Region. Concern is expressed about the way in which the King and Queen and Prime Minister are visiting the bombed areas, although the effect of their behaviour on public morale is fully appreciated.

MIDLANDS (Birmingham) There has been an enthusiastic reception for the Prime Minister's speech. This applies also to the new raid warning system. Various Information Committees have commented upon the display of car lights which are to be seen on trunk roads throughout the Region.

SCOTLAND (Edinburgh) Full approval is given to the Prime Minister's speech. It has enhanced the expectation of invasion, but the public are nevertheless confident about the outcome of such an enterprise. There are many rumours dealing with this subject.

NORTHERN IRELAND (Belfast) Investigations are being made into the accommodation available for the reception of Londoners rendered homeless through air raids. This problem is being considered by the Northern Ireland Cabinet. The local press alleges that the voluntary recruiting system has been unsatisfactory and that young men prefer the dole.

LONDON

Majority carrying on with calmness and courage even in heavily bombed areas. Most prevalent emotion anger with Germans and irritation over constant raids. Real hatred and savagery flash out at times from those who have come in contact with actual tragedies:

'we must wipe them off the face of the earth' is working man's comment heard today. AA barrage continues to be encouraging. Much talk today of invasion; expectancy but not fear expressed. Croydon contact reports local people 'determined to see it through' but that defeatist sentiments are voiced by isolated members of middle class. Noticeable friendliness everywhere among all classes and types of people. Everybody is trying to help everybody else – except motorists who are rousing angry bitterness at not offering lifts with empty cars to long queues of tired workers. Even when Home Guard asked motorists to give lifts in Balham to stranded workers they refused. Misuse of public shelters in Wandsworth reported; people push in with bedding and prevent strangers from getting a place; conditions described as dirty and unhygienic. Borough of Finsbury keeps its public shelters in excellent condition; result is that people come to large underground shelter from other boroughs in cars and crowd it out. Authorities feel they cannot turn people away as in present state of nervous tension there would be angry scenes.

SATURDAY 14 SEPTEMBER 1940

People in London are slightly less cheerful today. The decline in the activity of the anti-aircraft barrage has caused comment, and there are many questions about the effect of cloud and rain on the barrage.

Unplanned evacuation from London is continuing. Most people leave without giving any indication of their destination. A report on the reception of refugees in Oxford and Buckinghamshire will be provided on Monday.

Conditions in many shelters are still unsatisfactory. Complaints are mainly about insanitary conditions, lack of ventilation and overcrowding.

Many of our reports show criticism of the Lord Mayor's 'charitable appeal' for relief and consider the charge should properly be carried by the Government.

Exaggerated stories of damage and Haw-Haw rumours continue to circulate.

There is little interest in the possibility of invasion, nor does the prospect alarm people.

Public opinion about the bombing of Buckingham Palace is divided: most people feel a fresh bond with their leaders, others think that 'the King and Queen ought not to be exposed to such danger'.

Points from Regions

NORTH-EASTERN (Leeds) All eyes are still on London, and newspaper accounts of the behaviour of Londoners have stiffened public resolve in the North. Despite warnings about invasion, it cannot be said that most people take the threat seriously. The War Weapons Week has had a brilliant send-off in Leeds. Although morale is high, more people than for some time past are listening to Haw-Haw, and it seems that people hope to pick up hints about coming events. There is strong feeling because bombs fell again this week and there were no sirens sounded or AA fire.

EASTERN (Cambridge) The chief reactions to the bombing of London appear to be anxiety concerning communications. The accounts of the bombing of Buckingham Palace have captured public imagination. There has been an increase in rumours although not of an unduly alarmist nature. Complaints of non-arrival of postal packets sent to the USA have caused a suspicion that certain letters are being systematically stopped.

SOUTHERN (Reading) There is some anxiety as to the possibility of continued night raiding through the winter. An authoritative statement on the damage which is being done to Germany would undoubtedly have a tonic effect on many people. Although the public is alive to the possibilities of invasion, there is a general feeling that it can only be a disaster for the Germans. There is a feeling in some quarters that there is too much emphasis placed on damage by press photographs, and the attitude that 'we can take it', which suggests our ability to suffer rather than our power to hit back.

WALES (Cardiff) Interest is centred on activities in South East England, the prospect of invasion, and additions or improvements to shelters to meet winter conditions. The continued presence of the King and Queen in London and their tours has enhanced the respect felt by all. There is some call for reprisals by random bombing in Germany.

NORTH-WESTERN (Manchester) Today's topic of conversation is surprise at getting through a whole night without an alarm. There are fresh reports that Liverpool dockers are not cooperating and are far too ready to stop work for alarms. The deliberate bombing of Buckingham Palace is thought to be a blunder by Hitler.

SOUTH-EASTERN (Tunbridge Wells) Tunbridge Wells suffered considerable damage on Thursday as a result of a lightning raid. No siren was sounded but members of the Civil Defence behaved splendidly, but soon after the streets became full of curious sightseers who interfered with the work of the Fire Services. If the raider had returned there might have been many casualties.

MONDAY 16 SEPTEMBER TO SATURDAY 21 SEPTEMBER 1940

Between July and September 1940 about 2,500 children were evacuated to Canada, South Africa, Australia and New Zealand under the government-assisted scheme run by the Children's Overseas Reception Board. On the night of 17–18 September the passenger ship, *City of Benares*, carrying ninety children to Canada, was torpedoed and sunk by a U-boat. The children were transferred to lifeboats but it was several hours before a destroyer was able to come to the rescue. In rough seas and bitter cold, most of the children perished in the lifeboats and only thirteen survived. The news was not, however, released until the following weekend.

September the 15th marked the climax of the 'Battle of Britain', though the phrase does not appear in the Home Intelligence reports. The Air Ministry announced that 185 raiders had been shot down in daylight battles over London, 178 by fighter aircraft and 7 by anti-aircraft guns. Post-war research showed that only 60 German aircraft had been shot down, but the losses inflicted on the Luftwaffe were so great as to amount to a defeat and 15 September was to be celebrated as 'Battle of Britain Day' in years to come. On 20 September Hitler postponed plans for the invasion of Britain indefinitely.

One of the effects of the Blitz was a revival of rumour. Home Intelligence recorded that evacuees from London were spreading lurid and exaggerated accounts of the damage inflicted by raids. There were persistent rumours that an invasion was in progress, or that an invasion had been attempted and failed, leaving hundreds of German corpses floating in the Channel. The East End was alleged to have sent Churchill a 'petition for peace', a rumour that probably reflected the activities of Communists who were organising petitions in favour of bomb-proof shelters and the opening of the tube stations for shelter at night.

As the daily reports record, the people of London were already taking the initiative and converting the tubes into shelters in spite of official requests not to do so. The inadequacy of rest centres and the difficulties of finding accommodation for thousands of homeless people were a constant source of complaint and an administrative nightmare for central government and local government alike. Oxford alone had to cope with about 10,000 unexpected visitors.

Harold Nicolson, the Parliamentary Secretary to the Ministry of Information, feared that class bitterness would arise if the poor of the East End were bombed while the wealthier classes were unscathed. To his great relief the Luftwaffe bombed the City of London and the West End. Belatedly, as Home Intelligence noted, the BBC reported that Madame Tussaud's on Marylebone Road had also suffered bomb damage. Visiting the scene for the *Daily Express*, Hilde Marchant had found the waxwork of Hitler with a lump missing from the face, and Göring's uniform covered in soot and broken glass. Churchill, however, 'stood as firm as a rock, his glassy blue eyes sternly supervising the clearing of the wreckage'.

In North Africa, a column of Italian troops under the command of Marshal Graziani advanced about sixty miles into Egypt to occupy Sidi Barrani, where they were bombed by the RAF. To judge from the Home Intelligence reports, it was a news story that passed almost unnoticed amidst the drama of the London blitz.

MONDAY 16 SEPTEMBER 1940

Yesterday's aerial successes have produced enthusiastic praise for the RAF. There is, however, comment that the AA barrage last night seemed less intense than usual. This may be due to nothing more than people becoming used to it.

Most people anticipate an invasion within a few days, and are very confident that it will be a failure. Rumours that it has already been attempted and has failed are reported from many quarters. From the Northern Region it is stated that there are many requests for a public denial or an explanatory statement. From Nottingham comes the rumour that hundreds of German bodies have been floating in the Channel. In North Nottinghamshire the invasion is said to have been attempted on Lincolnshire and the South Coast. In Northampton it is said that the attack was launched on the West Coast. Invasion rumours are also reported in the South-Western Region and Scotland.

The people of London are in the great majority more optimistic, but unplanned evacuation of the 'jittery' to Bucks., Berks., Herts., Oxford and Kent continues. These evacuees magnify their adventures and the amount of destruction in London, thus alarming people in Reception Areas. Nightly migrations to public shelters which people regard as safe in the West End and elsewhere are now routine events. Tubes are also being used as shelters.

There is still criticism of lack of washing and other facilities at Rest Centres, and suggestions are made that these centres should cooperate more closely with the public baths.

The Lord Mayor's Fund for Air-Raid Relief is criticised on two scores: first that the matter is really a Government concern, and secondly that many towns have suffered considerably already but that no national fund has been opened for them.

In the excitement of aerial battles, air raids, and invasion threats, the situation in Egypt is being allowed to pass by the public with little comment.

Points from Regions

NORTHERN (Newcastle) Rumours of an attempted invasion which failed are widespread. There is much evidence that public feeling against the German people is rapidly hardening as a result of the more intensive raids. Complaints have been made that many people fail to hear the one minute warning when asleep, and it has been urged that after 10.30 p.m. the sirens should be sounded for at least two minutes. The heating of shelters is becoming a major concern for many people. Feeling is growing in working-class circles that certain classes are not pulling their weight in the financing of the war, in view of big interest-free loans made by working-class organisations.

NORTH-MIDLAND (Nottingham) Widespread rumours are prevalent that an invasion has already been attempted. The continued presence of the King, Queen and Government in London is appreciated. More news of our air raids on Germany is still desired, as there is a feeling that we can stand bombing better if the Germans are getting the same treatment. In Northamptonshire some workers express concern at the sparing use of alarms; they do not mind working through so long as they can feel their families can take cover in good time. War investments have increased in Nottingham mining areas as a result of local bombing.

MIDLAND (Birmingham) The relative calm of the past few nights is creating a belief that invasion is imminent and there is absolute confidence in the outcome. People are less worried by siren warnings than formerly, and go to bed until bombs are dropped. Licensing Justices of Birmingham are to consider the earlier closing of public houses in view of the disorderly behaviour of intoxicated people in public shelters.

NORTHERN IRELAND (Belfast) There is enthusiastic praise for the way in which the RAF has bombed enemy invasion bases, and brought down so many aircraft in London raids. There is some comment on the relatively small number of planes destroyed by AA fire. Anger is expressed at the renewed bombing of Buckingham Palace. The situation in Egypt is viewed with some uneasiness.

SOUTH-WESTERN (Bristol) Admiration is expressed for the exploits of the RAF in yesterday's raids, and many people are expressing the hope that retaliation will be made on Berlin. There are rumours of parachutists landing in Cornwall.

SCOTLAND (Edinburgh) In Dundee there is general scepticism about invasion, based on confidence in the Navy, but elsewhere there are vigorous rumours of an attempted invasion of North East Scotland. There is little talk about the Italian moves on the Egyptian border and this campaign seems to be regarded as a side issue. It is reported that on receipt of an air-raid warning in Glasgow last night many lights became visible, and ARP workers complain that they have no power to take effective action.

LONDON

Big trek each evening to find shelter accommodation for the night – from such areas as Bermondsey, Canning Town, and Paddington. Numbers of people including many children shelter in Underground Stations. In a West End district, it is reported that people bombed out of a public shelter were refused admittance to the large private shelter of a big store. A Stepney observer reports: 'need for clothes for refugees at Rest Centres; communal feeding centres working well, though many people ignorant of their existence, and uninformed of changed addresses as the result of fresh raids; many working men unable to obtain meal in evening owing to bombing of market, and lack of gas, electricity and water'; suggests temporary hostels for them. Watford observer reports that district making London refugees welcome; some anxiety about getting in touch with relatives. Improvement in the offering of lifts by private cars reported from several areas.

TUESDAY 17 SEPTEMBER 1940

While many continue to anticipate invasion, and indeed hope that it will come within the next few days, reports show that some people are suggesting that its likelihood has diminished. Rumours that it has already been attempted and has failed continue to be reported.

Regional reports continue to state that there is an increase in the amount of listening to German broadcasts.

The great delay in the receipt of the national morning papers in many parts of the provinces has led to requests that the BBC should revive their 10 o'clock morning news.

Londoners whose families have been re-billeted or who have evacuated themselves are having great difficulty in making contact with them. Suggestions are made that Rest Centres should keep careful records of the destinations of those they house temporarily, and that anxious relatives should be instructed to apply at these centres to trace their families.

Descriptions of our retreat from Sollum are criticised for attempting to disguise bad news as good news.

Points from Regions

NORTH-EASTERN (Leeds) Confidence throughout the Region is very high. Rumours are rife that attempts at invasion have been made. More people are listening to Haw-Haw and the New British Broadcasting Station appears to have a large number of listeners. Despite the bombing of London and local propaganda, there is no appreciable difference in the rate at which Leeds children are being registered for evacuation. Censorship of letters to Eire appears to cause some resentment. It is felt in some quarters that undue publicity has been given to the bombing of Buckingham Palace.

EASTERN (Cambridge) Morale still remains high, and once again some people feel the threat of immediate invasion has disappeared. New refugees from London are settling down, but it seems that billets earmarked for troops or compulsory evacuees are at present being occupied by them. There appears to be a slight increase in listening to German broadcasts. A number of stories are in circulation concerning alleged invasion, and it is said that isolated groups of vessels have been beaten off. There are increasing signs of a disposition to settle down to winter routine.

SOUTHERN (Reading) London's reaction to air raids, German air losses, and stories of the RAF attacks on invasion bases stimulate confidence and courage. Threatened cities such as Portsmouth and Southampton are effectively adapting themselves to war conditions. A fresh wave of evacuees from London is disquieting Local Authorities in the northern part of the Region, which already has refugees from coastal cities and evacuated children, and the billeting demands of the military are also increasing.

WALES (Cardiff) Air successes on Sunday and the bombing of the Channel ports has increased confidence in our ability to cope with the enemy. There is criticism of the report of the BBC observer in Egypt on our 'withdrawal' from Sollum: 'If we retreat, let us admit it.'

NORTH-WESTERN (Manchester) While Manchester and Liverpool have been heartened by London's resistance to a week of severe bombing, there is growing perturbation over stories of lack of shelters and accommodation for those who have been bombed; many people are worried over lack of shelters in this Region, and in one or two housing estates rent strikes have been staged until shelters have been provided. Many people are urging that municipal transport should continue to run until danger is imminent.

SOUTH-EASTERN (Tunbridge Wells) Stories of damage to London brought by lorry drivers are becoming increasingly lurid, and demands for reprisals equally emphatic. More information regarding results of air raids is urged from many parts of the Region. There is a demand that the sounding of sirens should be entrusted to Local Authorities when lone raiders are overhead. There is some dissatisfaction among Kent members of the Home Guard because, although in the 'front line', they are without steel helmets and respirators. Many hop pickers arriving in a hurry from London are saying 'What is the good of going on?' A report from Folkestone says that morale is adversely affected by the exodus of a large number of well-off people from London, and others from Folkestone, including ARP and Red Cross personnel who should be in the front line.

LONDON

Morale steady; public on whole settling down to new air-raid life cheerfully and show fewer signs of tiredness. Small pockets of bad morale reported from different districts especially with regard to over-crowded Rest Centres (this is now being dealt with by London Region Ministry of Health). Bermondsey contact reports 'talk against Government on account of inadequate number and poor equipment of local shelters. Shelters under railway arches have insufficient seats and people are forced to sit and lie on pavement.' This and other 'target' areas of the docks still need some voluntary scheme of evacuation of mothers and children, also old and infirm, state Social Workers and other responsible people. This less true of other bombed districts such as Lewisham, Stoke Newington, Finsbury, Battersea etc. where people cling to their homes at all costs. Stoke Newington contact states bombed people in district very philosophical: 'majority set to work to clean up mess at once and say "it might have been worse"'. Same contact reports many people would like to get their old parents out but that the old people are difficult to move. South Kensington contact states roundsmen upsetting housewives by gossip of air-raid damage and numbers of customers leaving the district. Suggests propaganda to stop this. Rumours of unexploded bombs far outweigh their numbers and it is suggested that people should not believe such rumours but look only for police warnings. West End businesswoman states her own class feel that more generous treatment should be given to East Enders who have lost homes or have to spend nights in shelters. Reports also 'bitterness against Government for not having built deep shelters to protect population'. Business circles ask for a definite lead on working hours and transport. Latter question increasingly difficult for workers although car drivers are giving lifts more readily than a few days ago. Working women reported to wish to use ground floors and basements of empty houses to sleep in to meet shelter difficulty. Day rest periods for workers, mentioned by Minister of Labour, being asked for by factory workers who are not sleeping well because of night raids.

WEDNESDAY 18 SEPTEMBER 1940

Provincial reports show that the bombardment of London is still the outstanding news interest. Sympathy for 'London's ordeal' is widely expressed, and there is reason to believe that the communiques describing detailed damage (but not the amount of London which still stands) and the newspaper pictures of ruined buildings are producing a greatly exaggerated picture in provincial minds. This is coupled with such expressions as 'if London can take it, so can we'. At the same time some people are beginning to wonder how long London will be able to go on taking it.

Rumours of damage to London, some accurate but many exaggerated, are common in the provinces and the Northern Region comments that the BBC's revelation on Saturday evening that a bomb fell on Madame Tussaud's was regarded as 'the most humorous remark on the wireless this year'; everyone had known about this for at least two days.

The rumour that invasion was attempted a few days ago and failed with considerable loss to the Germans is now reported to be causing excitement in the Midlands. There is also the rumour reported from the South-Western Region that British Marines have landed in Jersey.

It is again reported that listening to the German wireless is on the increase. This is attributed by many to the fact that when the 9 o'clock news has to cut out on account of raids, the English news from Germany is often audible without re-tuning.

Though strong demands for reprisals on German civilians are still reported, there are many who are satisfied that the wisest policy is to continue attacking invasion objectives.

Points from Regions

NORTHERN (Newcastle) Expressions of sympathy with London are numerous, and there is an atmosphere of expectancy. In some centres local ARP wardens are anxious to go to London to relieve those on duty there. It has been suggested that more broadcasts from the Service Ministers would be appreciated. There is little discussion of peace aims at present. Some complaints have been made by munitions contractors of the inexperience of Government inspectors.

NORTH-MIDLAND (Nottingham) London casualties have caused anger, and there is a growing feeling in Notts that we ought 'to dose Hitler with his own medicine'. Official statements that if we hold out for a period of weeks the major crisis will pass, have been interpreted by some as meaning the war will end with the crisis. A report from Leicester states that benefits which can be immediately claimed by air-raid victims for material losses appear inadequate, and the replacement of furniture is said to be particularly difficult.

SOUTH-WESTERN (Bristol) People are facing the prospect of attempted invasion calmly, and are confident of the ultimate outcome. Three reliable contacts in Devon say that people with the least satisfactory attitude towards the war are mostly found in the income group from £250–£750. Some dissatisfaction reported from Exeter and Penzance where bombs were dropped without the sirens being sounded. There are complaints from Weston-super-Mare that buses cease running in air raids. Evacuated Londoners are spreading highly coloured accounts of raids in Swindon. There is some speculation as to whether London can stand up to the bombing. The need for bombing barge concentrations is appreciated, and there is a decrease in demands for retaliations on Berlin.

MIDLAND (Birmingham) The rumour that an attempted German invasion last Sunday was frustrated with heavy losses is widespread. There is much feeling about lights on motor cars being left on after sirens are sounded. The question of earlier closing for public houses comes before the Justices tomorrow. There are complaints of lack of transport facilities for workers from Coventry.

SCOTLAND (Edinburgh) Middle-class people are beginning to ask 'What is going to be the end of this mutual bombing?' The chief reaction to the terror raids is one of anger with the enemy and admiration for those enduring the ordeal. There is some disquiet about the Italian advance. There is some adverse comment at the absence of AA fire in Glasgow, and the public would welcome some assurance that British fighters were up.

NORTHERN IRELAND (Belfast) There is some speculation as to the reason for the Secret Session in the House of Commons yesterday, although it is not presumed that the situation is more critical. It is generally felt that any attempt at invasion would be repulsed. In intellectual circles General Sir Alan Brooke's statement welcoming an invasion attempt is thought to be ill-advised. Ministry of Supply experts are investigating iron ore and bauxite sources in Ireland.

LONDON

Londoners still remain outwardly calm and are putting up with difficulties extremely well, but there are still numbers of people anxious to get out. One Earls Court Square has practically evacuated itself after bombing there; others in less fortunate position need scheme to help them. A certain amount of panic shown in individual cases where people have had horrible experiences but this is often due to temporary physical reaction. There are still criticisms about Rest Centres – inadequately staffed and equipped – although some districts report gradual improvement. Re-billeting of homeless still causing difficulties and organisation reported to be bad in some areas e.g. Chelsea, St Pancras. ARP warden in West End and also Social Workers in East End feel Mayfair billeting does not solve the problems of homeless East Enders – they feel homesick and lonely and food prices are beyond them. Still much criticism about inadequacy of shelter amenities. Many people have lost faith in surface shelters and now go to tubes where atmosphere is reported to be bad; more supervision and help required here. Transport difficulties increasing and several observers comment on number of half empty cars in congested streets. Harrow factory which carries on with production throughout the 'Alert' resents Government offices in the neighbourhood closing down; workers finding it more and more difficult to do essential shopping and transact necessary official business (Post Office, Labour Exchange, Stationery Office). Increase in unemployment reported in North London as many industries are without facilities for carrying on (water etc.), even where property remains undamaged; this is causing a certain amount of anxiety and distress.

THURSDAY 19 SEPTEMBER 1940

1. People are not so cheerful today. There is more grumbling. Elation over the barrage is not so strong: people wonder why it is not more effective in preventing night bombing and many avow it has decreased in intensity. There is also evidence that physical tiredness is beginning to have an effect on nerves.

2. There are increasing demands for reprisals and growing hatred against the Germans. Wild suggestions are made: 'Fill Buckingham Palace with prisoners', 'Shoot all captured airmen', etc. These expressions are common in public shelters in specially heavily bombed areas.

3. In London the following tension points continue:

> *Amenities of public shelters*
> *Inability of Local Authorities to remove people quickly from rest shelters*
> *Inadequate methods of evacuation to other parts of London and to the country*
> *Transport difficulties*
> *Curtailment of services, e.g. Post Offices, shops, Employment Exchanges, etc.*
> *Lack of a register of evacuated persons*
> *Determination of the public to use underground stations as shelters*
> *Rigidity of compensation regulations*

4. Last night the number of people taking shelter in underground stations greatly increased.

5. Rumours and exaggerated stories circulate widely in London and the provinces. The most important subjects are:

> *Terrors of the new magnetic mines dropped by parachute*
> *Invasion (in progress, repulsed, etc.)*

Spies (Fifth Column activities in shelters, signalling with torches, etc.)
Damage and casualties in London
Today several people reported 'a petition for peace' sent to the Prime
   Minister from the East End. This may be due to the petitions which
   the People's Vigilance Committees, Communist groups, etc. are organ-
   ising in shelters

6. Reports confirm that in the country outside London there is an exaggerated view of the damage and dislocation in London. 'Refugees' are spreading
highly coloured stories and the press continues to devote itself almost exclusively to accounts of damage.

7. The situation in Egypt is not raising popular concern. On the other hand
thoughtful people are disturbed and already speak of 'another Somaliland'.

Points from Regions

NORTH-EASTERN (Leeds) Some apprehension about events in Africa,
and doubt as to whether the power of the Navy in the Mediterranean
is enough to check the Italian advance. Expectations of invasion are
diminishing. Newsreels and pictures in papers of damage to London
have done much to improve black-out and Civil Defence precautions. Showing of King and Queen visiting the East End in newsreels has brought cheers everywhere. LIC at Sowerby Bridge passed
resolution urging need for discussion of war aims as a positive factor
in morale. Much discussion of deep shelters and many urge the need
for them.

EASTERN (Cambridge) Increasing belief that our strong defences
and the weather will defer invasion. Some demand for press pictures
of RAF damage to Germany, to offset continual pictures of damage
here. Requests for more information about our AA defences and
some anxiety at American statement that life of AA guns is very
short. Complaints continue about German wireless monopolising
ether. Some criticism of expense to Local Authorities of salvage
schemes; contractors suspected of excessive profits, sometimes quite
unfairly.

SOUTHERN (Reading) Local Authorities faced by big problem of East End refugees. Towns affected are Oxford, Windsor, Banbury, Chipping Norton, Aylesbury, Newbury, etc. Refugees spread despondency by lurid accounts of bombing. Growing demand that large empty country houses should have been taken over for refugees. Official statements about 'no retaliation' creating discussion. Belief expressed that in absence of retaliation indiscriminate bombing will get progressively worse, while retaliation might stop it. Some argue that civilian bombing *has* military value and instance bombing of Rotterdam. Criticism that we have not convinced neutrals of our own certainty of ultimate victory.

WALES (Cardiff) Complaints that Civil Defence equipment is impossible to obtain in both North and South Wales. Much criticism of cars parked in rows with side lamps lit outside hotels. Public believe these can be seen from the air. Curfew on beaches accepted as a wise precaution. Much interest, coupled with uneasiness, about situation in Africa. Suggestion is made that BBC interviews of victims of bombing do not ring true, as persons interviewed sometimes have difficulty in reading their apparently carefully prepared scripts.

NORTH-WESTERN (Manchester) Indignation reported in Merseyside area at daylight bombing without apparent resistance from fighters, and that sirens sounded after raid had started. Liverpool considers that for its size its losses have been as heavy as London's, and that it should have appropriate fighter protection. Increasing optimism about results of possible invasion but distinct uneasiness about Spain and Egypt; public sceptical when told of negligible value of abandoned territory. Growing anxiety about conditions which are likely if long winter nights have to be passed in cold shelters.

SOUTH-EASTERN (Tunbridge Wells) Some alarm expressed at German programmes overlapping and substituting BBC programmes on closely similar wave-lengths. Rumours that East Enders have sent a petition to the Prime Minister to stop the war. Sarcastic comments at closing of Post Offices whenever warnings sound. Increasing irritation at apparent immunity of German bombers which are thought to 'circle over' individual towns for hours at night. Rumours persist that invasions have taken place and have been repulsed.

LONDON

Some dismay expressed today at heavy raid last night and apparent inability of AA barrage to prevent it. Fear of mines dropped by parachute and the extent of the damage they cause is also evident. No break in morale, however, can be seen. Extreme annoyance again expressed by business people and other workers at closing down of public utility services during warnings, especially Post Offices and banks. Welfare Supervisor of large employing concern reports workers less worried over difficulty of transport than lack of sleep. 75% of these workers are sleeping in shelters where their rest is continually disturbed. Rest Centres and Communal Feeding Centres in heavily bombed areas now working far more smoothly but problem of re-billeting of homeless in East End districts still acute. People turned out of houses by time bombs are not catered for on regular system; one family in Greenwich reported to have been living in dugout for ten days waiting to go home when time bomb had exploded, and voicing resentment as they say that 'in Mayfair bomb would have been dealt with after two days'. Urgent need for some machinery by which contact can be kept with people who have left London so that relations can get in touch with them. Air-raid casualties reported by Hospital Almoner to be extremely brave and cheerful but anxious over welfare of relations. Local machinery needed to find out and report on these relations to hospital patients. Middle classes reported to be concerned over question of compensation when houses have been damaged or demolished. Complaints voiced that nothing is being done for them although they are hard hit by taxation and loss of business. Grievance also that full rates are charged for houses half demolished. Motorists willing to give lifts complain of confusion and delay in picking up people wanting to go in the same direction. Wish request could be made that people wanting lifts should hold out notices with names of places they are going to clearly marked. Bad feeling growing in North London suburbs about numbers of 'aliens' who go into street shelters with mattresses early in evening and leave no room for passers-by.

FRIDAY 20 SEPTEMBER 1940

In general morale is excellent and in particular people are more cheerful today. The feeling of being in the front line stimulates many people and puts them on their mettle in overcoming transport and shelter difficulties. Several of our reports comment on this characteristic.

There is, however, evidence of increasing physical tiredness.

Although there is no general demand for evacuation from heavily bombed areas there is evidence that certain classes of the community would welcome arrangements for them to go, e.g. wives and children of men working or serving elsewhere, infirm or invalid persons, old couples, widows. It is emphasised by our observers, however, that willing cooperation could only be got for a carefully thought out scheme which took into consideration the special needs and problems of these classes. Women with husbands are not in general prepared to go although evidence suggests that they might do so if proper arrangements were made for the men left behind.

In East and South East London there are many complaints that the whereabouts of evacuated persons are unknown.

Taking shelter in underground stations continued last night. People were orderly but conditions were very insanitary. There is evidence that people do not intend to pay attention to official requests not to shelter there.

Points from Regions

NORTHERN (Newcastle) Many statements have been made expressing fear that Hitler will not attempt invasion; it is generally felt that any attempt is bound to be unsuccessful and would shorten the war. Criticism of the closing of Post Offices and banks for long periods during warnings is widespread. The method of deducting income tax at source appears popular, but there is some criticism that it gives the employer too much information as to the private income of the employee.

NORTH-MIDLAND (Nottingham) There is a general feeling of admiration for the way in which 'the Cockneys are standing up to air raids'. The rumour that invasion has been attempted is prevalent.

There are some complaints by Grimsby people who have evacuated themselves to the Lake District that they are being exploited by landladies and others. There is grumbling at the shortage of eggs in Nottinghamshire and Leicestershire, and annoyance at official announcements that eggs are plentiful; a shortage of bagged coal is also reported.

SOUTH-WESTERN (Bristol) Despite official denial stories of attempted invasion still circulate. From Trowbridge and Weston come reports of a demand for the publication of pictures of damage done to German towns by RAF. Sympathetic concern for the bombing of London is shown everywhere. People in Exeter would like to be shown what damage has *not* been done to London, and to know how normal life continues despite the raids, as well as to learn of the damage effected. Evacuees from London and coastal towns are reported to be well received. After several days of comparative peace people of Plymouth are expecting a big attack, but except for a feeling that deep shelters should be provided, there is little concern and no alarm.

MIDLAND (Birmingham) It is generally felt that the bombing of the invasion ports is preventing invasion, and that the bombing of London calls for reprisals on Berlin. There are many complaints about shortage of coal, and protests against the 'means test' for supplementary Old Age Pensions.

SCOTLAND (Edinburgh) Italian moves in North Africa are discussed with some concern and the questions are asked: 'Are we going to hit Italy hard soon?' and 'Are our forces out there strong enough?' During a survey of ten cinemas held during a warning last night only one person was seen to move from the gallery to the ground floor, and nobody left the building. The fact that buses in Midlothian stop when a warning is sounded is causing some interference with colliery work.

NORTHERN IRELAND (Belfast) The manner in which Londoners are standing up to bombing continues to be praised. The bombing of ports in enemy hands is taken as a sign that Britain can maintain this preventive offensive indefinitely. Precautions are being taken against the possible development of enemy air activity over Ulster, and Civil Defence services in urban areas are to be strengthened. The Belfast Spitfire fund has now reached £72,000. Efforts are to be made greatly to increase Ulster's flax acreage in 1941.

LONDON

Morale still steady with growing anger against Germans. Many East End workers and others qualified to speak still feel that dispersal of non-essential population would ease the difficulties of London authorities. Large crowds, mostly women and children, still congregate in most tube stations for sleeping at night; little space left for travellers. Observer on Edgware line noticed quantities of rubbish still being swept up about nine o'clock this morning. Islington Social Workers report need for broadcasts in simple language informing people rendered homeless what they should do and what provisions are made for them; this need evident from criticism of lack of co-ordination between various services. Golders Green resident expresses concern at squads of cyclists on road showing too much light. Responsible official in Woolwich impressed by extraordinary determination of employers to carry on in spite of factories receiving repeated hits. Business and professional people now asking what compensation they will have when houses or business premises are damaged; big employers concerned not only about personal loss but about resulting unemployment among their workers. Rest Centres reported to be working more smoothly in many districts but more officials needed. Jewish Social Worker says spirit of the poor in East End not broken in spite of terrible ordeals; Westminster Council now helping to re-billet homeless East Enders and records being kept. Many would like to move from London. Heston professional man reports anxiety of many people about situation in Mediterranean, but no loss of confidence in present Government is expressed.

SATURDAY 21 SEPTEMBER 1940

There is little change in morale: yesterday's cheerfulness is maintained.

In London conversation is almost exclusively about air raids; it is gossipy, not panicky, and is centred in personal matters. There appears to be very little relationship between 'the bomb at the corner of our street' and the war as a whole. Interest in the total aspect of the war is very low, although demands for reprisals continue.

The necessity for seeking night shelter is accepted with resignation, and there are many examples of the fine spirit with which difficulties are met and overcome. At the same time, there are criticisms of obvious defects: shelter amenities, evacuation facilities, lack of information.

Taking shelter in underground stations is still on the increase. People are orderly, officials humane.

There are a number of reports showing that people are well aware of the damage and danger of 'land mines'. Terror stories are frequent. There are also tales of new weapons, e.g. plaster bombs, and evidence that people only begin to feel secure when they are below the surface: in tubes, basements, underground trenches, etc.

Time bombs are not regarded with undue alarm. The public feels that officials of various kinds are well aware of their dangers. There are, however, a number of enquiries about the duration of their effectiveness; people are very vague, some think they may be effective for a fortnight or longer; others that they cannot last more than a few hours. Evacuation on account of time bombs has brought hardship, but not alarm.

The AA barrage continues to cause a certain amount of disappointment: 'It's all very well, but they aren't bringing them down'. The idea that there is no protection against night bombing has not yet been accepted by most people. Protection is expected 'in time'. Only a few appear to contemplate much intensified bombing.

The public is increasingly anxious about black-out offences and there are many complaints about traffic lights, side lights, matches, torches, railway signals, etc. Many people appear to think that all lights are visible from the air.

Cinema attendances are low, and evidence shows that leisure time is not being profitably used.

There are fewer complaints about the warning system although today's

*incident in Bethnal Green has greatly perturbed people there. Their confi-
dence is again shaken.*

*From the provinces come reports that AA and fighter defences are consid-
ered inadequate.*

Points from Regions

NORTH-EASTERN (Leeds) No change in confidence except a slightly
growing feeling of stalemate. In view of recent rumours, people are
asking for clear statements as to whether there has or has not been
an attempted invasion. In an interview given to the *Yorkshire Post*,
the Leeds City Engineer says that brickwork is being done on non-
essential buildings and shelter contractors are unable to get the
labour they require.

EASTERN (Cambridge) The extent of damaged property in London
has been exaggerated by refugees, and it is thought that the East
End has been laid waste. There are still complaints about the limited
number of BBC stations broadcasting, and with the delay in the
distribution of London papers, there is increasing support for a
ten a.m. bulletin. Yesterday's announcement that Post Offices will
remain open during warnings is welcomed. Complaints about the
uncertain arrangements for running buses during air raids
continues, particularly from country districts where services are
few.

SOUTHERN (Reading) Many refugees from London have arrived in
the Region, and in Oxford where the number is about 10,000, the
problem of accommodation is serious. Although most of these people
appear to be in good heart, a small minority who have suffered from
a continued loss of sleep and are dazed by their experiences, have
tended to spread a somewhat defeatist attitude. There is discussion
on the question of reprisals, and the speech by the Air Minister does
not appear to have satisfied public opinion. Most people seem to
think that invasion will not now be attempted. The more thoughtful
section of the public is anxious about the position in Egypt, and
although appreciating the advantage of allowing the Italians to have

several hundred miles of desert communications, it hopes that the press accounts are not too 'rosy'.

NORTH-WESTERN (Manchester) There is much feeling in the Liverpool area over the apparent absence of local defence against bombers, and the inadequacy of shelters is also a subject of comment; yesterday a meeting of Merseyside Mayors was convened and a message sent to the Prime Minister on the latter subject. The news of heavy RAF raids on Germany and occupied areas causes great satisfaction.

SOUTH EASTERN (Tunbridge Wells) People are much concerned about the problem of countering night bombers, and such questions as 'why can't Spitfires be armed with searchlights?' are being asked. It is reported that people who left London on account of air raids and went hop-picking are now worried because they will have nowhere to go when the picking is finished.

LONDON

Great fear of land mines reported from many districts. For example, this fear has resulted in occupants of luxury flats in St John's Wood using the tube for shelter at night; also, after experiencing effects last night it is reported from Bethnal Green that many people wish to be evacuated. From Poplar and Bethnal Green it is stated that there is some ill-feeling because homeless are not re-billeted quickly enough and the Rest Centres are overcrowded. People feel that the victims of raids deserve the most generous treatment and that those who wish, homeless or otherwise, to leave London should be given facilities for doing so without delay. A Stoke Newington official points out the danger of fire in unoccupied houses if evacuation becomes too general in some districts. Observer in Islington says that undertakers are making excessive charges for funerals and a minimum charge should be instituted. Observation at different tube stations reveals that the number of people sleeping there is increasing. It has been suggested that tunnels used as shelters should have baffle walls to break blast.

MONDAY 23 SEPTEMBER TO FRIDAY 27 SEPTEMBER 1940

On the morning of 23 September an expeditionary force consisting of 4,200 British and 2,700 Free French troops arrived off the port of Dakar in French West Africa. The aim was to land the French troops in the hope of persuading the local authorities, who were loyal to the Vichy Government, to transfer the port to the Free French. The plan failed when the local Vichy French resisted and opened fire on the expedition. After two days of inconclusive action the attempt to seize Dakar was called off. Of the seven regions reporting on 26 September, five reported varying degrees of disquiet over this failed venture, which the Cardiff office described as 'the biggest blow since the fall of France'. Among the questions being asked, the Leeds office reported, were: 'Is our Intelligence Service any good?' and 'Are the Free French full of Fifth Columnists?'

The torpedoing of the *City of Benares* and the death of child evacuees provoked deep indignation, Home Intelligence reported, and the South-Western Region expressed 'bitter demands for reprisals against German civilians'. According to the summary of opinion for 24 September, 'most people feel that the evacuation of children to the Dominions should proceed'. Churchill, however, wanted to discontinue the scheme and it was ended on 3 October.

Nightly attacks on London continued, as did the exodus of refugees to the surrounding country, and the increasing use of tube stations as shelters. 'Tremendous crowds again used tube stations for sleeping last night,' the daily report recorded on 25 September. 'An observer remarked on the orderliness of the crowds; the obvious relief of mothers at feeling safe; that the kindness of LPTB [London Passenger Transport Board] workers was much appreciated.' Workers in charge of a rest centre at Hackney were worried about hygiene, 'as people are not examined for contagion and infection, and bedding is used by different people on successive nights'. On the topic of community spirit the evidence was mixed: 'In bombed areas of Kensington there is reported to have been much neighbourly help for raid victims . . . Resentment heard expressed against first-class passengers who show displeasure when third-class passengers overflow into their compartments.'

In a broadcast on 23 September King George VI announced a new honour specifically intended to mark the gallantry of civilians: the George Cross. It was to rank with the Victoria Cross and be supplemented by a more widespread award, the George Medal. 'The new George Cross,' commented the Leeds regional office, 'undoubtedly meets a general demand for recognition of civilian heroism.'

Mary Adams had intended for some months to introduce a weekly Home Intelligence report. The last of the daily reports, which appeared on 27 September, noted that Bristol had stood up magnificently to a heavy raid two days earlier. The Birmingham regional office reported: 'Those who a few weeks ago were not in favour of bombing German towns unless they contained military objectives are now wholeheartedly in favour of reprisals for the wanton attacks on London.'

MONDAY 23 SEPTEMBER 1940

There is anger and indignation about the torpedoing of the child evacuee ship. The effect has been to increase the demand for 'reprisals on German civilians'. A number of enquiries have been received about the seavacuation scheme: will it go on? Was the ship convoyed? etc. Many people appear to think that the scheme will be discontinued. This is the first piece of news for a fortnight which has deflected people's interest from air raids.

Further investigation into the situation in those places outside London where 'refugees' have gone shows that while there is much sympathy for these people, there is an increase of criticism about their dirty habits and inconsiderate behaviour. The exodus is still largely unorganised and is producing local irritation. Shortages of certain kinds of food have been reported and accounts of exaggerated stories continue.

People in London are cheerful but continue to enquire when there will be protection against night bombing.

Points from Regions

NORTHERN (Newcastle) There is evidence of growth in the demand for reprisals on the German civilian population, although more thoughtful people realise that no real military advantage can be secured thereby. Newsreels showing the King and Queen visiting victims of air raids have received unusually warm applause. There is a feeling that there is too much red tape and too little responsibility and encouragement given to Local Authorities when dealing with air-raid victims, and many quarters urge greater elasticity of administration. Complaints about the quality of reception of BBC programmes have noticeably increased during the last two weeks. The desire for a real military success against the Italians remains very strong.

SOUTH-WESTERN (Bristol) Bitter demands for reprisals against German civilians are reported as a result of the news of the sinking of the evacuee ship; Barnstaple reports that apprehension is felt as to the effect of the sinking on a scheme for transporting children to Barnstaple Massachusetts. Activity amongst troops and Home Guards during the weekend is said to have been responsible for a further crop of invasion rumours. In spite of wireless talks and press reports Salisbury states that the position of men working after the siren has sounded is still not clearly understood.

MIDLAND (Birmingham) The drowning of evacuee children due to U-boat action has evoked indignation throughout the Region. The fact that there have been no raids over the Region for the past two days has encouraged the belief that Hitler has abandoned his invasion plan. Rules for air-raid shelter conduct have been issued by the Chief Constable of Wolverhampton, and wardens may refuse permission to persons living near who have been provided with domestic shelters. Day Nurseries for children of women engaged on war work are opening in Birmingham.

NORTHERN IRELAND (Belfast) There is deep indignation at the sinking of the evacuee ship bound for Canada. The public is watching developments in the Mediterranean, and there is speculation as to the future policy of Spain. The appeal by the Minister of Aircraft Production for continued work in factories after the sounding of sirens is welcomed here as encouraging workers to intensify their efforts.

LONDON

Londoners trying to carry on as cheerfully and normally as possible, but many asking 'Can nothing be done to stop this night bombing?' Main concern still centres round shelter arrangements and re-billeting the homeless. Criticism reported from Bethnal Green, Stepney and Bermondsey over Rest Centres and rehousing of homeless, but matters are improving, though somewhat slowly. Outer London Boroughs coping with evacuees sent to their areas, but Social Workers feel that rehousing rather than billeting would be more acceptable; local Councils need to take more drastic steps about requisitioning empty premises. More workers of the right type still needed in Rest Centres and shelters. Great bitterness expressed over sinking of liner taking children to Canada; it is feared that this tragedy may upset the whole overseas evacuation scheme. Social Worker visiting hop fields at weekend suggests that East Enders might be allowed to stay in hop field hutments rather than return to devastated areas.

TUESDAY 24 SEPTEMBER

1. In London people remain determined, but cheerfulness varies. People are anxiously considering night life in shelters under winter conditions.

2. The King's speech was generally praised, and the creation of the George Cross and Medal has been widely welcomed.

3. Reports show that most people feel that the evacuation of children to the Dominions should proceed. To many the torpedoing was felt as a challenge to go ahead.

4. Rumours and exaggerated stories continue: in particular there are stories of poisonous substances dropped from enemy planes and of 'secret weapons' with which we shall eventually stop night bombing.

5. There is a steady drift towards public and away from private shelters.

6. Except in certain areas invasion talk has receded into the background.

7. 'Refugees' continue to move into the country round London. Here a general comment is 'no one has learned anything from the problems and failures of last September'.

Points from Regions

NORTH-EASTERN (Leeds) The King's speech was widely listened to and has been the subject of much favourable comment; many people seem to have expected him to announce grave news, and so the speech came as a relief. The new George Cross undoubtedly meets a general demand for recognition of civilian heroism. The sinking of the 'Mercy' ship is much discussed and the questions 'Why was it not convoyed the whole way?' and 'Was it convoyed at all?' are being asked. There are rumours of poisonous substances being dropped by enemy planes.

EASTERN (Cambridge) The effect of the King's broadcast has been particularly marked on women. The news of the ship carrying evacuees to Canada has aroused considerable anger; one reaction is 'I thought it would happen'. The publication of pictures showing damage by the RAF to German-occupied territory has been effective, but there is criticism of the small number and poor quality of the photographs. Criticism that vivid pictures illustrating conditions in an underground railway tunnel published in a Sunday picture paper are a useful gift to German propagandists.

SOUTHERN (Reading) The exodus of refugees from London continues, and although the great majority is far from defeatist their stories support newspaper criticism that ARP preparations have been unequal to the emergency. There is renewed criticism of Chamberlain's continued presence in the Government. Some resentment is felt among workers at the alleged unwillingness of the middle classes to receive refugees. There is keen satisfaction that we have taken the initiative at Dakar.

Intellectual circles eagerly await news from Egypt. Reports from South Coast cities which have been bombed indicate that the exodus has been small. Rumour, which is rife, concentrates upon invasion and damage due to raids. The proportion of Jews among evacuees is causing anti-Semitic talk.

WALES (Cardiff) Interest still centres around the bombing of London, and admiration is expressed for the courage of Londoners. There is some exaggeration of damage in bombed areas by people enlarging upon their experiences. Reports from North Wales express uneasiness in regard to the slowness of Civil Defence preparations by Local Authorities. America's increased friendliness gives satisfaction, and there is hope that all efforts are being made to rally Morocco to de Gaulle. The recent broadcast talk on Rumour was much appreciated and there is a call for similar talks in Welsh, and for talks on the Egyptian situation. Rumours of invasion persist. Haw-Haw's alleged references to local places have a disturbing effect.

SOUTH-EASTERN (Tunbridge Wells) Complaints of the immunity with which enemy bombers fly over towns by night are still on the increase. Despite denials of reports of attempted invasion, the belief in the attempts is still widespread. There is some uneasiness over the system of warnings, in view of the fact that this morning two fairly large formations of enemy bombers circled over the town some minutes after 'Raiders Passed' had been given, and when hundreds of school children were setting off for school. People in Canterbury are asking for Anderson shelters left in evacuated coastal towns. There is some renewal of talk of the Government going to Canada.

LONDON

Morale still steady, but transport difficulties remain one of the greatest problems for London workers. West End staffs feel that Government does not cope with disrupted communications efficiently. Shelter problems still acute but Home Security's statement issued yesterday has given a certain amount of reassurance; Willesden contact, however, states that surface shelters in this area will not be blast-proof as poor material has been used. Tubes in some places said to be more crowded than ever. Rest Centres generally are said to be improving. Women with young children still asking to be sent to a safe area and seem to be unaware of the various Government schemes. Factory Supervisor, Clerkenwell, with depots all over London, reports that his Home Guard numbering 400 are still without uniforms and arms and are losing interest; he states that some large firms have disbanded their units because of this. Land mines are still giving rise to much talk and exaggerated stories about their effects are spreading. The question of liability for rents and rates by people whose homes are damaged or who must leave on account of time bombs is causing a good deal of anxiety in Willesden. Difficulty is experienced in getting hot meals in some districts in East End and more mobile canteens and kitchens would ease the situation considerably.

WEDNESDAY 25 SEPTEMBER 1940

Points from Regions

NORTHERN (Newcastle) As a result of the sinking of the *City of Benares* there have been a number of cancellations for overseas evacuation in Middlesbrough; on the other hand, one or two statements have been received that parents think there is serious risk for their children whether they go or stay. The news of Gen. de Gaulle and Dakar is considered confusing. Criticism is voiced of the regular publication in the press of pictures showing widespread damage in London. There is said to be confusion in the minds both of people and traders as to the methods of imposition of the Purchase Tax. Rumours that the bodies of German soldiers are being washed up on the East Coast are prevalent.

NORTH-MIDLAND (Nottingham) As a result of hearsay, correspondence and newspaper pictures, exaggerated stories of damage to London are being spread. More complaints are received of the poor reception of broadcasts, and it is suggested that as a consequence people are inclined to listen to German stations which are clearly heard. There is dissatisfaction at COs being able to derive financial advantages through exemption. There are reports of the freedom with which soldiers speak in canteens and elsewhere.

MIDLAND (Birmingham) There is little to indicate that the torpedoing of the *City of Benares* has caused opposition to trans-Atlantic evacuation, and it is felt that such misfortunes are exceptional. A mutual fund for helping people suffering air-raid damage has been started at Rubery, near Birmingham; Coventry is also making good progress with a fund to provide supplementary assistance to that offered by the Government.

NORTHERN IRELAND (Belfast) It is generally thought that the RAF is inflicting heavier damage on Germany than is being received by London and South East England. The possibility of invasion is still

sent the British working classes being sacrificed for capitalism in an un-winnable war.

Brooke, General Sir Alan: from 20 July 1940, Commander-in-Chief, Home Forces.

Burma Road: overland supply route which connected Burma with China and helped to support Chiang Kai-shek's nationalist forces fighting the Japanese.

Butler, R. A.: from 26 February 1938, Parliamentary Under-Secretary of State for Foreign Affairs.

Carol, King: Carol II of Romania.

Casement, Roger: Irish nationalist. Executed by the British for high treason in 1916.

Chamberlain, Neville: Prime Minister from 28 May 1937 to 10 May 1940; from 11 May 1940, Lord President of the Council.

charabanc: a bus used for pleasure trips.

Churchill, Winston: from 10 May 1940, Prime Minister and Minister of Defence.

City of Benares: British passenger ship sunk by a German U-boat in the North Atlantic en route to Canada, 250 miles south-west of Rockall, on 18 September 1940. Of the 260 lives lost, 77 were child evacuees.

contex filter: special filter attached to gas masks to protect against arsine gas attack.

'Cooper's Snoopers': name coined by the press for the investigators employed by the Social Survey.

Cotswold Bruderhof: a German Hutterite community founded in 1936 at Ashton Keynes in Wiltshire.

Craigavon, Lord: Prime Minister of Northern Ireland.

Cripps, Sir Stafford: from 12 June 1940, British ambassador in Moscow.

Croix de Feu: a French far-right organisation established by veterans of the First World War.

Cross, Ronald: from 14 May 1940, Minister of Shipping.

Croydon incident: air raid on Croydon aerodrome in the London suburbs on 15 August 1940, when no sirens were sounded until seventeen minutes after the first bombs were dropped. Sixty-two people were killed.

Daily Worker: newspaper of the Communist party of Great Britain.

Dakar: expedition by British and Free French troops in September 1940 to secure the Vichy-controlled West African port of Dakar. The operation ended in failure and had to be abandoned.

Dalton, Hugh: from 15 May 1940, Minister of Economic Warfare.

Defence Regulations: measures taken by the government under the Emergency Powers (Defence) Act of 1939 that were thought necessary to secure public safety, the defence of the realm, the maintenance of public order, and the efficient prosecution of the war.

Defence Area: designated coastal areas in which all persons were liable to be questioned by the police or military authorities as to their reasons for entry into, or presence in, the area. If they were unable to provide satisfactory evidence that they were engaged in business, or had other good reason to be in the area, they would be required to leave. This applied to all holiday-makers.

Derby, Lord: Lord Lieutenant of Lancashire and former British ambassador in Paris.

De Valera, Eamon: the Taoiseach: head of the Irish government.

'Dig for Victory': Ministry of Agriculture slogan to encourage those with gardens and allotments to grow their own food.

Dill, General Sir John: from 27 May 1940, Chief of the Imperial General Staff.

Duff Cooper, Alfred: from 12 May 1940, Minister of Information.

Eden, Anthony: from 12 May 1940, Secretary of State for War.

Eisteddfod: annual festival of Welsh music and poetry.

Elizabeth, Princess: King's elder daughter and later to become Queen Elizabeth II.

Elles, General Sir Hugh: Chief of the Operational Staff of the Civil Defence Services at the Ministry of Home Security.

Emergency Powers Bill/Act: the Emergency Powers (Defence) Act of May 1940 extended the government's emergency powers to include the conscription of people as well as property.

Fields, Gracie: music-hall entertainer and film actress.

Fifth Column: term originating from the Spanish Civil War to denote those within the country who were thought to be sympathetic to, or working for, the enemy.

Franco, General Francisco: Spanish dictator.

Gamelin, General Maurice-Gustave: Commander-in-Chief of the French army, and Supreme Allied Commander, who was dismissed on 19 May 1940.

Gardner, Charles: BBC correspondent.

Gaulle, General Charles de: leader of the Free French.

GB cinema: Gaumont-British cinema.

George Cross/Medal: decorations intended to reward men and women for civilian gallantry. The George Cross was to rank next to the Victoria Cross; the George Medal more widely distributed.

Gestapo: German secret police.

Glorious: British aircraft carrier sunk by the German navy on 8 June 1940 in the Norway Sea. Over 1,500 lives were lost.

Goebbels, Joseph: Nazi propaganda minister.

Gort, General Lord: Commander-in-Chief of the British Expeditionary Force.

Greenwood, Arthur: from 11 May 1940, Minister without Portfolio and Chairman of the Production Council.

Grenfell, David: former coal miner who, from 15 May 1940, was Secretary for Mines in the Ministry of Fuel and Power.

Grigg, Sir Edward: from 12 May 1940, Parliamentary Under-Secretary of State for War.

Hackett, Fred: unknown broadcaster who gave a talk on the BBC's *Once a Week* programme on 2 August 1940.

Haile Selassie: exiled Emperor of Abyssinia.

Halifax, Lord: from 1 March 1938, Secretary of State for Foreign Affairs.

Harewood, Lord: Lord Lieutenant of the West Riding of Yorkshire.

Harlech, Lord: North-East Regional Commissioner for Civil Defence.

Haw-Haw, Lord: nickname given to William Joyce, former member of the British Union of Fascists, who broadcast German propaganda to Britain.

Healy, Maurice: barrister and broadcaster.

Hearst, William Randolph: American newspaper magnate.

Hi Gang: BBC variety show featuring Americans Vic Oliver, Bebe Daniels and Ben Lyon.

Hibberd, Stuart: BBC announcer.

Hicks, George: Labour MP and General Secretary of the Amalgamated Union of Building Trade Workers.

Highlander: British merchant ship whose gunners shot down two German aircraft over the North Sea near Stonehaven on 1 August 1940.

Hilton, Professor John: social scientist and broadcaster.

Hitler, Adolf: leader of Nazi Germany.

Hoare, Sir Samuel: British ambassador in Madrid.

Hoare–Laval Pact: plan drawn up in 1935 by Sir Samuel Hoare, the British Foreign Secretary at this time, together with the French premier, Pierre Laval, to partition Abyssinia in order to end the Italian–Abyssinian war. The plan was leaked to the press and denounced as a sell-out of the Abyssinians. Hoare and Laval were forced to resign.

Holesworthy, Suffolk: possible reference to Holsworthy, Devon.

Hooper, Frederic: businessman and broadcaster.

Hoover, Herbert: former US president who proposed that Britain should permit the passage of food ships through its blockade to feed the starving populations of occupied Europe.

Hore-Belisha, Leslie: Secretary of State for War from May 1937 to January 1940.

'Idle workers scheme': appeal by Bevin to employers engaged in munitions production to make available to factories elsewhere workers who were temporarily without occupation.

Ironside, General Sir Edmund: from 27 May to 20 July 1940, Commander-in-Chief, Home Forces.

Johnstone, Harcourt: from 15 May 1940, Secretary of the Department of Overseas Trade.

Joubert, Air Marshal Sir Philip: Assistant Chief of the Air Staff.

Juliana, Princess: daughter of Queen Wilhelmina of the Netherlands.

Kassala: Sudanese town close to the Eritrean border. The town was attacked by the Italians and the British garrison forced to withdraw.

Kent, Duchess of: Princess Marina of Greece and Denmark, wife of the fourth son of George V.

Kerry Head: Neutral Irish merchant ship bombed by a German aircraft off the south coast of Ireland on 1 August 1940. No one was injured.

Kindersley, Sir Robert: merchant banker and President of the National Savings Committee.

King: George VI.

King-Hall, Commander Stephen: writer, broadcaster, National Labour MP and personal assistant to the head of the Factories Defence Section of the Ministry of Aircraft Production.

Knox, Colonel Franklin: US Secretary of the Navy.

Lancastria: British troopship sunk by German aircraft off St Nazaire on 17 June 1940 whilst evacuating British troops and civilians from France. Over 4,000 lives were lost.

League of Reconciliation: possible reference to the Fellowship of Reconciliation, a Christian pacifist organisation established in 1914.

Leopold, King: Léopold III, King of Belgium, who surrendered his country unconditionally to the Germans on 28 May 1940.

Limitation of Supplies Order: measure to restrict the supply of consumer goods to the home market by imposing quotas on the production of various non-essential articles, ranging from pyjamas to cigarette cases to lawnmowers.

Lindbergh, Charles: American aviator who advocated that the USA should stay out of the war.

Lloyd George, David: Prime Minister from December 1916 to October 1922.

Lloyd George, Megan: David Lloyd George's daughter. Chairman of the Women MPs' Advisory Committee on Salvage.

Local Defence Volunteer Corps: renamed the Home Guard in July 1940.

MacCarthy, Desmond: literary critic and broadcaster.

MacDonald, Malcolm: from 13 May 1940, Minister of Health.

Macmillan, Harold: from 15 May 1940, Parliamentary Secretary at the Ministry of Supply.

Madame Tussaud's: waxworks museum on Marylebone Road.

Maginot Line: series of French fortifications constructed between the wars to deter a German offensive into France.

Mais, S. P. B.: writer and broadcaster.

Margaret Rose, Princess: King's younger daughter and later to become Countess of Snowdon.

Maurois, André: French author.

Meknès **incident**: neutral French passenger ship, *Meknès*, sunk by a German motor torpedo boat off Portland on 24 July 1940 whilst en route from Southampton to Marseilles to repatriate French naval personnel who wished to return to unoccupied France under the terms of the armistice. Nearly 400 lives were lost.

'Men of Munich': politicians associated with the appeasement of Hitler at the Munich conference of 1938.

Milne, Field Marshal Lord: appointed Colonel Commandant of the Auxiliary Military Pioneer Corps.

Mitford, Unity: Nazi sympathiser. Fourth of six daughters of Baron Redesdale.

Molotov, Vyacheslav: Soviet Foreign Affairs Minister.

Moral Rearmament: international movement established in 1938 to promote spiritual and moral renewal. Led by American evangelist Dr Frank Buchman who was of Swiss–German descent.

Morrison, Herbert: from 12 May 1940, Minister of Supply.

Mosley, Sir Oswald: leader of the British Union of Fascists.

Moyale: frontier town on the Kenya–Abyssinia border. The Italians attacked the town and the British garrison was compelled to withdraw.

Mussolini, Benito: Italian dictator.

Narvik: Norwegian port around which British and allied troops fought the Germans until evacuated between 4–8 June 1940.

New British Broadcasting Station: German radio station broadcasting 'black' propaganda to Britain. Presented itself as a forum for a group of patriotic British dissidents opposed to war with Germany.

Nicolson, Harold: from 17 May 1940, Parliamentary Secretary at the Ministry of Information.

Norman, Montagu: Governor of the Bank of England.

Ogilvie, F. W.: Director-General of the BBC.

'Onlooker': radio name for barrister and broadcaster, Norman Birkett.

Oxford Group Movement: organisation out of which Moral Rearmament grew.

Packard: American motor car company.

parashot: someone who would stand guard with a weapon waiting for parachutists to descend.

Peace News: journal of the Peace Pledge Union, a pacifist organisation founded in 1934.

People's Vigilance Committee: communist-inspired group which campaigned for practical measures, such as improvements to air-raid shelters, as well as promoting broader political aims, such as a 'people's government' and a 'people's peace'.

Pétain, Marshal Phillippe: replaced Reynaud as French Prime Minister. Concluded an armistice with Germany on 22 June 1940.

Portsea, Lord: Jerseyman.

Postscripts: series of talks broadcast on the BBC, usually after the 9.00 p.m. news on a Sunday night.

Priestley, J. B.: novelist and playwright.

Protected Area: designated areas in which people had to have a permit in order to remain or visit.

Purchasing Commission: British Purchasing Commission in New York.

purple warning: night-time air-raid warning issued to premises with exempted external lighting as an order to extinguish their lights.

Queen: Elizabeth, consort of George VI. Later styled Queen Elizabeth, the Queen Mother.

Quisling: synonym for collaborator or traitor. Derived from Vidkun Quisling, the Norwegian fascist leader, who collaborated with the Germans after they occupied his country in 1940.

Reception Areas: areas of the country to which those evacuated from cities were sent to escape the bombing.

red warning: air-raid 'action' warning following the preliminary yellow warning (see below). Was the signal for the public sirens to be sounded.

Region: the Ministry of Information regions were coterminous with the twelve Civil Defence regions in England, Wales and Scotland, with the addition of a Northern Ireland region in April 1940.

Regional Commissioners: these officials, who coordinated Civil Defence measures across the country, were given additional powers, subject to control by the Ministry of Home Security, to issue any directions or orders required for the purposes of defence within their respective areas.

Reynaud, Paul: French Prime Minister. Resigned on 16 June 1940.

Roosevelt, Franklin D.: President of the United States of America.

Scharnhorst: German battleship reported to have been damaged by RAF aircraft during a raid on the Kiel Canal on 1 July 1940.

Secret Session: debate in the House of Commons held in secret.

Shakespeare, Geoffrey: from 15 May 1940, Parliamentary Under-Secretary of State for the Dominions. Also chairman of the Children's Overseas Reception Board.

Siegfried Line: German fortifications opposite the French Maginot Line.

Silent Column campaign: appeal launched by the Ministry of Information to persuade people to join an imaginary regiment, 'the silent column', composed of men and women who were resolved to say nothing that could help the enemy.

Simon, Lord: from 12 May 1940, Lord Chancellor.

Sinclair, Sir Archibald: from 11 May 1940, Secretary of State for Air.

Smuts, General Jan Christiaan: Prime Minister of South Africa.

Social Survey: organisation known as the Wartime Social Survey, operating under the auspices of the National Institute of Economic and Social Research, which compiled reports on public opinion for the Ministry of Information's Home Intelligence department and whose investigators interviewed householders.

Sollum: harbour on the Egyptian–Libyan border occupied by the Italians.

Spitfire funds: public subscriptions to raise money for the production of new Spitfire fighters.

Stalin, Joseph: Soviet dictator.

Stephenson, J. W.: president of the Confederation of Shipbuilding and Engineering Unions.

Stimson, Henry: US Secretary of War.

Stokes, Richard: Labour MP and founder of the Parliamentary Peace Aims Group in 1939.

Stubbs, Bernard: BBC correspondent.

Swan & Edgar Ltd: department store at Piccadilly Circus.

Swing, Raymond Gram: American journalist and broadcaster.

Swinton Committee: Lord Swinton's Home Defence (Security) Executive.

Thompson, Dorothy: American journalist and broadcaster.

tocsin: an alarm bell or signal.

Tredegar, Lord: eccentric Welsh aristocrat.

Trenchard, Lord: former Chief of the Air Staff who appealed for more bomber aircraft in order for Britain to go on to the offensive against Germany.

Vichy government: term for Pétain's French collaborationist regime based in the city of that name.

War Weapons Week: campaign launched by the Chancellor of the Exchequer to raise money towards the cost of bombers.

War Zone Emergency Courts Bill: legislation to enable special courts to be set up in areas where, as a result of enemy action, the military situation was such that criminal justice could not be administered by the ordinary courts with sufficient expedition.

Ward, Edward: BBC correspondent.

Weygand, General Maxime: replaced Gamelin as Commander-in-Chief of the French Army, and Supreme Allied Commander, on 20 May 1940.

Wilkinson, Ellen: from 17 May 1940, Parliamentary Secretary at the Ministry of Pensions.

Windsor, Duke of: formerly Edward VIII. Abdicated in 1936.

Wood, Sir Kingsley: from 12 May 1940, Chancellor of the Exchequer.

Wood, Dr Thomas: composer and broadcaster.

Woolton, Lord: from 3 April 1940, Minister of Food.

yellow warnings: preliminary air-raid warning sent confidentially to police, Civil Defence services, government offices and large industrial concerns.

Index

In addition to counties see also specific towns within those counties

lorry drivers 144, 156, 194, 355, 410, 429
Loughborough 176
Lowdham 218
Lowestoft 40, 56, 219, 354
LPTB *see* London Passenger Transport Board
Luton 16, 389
luxury trade 98, 143, 150, 195, 200, 239, 253, 269

Mablethorpe 139
McCarthy, Desmond 110, 467
MacDermott, John (Northern Ireland Minister of Public Security) 139, 158
MacDonald, Malcolm (Minister of Health) 43, 64, 114, 119, 177, 201, 467
Macmillan, Harold 294, 467
Madame Tussaud's (London) 424, 431, 467
Madge, Charles xii
Maginot Line 12, 13, 25, 467
Maidstone 66, 242, 288
Mais, S. P. B. 395, 467
Malden 339, 346, 373
Maltese refugees 367
Man, Isle of 52, 61, 352
Manchester 281, 293, 374, 410, 429
Mansfield 84
Marchant, Hilde 424
Marconi Works 141
Margaret, Princess 2, 12, 13, 105, 142, 153, 234, 468
Margate 51, 56, 105, 108, 212–13, 246, 303–4
Marylebone (London) 74, 128, 187, 189, 224, 424
Mass Observation (M-O) xii–xiii, xiv, xvi, 9
matches, lighting of 89
Maurois, André 104, 105, 107, 468
Mayfair (London) 277, 285, 398, 433
means tests 271, 389, 439
meat rationing 61, 201
Meknès incident 272, 468
Melksham 357
'Men of Munich' 173, 184, 246, 279, 468
Mers-el-Kebir (Algeria) 171
Merseyside 326, 399–400, 436, 443, 455
MI7 145, 152, 207, 461
Middlesbrough 102, 128, 136, 159, 198, 221, 280, 322
    evacuation from 156, 190, 211, 452

Middleton and Prestwich by-election 22, 54
Midlothian 439
military bands and parades, requests for 195, 205–6, 207, 213, 222, 246, 257, 269, 308
military training, demands for 116, 132, 135, 157
milk 276, 295, 298, 328, 365, 388, 389
Mill Hill (London) 220, 273, 458
Milne, Field Marshal Lord 190, 468
miners 50, 77, 78, 85, 105, 112, 178, 245, 271, 320, 391, 426
    absenteeism 215, 226, 409
    Spitfire fund 363
    unemployment 131, 186, 223, 280, 410
    Welsh 105, 193, 375, 410
    Yorkshire 16, 55, 72, 81, 198, 215, 226, 257, 260, 267
Ministry of Food 300, 307, 309, 356
Ministry of Information (MOI) xi–xii, xiv, xv, 78, 255, 258, 260, 263, 270
    Anti-Lies Bureau 70, 87–8, 463
    films 181, 265, 273, 298, 308, 365
    invasion pamphlet 130, 131, 137, 140, 144
    press campaign against 254, 270, 294, 297, 298, 300, 301
    see also 'Silent Column' campaign
Mitcham 133, 273, 336, 373
Mitford, Unity 60, 468
M-O *see* Mass Observation
mobile canteens 409, 412, 451
mobilisation of manpower *see under* Government
MOI *see* Ministry of Information
Molotov, Vyacheslav 291, 292, 296, 468
Montrose 114, 268, 414
Moral Rearmament 198, 215, 333–4, 468
morale, civilian 5–6, 7–10, 18–21, 41, 53, 58, 76, 161, 165, 175, 179–80, 197, 202, 258, 263, 274, 278, 329–30, 345–6, 375
    and class 10, 13, 32, 41, 96, 108, 123, 203, 247, 248
    complacency 15, 31, 36, 61, 73, 223, 238, 264, 274, 279, 280, 289, 290, 291, 302, 309
    after Dunkirk 49
    and gender 15–16, 19, 20, 25, 31, 32, 108
    and return of BEF 40, 63